21.69
650

FOUNDATION QUANTITATIVE METHODS FOR BUSINESS

FINANCIAL TIMES
MANAGEMENT

About our books

We work with leading authors to develop the strongest ideas in business and finance, bringing cutting-edge thinking and best practice to a global market.

Under the Financial Times Pitman Publishing imprint we craft high quality books which help readers to understand and apply their content, whether studying or at work.

To find out more please visit our website:
www.ftmanagement.com

FOUNDATION QUANTITATIVE METHODS FOR BUSINESS

Mik Wisniewski

Director, Management Development Unit,
University of Stirling

with

Richard Stead

Principal Lecturer, Leeds Business School,
Leeds Metropolitan University

FINANCIAL TIMES
PITMAN PUBLISHING

FINANCIAL TIMES
MANAGEMENT
LONDON · SAN FRANCISCO
KUALA LUMPUR · JOHANNESBURG

*Financial Times Management delivers the knowledge,
skills and understanding that enable students,
managers and organisations to achieve their ambitions,
whatever their needs, wherever they are.*

London Office:
128 Long Acre, London WC2E 9AN
Tel: +44 (0)171 447 2000
Fax: +44 (0)171 240 5771
Website: www.ftmanagement.com

A Division of Financial Times Professional Limited

First published in Great Britain in 1996

ISBN 0 273 60765 0

British Library Cataloguing in Publication Data
A CIP catalogue record for this book can be obtained from the British Library

10   9   8   7   6   5   4   3   2

Typeset by 🌀 Tek-Art, Croydon, Surrey
Printed and bound in Great Britain by Redwood Books, Trowbridge, Wiltshire

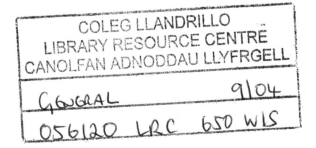

CONTENTS

Contents

PREFACE

This text has been written for students who are studying the use of quantitative techniques – statistical and mathematical – in a business context, perhaps as part of a business studies course, and for whom this is almost certainly the first time they have had to develop extensive quantitative skills and knowledge.

In this text the focus is very much on developing the basic knowledge and skills which form the platform from which future professional and business competence can be developed. In particular the text aims to equip students with the ability to:

- apply a number of commonly used quantitative concepts and techniques;
- analyse and solve business problems using quantitative techniques;
- evaluate information derived from applying quantitative techniques in a business context;
- present quantitative business information in a logical format;
- communicate quantitative information in a business context.

The text has been specifically written so that techniques are introduced in a logical and progressive manner and so that the student can understand the need for them in business decision-making and their role. The author has written the text to be as user-friendly as possible, bearing in mind that most students will have little enthusiasm for this topic area when they first encounter it in their studies.

 A key feature of the text is the selection of extracts from the *Financial Times* which help to relate the theory to the real world of business.

Also available from the publishers is a PC compatible disk which contains many of the data sets used throughout this text. These data sets can be accessed directly by most spreadsheet programs.

Whilst no specific prior knowledge is assumed certain basic arithmetic and mathematical skills are expected. For those students whose recollection of these is vague a special chapter is provided to help revision.

1 INTRODUCTION

Students have probably bought this text in the fervent hope that it will help them pass an exam that they shortly will face in a subject about which they probably have considerable concern.

One of the major reasons for writing this text was to provide students with a comprehensive coverage of the syllabus content that is both relevant to their own studies and also easy to read and to understand. The text is aimed primarily at students in the business studies area, including economics, accounting and finance, management and business studies. The text is *not* directed at students whose main interest is in statistics, mathematics or computing. We assume that, like ourselves, students in the fields of management, accountancy, finance and business have no interest in these subject areas in their own right but rather in the practical *applications* of such topics and techniques to business. However, whilst the text was written to help students pass their exams it also has a wider purpose.

The reason why *all* students in the business area nowadays have to take an examination in the quantitative analysis area is that a working knowledge of these topics is essential for present and future managers. In order to work effectively in a modern business organization – whether the organization is a private commercial company, a government agency, a state industry or whatever – a student today must be able to *use* quantitative techniques and *understand* their use and results in a confident and reliable manner.

Today's students are striving to become tomorrow's managers. Practising accountants will make decisions based on the information relating to the financial state of the organization. Economists will make decisions based on the information relating to the economic framework in which the organization operates. Personnel managers will make decisions based on the information relating to the levels of employment in the organization and so on. Such information is increasingly quantitative and it is apparent that managers (both practising and intending) need a working knowledge of the procedures and techniques appropriate for analysing and evaluating such quantitative information. Such analysis and certainly the business evaluation based on it cannot be delegated to the professional statistician or mathematician who, adept though they might be at sophisticated numerical analysis, will frequently have little overall understanding of the business relevance of such analysis.

A survey* conducted by the author of this text into the use of quantitative techniques by UK managers found that:

- 81% of managers were using quantitative techniques;
- on average, managers were aware of 13 different quantitative techniques;
- the major reason managers cited for not using techniques was lack of training/education.

LEARNING OBJECTIVES

By the end of this chapter you should be able to:

- explain why quantitative methods are important to a manager;
- explain the main terms used in statistical and mathematical terminology;
- describe the difference between the main types of variable;
- explain the difference between raw and aggregated data;
- explain the difference between primary and secondary data;
- understand the difference between descriptive and inferential statistics.

---

*M. Wisniewski, K. Kristensen, H. Madsen, P. Ostergaard and C. Jones (1994) 'Does anyone use the techniques we teach?' *Operational Research Insight*, Vol. 7, No. 2, pp. 2–7

INFORMATION AND DECISION-MAKING

One of the major problems facing a manager in any business organization – public or private sector, large or small – is that of uncertainty. Many aspects of managing a business activity are uncertain. A company will not know for certain what will happen to its sales, its profitability, its costs, its markets, its customer demand. A public sector organization, like a hospital, will also face uncertainty: how many patients will need treatment next year, how fast drug prices will increase, what level of government funding will be made available, what major advances in medical technology will become available, and so on. For any one of these areas of uncertainty we can think of several factors which will contribute to it. Uncertainty over sales, for example, will stem from uncertainty over customer demand, future prices, inflation, tax levels.

Uncertainty then is all around the business decision-maker. The role of quantitative techniques in business decision-making is to clarify and quantify – as much as is possible – the uncertainty that may exist in the decision-making process. In doing this it helps a manager to take reasonably rational and consistent decisions.

It is evident, even at this stage in the text, that information is required as a basis for management decision-making and the gathering and analysis of data must form the basis of this information. Many business situations arise in which it is necessary to gather and analyse data to provide the basis for a rational, informed decision – this could be a relatively straightforward accept-or-reject decision for goods arriving at a factory, or it could be a decision as to how to manage an important project which has overrun its specified time and budget to completion.

There are also many situations which occur in management which can be analysed using either statistical methods or the models which are common to what is known as management science – the systematic application of quantitative techniques to business and management problems. Much of the data which is available to management in any organization is collected on an ongoing basis:

- the organization's salary costs;
- income received from products or services supplied;
- the amount of output produced or services provided;
- the costs incurred in providing a product or service.

Quantitative techniques provide the tools with which this data may be analysed so that it is presented in a more meaningful way as information to managers. We distinguish between data and information in that data are the raw numbers and information is the result of processing the data in a way which makes it relevant to the problem and provides a basis for management action.

The availability of computers and associated software allows the processing of data in a number of ways and in a time scale which would previously have been impossible. This has resulted in the widespread use of statistical techniques which need to process large quantities of numbers very quickly. Not only are data processed more quickly but there is now the opportunity to engage in 'what if' scenarios to investigate the likely effects of different decisions. Because of the possibilities offered by computing, the immediacy with which information may be presented and the ability to investigate 'what if' situations, the use of quantitative techniques is becoming more widespread. This is not to say that the use is in fact better but certainly the desire to use them is greater.

The techniques which are introduced in this book will enable you to analyse data, present information, and investigate the effects of decision-making. However, it is important to realize that business problems cannot be solved simply through the use of quantitative techniques. Such techniques – if properly used and properly understood – can supply useful information about a problem but such information is rarely enough by itself. It must be supplemented by that available from other sources – the finance department, the personnel department, production, etc. as well as the experience, expertise and 'gut-feel' of the manager who has to take an appropriate decision based on these various and varying sources of information.

APPROACH OF THE TEXT

As indicated this text has been written for the business student. Accordingly, the material presented in the text focuses on the practical and applied areas of relevance to business organizations. Students are assumed to have no previous knowledge or use of the quantitative techniques covered. The necessary introduction to any techniques will be provided in the text itself. However, we do assume that students are able to deal with the elementary mathematics (in terms of arithmetic and simple algebra) that are prerequisites for this type of material. For those whose recollection of basic numerical principles is uncertain we have provided a review in Chapter 2 and if you are in any doubt about your own numerical abilities you are strongly encouraged to read through this chapter first. Similarly, if you find some of the later chapters difficult to understand then come back to Chapter 2 and read the relevant supporting section.

The text adopts a twin focus to the topics covered. On the one hand, it is necessary for you to develop the appropriate skills to be able to solve a typical problem, in other words to be able to find 'the answer' to a quantitative problem set. On the other hand, however, it is also necessary to develop a critical understanding and awareness of the techniques and methods covered. It is plainly inadequate simply to provide the solution to a quantitative problem if you cannot also interpret and evaluate the solution in the business context in which it is set. After all, these days computers are far more efficient at finding 'the answer' than people. A computer system cannot, however, formulate the problem, decide which method of analysis is appropriate, assess the business relevance of the solution and interpret the 'answer' in terms that the managing director can understand! Accordingly we hope that you will not use this text simply to be able to work out the solution to a problem but also to gain a wider awareness of the role and function of quantitative analysis in business.

ORGANIZATION OF THE TEXT

Each chapter in the text takes the following general format. First, we provide an Introduction to the focus of that chapter. Second, we establish the Learning Objectives for that chapter so on completing each chapter you will be able to assess for yourself whether these learning objectives have been achieved. Then each chapter introduces the relevant topics and places them in a typical business context. Typically in each chapter an example problem is thoroughly investigated and discussed both in terms of determining a solution to the problem and discussing the wider business applications of the technique.

Within each chapter you will also find a number of Student Activities. These are tasks for you to complete at that point in your reading of that chapter. Whilst you may be tempted to 'skip over' an activity we would strongly encourage you not to do so. The activities are an integral part of the learning process and will typically lead you into the next part of that chapter. At the end of each chapter a summary of the major points in the chapter is presented. Finally, starting in Chapter 3 we present a fully worked example, or details of an application, illustrating the techniques introduced in that chapter. A series of Self-Review Questions are presented which allow you to test your own understanding of the topic covered. The relevant answers to these questions are to be found in Appendix 1 at the end of the book. Lastly, a set of Student Exercises are presented. These fulfil two functions. First, they develop ideas and applications introduced in the chapter. Second, they provide practice at the type of question you may well face in the examination.

The text has been written in such a way that is effectively self-contained. It may, therefore, be used by the student working alone or by a student receiving tuition in this subject. It is essential, however, that the text is used in the correct way if you are to gain the most from it in your studies. Much of the material is presented in sequential order and it is, therefore, important that you thoroughly understand one chapter before progressing to the next. To this end it is also essential that you attempt both the Self-Review Questions and the Student Exercises at the end of each chapter to ensure that you have understood both the major concepts and the methods of solution. The Student Exercises in particular are designed to supplement the material presented in the chapter and to encourage you to think about the wider implications of the topics in business.

COMPUTERS

The text has been written in such a way that direct access to computing facilities is not essential in following the material presented. However, you will find your knowledge and understanding of business computing systems considerably enhanced if you can gain access to such equipment. If at all possible you should access and use relevant computer software. This may simply be general business software that can be adapted for use in mathematics and statistics – computer spreadsheets are ideal for many of the repetitive calculations required. Alternatively, you may have access to purpose-written software designed for use with these techniques. There are a variety of such packages available. At the end of some chapters we have introduced additional Student Exercises designed for use with a computer spreadsheet. A disk is available containing the relevant data files.

However, you should not fall into the trap of assuming you do not need to understand the quantitative techniques simply because they are available on 'the computer'. There is no substitute for knowledge and a conceptual understanding of the calculations underpinning some techniques (even if you are not actually doing those calculations yourself). To have confidence in the information that such techniques generate you must have confidence in your own ability to assess that quantitative information and evaluate it in a business context.

TERMINOLOGY AND VOCABULARY

In the remainder of this chapter we will be introducing much of the specialized terminology that is used in dealing with statistical and mathematical techniques in business. Like any specialized subject, mathematics and statistics have their own vocabulary and in order to proceed we shall need to understand the meaning of the more important terms. Just as the words 'debits and credits', for example, probably don't mean a great deal to the ordinary person but have a very specific and specialized meaning for the accountant, the same is true in quantitative methods.

Variables

We often use the term 'variable' when dealing with data. Simply defined, a variable refers to whatever feature or factor we are interested in or are investigating. So, if we are looking at company profits, for example, this would be our defined variable. Normally, the variable we are looking at will fall into one of three general categories. It may be:

- discrete;
- continuous;
- attribute.

Let us look at each of them in turn. A *discrete* variable is one which can only have certain numbers (or take certain fixed values). If our variable were the number of employees in a particular company then this would be an example of a discrete variable. The number of employees might be 50 or 51 or 52, for example, but it cannot possibly be 50.2 or 51.3428 since you can't employ a fraction of a person.

On the other hand, a *continuous* variable is one which can take any numerical value within a given range. If the variable were the amount of floorspace available in a supermarket then we could, technically, measure this variable to any degree of accuracy that we wanted. We might, for example, measure the variable to the nearest metre, or the nearest centimetre, or the nearest millimetre and so on. The only thing stopping us would be the accuracy of the measuring equipment.

Finally, the last type of variable is an *attribute* variable. Some variables that we might be interested in may not be shown in terms of numbers at all. For example, suppose our chosen variable was the sex of the employees in a particular company. We cannot express this variable sensibly as a number.

Student activity

Take a look at the following variables and decide which of the three types of variable it is:

- *your height;*
- *the colour of your eyes;*
- *the number of brothers and sisters you have.*

Height is a continuous variable because we could, if we wanted, measure it as closely as we wanted to the nearest centimetre, or to the nearest millimetre, and so on. Eye colour is an attribute variable because we cannot sensibly relate the variable to a number. Brown, for example, has no obvious numerical equivalent. Finally, the number of brothers and sisters is a discrete variable as it can only take certain fixed values from 0 upwards.

Primary and secondary data

Next we must distinguish between data which is classed as *primary* and that which is classed as *secondary*. Primary data refers to data that has been collected by the person who will use it, or at least that person has been responsible for supervising and organizing the collection. Typically, primary data has been collected directly for the purpose for which it is to be used. Secondary data, on the other hand, refers to data that has been collected for another purpose than the one for which it is to be used.

For example, a supermarket will collect data on the daily sales figure achieved. Such data, as far as the store is concerned, would be primary data – collected at first hand and for the store's own use. The head office of the supermarket chain may require all stores in the group to submit details of their daily sales on a regular basis perhaps to analyse how well different product lines are selling, or perhaps to assess which types of credit card customers tend to use. To the head office such data would be secondary.

Student activity

Why do you think it is important to distinguish between what is primary and what is secondary data?

Some of the reasons you may have thought of are:

- Primary data is usually more reliable because we know more about it – how it was collected, who collected it, why it was collected, and so on.
- Primary data has been collected specifically for a purpose so will only really suit one person's exact requirements.
- Secondary data is less reliable because we may not know how, when or why it was originally collected.
- Secondary data may not be exactly what we need for our investigation as it was originally collected by someone else for their own uses, not for ours.

Overall, if we are using secondary data we would need to be careful about its accuracy and reliability before using the data in any analysis. The distinction between primary and secondary data is important because it affects the potential reliability – and hence managerial usefulness – of any quantitative analysis undertaken. For secondary data we would need to ask a number of questions before using, analysing and reaching conclusions about the data:

- What data was collected?
- Who collected the data?
- For what purposes was the data collected?
- How was the information collected?
- Where and when was the information collected?
- Has any preliminary analysis been carried out on the data?

If we are dealing with primary data, however, the reliability of the information is much higher.

Raw data and aggregated data

Data may also be categorized as either raw or aggregated. Raw data refers to data in its original format that typically has not been processed or analysed in any way. Aggregated data, on the other hand, refers to data that has in some way already been processed and analysed. Raw data is generally of little use to management as it normally consists of a mass of individual numbers and, as we shall soon see, it is difficult to pick out the main features from such a mass of data. It is usually necessary to aggregate raw data by applying relevant quantitative techniques. As we shall see shortly in one of the subsequent chapters, when we aggregate raw data we lose some of the detailed information contained in it. For that reason we generally prefer to start off with raw data wherever possible and perform the necessary aggregation ourselves. For example, the manager of a modern supermarket could, in principle, have a computer printout of every single customer's purchases. Far more useful, however, would be an aggregation of this into a total daily sales figure for the store.

Populations and samples

In the process of analysing data we must usually distinguish between a sample and the statistical population. (Note that the word 'population' in statistics does not necessarily refer to people.) A population in statistics refers to the entire set of data that exists for some variable. A sample, on the other hand, refers to a carefully chosen, and representative, part of the population.

The distinction between sample and population is very important in statistics. Let us suppose that we wished to collect data on daily sales for all the supermarkets owned by a company. The population would, therefore, consist of all the stores and, in this case, we could easily collect the data relating to the population.

Frequently, however, we cannot collect data on the statistical population. For example, suppose the company is thinking of introducing a new item for sale in its stores, let's say a portable compact disc player. Before doing so they want some idea as to how well this item will sell. They, therefore, decide to ask customers whether they would buy such an item if it were on sale.

Student activity

Why do you think in this case we couldn't collect data on the population?

There are a number of reasons.

First, it is clear that the population in this case would be made up of all customers. Asking all customers if they would buy this item would:

- take too much time;
- be very difficult to organize;
- be very costly;
- provide far too much data for us to analyse.

For such reasons we would probably decide instead to ask a *sample* of customers – a selected cross section of the population. We would need to ensure that the sample was properly representative of the population and a subsequent chapter (see Chapter 3 on 'data collection') will discuss how this is achieved. Almost always our interest lies in analysing the statistical population. Almost always, however, we are forced to analyse instead only part of the population – a sample. The reasons why we are usually forced to investigate a sample may be several:

- there may be too many items in the population;
- it may take too long to collect data on the population;
- even if we collected data on the population it might take too long to analyse;
- the costs of collecting population data may be prohibitive.

There may be other reasons for restricting our data collection to a sample. The important point is that our analysis of the sample will still reveal the key characteristics of the population *provided* that the sample is properly representative of the population from which it is taken. This is a key assumption whenever we are analysing data collected from a sample. For the results of any statistical analysis to be valid we must be sure the sample is a fair cross section of the statistical population.

Occasionally, of course, it is possible to undertake analysis of populations rather than samples. Governments regularly collect data relating to some statistical population – usually referred to as a census. Increasingly, with computer-based storage of data it becomes possible to access and analyse population data. A company may have all employee records stored on a computer database, for example, which permits statistical analysis of the entire employee population rather than restricting the analysis to only a sample of the workforce.

Descriptive and inferential statistics

The final piece of vocabulary that we need to introduce at this stage relates to the difference between *descriptive* and *inferential* statistics. Descriptive statistics as a subject is concerned with the techniques for aggregating, summarizing and presenting data: quite simply with those techniques which allow us to describe the main features of a set of data. So, going back to the example of a survey of customers, we might describe how many male customers would buy the product and how many female customers. Inferential statistics is concerned with trying to reach a conclusion (literally making inferences) about a set of data when only part of the data set is available. Typically, inferential statistics is concerned with reaching conclusions about the population based on the descriptive statistics of the sample. So, in this example, we would try and determine, based only on the sample, how likely it was that the new product would be profitable.

SUMMARY

Now you have completed this section you will appreciate that:

- Managers in any type of business organization need an adequate understanding of common quantitative techniques and their relevance for business decision-making.
- An adequate understanding of the more important terminology used in statistics is essential for accountants and managers.
- Variables fall into one of three types: discrete, continuous or attribute.
- Data can be classified as primary if it has been collected first-hand or secondary if it has not.
- Data may be classified as raw if it is in its original, unprocessed form or aggregated if it has already been processed in some way.
- The data may relate to a statistical population or to only part of that population – a sample.

 ## SELF-REVIEW QUESTIONS

1 *What is the main difference between primary and secondary data and why is this difference important?*

2 *What is the difference between a sample and a population?*

3 *Why is it necessary to analyse a sample rather than a population?*

4 *What is the difference between descriptive and inferential statistics?*

5 *Why is it usually necessary to aggregate raw data?*

6 *What is the key feature of a sample that makes it possible to infer population characteristics from it?*

 ## STUDENT EXERCISES

1 Put yourself in the position of a manager in each of the following types of organization. Draw up a detailed list of the key pieces of data you would like to have about the operation of that organization and consider how such data might be used to help you manage that organization:

   (a) a car manufacturer;

   (b) a hospital;

   (c) a McDonald's restaurant;

   (d) a supermarket.

2 For the lists of key data that you produced for exercise 1 above, determine for each data item:

(a) what type of variable it would represent;

(b) whether the data is likely to be primary or secondary;

(c) whether the data is likely to be raw data or aggregated;

(d) whether the data is likely to be based on a population or a sample.

2 TOOLS OF THE TRADE

INTRODUCTION

We tried to convince you in the last chapter that managers and other business professionals need to have appropriate and relevant quantitative skills if they are to pursue a successful career and be effective in their jobs. Throughout the rest of this text we shall gradually be introducing you to a number of the common quantitative techniques and methods that are used by many businesses. However, before we do that we have to make sure that you have the relevant skills and knowledge to be able to understand those topics.

What we intend to do in this chapter is provide you with a basic set of numerical skills – what we can refer to as *tools of the trade* – that you will need before we go any further. We have kept these to the absolute minimum in this chapter and we shall introduce other basic skills as and when we need them in later chapters.

Naturally, different people will start using this text with different backgrounds, different experiences and different skills that they have already acquired. Above all in this chapter you should use your common sense to decide which of the topics covered you need to read and which you don't. Some of you will already be familiar with some of the topics we introduce in this chapter. If you are, then skip over that topic and move onto those topics which you need to read. However, don't do this simply to avoid work!

We've introduced the topics in this chapter because you really do need to have these related skills before we go on. To help you decide if you need to read a particular topic we've provided a 'self-assessment' section at the start of most sections. You should look at these questions and try and answer them without any further reading. When you've got your answers check them with ours. If *all* your answers are right and you feel comfortable with how you arrived at your answers then you don't really need to read that topic and can jump on to the next one. However, there's no point cheating since you'll only fool yourself and may well have difficulty with later topics.

CHAPTER STRUCTURE

The chapter introduces the basic topics shown below. They are written in such a way that you can jump from one to another but they are best read as a sequence. However, as you're working your way through the text, if you have difficulty with one of the later topics then come back and browse through the sections in this chapter to help you develop the prerequisite knowledge.

Section	Needed no later than Chapter:
Numbers	4
Basic arithmetic	4
Rounding	4
Estimating	4
Negative numbers	4
Fractions	4
Decimals	4
Percentages	4
Powers, exponents and scientific notation	6
Symbols and equations	6
Roots of numbers	6
Logarithms	14
Other mathematical operators	5

We are assuming that your level of numerical ability as you start this text is fairly limited. However, we are assuming that you:

- can count;
- can perform simple arithmetic using addition, subtraction, multiplication and division (using a pocket calculator and with pen and paper);
- are familiar with common number systems like £s and pence, miles, kilometres and so on.

You can probably do more than this and if you can you'll be able to work through the material in this chapter very quickly. You'll also need a calculator (and be able to use it) not just for sections in this chapter but for the whole of the text. It doesn't have to be a particularly sophisticated one but in addition to the usual basic keys it will need to have the following special abilities:

- a memory for storing numbers;
- keys marked as the following (or equivalent):

log

10^x

$\sqrt{}$

NUMBERS

Much of quantitative business analysis is about *numbers:* using numbers to represent a business situation, working with numbers to provide a solution to a problem, presenting numbers about some situation to a manager. Before we go any further we need to ensure that we understand properly what a

Record profits of £472m

number represents and how the basic number system works, and we need to develop some self-confidence when dealing with numbers. This last point is particularly important for would-be managers: you need to feel confident that you can handle information in the form of numbers easily, quickly and reliably. Unfortunately there is no magic solution to develop this level of confidence: it's a matter of hard work, determination and practice (and of course a well-written textbook!). You also need to remember that it's not just you that has initial difficulty with numbers and calculations. Many people do and research shows that many managers are particularly poor at analysing and understanding numerical information.

With a little bit of thought it soon becomes clear why we need a formal way of dealing with numbers. We use numbers to provide information: about an organization, a country, ourselves. Picture a simple scenario. We have a long street of houses and someone who regularly has to deliver letters and parcels to the right houses. Imagine that we did not have a number system, that is that none of the houses had a number showing on the front door. The person's task would not be an easy one. Picture a letter addressed to 'the house on Acacia Avenue with three windows and a green door next to the house with a red door'. A number system which says deliver this letter to 156 Acacia Avenue is better all round. Picture again what the (intelligent) person might do if no such numbering system existed. (S)he might actually create one to make life easier, perhaps using a simple tally, or marking, system. So, the first house might be marked as I, the second house as II, the third house as III and so on. The problem with such a tally system is that by the time we're a good way down the road we're at house number:

IIIIIIIIIIIIIIIIIIIIIIIIIIIIIIIIIIIIIIIIIIIIIII

or 46. Clearly such a tally system is not an efficient way of representing numbers, especially large ones. What we could do instead is develop a numbering system where we grouped sets of such tally marks, say in groups of 10. So we might have:

IIIIIIIIII   IIIIIIIIII   IIIIIIIIII   IIIIIIIIII   IIIIII

So we have four groups of 10 with 6 left over. However, we might as well go one stage further and rather than use tally marks to represent a number we use special symbols instead. These symbols – numbers – we are already familiar with:

0   1   2   3   4   5   6   7   8   9

Now think carefully about the implications of these symbols. There are only ten of them. And yet with these ten symbols we can write any number of any size!

The number system that most of us are familiar with is called the *decimal*, or denary, system. It's called this because all the numbers we use are made up of combinations of 10 numbers: 0,1,2,3,4,5,6,7,8,9. We take it for granted that we count things in groups of ten (after all we tend to have 10 fingers and 10 toes which helps us with basic counting). However, this isn't the only way of counting. At different times different cultures have used different counting systems. The Mayan civilization in Central America used a system which had 20 as its base (rather than our 10). The ancient Babylonians used 60 as the base (which is thought to be the reason why we still have 60 seconds in a minute and 60 minutes in an hour). More up to date, computer systems use the binary system for numbers where all numbers are represented as combinations of 0 and 1. To us, with the decimal system the number:

100

we see as one hundred. To a computer system, however, it would represent the decimal number 4! (To a computer 1100100 represents our 100.) So, for our decimal number system any number is made up of individual numbers between 0 and 9. These individual numbers we refer to as *digits* and what is known as the *place* of the digit in a number contributes to the value of that number. To help explain this we can think of a number – like 2932 – as being written as:

	Ten thousands	Thousands	Hundreds	Tens	Ones
Number	—	2	9	3	2

That is, our number is actually made up of:

two thousands
nine hundreds
three tens
two ones

One interesting – and important – point is that moving the position of any particular digit one place to the *left* multiplies its value by 10. So, for example, the digit 2 at the very right of the number represents 2 (units). If it had been in the column to the left it would have represented:

20 (two tens or 2 × 10)

One place to the left again and it would have been:

200 (two hundreds or 2 × 100 or 2 × 10 × 10)

One place again to the left and we would have:

2000 (two thousand or 2 × 1000 or 2 × 10 × 100)

It will be helpful for your studies if you can quickly recognize the *size* of numbers – that is recognize whether the number is in hundreds, thousands, millions and so on. One easy way of doing this is to see how many 0s there are in the right-hand part of the number. The number:

10   has one 0 on the right and we recognize this as ten.

The number 100 has two 0s and we recognize this as one hundred. It quickly becomes clear that each time we add a 0 to the right we are increasing the number tenfold:

10	ten
100	hundred
1,000	thousand
10,000	ten thousand
100,000	hundred thousand
1,000,000	million
1,000,000,000	billion

Notice that when we get to 1,000,000 rather than call this one thousand thousand (which is what it is) we tend to use the term million instead. Similarly the last number is actually one thousand million but is more usually called a billion – although there is a further confusing point to note about the term 'billion'. We have shown a billion as one thousand million. Some people refer to a billion when they have one million million (1,000,000,000,000). In this book we shall always use one thousand million when we refer to billion but in other books and when you see the word billion used by someone else you need to check which number they actually mean.

Notice also that we have used a comma (,) to separate each group of three 0s in the numbers above. This can be helpful when writing out large numbers with lots of 0s (or other digits) in them, although not all large numbers are written in this way. You might find it helpful for yourself to do this to begin with. Notice that we start counting the digits/0s from the right of the number and clearly each set of three 0s represents a multiple of a thousand. For example, for the number:

10000000000

we would start with the right-hand zero and count three 0s to the left and then put in a comma:

10000000,000

count another three 0s to the left and insert another comma:

10000,000,000

and then another:

10,000,000,000

until we can't put any more commas in. Notice also that some people might use a space rather than a comma:

10 000 000 000

Either way we recognize the number as ten billion.

BASIC ARITHMETIC

Self-assessment 1

Answer the questions set out below as best as you can. Check your answers against ours on p. 80.

If you've got them all right move on to the next self-assessment on p. 21.

Without using a calculator work out:

(a) $10 \times 3 - 5 \times 2$

(b) $15 \div 3 + 2 - 3$

(c) $15 \times 2 - 1 \times 4$

We said earlier in this chapter that we are assuming that you can count and can do simple arithmetic using addition, subtraction, multiplication and division either manually on a piece of paper or by using a calculator. If these basic calculations give you trouble you might want to look at a few chapters in another book which might help: *A Way with Numbers* by Terry Riley (published in 1990 by BBC Books, ISBN 0 563361638) which will remind you of how to do basic arithmetic.

However, one thing that can give people difficulty is when you have to do arithmetic which involves several numbers in a sequence. For example, working out:

$$9 + 8 + 2 + 3$$

is fairly straightforward to do even though it involves several numbers. The reason it is fairly easy (and the answer is 22 by the way) is that all the arithmetic is of the same sort – it involves addition. We often will have to do arithmetic on a string of numbers like this where the arithmetic is of different sorts. For example, we might want to work out:

$$9 + 8 - 2 \times 3$$

You might think that we can do the arithmetic simply by starting with the number on the left and working our way through until we get to the number on the right as we did with the last calculation. That is:

$9 + 8$ is 17

$17 - 2$ is 15

15×3 is 45

giving an answer of 45. Whilst this seems simple enough, unfortunately it's wrong! The reason is that there is a recognized (but not always explicitly stated) way of tackling this type of arithmetic. We do this by considering what are known as the *arithmetic operators* that we have to use. An arithmetic operator is just a fancy word for the specific arithmetic calculation. The arithmetic operators you are already familiar with are:

+ (add)

− (subtract or minus)

× (multiply or times)

÷ (divide, sometimes shown as /)

If we're doing arithmetic which involves more than one of these operators then we have to use them in a specific sequence:

- we must do any arithmetic involving × or ÷ first in the order in which they appear;
- then we do any arithmetic involving + or − again in the order in which they appear.

What 'in the order in which they appear' means is that if we have some arithmetic where both × and ÷ appear then if the × comes first we do this arithmetic first and then anything involving ÷. If the ÷ appears first then we do this bit of the arithmetic followed by anything involving ×. The same applies to + and −. You may actually have a calculator which is preprogrammed to do arithmetic in this way and computer programs have these 'rules' already built into them. In our case we would work out the answer for:

9 + 8 − 2 × 3

as:

- 2 × 3   which is 6

which then means we have to work out:

9 + 8 − 6

- 9 + 8 is 17 (there is no division to do)

which means we have to work out:

17 − 6

- 17 − 6 is 11 which is our answer.

Rather different from the first answer of 45 we got! It might seem odd that we have to do the arithmetic in a different way from how it is written in the problem but this arithmetic operator precedence is standard practice and we just have to get used to it. It will probably be worthwhile at this stage using your own calculator and seeing whether it uses such precedence rules automatically.

On your calculator press the following keys:

9

+

8

−

2

×

3

=

If it gives you the answer 11 then your calculator is automatically using the rules we set out. If it doesn't show this answer then you need to be careful when doing this sort of arithmetic as you'll have to remember the rules for yourself.

Student activity

Work out the following and check your answer against ours below. We suggest that you use pen and paper first and then work it out on your calculator.

(a) $8 + 9 + 5 \times 2 - 2$

(b) $6 \div 2 \times 3 - 6 + 5$

(c) $3 \times 5 \div 3 + 5 - 4$

You should have got the following answers (and if you didn't then go back through your workings and check them carefully against ours):

(**a**) Answer 25

> 5×2 is 10 giving $8 + 9 + 10 - 2$
>
> $8 + 9$ is 17 giving $17 + 10 - 2$
>
> $17 + 10$ is 27 giving $27 - 2$
>
> $27 - 2$ is 25 which is the answer.

(**b**) Answer 8

This one involves both × and ÷ but the ÷ appears first so we must do this first:

> $6 \div 2$ is 3 giving $3 \times 3 - 6 + 5$
>
> 3×3 is 9 giving $9 - 6 + 5$
>
> $9 - 6$ is 3 giving $3 + 5$
>
> $3 + 5$ is 8 which is the answer.

(**c**) Answer 6

Again we have × and ÷ but the × appears first. So we have:

3 × 5 is 15 giving 15 ÷ 3 + 5 −4

15 ÷ 3 is 5 giving 5 + 5 − 4

5 + 5 is 10 giving 10 − 4

10 − 4 is 6 which is our answer.

The = sign

One further mathematical operator which will be useful to us is one with which you're probably already familiar, the equals sign shown as =. Whenever we see this it simply means that the numbers, or expressions, on the left-hand of the sign are exactly the same as those on the right-hand side (even though they might look different). So we have:

2 × 2 = 4

5 − 3 + 2 − 1 = 3

and so on.

Brackets

Self-assessment 2

Answer the questions set out below as best as you can. Check your answers against ours on p. 80.

If you've got them all right move on to the next self-assessment on p. 25.

Without using a calculator work out the following:

(a) (3 × 2) − (5 + 2)

(b) (3 × 2 − 5 × (3 + 1))

(c) 10 + (15 ÷ 3) × 2

(d) (((3 × 4) −5) × 2)

Sometimes, for more complicated calculations, we might want to make sure that someone understands how arithmetic is to be done by using brackets, ( ), in the expression. We use brackets as a pair – that is one on the left (and one on the right) to show the bits of the calculation that must be done first. For the calculations in the previous activity we could have written:

(**a**) 8 + 9 + (5 × 2) − 2

to make it clear that the bit inside the brackets had to be calculated first. For (**b**) we could have written:

(**b**) ((6 ÷ 2) × 3) − 6 + 5

This looks quite complicated since it involves two sets of brackets, one inside the other. Whenever we see multiple brackets like this we can work out the arithmetic simply by looking for the inside pair of brackets and working that out, then finding the next pair and working that out, and so on. Here the inside pair is that around $(6 \div 2)$ so we would work this out first as 3 and then we would have:

$$(3 \times 3) - 6 + 5$$

so we would work the next pair out as (3×3) or 9 and then complete the rest of the arithmetic in the usual way. In this way quite complex arithmetic can be expressed but as long as we remember to start with the inside set of brackets and then work outwards we should be OK (although remember that with more complicated arithmetic it is always worthwhile double-checking your answer to make sure you've not made any obvious mistakes – especially in an exam).

Student activity

For (c) in the last activity use brackets to indicate the arithmetic sequence.

Work out the following:

(a) $(3 - 2) \times 5 - 2$

(b) $6 + ((3 \times 2) - 5)$

(c) $(9 \div 3) \times (2 + 1)$

For (**c**) in the last activity we would write:

$$((3 \times 5) \div 3) + 5 - 4$$

indicating that 3×5 is to be done first before dividing by 3.

For part (**a**) of the activity above we have:

$$(3 - 2) \times 5 - 2$$

or:

$$1 \times 5 - 2$$

giving $5 - 2$ or 3 as the answer. Notice that in this case we have used brackets to force a calculation which goes against the normal rules of precedence (when we would have normally multiplied first before subtracting if there had been no brackets). This is quite a common use of brackets.

For (**b**) we have:

$$6 + ((3 \times 2) - 5)$$

giving $6 + (6 - 5)$ which in turn gives $6 + 1$ or 7 as the answer.

For (**c**) we have:

$$(9 \div 3) \times (2 + 1)$$

Here we have two sets of bracket but they're not inside each other. So we work them out together giving 3 × 3 with an answer of 9.

It is worth remembering that brackets *must* be used in pairs. So, if you're using brackets in some arithmetic always check that you have an even number of them otherwise you've made a mistake. This often happens in exams. An expression like:

(3 + 2) × ((6 − 1) × 5 − 3

is incorrect since a bracket is missing (there are only five and we must always have an even number of brackets) and the arithmetic can't be completed since we don't know where the missing bracket should go (which of course will affect the answer we get).

Student activity

Suppose the missing bracket should have given:

(3 + 2) × ((6–1) × 5) − 3

What would the answer be?

With the missing bracket as (3 + 2) × ((6 − 1) × 5) − 3 then we start with:

((6 − 1) × 5) and work out the inside pair first:

(6 − 1) is 5 giving

(3 + 2) × (5 × 5) − 3

We work out each of the next two pairs together giving:

5 × 25 − 3

and then our normal operator precedence rules apply so we must do the multiplication first: 5 × 25 is 125 and subtracting 3 gives an answer of 122.

Notice that we might see the expression written as:

(3 + 2) ((6 − 1) × 5) − 3

which, if you look carefully, has had the multiplication sign between the brackets removed. This is quite common. If two expressions in brackets are to be multiplied together then we might not bother showing the multiplication sign itself. We can only do this with brackets, however, and not with numbers themselves – that is we couldn't write 53 instead of 5 × 3 since we couldn't distinguish this from the number fifty-three.

One other useful thing to remember about basic arithmetic is that if we're multiplying or dividing and one of the numbers ends in 0 then the job is much easier. If we wanted, for example, 15 × 10 then all we have to do is add a 0 to the end of the first number:

15 × 10 = 150

This works for any whole number:

$$134 \times 10 = 1,340$$
$$15,629 \times 10 = 156,290 \text{ and so on.}$$

If we multiply by a number with more than one zero the same principle applies but this time we add as many 0s as there are on the number we're multiplying by:

$$15 \times 100 = 1,500$$
$$134 \times 1,000 = 134,000$$
$$15,629 \times 10,000 = 156,290,000$$

and so on. Similarly, if we're dividing one number by another number which ends in zero we can simply knock off a zero from the end of the first number. For example:

$$1,500 \div 10 = 150$$
$$134,000 \div 1,000 = 134$$

that is, knocking off one 0 from 134,000 for each 0 in the dividing number.

Student activity

Work out the following:

(a) 134,000 ÷ 10

(b) 134,000 ÷ 100

(c) 134,000,000 ÷ 10

(d) 134,000,000 ÷ 10,000

The arithmetic is quite simple: we simply knock off the appropriate number of 0s from the end of the first number:

(a) 134,000 ÷ 10 = 13,400̸ or 13,400

(b) 134,000 ÷ 100 = 134,0̸0̸0̸ or 1,340

(c) 134,000,000 ÷ 10 = 134,000,00̸0̸ or 13,400,000

(d) 134,000,000 ÷ 10,000 = 134,00̸0̸,0̸0̸0̸ or 13,400

Notice when we're dealing with a number with lots of 0s we have to be careful not to miss one out (or put in one too many). Double-check your answers whenever possible.

ROUNDING

Self-assessment 3

Answer the questions set out below as best as you can. Check your answers against ours on p. 80.

If you've got them all right move on to the next self-assessment on p. 29.

1 You read in the paper that a particular company made a profit last year of £3,873,584. What would this be to the nearest:

   (**a**) hundred pounds?

   (**b**) ten thousand pounds?

2 Without using a calculator or pen and paper work out roughly how much 2,908,235 + 1,865,871 would be.

National Lottery sales pass £3bn mark

We all know that accountants are very fussy about the accuracy of data and numbers that they use. An accountant would want to know down to the last penny what something cost, for example. However, for many managers such detail is very often not necessary and for many of us trying to remember numbers in very precise terms can be very difficult and in many cases is probably not necessary anyway. Think about question 1 in the last self-assessment where we said that we'd seen in a paper that a particular company had made £3,873,584 profit last year. Of course the accountant will need to have this figure in all the detail shown (and the Inland Revenue will as well). But for the rest of us it's much easier to remember that the company made a profit of about £4 million. That type of number stays in our memory much more easily than the detailed one. Obviously what we've done is to round the original number into something that is more convenient and easier to remember.

The process of rounding a number is simple enough, although we have to be clear about how much rounding is to take place. In our example we could round the profit figure of £3,873,584 to the nearest £10, the nearest £100, £1,000, £10,000, £100,000 or million (£1,000,000).

Rounding to the nearest 10

To round to the nearest 10 we take the last two numbers in the profit figure of £3,873,584 (84) and look at the last number in the figure (known as the last digit), 4 in our example. We then use a simple rule:

Last digit:	1 2 3 4	5 6 7 8 9
What we do:	Round down to next lowest 0	Round up and add 1 to next digit on the left

So, if the last digit is between 1 and 4 we round the two digit number down but if it is between 5 and 9 we round it up. In our case our number is 84, the last digit is 4 so we round down to 80 and say that profit is £3,873,580 to the nearest £10. If the last two digits had been 86 instead we would round up to 90, that is setting the last digit to 0 and adding 1 to the previous digit.

There are two other things to say. The first is that if the last digit is 5 we've said to round up. Some people might tell you to round down with a 5. Which you actually do is quite arbitrary as long as you're consistent and do it the same way every time. In this book we'll always round up. The second thing we have to say is that if the last digit ends in 0 we don't actually need to round at all.

Student activity

Round the following numbers to the nearest 10:

(a) 39

(b) 33

(c) 55

(d) 80

(e) 96

Our answers are as follows:

(**a**) We round the 9 up and add 1 to the next digit to give 40.

(**b**) We round down to give 30.

(**c**) We round up to give 60.

(**d**) We don't need to round this at all as it's already to the nearest 10.

(**e**) We round up and add 1 to the next digit. But this gives the next digit as 9 + 1 or 10 so the number is then rounded as 100.

Rounding to the nearest 100

Like a lot of the things we'll be looking at, once we've learned how to round to the nearest 10 rounding to the nearest 100 (or 1,000) is more or less the same. To round to the nearest 100 we take the last three digits of the figure. Our rounding rule is then:

Last two digits:	1 to 49	50 to 99
What we do:	Round down	Round up

Our last three digits in the profit figure are 584 and the last two are 84. This puts us between 50 and 99 so we round up to 600 and would say that profit was £3,873,600 to the nearest £100. If the last three digits had been 548 instead we would have rounded down to 500.

Student activity

Round these numbers to the nearest 100:

(a) 237

(b) 871

(c) 560

(d) 42

The solutions are:

(a) Last two digits are between 1 and 49 so round down to 200.

(b) Last two digits are between 50 and 99 so round up to 900.

(c) Last two digits are between 50 and 99 so round up to 600.

(d) Last two digits are between 1 and 49 so round down. But the original number is already less than 100 so we round down to 0.

It's now fairly clear that the 'rules' for rounding are virtually the same for 10s and for 100s. Obviously we could go on to look at 1,000s, 10,000s and so on. However, the overall principles will still be the same. This gives us a simple set of 'rules' for rounding:

	Round down	*Round up*
Nearest 10	0 to 4	5 to 9
Nearest 100	0 to 49	50 to 99
Nearest 1,000	0 to 499	500 to 999
Nearest 10,000	0 to 4,999	5,000 to 9,999
Nearest 100,000	0 to 49,999	50,000 to 99,999
Nearest 1,000,000	0 to 499,999	500,000 to 999,999

and so on.

Student activity

(a) *What would the 'rules' be for rounding to the nearest 10 million?*

(b) *Round the following numbers:*

8,759   12,345   789   198,567   25,765,341   8,347,078

(i)   to the nearest 1,000;
(ii) to the nearest 100,000;
(iii) to the nearest million.

(a) We would have:

Nearest 10,000,000
Round down 1 to 4,999,999
Round up 5,000,000 to 9,999,999

(**b**) Rounding the numbers we would have:

(i) to the nearest 1,000:
8,759 rounds up to 9,000
12,345 rounds down to 12,000
789 rounds up to 1,000
198,567 rounds up to 199,000
25,765,341 rounds down to 25,765,000
8,347,078 rounds down to 8,347,000

(ii) to the nearest 100,000:
8,759 rounds down to 0
12,345 rounds down to 0
789 rounds down to 0
198,567 rounds up to 200,000
25,765,341 rounds up to 25,800,000
8,347,078 rounds down to 8,300,000

(iii) to the nearest million:
8,759 rounds down to 0
12,345 rounds down to 0
789 rounds down to 0
198,567 rounds down to 0
25,765,341 rounds up to 26,000,000
8,347,078 rounds down to 8,000,000

Rounding a complex number then can help us make more sense of the thing the number relates to and help us better remember the number. But we do have to be a little careful. We now realize that any rounded number is just an approximation of the original number. If we forget this we may mislead ourselves – and others – when using such numbers. For example, let us suppose we read in the press that a particular company operating both in the food sector and the drinks sector made the following profits last year:

Food sector profit: £3 million
Drinks sector profit: £2 million

We then conclude that obviously (!) the company made a total profit of £5 million. However, knowing what we now know about rounding we realize that each of these figures is rounded to the nearest million. We can work out that the first figure of £3 million (rounded) could have been anywhere between £2,500,000 and £3,499,999 since any number between these two would be rounded to £3 million.

Student activity

What would be the corresponding range of numbers for the profit figure of £2 million for the drinks sector?

The equivalent figures for £2 million would be £1,500,000 to £2,499,999. So, this means that actual profits could be:

	Lowest	*Highest*
Food sector	£2,500,000	£3,499,999
Drinks sector	£1,500,000	£2,499,999
Total	£4,000,000	£5,999,998

anywhere between £4 million and £6 million!

The moral is that although it can be very useful to round numbers we must be careful about using such numbers.

Significant digits

Self-assessment 4

Answer the questions set out below as best as you can. Check your answers against ours on p. 80.

If you've got them all right move on to the next self-assessment on p. 30.

We have a number 53,467.

(a) Show this to two significant digits.

(b) How many significant digits does the original number show?

When presenting data for some variable a choice must often be made as to the level of accuracy of the numbers given, as in the example of reporting company profits. If data on, say, company profits were being presented – with actual profits being £3,873,584, these could be shown to the nearest £ million (e.g. £4 million) or to the nearest £100,000 (£3.9 million) and so on down to the nearest pound or even the nearest penny if desired. A distinction is made, therefore, in a number between those digits representing accurate information and those which provide information only about the size, or magnitude, of the number. For example, we would say that both the numbers below have one significant digit:

4 million
4,000,000

In either case, the number is reliable only to the nearest million. If, however, the numbers were calculated to the nearest 100,000 then they would have two significant digits:

3.9 million
3,900,000

The importance of determining the number of significant digits associated with a particular set of numbers becomes apparent when considering the rounding of numbers. Frequently figures are rounded (to the nearest whole unit, to the nearest thousand, to the nearest million and so on) to simplify the numbers that have to be dealt with. It is, after all, much easier to appreciate that profit was £4 million (to the nearest £1,000,000) than to say that profit was £3,873,584. To round a number to the nearest unit we must determine the number of significant digits we require. Examples of rounding are shown below:

Rounding an actual figure of £3,873,584 for example:

To the nearest £1:	£3,873,584	(7 significant digits)
To the nearest £10:	£3,873,590	(6 significant digits)
To the nearest £100:	£3,873,600	(5 significant digits)
To the nearest £1,000:	£3,874,000	(4 significant digits)
To the nearest £10,000:	£3,870,000	(3 significant digits)
To the nearest £100,000:	£3,900,000	(2 significant digits)
To the nearest £1,000,000:	£4,000,000	(1 significant digit)

The importance of significant digits and rounding also becomes apparent in the calculation of statistical measures and their presentation. With the advent of pocket calculators (and computers) we can perform the relevant calculations to five, six or more decimal places. The danger is that the person seeing such a long string of digits can easily forget that the data being analysed is significant to far fewer digits than shown on the calculator or computer printout.

As a general rule when performing calculations you should use as many significant digits as possible in the intermediate stages of the calculation and only perform the appropriate rounding at the end of the calculation. We shall see how important this is later in this chapter.

ESTIMATING

Self-assessment 5

Answer the questions set out below as best as you can. Check your answers against ours on p. 80.

If you've got them all right move on to the next self-assessment on p. 33.

Answer these questions *without* using a calculator and *without* using pen and paper to do the calculations.

1 You meet some five friends in a coffee bar and offer to buy them all a coffee (you have one as well). Coffee costs 52p per cup. Roughly how much will the cost of six coffees be?

2 You've recently bought yourself a car and are checking around for car insurance. One company says it will provide insurance for £47 per month. Roughly how much will this cost a year?

Very often when we're dealing with figures we want a rough idea of the answer to some problem – like the bill in a restaurant or supermarket – and we want this quickly and easily which usually means doing the sums in our head rather than on a calculator or on paper. To make such an estimate quickly and easily we can use the principles of rounding numbers. We can use the examples from the last Self-assessment to illustrate. In the first question we're asked for a rough idea of the cost of six coffees which cost 52p each.

52p rounds easily to 50p and 50p × 6 = 300p or £3. So, when it comes time to pay the bill we'd be expecting to pay about this much. If the bill came to £4 we'd now know that something looked wrong and we might ask to check the bill again. Similarly if the bill came to £2 we might decide to pay up quickly and leave before the cafe realized its mistake! Similarly with the car insurance example – the insurance costs about £50 each month so the cost each year would be £50 × 12 months or about £600.

Student activity

You're in charge of ordering floppy disks for the computer in the office where you work. You place an order for 50 disks at £0.99 each. Roughly how much will they cost altogether?

The disks cost about £1 each so 50 × £1 is about £50.

As we shall see as we begin to investigate the various quantitative techniques used by business it is very useful to do this sort of estimating in a problem so that you have a rough idea of what answer we should get to some problem before we actually calculate it. Even people who have a lot of practice at performing calculations still make mistakes. They make a mistake when using a calculator, they put a decimal place in the wrong spot, they subtract when they meant to add and so on. When using a computer system to do such calculations we might make a mistake entering the numbers for example.

Unless we know *in advance* roughly the sort of answer to expect we might not spot such mistakes. In the case of the last Student activity if we suddenly got an invoice from the supplier of the computer ribbons for £500 we would obviously realize a mistake had been made somewhere. But suppose the bill had been for £60? Having estimated the rough cost we would now know that the invoice looks too high and would know that it needed checking. Without the rough estimate we might just have paid it!

Student activity

Without using a calculator try estimating the answer you should get to each of the following:

(a) 383 + 92   **(c)** 18,321 + 509   **(e)** 14,962 × 2,031

(b) 508 − 215   **(d)** 1,987 × 23

When you have an estimate of the results use your calculator to check whether you were right.

Remember that the idea behind estimating is not to give you an accurate answer to the question but to provide a rough idea as to what sort of answer to expect – should the answer be in hundreds, thousands, millions and so on. You would probably be surprised at the number of senior managers and executives in a variety of organizations the author has worked with who have accepted reports, estimates, budgets with obvious (!) arithmetic errors in them. This approach – of estimating an approximate answer wherever possible before doing the arithmetic is particularly helpful in exams when pressures of time and of nerves can lead you to careless mistakes when using your calculator. Taking each part of the question in turn:

(a) 383 rounds to 400

92 rounds to 100

so 400 + 100 is 500 (actual answer is 475).

(b) 508 rounds to 500

215 rounds to 200

so 500–200 is about 300 (actual answer is 293).

(c) 18,321 is about 18,000

509 is about 500

so 18,000+500 is about 18,500 (actual answer is 18,830).

(d) 1,987 is about 2,000

23 is about 20.

Remembering that 20 is 2 × 10 we then have:

2,000 × 2 × 10

2,000 × 2 is 4,000 whilst 4,000 × 10 is 40,000 (we just add one 0 to the 4,000 when multiplying by 10). (Actual answer is 45,701).

(e) 14,962 is about 15,000 whilst 2,031 is about 2,000.

15,000 × 2,000 is 15,000 × 2 × 1,000 or 30,000 × 1,000. We can add three 0s to 30,000 to get an estimate of 30,000,000 (30 million). (Actual answer is 30,387,822.)

NEGATIVE NUMBERS

Self-assessment 6

Answer the questions set out below as best as you can. Check your answers against ours on p. 80.

If you've got them all right move on to the next self-assessment on p. 35.

1 You have £25 left in your bank account. However, the bank has just told you that you owe it £40 in bank charges and has deducted this from your account. How much is left in your account?

2 Work out −30 + 15 − 20

We shall often need to be able to incorporate negative numbers into our calculations and we need to understand what we are doing when we do this. Adding numbers together doesn't usually cause any difficulty. If we wanted 5 + 2, for example, we can work out in our heads that this is 7. What we are actually doing (even without realizing it) is to think of the arithmetic like the diagram below:

We start at the first number, 5, and move 2 to the right to get to 7. Similarly, if we want to subtract one number from another we would find the first number point and then move to the *left*. For example 9 − 6 means that we locate 9 and move 6 to the left to give an answer of 3:

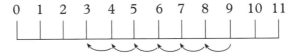

But what if we want to subtract a further 6 from this result? That is, 3 − 6. We clearly want to move 6 to the left so it seems logical to extend the scale to the left to allow us to do this:

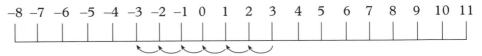

where the numbers to the left of 0 are known as negative numbers. We see that 3 − 6 would give −3 as the result. So, it will help us if we remember that when adding a number we are effectively moving to the right of this scale and when we subtract a number we are moving to the left. Sometimes when subtracting, the result is itself a negative number. Consider the first question in the last Self-assessment exercise. We were told that we had £25 in the bank account but that the bank was charging us £40 in bank charges. To find out the amount in our account after these charges are deducted we need:

$$25 - 40$$

which is −£15: that is, we are overdrawn to the extent of £15, effectively we owe the bank this much.

We already know how to do basic arithmetic with negative numbers (since we are simply subtracting some number from another). However, some arithmetic involving negative numbers can get a little more complicated and we need to ensure you are familiar with the 'rules' involved. Let us return to our bank account example. We now have −£15 in the account. Suppose the bank now tells us that a cheque for £10 that you'd written (but forgotten about) has now been cashed: that is a further £10 has to be debited from your account. We now require:

$$-15 - 10$$

This will now give −£25 since, again, we move 10 units to the left of our number scale and since this was already at −15 it moves to −25. But what about subtracting a negative number?

To see what this means think again about the bank. It has now realized that the £10 it subtracted from your account was a mistake and it wants to rectify this mistake. That is, it wants to subtract the subtraction that it has just done. In arithmetic terms:

$$-15 - (-10)$$

It wants to subtract the amount it had mistakenly subtracted. This implies it wants to subtract a negative number. Without going into the why's and wherefore's we say that:

subtracting a negative number is exactly the same as adding a positive number.

That is:

−15 − (−10) is the same as −15 + 10
(both giving an answer of 5)

So the two negative signs together become a positive sign. In the bank example you can see why this works. Subtracting the previous subtraction (the two minuses) is just the same as the bank adding £10 to your account to rectify its earlier mistake. So, whenever we are performing arithmetic and we see that we are subtracting a negative number we can simply add this number instead. When using a calculator with this type of arithmetic you need to be careful since most will not properly recognize this double negative operation.

For example, on my calculator if I press:

$\overline{}$

15

$\overline{}$

$\overline{}$

10

=

I get an answer of 25! To get the correct answer I must use a key sequence of:

15

+/– (this is usually a special key which reverses the sign of the number you have just keyed in)

$\overline{}$

10

+/–

=

and this gives an answer –5.

Multiplying and dividing with negative numbers

> ### *Self-assessment 7*
>
> Answer the questions set out below as best as you can. Check your answers against ours on p. 80.
>
> If you've got them all right move on to the next self-assessment on p. 38.
>
> Work out the following:
>
> **(a)** 10×-5 **(d)** $10 \div -5$
>
> **(b)** -10×-5 **(e)** $-10 \div -5$
>
> **(c)** -10×5 **(f)** $-10 \div 5$

There are times when we will need to multiply or divide by a negative number. Without explaining why we provide the following rules:

Multiplication:

positive × positive = positive   e.g. $2 \times 2 = 4$
number   number   number

positive × negative = negative   e.g. $2 \times -2 = -4$
number   number   number

negative × positive = negative   e.g. $-2 \times 2 = -4$
number   number   number

negative × negative = positive   e.g. $-2 \times -2 = 4$
number   number   number

Division:

positive ÷ positive = positive   e.g. $10 \div 2 = 5$
number   number   number

positive ÷ negative = negative   e.g. $10 \div -2 = -5$
number   number   number

negative ÷ positive = negative   e.g. $-10 \div 2 = -5$
number   number   number

negative ÷ negative = positive   e.g. $-10 \div -2 = 5$
number   number   number

All of this boils down into a simple rule for multiplication and division:

- *If both numbers are the same sign the result will be positive.*
- *If the two numbers have different signs the result will be negative.*

Again, when using your calculator you will probably have to use the +/– key. For example to get $10 \div -2$ we key in:

10
÷
2
+/–
=

to get –5.

Student activity

For each of the following:
- *first decide whether the answer would be positive or negative;*
- *use your calculator to work out the answer.*

(a) 104×-5

(b) $-86 \div -2$

(c) $(-86 \div -2) \times 5$

(d) $(-86 \div -2) \times -5$

    (e) $(-86 \div -2) \times (-5 \times 3)$

    (f) $(-86 \div -2) \times (-5 \times -3)$

    (g) $(-3 \times -2 \times -5) \div 10$

(a) We have a + and a – so the answer will be negative. With a calculator we get –520 (keystrokes are 104, ×, 5, +/–,=).

(b) Both signs are the same so we get a positive answer. With the keystrokes 86, +/–, ÷, 2, +/–, = we get an answer of 43.

(c) This is a little more complicated but we follow our earlier rule of working out things in brackets first. The term inside the bracket will be positive (since the two signs in the bracket are the same). We'll then be multiplying this positive answer by another positive number so the final result will be positive.

    With a calculator we have: 86, +/–, ÷, 2, +/–, ×, 5, = to give an answer of 215.

(d) Using the same logic as in (**c**) the term in brackets will be positive but we're now multiplying by a negative number. We have two numbers with different signs so we'll get a negative answer.

    With a calculator we have: 86, +/–, ÷, 2, +/–, ×, 5, +/–, = to give an answer of –215.

(e) This time we've got two sets of brackets. The arithmetic inside the first pair will give a positive answer. The arithmetic inside the second pair will give a negative answer. So we'll end up multiplying a positive number by a negative so the final result will be negative also.

    With a calculator we have: 86, +/–, ÷, 2, +/–, ×, 5, +/–, ×, 3, = to give an answer of –645.

(f) Following the logic in (**e**) we'll now get a final answer which is positive since the arithmetic in the second pair of brackets will now give a positive result.

    With a calculator we have: 86, +/–, ÷, 2, +/–, ×, 5, +/–, ×, 3, +/–, = to give an answer of 645.

(g) The term in the brackets involves multiplying three negative numbers. Multiplying the first two will give a positive result. Multiplying by the third (negative) number will turn this answer back into negative. And dividing through by a positive number will give a final answer which is still negative.

    With a calculator we have: 3, +/–, ×, 2, +/–, ×, 5, +/–, ÷, 10, = to give an answer of –3.

FRACTIONS

Self-assessment 8

Answer the questions set out below as best as you can. Check your answers against ours on p. 80.

If you've got them all right move on to the next self-assessment on p. 45.

Work out the following without using a calculator:

(a) $\frac{3}{4} + \frac{2}{5}$ (c) $\frac{3}{5} \times \frac{1}{7}$

(b) $\frac{6}{7} - \frac{2}{3}$ (d) $\frac{5}{6} - \frac{8}{9}$

So far you might have noticed that we've only been working with whole numbers (often referred to as *integers*). There are frequently times when we need to deal with numbers which are non-integer – they are shown in parts or, in mathematical terms, as a *fraction*. A fraction is simply part of a whole. If you buy a bar of chocolate and share it with a friend then you may have half a bar each, shown as $\frac{1}{2}$ (assuming of course you share the bar equally between you!). If the bar is one of those which is divided into small squares of chocolate then, if there are 20 squares of chocolate, you might have $\frac{10}{20}$ squares each. We can show this quite simply in diagram form as in Fig. 2.1.

Fig. 2.1   Dividing a bar of chocolate

Student activity

For the bar in 20 parts what would be the fraction if you kept 16 of the squares? How many would your friend get as a fraction?

Fairly obviously, we would have $\frac{16}{20}$ pieces and our friend would have the reminder which must be $\frac{4}{20}$ pieces.

You may remember if you've met fractions before that the number on the top of the fraction expression is referred to as the *numerator* and the one on the bottom as the *denominator*. One thing about fractions that can puzzle people to begin with is that a particular fraction – like $\frac{16}{20}$ – might be written in a different way, or in fact in several different ways. Fractions which are equal to each other but which have different numerators and denominators are called *equivalent fractions*. Equivalent fractions can be found by multiplying or dividing both the numerator and denominator by the same number. Let us consider $\frac{16}{20}$. Suppose we divide both numerator and denominator by 2. We then get:

$$\frac{16}{20} = \frac{16 \div 2}{20 \div 2} = \frac{8}{10}$$

as two equivalent fractions. That is, $\frac{16}{20}$ and $\frac{8}{10}$ are exactly the same. We could divide $\frac{8}{10}$ by 2 again to get:

$$\frac{16}{20} = \frac{8}{10} = \frac{4}{5}$$

Similarly if we took our original fraction, $\frac{16}{20}$, and multiplied by 2 we would get:

$$\frac{16}{20} = \frac{8}{10} = \frac{4}{5} = \frac{32}{40}$$

and so on. All these fractions are equal and it doesn't matter which we actually use. In the chocolate bar context, it wouldn't matter if you got $\frac{16}{20}$ths of the bar or $\frac{4}{5}$ths since the amount you got relative to the total would be the same in both cases.

Sometimes we might be asked to find the *simplest form* of a fraction. This is simply the equivalent fraction shown in its smallest numerical form and where the numerator/denominator cannot be divided by any number other than one. In our example, $\frac{4}{5}$ would be the simplest form of the fraction. We cannot divide 4 or 5 by the same number to get integers – dividing through by 2, 3, 4 or 5, for example, would not work.

Student activity

You work in a small company with a total of 25 employees: 10 of the employees are female; 4 are under 25 years of age; 10 have been with the company over 10 years. Write as fractions:

(a) *the number of female employees;*

(b) *the number of employees under 25;*

(c) *the number of employees who have been with the company no more than 10 years;*

(d) *for each fraction find the equivalent fraction when the denominator is 100;*

(e) *for each fraction find its simplest form.*

For part (**a**) we have:

$\dfrac{10}{25}$ as the fraction who are female.

Similarly we have for (**b**):

$\dfrac{4}{25}$ as the fraction who are under 25 years of age.

For (**c**) we hope you read the question carefully! We were told that 10 had been with the company more than 10 years, as a fraction $\frac{10}{25}$. But we weren't asked for this. We were asked for the fraction who had been with the company no more than 10 years. Clearly this must be $\frac{(25-10)}{25}$ which is:

$\dfrac{15}{25}$

We are also asked in (**d**) to find the equivalent fractions which have a denominator of 100. To get a denominator of 100 from one of 25 we must multiply by 4. To keep the fractions equivalent we must also multiply the numerator by 4. This gives:

(a) $\dfrac{10 \times 4}{25 \times 4} = \dfrac{40}{100}$

(b) $\dfrac{4 \times 4}{25 \times 4} = \dfrac{16}{100}$

(c) $\dfrac{15 \times 4}{25 \times 4} = \dfrac{60}{100}$

For part (**e**) we are asked to find the simplest form of the fraction. Taking each in turn from the answer to part (**d**) we have:

(a) $\dfrac{40}{100}$

With practice it usually becomes clear what dividing numbers to use. Until then we can just keep trying by hit and miss: numbers like 2, 5, 10 will often work. If we divide both by 10 we get:

$\dfrac{4}{10}$

Both numerator and denominator are even numbers so we can always divide by 2 to give:

$$\frac{2}{5}$$

The only number other than one that we can divide the numerator by is 2 and this will not give an integer result for 5 so this fraction, $\frac{2}{5}$, is the simplest form of the fraction $\frac{40}{100}$.

Repeating this for (**b**) but without the discussion we get:

$$\frac{16 \div 2}{100 \div 2} = \frac{8 \div 2}{50 \div 2} = \frac{4}{25}$$

which we can't simplify further.

For (**c**) we have:

$$\frac{60 \div 2}{100 \div 2} = \frac{30 \div 2}{50 \div 2} = \frac{15 \div 5}{25 \div 5} = \frac{3}{5}$$

Working with fractions

Sometimes, just as we need to do arithmetic on integers (adding, subtracting, multiplying, dividing) so we might have to do similar arithmetic on fractions. We shall look at this arithmetic in the order:

- multiplication;
- division;
- addition/subtraction.

Multiplication

To multiply two (or more) fractions together we multiply the numerator terms together and then we multiply the denominator terms together. For example:

$$\frac{3}{10} \times \frac{2}{5} = \frac{3 \times 2}{10 \times 5} = \frac{6}{50}$$

But we see that we can simplify this by dividing by 2 to give $\frac{3}{25}$ as the result of the multiplication.

Division

To divide one fraction by another we invert (turn upside down) the fraction we are dividing by and then multiply the two fractions together:

$$\frac{3}{10} \div \frac{2}{5} = \frac{3}{10} \times \frac{5}{2} = \frac{15}{20}$$

which in its simplest form is $\frac{3}{4}$.

Student activity

Work out the following fractions. Put each into its simplest form:

(a) $\dfrac{3}{10} \times \dfrac{5}{6}$

(b) $\dfrac{3}{10} \div \dfrac{5}{6}$

(c) $\dfrac{4}{7} \times \dfrac{2}{3} \times \dfrac{4}{5}$

(d) $\dfrac{4}{7} \div \dfrac{2}{3} \div \dfrac{4}{5}$

For (**a**) we have:

$$\frac{3}{10} \times \frac{5}{6} = \frac{15}{60} = \frac{3}{12} = \frac{1}{4}$$

(dividing $\frac{15}{60}$ through by 5 and $\frac{3}{12}$ through by 3).

For (**b**) we have:

$$\frac{3}{10} \div \frac{5}{6} = \frac{3}{10} \times \frac{6}{5} = \frac{18}{50} = \frac{9}{25}$$

For (**c**) we have:

$$\frac{4}{7} \times \frac{2}{3} \times \frac{4}{5} = \frac{4 \times 2 \times 4}{7 \times 3 \times 5} = \frac{32}{105}$$

which is in its simplest form. Notice how we have simply extended the principles to deal with three fractions rather than just two.

For (**d**) we have:

$$\frac{4}{7} \div \frac{2}{3} \div \frac{4}{5} = \frac{4}{7} \times \frac{3}{2} \times \frac{5}{4} = \frac{4 \times 3 \times 2}{7 \times 2 \times 4} = \frac{60}{56} = \frac{30}{28} = \frac{15}{14}$$

(inverting the fractions we are dividing by and then multiplying the whole thing in one go).

Addition/subtraction

To add or subtract two fractions we put them over what is known as a *common denominator* and add/subtract the numerators. We will illustrate this with a numerical example. We require:

$$\frac{3}{4} + \frac{1}{2}$$

A common denominator is a number which is exactly divisible into both denominators. In this case one common denominator would be 4 since the denominator 4 goes into this exactly once and the other denominator 2 goes into this exactly twice. We then use these multiples (1 and 2) to multiply the respective numerators. That is:

$$\frac{3}{4} + \frac{1}{2} = \frac{(1 \times 3) + (2 \times 1)}{4} = \frac{3 + 2}{4} = \frac{5}{4}$$

Note that we have multiplied the first numerator, 3, by 1 since its denominator (4) goes into the common denominator exactly once. We have multiplied the second numerator (1) by 2 since its denominator goes into the common denominator exactly twice.

Choosing a common denominator

Often when we are trying to decide on a common denominator to use it is clear that some obvious number will be exactly divisible by each of the two fraction denominators. There are times, however, when such a value is not immediately obvious. In such a case an easy approach is simply to use a common denominator which is the product of multiplying the two fraction denominators together. For example:

$$\frac{3}{5} + \frac{2}{3}$$

there is no obvious common denominator that springs to mind so we choose to use 15 (5 × 3). The arithmetic would then be:

$$\frac{(3 \times 3) + (2 \times 5)}{5 \times 3} = \frac{9 + 10}{15} = \frac{19}{15}$$

Student activity

Simplify each of the following:

(a) $\frac{2}{5} + \frac{3}{4}$ **(b)** $\frac{5}{6} + \frac{3}{7}$ **(c)** $\frac{2}{5} + \frac{1}{3} + \frac{5}{8}$

For **(a)** we use a common denominator of 20 (5 × 4) to give:

$$\frac{(2 \times 4) + (3 \times 5)}{5 \times 4} = \frac{8 + 15}{20} = \frac{23}{20}$$

(b) $\frac{5}{6} + \frac{3}{7}$: We have a common denominator of 42 (6 × 7) giving:

$$\frac{(5 \times 7) + (3 \times 6)}{6 \times 7} = \frac{35 + 18}{42} = \frac{53}{42}$$

(c) $\frac{2}{5} + \frac{1}{3} + \frac{5}{8}$: Although we have not explicitly looked at three fractions being added together, we can simply add the first two and then add this product to the third (although with practice we might be able to perform the arithmetic in one step rather than two).

We have:

$$\frac{(2 \times 3) + (1 \times 5)}{5 \times 3} = \frac{11}{15}$$

43

and then:

$$\frac{11}{15} + \frac{5}{8} = \frac{(11 \times 8) + (5 \times 15)}{120} = \frac{99 + 75}{120} = \frac{174}{120}$$

Subtraction

Although we have only looked at addition of fractions exactly the same approach applies to subtraction. For example:

$$\frac{3}{5} - \frac{2}{3} = \frac{(3 \times 3) - (2 \times 5)}{15} = \frac{9 - 10}{15} = -\frac{1}{15}$$

using a common denominator or 15 (5 × 3). Notice also that there's no reason why we shouldn't have negative fractions just as we have negative integers.

Student activity

Work out each of the following expressions:

(a) $\frac{3}{4} - \frac{1}{3}$ (b) $\frac{3}{5} - \frac{1}{9}$ (c) $\frac{1}{5} - \frac{4}{7} + \frac{3}{8}$

For (**a**) we have:

$$\frac{3}{4} - \frac{1}{3} = \frac{(3 \times 3) - (1 \times 4)}{4 \times 3} = \frac{9 - 4}{12} = \frac{5}{12}$$

For (**b**):

$$\frac{3}{5} - \frac{1}{9} = \frac{(3 \times 9) - (1 \times 5)}{5 \times 9} = \frac{27 - 5}{45} = \frac{22}{45}$$

For (**c**):

$$\frac{1}{5} - \frac{4}{7} + \frac{3}{8}$$

We'll do this all in one go, although you might have done it in two steps:

$$\frac{1(7 \times 8) - 4(5 \times 8) + 3(5 \times 7)}{5 \times 7 \times 8} = \frac{56 - 160 + 105}{280} = \frac{1}{280}$$

Arithmetic involving integers and fractions

Sometimes we might have to perform arithmetic involving a mixture of integers and fractions. For example:

(a) $3 \times \frac{1}{5}$

(b) $6 + \frac{15}{22}$

The easiest way to do this is simply to convert the integer into the form of a fraction. We can do this by giving an integer a denominator of 1 (since dividing an integer by 1 still leaves the integer unchanged):

(a) $\frac{3}{1} \times \frac{1}{5}$

(b) $\frac{6}{1} + \frac{15}{22}$

and we can use the rules we developed in the previous section for performing this type of arithmetic. For **(a)**, for example, we would then have:

$$\frac{3}{1} \times \frac{1}{5} = \frac{3}{5}$$

and for **(b)**:

$$\frac{6}{1} + \frac{15}{22} = \frac{6(22) + 15(1)}{22} = \frac{132 + 15}{22} = \frac{147}{22}$$

DECIMALS

> ### Self-assessment 9
>
> Answer the questions set out below as best as you can. Check your answers against ours on p. 80.
>
> If you've got them all right move on to the next self-assessment on p. 50.
>
> Without a calculator work out:
>
> **(a)** 167.304 × 10,000
>
> **(b)** 18.67 ÷ 1,000

For some types of fraction we can express the fraction in a very specific way by using what is known as *decimal notation* – that is showing a number in decimal form. Such decimals make use of the decimal point when expressing a number like:

      10.6   (pronounced 10 point 6)

or 3.5   (pronounced 3 point 5)

or 0.8   (pronounced nought point 8)

or 0.014 (pronounced nought point nought one four and not point nought fourteen)

A decimal like 10.6, for example, indicates that we have a number made up of two parts: an integer part (10) and a decimal (or fraction) part (6). You'll remember in section 2.1 that we talked about the *place* of a digit – its position, in relation to adjacent numbers, indicated whether the number was in units of ones, tens, hundreds, thousands and so on. We can use this same place system to help us understand decimals but this time we are looking at places as they move to the right of the number rather than the left (see Fig. 2.2).

10,000 ten thousands	1,000 thousands	100 hundreds	10 tens	1 ones	$\frac{1}{10}$ tenths	$\frac{1}{100}$ hundredths	$\frac{1}{1,000}$ thousandths	$\frac{1}{10,000}$ ten thousandths
8	5	3	2	6				
	8	5	3	2	6			
		8	5	3	2	6		
			8	5	3	2	6	
				8	5	3	2	6

Fig. 2.2 The decimal system

So, a digit one place to the *right* of the decimal point is in tenths. A digit two places to the right of the point is in hundredths, three places to the right in thousandths and so on. Decimal digits then follow a simple rule system:

$$0.1 = 1 \div 10 = \frac{1}{10}$$

$$0.01 = 1 \div 100 = \frac{1}{100}$$

$$0.001 = 1 \div 1,000 = \frac{1}{1,000}$$

and so on. Similarly, 0.5 would be $\frac{5}{10}$ths, 0.05 would be $\frac{5}{100}$ths and 0.005 would be $\frac{5}{1,000}$ths. Notice that in the last case we still had to include the first two zeroes after the decimal point to properly indicate the place value of the 1 that appears in the third decimal place. Notice that we have also put a zero in front of the decimal point. This is not strictly necessary. Sometimes you will see numbers written as .1, .01, .001 and so on. Which way you choose is up to you.

Remembering this rule helps us to decide which number is bigger when looking at decimals. Suppose we had two integers: 305 and 350. We would have no trouble deciding that 350 was a bigger number than 305. However, with decimals we have to be a little more careful. Suppose we had two decimals 3.05 and 3.025. The second number *looks* bigger because it has more digits in it. However, the first number is numerically larger. We see this because it consists of an integer 3 plus 5 hundredths:

$$3 + \frac{5}{100}$$

The second number consists of the same integer but now has two hundredths and also five thousandths (which are smaller):

$$3 + \frac{2}{100} + \frac{5}{1,000}$$

Remembering our work on fractions in an earlier section we can find an equivalent fraction to $\frac{5}{100}$ as:

$$\frac{5 \times 10}{100 \times 10} = \frac{50}{1,000}$$

that is, whilst 0.05 is five hundredths this is also exactly the same as 50 thousandths. The equivalent fraction for 0.025 is then:

$$\frac{2 \times 10}{100 \times 10} + \frac{5}{1,000} = \frac{20}{1,000} + \frac{5}{1,000} = \frac{25}{1,000}$$

So 0.025 is 25 thousandths, confirming that 3.05 is larger than 3.025. Most of the arithmetic we will be doing with decimals we'll be doing on a calculator. However, we need to look at some simple decimal arithmetic so you understand what is actually happening when you use the calculator (and again so you'll have some idea of the answer to expect, in case you've keyed in the wrong numbers or the wrong sequence).

Student activity

Without using a calculator write the following as decimals:

(a) $\frac{5}{10}$

(b) $\frac{6}{1,000}$

(c) $\frac{12}{1,000}$

Write as fractions:

(d) 0.03

(e) 0.303

(f) 0.033

We have:

$$\frac{5}{10} = 0.5 \qquad \frac{6}{1,000} = 0.006 \qquad \frac{12}{1,000} = 0.012$$

Similarly:

$$0.03 = \frac{3}{100} \qquad 0.303 = \frac{303}{1,000} \qquad 0.033 = \frac{33}{1,000}$$

Multiplying decimals by 10s

Suppose we have a decimal number 12.347 and we want to multiply this by 10. This is actually quite simple and doesn't need us to use a calculator or our brain cells. When multiplying a decimal number by 10 we simply move the decimal point one digit to the right. That is:

$$12.347 \times 10 = 123.47$$

Multiplying a decimal by 100 means we move the decimal point *two* places to the right:

$$12.347 \times 100 = 1,234.7$$

and we can easily extend this to multiplying by 1,000, 10,000 and so on. But what happens if we multiply by a number and run out of digits to move the decimal place past? For example:

$$12.347 \times 1,000 = 12,347$$

and we'd normally show this as an integer, 12,347, or with an extra 0 added past the point, 12,347.0. But what about:

$$12.347 \times 10,000 = ?$$

Well, all we do is add extra 0s to allow us to keep moving the decimal point. After all we could write 12.347 as:

$$12.347 = 12.3470 = 12.34700 = 12.347000$$

and so on since the extra 0s on the right don't alter the value of the number at all. So we have:

$$12.3470 \times 10,000 = 123,470.0$$

Dividing by 10s

We can use a similar rule when we want to divide a decimal number by 10 (or 100 etc.). For example:

$$12.347 \div 10$$

This time we move the decimal point one place to the *left*:

$$12.347 \div 10 \quad = 1.2347$$
$$12.347 \div 100 \quad = 0.12347$$
$$12.347 \div 1{,}000 = 012.347 \div 1{,}000 = 0.012347 \text{ and so on.}$$

Arithmetic involving decimals is best carried out on a calculator. As with any calculation, however, it is worthwhile trying to estimate the answer you expect. Most calculations are straightforward. For example, if we want to multiply 10.324 by 5.129 then we would estimate an answer of about 50 (10 × 5) – the actual answer from a calculator is 52.95176. Similarly if we were dividing 103.45 by 8.627 we would expect an answer of about 10 (100 ÷ 10) – the actual answer is 11.9914222789. However, when we're dealing with decimals which are less than 1 we get results which might take a bit of getting used to. For example, if we multiply 153.2 by 0.05678126 we might think that because there are a lot of digits in the numbers we're multiplying together then we'll get a large number as a result. But we don't: from the calculator we get 8.698889032. Similarly if we divide 153.2 by 0.05678126 we get 2,698.07327277.

The results we get when one of the decimals is small (less than 1) can be a bit of a surprise and students sometimes assume they've done something wrong. The reason the answer is so different from the original numbers lies with what the decimal represents. 0.06 (we've rounded it) is, you'll remember, 6 hundredths or $\frac{6}{100}$. So, if we multiply a large number like 153.2 we're effectively multiplying by $\frac{6}{100}$ which will reduce the answer considerably. In fact we can use this to estimate the size of the result. 153.2 is about 150. We know that we're multiplying by $\frac{6}{100}$. As with any fraction this means we're multiplying by 6 and dividing by 100. But we know an easy way to divide by a hundred. We simply move the decimal point two places to the left to give 1.5. Multiplying this by 6 gives an expected answer of 9 – which isn't far from what we actually got at 8.698889032. Similarly if we want to divide 153.2 by $\frac{6}{100}$. Recollect that to divide by a fraction we invert it (turn it upside down) and then multiply. Inverting gives $\frac{100}{6}$. Multiplying by 100 gives 15,000 (just adding two 0s). If we say the 6 is close to a 5 (to make the arithmetic easier) we have $\frac{15{,}000}{5}$ which is about 3,000 as our expected answer. This compares with the precise answer of 2698.07327277.

One last point about working with decimals brings us back to rounding and significant digits. It will be clear that when we're working with decimals we'll often end up with answers which have a large number of decimal places. When presenting an answer to a problem we may want to round a decimal to some 'sensible' number of decimal places. What 'sensible' means will depend very much on the context of the problem. If we were working with financial figures, for example, we would certainly round to two decimal places (often shown as 2 DP) since this would give a result to the nearest penny. We might even want to round to 0 DP (i.e. to the nearest £). Like much of what we do you will need to use your judgement and common sense when rounding. One acceptable approach is to see what the maximum number of DPs is in any of the initial numbers and then round to the maximum of these in the final answer.

For example if we wanted:

$$12.3 \times 105.23 \times 16.83$$

then the maximum number of decimal places in any of the initial numbers is two. Our final answer could then reasonably be rounded to 2 DP also. Since the precise answer would be 21,783.55707 we might round this to 21,783.56.

One important point though with decimals in particular is that you must always round *at the very end* of the calculation and not part way through. Always use as many DPs as your calculator allows when performing the calculations and only round the number at the very end. A simple illustration will show this. Suppose we wanted:

$$23.5 \times 456.75 \div 0.00126$$

Multiplying the first two numbers we get 10,733.625. We might – wrongly – decide to round this to 10,733.6 before doing the next calculation. So we would then have:

$$10,733.6 \div 0.00126 = 8,518,730.15873$$

instead of the precise answer of 8,518,750 – a difference of 20 in the final answer.

PERCENTAGES

> ### *Self-assessment 10*
>
> Answer the questions set out below as best as you can. Check your answers against ours on p. 80.
>
> If you've got them all right move on to the next self-assessment on p. 54.
>
> Without a calculator work out:
>
> **(a)** 10% of £15.85.
>
> **(b)** 25% of 300.
>
> **(c)** express as a percentage $\frac{10}{20}$.

We've looked at fractions and decimals in earlier sections. In this section we look at numbers which are related to both of these: *percentages*. A percentage is a fraction or proportion of some number expressed out of 100. So if we wanted 25 as a percentage of 100 we would have:

$$\frac{25}{100} \text{ as } 25\%$$

where the symbol % stands for percentage. So, 25% is exactly the same as $\frac{25}{100}$. It will be clear that fractions, decimals and percentages are interchangeable:

$$\frac{25}{100} = 25\% = 0.25 = \frac{1}{4}$$

and it doesn't really matter which way we use to express some number since they're all effectively the same. In this example, working out the percentage (as a number out of 100) was easy since the fraction was already out of 100. $\frac{53}{100}$ would be 53%, $\frac{7}{100}$ would be 7% and so on. But how would we go about working out a fraction as a percentage in other cases? Suppose we had $\frac{8}{15}$ and we wanted to show this as a percentage. We can work this out very easily:

$$\frac{8}{15} \times 100$$

That is, we multiply the fraction by 100. The result will give us the percentage which is identical to the original fraction. Here (using a calculator) we would get 53.3% (to 1 DP). That is, $\frac{8}{15}$ as a percentage is 53.3%. It is also important to remember what a percentage number shows. Like a fraction it shows the part of a total (expressed as 100) represented by the fraction numerator. So, this number, $\frac{8}{15}$, is just over half. So, to convert a fraction to a percentage we multiply the fraction by 100 and work out the answer. If we have a decimal number we can get the comparable percentage in much the same way. If we had a decimal of 0.4 and multiply this by 100 it gives the equivalent percentage:

$$0.4 \times 100 = 40\%$$

Using percentages

We actually encounter and use percentages quite a lot without most people thinking about it. For example, when you have a job your employer will deduct a percentage of your wage or salary. A certain percentage will be deducted for National Insurance and pension payments and another percentage will be deducted to pay income tax. Many products that we buy will have a percentage of the cost added to the price for VAT (value added tax), currently at 17.5% in the UK. In a restaurant there might be a 10% service charge added to the bill. We need to be able to work comfortably with such percentages.

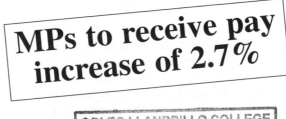

MPs to receive pay increase of 2.7%

Student activity

Work out the following:

(a) *Your bank charges you extra if your account is overdrawn. If you are overdrawn it charges you 10% of the amount you are overdrawn. Your account is overdrawn by £25.68 so how much will be the bank charge?*

(b) *In a restaurant there is a service charge of 15% added to the bill. The bill comes to £46.75, so how much will the service charge be?*

(c) *A shop selling clothes has a pair of jeans at £24.99 but has to add VAT at 17.5%. How much will the jeans cost altogether?*

(d) *A friend paid £32.67 recently for a meal which included a service charge of 15%. How much was the meal without the service charge?*

(a) We want 10% of £25.68. Remembering that percentages, fractions and decimals are interchangeable this means we want to calculate:

$$\frac{1}{10}(£25.68) \text{ or } 0.1(£25.68)$$

which will be £2.568 or £2.57 rounded (and you shouldn't even need a calculator to do this simple arithmetic).

(b) The bill for the meal is £46.75 but we have to add 15%. We can work out 15% of £46.75 as:

$$0.15(46.75) = 7.0125 \text{ or } 7.01 \text{ rounded}$$

So the final bill will be £46.75 + £7.01 or £53.76. We could also work this out in a slightly different way. That is as:

$$46.75 + 0.15(46.75)$$
$$\text{or } 1(46.75) + 0.15(46.75)$$
$$\text{or } 1.15(46.75) = 53.76$$

Multiplying 46.75 by 1.15 is effectively the same as taking the original amount (46.75) and adding 15%. This is a quick and easy way of working out a new total when adding a percentage to some initial number.

(c) This is quite easy. If the jeans cost £24.99 but must have 17.5% added then the selling price will be:

$$1.175(24.99) = 29.36$$

(d) This one is slightly different. We know that the final bill came to £32.67 and that this included a 15% service charge. We might be tempted to say the service charge was 0.15(32.67) or £4.90 but on reflection this would be wrong. This £4.90 is 15% of the final bill whereas the service charge is already included in this final bill. Without explaining why it works for the moment we can work out this sort of problem by dividing the final bill by 1.15:

$$\frac{32.67}{1.15} = 28.41$$

as the cost of the meal without the service charge. We can check that this works by taking the cost of the meal, £28.41, adding 15% service charge and it should come to £32.67:

1.15(28.41) = 32.67

In fact you can see how the arithmetic works from this. If we take this arithmetic:

1.15(28.41) = 32.67

then, as we did with fractions, we can divide through by 1.15 to give:

$$\frac{1.15(28.41)}{1.15} = \frac{32.67}{1.15}$$

but in the expression on the left we know that $\frac{1.15}{1.15}$ must equal 1 so this gives:

$$28.42 = \frac{32.67}{1.15}$$

This type of calculation involving percentages – working backwards from a known total – is quite common.

Percentage increases and decreases

Very often in business problems we want to work out percentage changes – either increases or decreases – similar to those in the last activity. What sometimes is forgotten is that the same percentage will have different results when we use it to increase a number compared with when we want to decrease it. For example, suppose a shop is selling jeans at £24.99. The company decides to put its prices up by 10%. This means that the new selling price would be:

1.1(24.99) = 27.49

Suppose a few weeks later the shop has a sale and reduces its prices by 10%. This means the jeans would now be:

27.49 − 0.1(27.49) = 27.49 − 2.75 = 24.74

That is, we took the current price at £27.49 and subtracted 10% of this to give £24.74. You will see that the new selling price of £24.74 is *not* the original selling price of £24.99 even though we first added 10% and then subtracted 10%. The reason for this is that we are adding 10% to one number and then subtracting 10% from a different number.

POWERS, EXPONENTS AND SCIENTIFIC NOTATION

> ### *Self-assessment 11*
>
> Answer the questions set out below as best as you can. Check your answers against ours on p. 80.
>
> If you've got them all right move on to the next self-assessment on p. 58.
>
> Without using a calculator write the following as an ordinary number:
>
> **(a)** 10^4
>
> **(b)** 10^{-4}
>
> **(c)** 4^4
>
> **(d)** 1.04×10^4

In this next section we want to introduce the concepts of *powers* and *exponents* and introduce something you may already have seen on your calculator: *scientific notation*. We all know that:

$$10 \times 10 = 100$$

and that:

$$10 \times 10 \times 10 = 1,000 \text{ and so on.}$$

But we will find it convenient later on in the text to write an expression like 10×10 or 100 in a different way as 10^2 (pronounced 10 squared or 10 to the power 2) where:

$$10^2 = 10 \times 10 = 100$$

Similarly, 10^3 (10 cubed or 10 to the power 3) is:

$$10^3 = 10 \times 10 \times 10 = 1,000$$

The number appearing at the top right corner of the number 10 (the ^{2} or ^{3}) is known as the power or the exponent of the number and simply indicates how many times we multiply the number (10) by itself.

Student activity

Write out what would be meant by:

$10^4 \quad 10^5 \quad 2^2 \quad 2^3$

We have:

$$10^4 = 10 \times 10 \times 10 \times 10 = 10,000$$

$$10^5 = 10 \times 10 \times 10 \times 10 \times 10 = 100,000$$

For 2^2, although we've only shown powers for the number 10 there is no reason why they can't be used in the same way for any number. So:

$$2^2 = 2 \times 2 = 4$$

Similarly:

$$2^3 = 2 \times 2 \times 2 = 8$$

and obviously any number could be raised to a power. So, a number like 10, or 2, can be raised to some power and all it means is that we multiply that number by itself a given number of times.

But what about decimals and powers? For example, if we can express 1,000 as 10^3 can we express 0.001 as 10 to some power? The answer is that we can, and to see how let us look at the pattern of what we have been doing. We have:

10,000	1,000	100	10
10^4	10^3	10^2	10^1

The pattern we see is that as we 'lose' a zero from the end of each number (10,000 to 1,000 to 100 to 10) then the power term reduces by 1 each time from (^{3} to ^{2} to ^{1} – although notice that we probably wouldn't normally write 10^1 but just 10). So how would we express in power terms a number like 0.1 (1/10)? Well, for 0.1 we've effectively 'lost' two 0s compared with 10 (we've really moved the decimal point two places to the left which is the same thing). This suggests that we should reduce the power term by 2 also (giving $^{1-2=-1}$). This would give:

$$0.1 = 10^{-1}$$

which although it looks strange is the way of showing a decimal in exponent form. So, when we see a negative power it means we have a decimal (or a fraction with the numerator of 1 and a denominator equal to the number itself).

 ### *Student activity*

How would you write 0.01 and 0.001 in exponent form?

What about 0.2, 0.02 and 0.002?

We would have:

$$0.01 = 10^{-2} = \frac{1}{100} = \frac{1}{10^2}$$

$$0.001 = 10^{-3} = \frac{1}{1,000} = \frac{1}{10^3}$$

For 0.2 this is the same as:

$$0.2 = 2 \times 0.1$$

and since we already have an exponent expression for 0.1, this means we have:

$$0.2 = 2 \times 0.1 = 2 \times 10^{-1} = \frac{2}{10} = \frac{2}{10^1}$$

and then:

$$0.02 = 2 \times 0.01 = 2 \times 10^{-2} = \frac{2}{100} = \frac{2}{10^2}$$

and:

$$0.002 = 2 \times 0.001 = 2 \times 10^{-3} = \frac{2}{1,000} = \frac{2}{10^3}$$

Clearly we could write any number – integer or decimal – in such a way using an expression like 10^3 or 10^{-2}. Whilst this way of writing numbers may seem odd it is actually referred to as *scientific notation* where we have:

$$\text{a number} = \left(\begin{array}{l}\text{a number between}\\ \text{1 and 10}\end{array}\right) \times 10^{\text{power}}$$

So, for example:

$$
\begin{array}{ll}
13.58 & = 1.358 \times 10^1 \\
135.8 & = 1.358 \times 10^2 \\
0.1358 & = 1.358 \times 10^{-1} \\
0.001358 & = 1.358 \times 10^{-3} \\
-13.58 & = -1.358 \times 10^1
\end{array}
$$

Student activity

Write the following numbers in scientific notation:

(a) 56.2

(b) −108

(c) 0.023

We have:

(a) 56.2 $= 5.62 \times 10^2$

(b) −108 $= -1.08 \times 10^2$

(c) 0.023 $= 2.3 \times 10^{-3}$

Sometimes on some calculators and computer programs you may find scientific notation used in a slightly different way. Whilst we would write a number like 1,358.7 as:

$$1,358.7 = 1.3587 \times 10^3$$

an alternative form used would be:

$$1{,}358.7 = 1.3587\text{E}^3$$

where the term E is used instead of 10. There is no difference in how we would use such notation.

One last thing we need to note about powers is that any number to the power 0 equals 1. Whilst this might seem odd we can see the logic from the sequence pattern:

10,000	1,000	100	10	1	0.1	0.01	0.001	0.0001
10^4	10^3	10^2	10^1	?	10^{-1}	10^{-2}	10^{-3}	10^{-4}

which suggests that logically $10^0 = 1$. You'll simply have to accept from us that the same applies to any number. For example, $6^0 = 1$, $153^0 = 1$, and so on.

Arithmetic involving powers

It is often the case that arithmetic is performed on such power terms. In general this will involve two types of such arithmetic: multiplication and division.

For multiplication suppose we have:

$$10^2 \times 10^3 = ?$$

This can be re-written as:

$$(10 \times 10) \times (10 \times 10 \times 10) = 10 \times 10 \times 10 \times 10 \times 10 = 10^5$$

In general then, for an expression in the form:

$$10^b \times 10^c$$

where b and c are any two numbers (like ^{2} and ^{3}) then the result can be expressed as:

$$10^{(b+c)} \qquad \text{for example: } 10^2 \times 10^3 = 10^{2+3} = 10^5$$

The same will apply for any number in place of 10. For example:

$$2.345^2 \times 2.345^4 = 2.345^6$$

For division the equivalent rule is:

$$\frac{10^b}{10^c} = 10^{(b-c)}$$

So: $\dfrac{10^2}{10^3} = 10^{2-3} = 10^{-1}$

We can see this if we work it out without using exponents:

$$10^2 = 100$$
$$10^3 = 1{,}000$$

so: $\dfrac{10^2}{10^3} = \dfrac{100}{1{,}000} = \dfrac{1}{10} = 10^{-1}$

SYMBOLS AND EQUATIONS

> ### *Self-assessment 12*
>
> Answer the questions set out below as best as you can. Check your answers against ours on p. 80.
>
> If you've got them all right move on to the next self-assessment on p. 69.
>
> You are paid a salary each month by the company you work for. From this is deducted £200 each month for various pension contributions, health insurance and so on. You also pay tax on your salary of 20%.
>
> Using *S* as salary and *T* as take-home salary (i.e. salary less all deductions and tax) write an equation showing your take-home pay

For many business problems it can be helpful to express the problem not using words but using *symbols* and *equations*. For example, suppose you work in the payroll section of a company and you are responsible for calculating the weekly wages of some of the staff. Let us suppose that someone's weekly wage is based on the number of hours they worked and the amount they get paid, in £s, each hour they work. To work out someone's wage then we would take the number of hours worked and multiply by the hourly rate. For example, if the hourly rate were £10 and I worked 40 hours then my weekly wage would be:

$$40 \times 10 = £400$$

Sometimes, though, we want to show a calculation without using specific numbers. This might seem an odd thing to want to do but it means we want to write a general expression for working out someone's wage without worrying about the specific numbers. After all, the hours I work and the hourly rate might change but our general expression will still tell us how to work out my wages no matter what the specific numbers. This is where symbols come in useful. Let us define the following symbols:

W is the weekly wage;
H is the number of hours worked;
R is the hourly rate of pay.

Then we can use these symbols to calculate the weekly wage:

$$W = H \times R$$

You'll see that all we've done is to use these symbols to show the calculations we did earlier (and we could have chosen different letters for the symbols if we wanted). The advantage of symbols, and the equation we have written, is that it is a concise, shorthand way of expressing some calculation or some relationship. For some reason many students think there's something 'mystical' about symbols/variables and such equations but there isn't. It's just a form of shorthand. However, the shorthand can help us when we want to do other calculations. Suppose I got £440 in my wage packet last week. I know that I worked 40 hours so I'm wondering how much I got paid each hour. From the equation:

$$W = H \times R$$

we see that we now know W and H (that is we have specific numbers for these) and we're trying to work out R. The easiest way of doing this is to rearrange the equation so that we have $R =$ something. That is, in mathematical jargon, we rearrange the equation to put the unknown symbol on the left-hand side of the equation and everything else on the right.

We can do this with some simple arithmetic. This arithmetic is based on a simple principle: we can change one side of an equation (by adding, subtracting, multiplying, dividing) and the equation remains the same *as long as* we change the other side in exactly the same way. For example if we had:

$$2 \times 2 = 4$$

then multiplying both sides by, say, 10 really leaves the equation intact since $10(2 \times 2)$ still equals $10(4)$. So if :

$$W = H \times R$$

then we can divide both sides through by H to give:

$$\frac{W}{H} = \frac{H \times R}{H}$$

but the H on top and bottom of the right-hand side cancel out to give:

$$\frac{W}{H} = \times \frac{\cancel{H} \times R}{\cancel{H}} = R$$

We can now swap the two sides over to give:

$$R = \frac{W}{H}$$

That is, R can be calculated by dividing W by H (here it would give $R = 440/40 = £11$ as the hourly rate of pay). Notice that this cancelling out process is quite common when we're dealing with equations and symbols. We can cancel out a term in the numerator with a term in the denominator as long as the two terms are identical.

Student activity

Work out an equation so that H = something.

We have:

$$W = H \times R$$

so:

$$\frac{W}{R} = \frac{H \times R}{R}$$

and cancelling gives:

$$\frac{W}{R} = \frac{H \times \cancel{R}}{\cancel{R}} = H$$

or:

$$H = \frac{W}{R}$$

Coefficients and variables

In the previous example we had an equation $W = H \times R$ where all the symbols represented what are known as *variables* (literally something that can vary, or take different values). Equations often also involve something known as *coefficients*.

Let's consider someone who uses their car for travelling around on company business. The company pays that person a fixed monthly amount of £50 to compensate for wear and tear of the car. Also, they pay the person an agreed mileage rate: so much for each mile travelled on company business. This compensates for petrol and the like and the rate is currently 25p per mile. We can derive a simple equation to show how much this person would get reimbursed. Let us define the following variables:

A = amount reimbursed;

M = number of miles travelled on company business.

To work out how much they would get in travelling expenses each month we would then have an equation:

$$A = 50 + 0.25M$$

Note that we write the last term involving a variable and a number as $0.25M$ and not $0.25 \times M$ – the multiplication sign is not needed since it is implied in the way the expression is written. The two numbers, 50 and 0.25, are known as the coefficients in the equation. Unlike the variables in the problem these coefficients take a fixed value (that is they don't vary in the problem as it is set out). Notice that we have had to be careful about ensuring that all numbers in the equation, £50 and 25p, are shown in the same units of measurement – here both are shown in £s. We cannot mix numbers with different units of measurement in such an equation. We can actually go one stage further to say that we can replace the specific coefficient numbers with symbols also. If we let:

f = the fixed amount per month (here £50);

r = the rate paid per mile (here 0.25).

then we have:

$$A = f + rM$$

as a general equation. It is conventional to use capital letters to show variables and small letters to show coefficients.

Student activity

Let us return to the problem set in the last self-assessment.

You are paid a salary each month by the company you work for. From this is deducted £200 each month for various pension contributions, health insurance and so on. You also pay tax on your salary of 20%.

Using 'S' as salary and 'T' as take-home salary (i.e. salary less all deductions and tax) write an equation showing your take-home pay.

Using 'd' as the fixed deductions (currently £200) and 't' as the tax rate as a decimal write a general equation for take-home salary.

We know that our salary is S. From this we must deduct £200 and a further 20% of salary as tax. This means we have an equation so that:

$$T = S - 200 - 0.20S$$

(We shall see soon how we can simplify this equation.) Replacing the numerical coefficients with d and t we then have a general equation so that:

$$T = S - d - tS$$

Working with equations

Whilst we may want to derive equations from a problem we have been given we will also frequently want to work with such equations. Going back to the mileage problem we had:

$$A = f + rM$$

as the general form of the equation and:

$$A = 50 + 0.25M$$

as the specific form, using the numerical values for the two coefficients. It is clear that we can now use the equation to calculate A for any given value for M. If we travel, say, 100 miles then $M = 100$ and we have:

$$A = 50 + 0.25(100)$$
$$\text{or } A = 50 + 25$$
$$\text{or } A = 75$$

That is, for a monthly mileage of 100 miles we would receive a total of £75 mileage expenses made up of £50 as a monthly fixed amount and £25 linked to the exact mileage we had covered.

Substituting a numerical value for M allows us to work out A. But we can also work out M if we know A. This is quite an important point. In the equation we have two variables, A and M, and to begin with they are both 'unknown', that is we do not have numbers for them. In general, with two unknowns in an equation we can work out the value of either unknown if we have a value for the other one. Just now, we knew the value of M (at 100) so we could work out the other unknown, A. But if we know a value for A we can work out M.

Suppose last month you got paid mileage expenses of £100. How many miles did you cover on company business? The best way of finding this out is to take the equation and to rearrange it so we have $M =$ something. That is, to rearrange the equation so that all the 'knowns' are on the right-hand side and the 'unknown' is on the left. This is very common in business mathematics. We have:

$$A = 50 + 0.25M$$

Using the principle that we can rearrange an equation by performing the same arithmetic on both sides we have:

- Subtracting 50 from both sides:

  $A - 50 = 50 + 0.25M - 50$ (and the $+ 50$ and -50 on the right-hand side cancel)

  so $A - 50 = 0.25M$

- Dividing both sides by 0.25:

  $$\frac{A - 50}{0.25} = \frac{0.25M}{0.25} = 1M = M \text{ (since } 0.25M/0.25 = 1M)$$

- And swapping both sides around:

  $$M = \frac{A - 50}{0.25}$$

We could also show this as:

$$M = \frac{A}{0.25} - \frac{50}{0.25} = 4A - 200$$

So, when A is £100 we can work out M by:

$$M = 4A - 200 = 4(100) - 200 = 400 - 200 = 200$$

That is, we must have done 200 miles on company business last month in order to get a mileage expense of £100.

Student activity

Return to the take-home pay equation for the last activity. If your monthly salary is £1,000 what will your take-home pay be?

We had:

$$T = S - 200 - 0.2S$$

With S at 1,000 we then have:

$$T = 1,000 - 200 - 0.2(1,000) = 1,000 - 200 - 200 = £600$$

Equations and brackets

There are times when we're dealing with equations when we encounter quite complex expressions and these often involve brackets. It's often helpful to try to simplify complex equations. We can often do this by *collecting like terms together*. This means that if we see the same variable more than once we can collect these together into one expression. Similarly we can collect coefficients together (taking care over + and − signs). For example, suppose we had equations so that:

$$A = B + C$$
$$\text{and } B = 30 + 5C$$

We could then substitute the second equation into the first:

$$A = B + C$$
$$A = 30 + 5C + C$$

We have two terms involving C so we can collect these together. We have $5C + C$ which clearly equals $6C$. So we then have:

$$A = 30 + 6C$$

We can do this for more complex equations. Suppose we have:

$$A = B + C$$
$$\text{and } B = 30 + 5D$$
$$\text{and } C = 50 + 2D$$

We then have:

$$A = B + C = 30 + 5D + 50 + 2D$$
$$A = 80 + 7D$$

where we have now collected together terms involving just numbers (the coefficients 30 and 50) and the terms involving D ($5D + 2D$).

In this simple example the arithmetic involved in collecting like terms together is quite straightforward. It's often better to use brackets to help the arithmetic along when we have more difficult situations. For example, suppose we change the problem to:

$$A = B - C$$
$$\text{and } B = 30 + 5D$$
$$\text{and } C = 50 + 2D$$

We might be tempted to write:

$$A = B - C = 30 + 5D - 50 + 2D$$

giving:

$$A = -20 + 7D$$

where we are subtracting 50 but still adding $2D$. This is wrong because C is *both* 50 and $2D$ so we must subtract both of these, that is:

$$A = B - C = 30 + 5D - 50 - 2D$$

Collecting like terms together we would then have:

$$A = -20 + 3D$$

where -20 is $(30 - 50)$ and $3D$ is $(5D - 2D)$.

One easy way to avoid this type of mistake (and it's a very common one) is to use brackets so we are clear about what we have to subtract:

$$A = B - C = (30 + 5D) - (50 + 2D)$$

where we have used brackets to show the terms which relate to B and those which relate to C. It is now clear that we have to subtract everything in the second set of brackets. We do this by multiplying everything in the second brackets by $-$, to give $(-50 - 2D)$.

One tip about this type of arithmetic is to check by using numbers and looking at your answer. For example we have:

$$A = B - C$$
$$\text{and } B = 30 + 5D$$
$$\text{and } C = 50 + 2D$$

Suppose we choose D to be 2 (the actual number doesn't matter). We then have:

$$B = 30 + 5D = 30 + 5(2) = 30 + 10 = 40$$
$$C = 50 + 2D = 50 + 2(2) = 50 + 4 \ = 54$$

and so:

$$A = B - C = 40 - 54 = -14$$

We ought to get exactly the same answer for A from our simplified equation – as long as we simplified it correctly. We had:

$$A = -20 + 3D = -20 + 3(2) = -20 + 6 = -14$$

confirming that our simplified equation for A was correct.

An incorrect version would have given a different answer:

$$A = -20 + 7D = -20 + 7(2) = -20 + 14 = -6$$

which is different from the answer we got from the original three equations. If this happens we know we've gone wrong in our simplification somewhere and need to go back and check.

Student activity

Return to the equation for take-home salary:

$T = S - 200 - 0.2S$

Obtain a simplified equation for T.

If your take-home pay last month was £800 what was your monthly salary and how much tax did you pay in £s?

We can simplify the equation quite easily:

$$T = S - 200 - 0.2S$$

We have two terms involving S so we have:

$$T = -200 + (S - 0.2S) = -200 + 0.8S$$

(We can easily check by using $S = 1,000$ as we had in the last activity and confirming that this gives $T = 600$.) So we have:

$$T = -200 + 0.8S$$

We now are told $T = £800$ and we need to work out S. We need to rearrange the T equation to get S on the left-hand side and everything else on the right. We do this in a series of calculations each one rearranging the equation closer into the form we need it to work out S.

We need to get S on to the left of the equation. We can do this if we subtract $0.8S$ from both sides:

$$T - 0.8S = -200 + 0.8S - 0.8S = -200$$

We need to get T on the right-hand side and we can do this if we subtract T from both sides:

$$T - T - 0.8S = -200 - T$$
$$\text{or } -0.8S = -200 - T \text{ (since the } T\text{s on the left cancel)}$$

We need to get $-0.8S$ on the left as $1S$ (or S) and we can do this if we divide through by -0.8:

$$\frac{-0.8S}{-0.8} = \frac{-200 - T}{-0.8}$$

The two –0.8s on the left cancel leaving S. If we divide –200 by –0.8 and $-T$ by –0.8 (remembering that two minuses make a plus) we get:

$$S = 250 + 1.25T$$

and since T is £800 we can work out S as:

$$S = 250 + 1.25(800) = 250 + 1,000 = 1,250$$

We know that tax is 20% of S so we would have paid $0.2(125) = £250$ in tax last month.

This may seem complicated but we just have to be methodical and rearrange the equation one step at a time, gradually getting the variable we want to solve on the left by itself and all other variables and coefficients on the right.

Brackets in more complicated equations

We've started to use brackets for some types of algebraic arithmetic. The principles of using brackets with equations are exactly the same as with numbers and as we discussed in section 2.2. Suppose we have a fairly simple equation:

$$Y = 100 + 15(X - 3)$$

We can simplify this by expanding the brackets, that is by multiplying everything inside the brackets by the coefficient immediately preceding, 15. We then have:

$$Y = 100 + 15X - 45 \text{ (since } +15 \times -3 \text{ is } -45)$$

Collecting like terms together we then have:

$$Y = 55 + 15X \text{ (since } 100 - 45 \text{ is } 55)$$

Sometimes, though, we might come across more complex equations which we need to simplify:

$$Y = 100(X + 2) + 15(X - 3)$$

which would simplify to:

$$Y = 100X + 200 + 15X - 45$$
$$Y = 155 + 115X$$

Even more complicated would be:

$$Y = (100 - X)(X + 2) + 15(X - 3)$$

We now have two sets of brackets which we need to multiply together. Remember what we did with a coefficient and a bracket: we multiplied each term inside the brackets by the coefficient. With two sets of brackets to multiply we follow a similar approach: we take the first term in the first set of brackets and multiply each term in the second set by this. We then take the second term in the first set of brackets and multiply each term in the second set by this.

This sounds very complicated but is quite straightforward. Let us just look at the part of the equation:

$$(100 - X) (X + 2)$$

The first term in the first bracket is 100, so we multiply everything in the second bracket by this:

$$100(X + 2) = 100X + 200$$

The second term in the first bracket is $-X$ (remember the minus sign). We multiply everything in the second bracket by this also:

$$-X(X + 2) = -X^2 - 2X$$

If we now collect these two together we have:

$$(100 - X) (X + 2) = (100X + 200) + (-X^2 - 2X)$$

(We've used brackets just to show the two calculations.) Simplifying gives:

$$(100 - X) (X + 2) = 100X + 200 - X^2 - 2X$$
$$(100 - X) (X + 2) = 98X + 200 - X^2$$

But in our original equation we had another expression. The original equation was:

$$Y = (100 - X) (X + 2) + 15(X - 3)$$

which will simplify to:

$$Y = (98X + 200 - X^2) + (15X - 45)$$
$$Y = 113X + 155 - X^2$$

It is usual to rearrange a complex equation into a better order like:

$$Y = 155 + 113X - X^2$$

where we have put the coefficient first, then the X term then the X^2 term. How would we use such an equation to work out a value for Y given some value for X? The answer, like any equation, is just by substituting the X value into the simplified equation. For example, suppose $X = 5$ then:

$$Y = 155 + 113(5) - 5^2$$
$$Y = 155 + 565 - 25 = 695$$

Of course we would have got exactly the same value for Y from the original equations $Y = (100 - X)(X + 2) + 15(X - 3)$ and, again, this is a useful way of checking that your simplified equation is the same as the original.

Student activity

Simplify the following:

$Y = (X–2)(3+X)$

$Y = 5(4+X) – (X–5)(X+5)$

$Y = 3X(5X – 2) – (X+2)(X–3)$

These look pretty complicated but if we take a methodical approach we can simplify them. Remember also that if you're unsure as to whether you've got it right choose a number for X (like 2), substitute into each of the original equations and work out Y. Then do the same with the simplified equations and, of course, you should get the same answer if you've simplified it without a mistake.

For $Y = (X – 2)(3 + X)$

We take each term in the first bracket and multiply each term in the second bracket by it. Taking the X in $(X – 2)$ first:

$X(3 + X) = 3X + X^2$

Taking $–2$ in $(X – 2)$:

$–2(3 + X) = –6 – 2X$

and collecting the two calculations together we get:

$Y = 3X + X^2 – 6 – 2X = 1X + X^2 – 6 = –6 + X + X^2$

For $Y = 5(4 + X) – (X – 5)(X + 5)$.

We'll work out the first part and then do the second part:

$5(4 + X) = 20 + 5X$

$(X – 5)(X + 5) = X^2 + 5X – 5X – 25 = X^2 – 25$

So:

$Y = 5(4 + X) – (X – 5)(X + 5) = 20 + 5X – (X^2 – 25)$

$= 20 + 5X – X^2 + 25$

$= 45 + 5X – X^2$

Finally for $Y = 3X(5X – 2) – (X + 2)(X – 3)$:

$3X(5X – 2) = 15X^2 – 6X$

$(X+2)(X–3) = X^2 – 3X + 2X – 6 = X^2 – X – 6$

So:

$Y = 5(4+X) – (X–5)(X+5) = 15X^2 – 6X – (X^2 – X – 6)$

$= 15X^2 – 6X – X^2 + X + 6$

$= 14X^2 – 5X + 6$

ROOTS OF NUMBERS

Self-assessment 13

Answer the questions set out below as best as you can. Check your answers against ours on p. 80.

If you've got them all right move on to the next self-assessment on p. 71.

What is:

(a) $\sqrt{100}$

(b) $\sqrt{25}$

(c) $\sqrt{16.37}$

You might remember from school or an earlier course at college – with some dismay – the idea of a *square root*. We will see later in the text that we will need to be able to do arithmetic with these things and to understand what they are. Although it sounds very complicated we can say that:

The square root of a given number is another number which when multiplied by itself will give the original number.

For example, we would say that the square root of 100 is 10 because $10^2 = 100$. That is, 10 is the square root of 100 because when we square 10 (the square root) we get the original number again. In symbol form this would be:

$$\sqrt{100} = 10$$

where $\sqrt{}$ is the symbol for square root. For simple numbers some mental arithmetic is probably all we need to figure out the square root. So:

$$\sqrt{25} = 5 \text{ (since } 5^2 = 25)$$
$$\sqrt{36} = 6 \text{ (since } 6^2 = 36)$$

and so on. However, any positive number can have a square root. Usually we will find the square root using a calculator and you should check yours by looking for a key with the symbol $\sqrt{}$. For example, if we use the following keys:

$\sqrt{}$
100
=

we get an answer of 10. If we key in:

$\sqrt{}$
53.67
=

we get 7.32598116296 as the square root of 53.67 since $7.32598116296^2 =$ 53.67. Sometimes you might see a square root written in a different way as:

$10^{1/2}$ that is, 10 to the power $\frac{1}{2}$.

or $53.67^{1/2}$ and so on. This might look strange, but if you remember the earlier section on powers and exponents you might see why we can write it in this way. Suppose we had:

$53.67^{1/2} \times 53.67$ (that is the square root times the square root)

We know from the arithmetic using powers that this would be:

$53.67^{1/2+1/2} = 53.67^1 = 53.67$

which confirms our 'definition' of a square root as being a number which when multiplied by itself gives the original number.

There are also other roots beside square roots. We might have a cube root:

$\sqrt[3]{1,000}$

where $\sqrt[3]{}$ indicates the cube root. This would be a number which when multiplied by itself three times would give the original number. You may be able to see that the cube root of 1,000 would be 10, since $10 \times 10 \times 10 = 1,000$. We might have roots involving higher powers also:

$\sqrt[4]{}$ pronounced root 4

$\sqrt[5]{}$ pronounced root 5 and so on.

We have to wait for the next section before we can work these out though.

We should also note that, as with every calculation, it is worthwhile estimating the sort of answer you expect from a square root calculation (by rounding the number you're working out a square root for to some convenient integer). However, square roots of numbers less than 1 can be surprising. For example, using a calculator we get:

$\sqrt{100} = 10$

$\sqrt{10} = 3.16228$

$\sqrt{1} = 1$ (i.e. $1 \times 1 = 1$)

$\sqrt{0.1} = 0.316228$

The last one might be a bit surprising: the square root of 0.1 is 0.316228 which is larger than the original number. We can check that our calculator hasn't gone berserk by squaring 0.316228 to confirm that it does in fact give 0.1 as an answer. Similarly:

$\sqrt{0.01} = 0.1$ (since $0.1^2 = 0.01$, or $\frac{1}{10} \times \frac{1}{10} = \frac{1}{100}$)

The square root of any number less than 1 will give an answer which is larger than the original (but still less than 1).

Finally you should note that with our arithmetic we cannot find the square root of a negative number. That is:

$$\sqrt{-100}$$

is not possible for us to calculate. The reason goes back to the meaning of a square root: it's a number which we multiply by itself to give the original number. For us there is no way we could multiply a number by itself and get a negative answer. For example, 10^2 is actually $+10 \times +10$ which will give $+100$. Similarly, -10^2 is -10×-10 which will also give $+100$. And multiplying $-10 \times +10$ contradicts our definition of a square root since -10 and $+10$ are technically different numbers. What this means is that if you're working through a calculation and end up trying to find the square root of a negative number you've done something wrong at an earlier stage in the calculation.

LOGARITHMS

Self-assessment 14

Answer the questions set out below as best as you can. Check your answers against ours on p. 80.

If you've got them all right move on to the next self-assessment on p. 76.

What is the logarithm of:

(a)   154.3

(b)   6.019

Use logarithms to work out:

(c) 108.2×23.1

(d) $16.5 \div 0.234$

Frequently, the arithmetic necessary in some calculations – and this is especially the case in the calculations of many financial statistics that we shall be looking at later in the text – is extremely time-consuming and tedious using ordinary arithmetic. Using a particular type of arithmetic – that relating to something called *logarithms* – such calculations can be performed easily and quickly. In the section that follows we shall focus on the use of logarithms and we shall assume that you have available a pocket calculator which has such logarithmic functions available. Logarithmic arithmetic is based on the principles covered in an earlier section on powers and exponents (Section 2.9).

We know that the number 100 can be written in the form 10^2. We then define the logarithm of 100 as being 2.0. That is,

$$100 = 10^2$$

and the logarithm of 100 = 2.0

That is, we define the logarithm of a number as the exponent of 10 which equals that number. The logarithm of 100 is 2.0 because a logarithm is simply the exponent of 10 which equates to 100. We would often write this as log 10.

$$\text{Similarly } \log 1,000 \ = 3.0 \qquad (\text{given that } 10^3 = 1,000)$$
$$\log 10,000 = 4.0 \qquad (\text{given that } 10^4 = 10,000)$$

and so on. In general any number can have its logarithm defined in this way. On your calculator find the keys marked as log and as 10^x (your keys may be marked slightly differently but should be similar to these). Now use the following keystrokes:

log
5
=

You should get an answer 0.69897 (we've rounded this from what you'll see on your calculator). What does this mean? This is simply the log of the number 5:

$$\log 5 = 0.69897 \qquad (\text{given that } 10^{0.69897} = 5)$$

Similarly $\log 17.9 = 1.252853$ (given that $10^{1.252853} = 17.9$), and so on for any number.

Student activity

Use your calculator to find the log of:

(a) 152.3
(b) 0.145
(c) −19.3

For (**a**) we have:

$$\log 152.3 = 2.1826999$$

For (**b**) we have:

$$\log 0.145 = -0.838632$$

A negative log indicates a number less than 1 since:

$$\log 0.145 = -0.838632 = 10^{-0.838632} = \frac{1}{10^{-0.838632}}$$

For (**c**), since $\log x$ is simply 10^x then $\log -x = -10^x$, so

$$\log -19.3 = - 1.2855573 \text{ (which is just } -10^{1.2855573})$$

If you try to work out the log of –19.3 directly on your calculator you'll get an error message.

Anti-logs

We can also define something known as the *anti-logarithm* or anti-log as the exact opposite of taking the log of a number. That is, an anti-log takes a logarithm and converts it to a comparable 'proper' number.

anti-log 0.69897 = 5
anti-log 1.252853 = 17.9

That is, if we know a logarithm we can find the comparable number (like 5 or 17.9) by using the anti-log. The key marked 10^x is usually the anti-log key on a calculator. Use the following keystrokes:

10^x (on your calculator you might need to use the SHIFT key
          to get this)
.69897
=

and you will get an answer 4.99999999 (which is as near to 5 as we need it).

Student activity

Find the numbers corresponding to the following logs:

(**a**) 0.37383114507

(**b**) 4.40862997659

(**c**) –1.90308998699

Taking each in turn and using the anti-log key on the calculator you should get:

(**a**) log 2.365 = 0.37383114507

(**b**) log 25623 = 4.40862997659

(**c**) log 0.0125 = –1.90308998699

Using the ideas introduced in the earlier section on powers we can now use logarithms to undertake a variety of forms of arithmetic. Suppose we wished to work out:

5 × 17.9

Whilst we could use ordinary arithmetic we can also use logarithms and this would become:

0.69897 + 1.252853 (i.e. $10^{0.69897} \times 10^{1.252853}$)

giving log (5 × 17.9) = 1.95175. Taking anti-log (1.95175) we have 89.485 which if you check using normal arithmetic is effectively the product of 5 × 17.9

(which using ordinary arithmetic is 89.5). The reason there is a slight difference between our answer using logs and using ordinary arithmetic is because we rounded the logs. You really need to use as many decimal places in log calculations as there are on your calculator. If you do this then the difference in the answer will be negligible.

In general there will be four main types of logarithmic calculations that we wish to undertake:

- multiplication;
- division;
- obtaining powers;
- obtaining roots.

The rules for performing such arithmetic through the use of logarithms are straightforward and are described below.

Multiplication

1 Find the logarithm of each of the numbers to be multiplied together.
2 Add the logarithms together.
3 Find the anti-log of this total.
4 The resulting number is the product of the multiplication.

For example: $18{,}756 \times 13.567 \times 1{,}987.1 \times 0.98$

$\log 18{,}756 = 4.273140224$
$\log 13.567 = 1.132483825$
$\log 1987.1 = 3.298219723$
$\log 0.98 \quad = -0.008773924308$
Totalling gives: 8.695069848

Taking the anti-log gives 495,529,880.9 which is the result for the original multiplications.

Note two points:

- the importance of using as many significant digits as possible;
- the fact that an answer derived via the use of logarithms will almost invariably be slightly less accurate than that using normal arithmetic.

Division

1 Find the logarithm of each of the numbers to be divided.
2 Subtract the logarithm of the number at the bottom of the division from that on the top (the denominator from the numerator).
3 Find the anti-log of this total.
4 The resulting number is the product of the division.

For example:

<u>1276.58</u>
  32.59
log 1276.58 = 3.106048036
log 32.59   = 1.51308436
log 1276.58 –log 32.59 = 3.106048036 –1.51308436
                 = 1.592963676
anti-log 1.592963676   = 39.171   which is the result.

Obtaining Powers

1 Find the logarithm of the number which is to be raised to some power.
2 Multiply the logarithm by the power number.
3 Find the anti-log of this total.
4 The resulting number is the original number raised to the stated power.

For example:

14.78^6
log 14.78 = 1.169674434
6 × log 14.78 = 6 × 1.169674434 = 7.018046604
anti-log 7.018046604 = 10,424,292.86   which is the result.

Obtaining Roots

1 Find the logarithm of the number for which the root is to be found.
2 Divide the logarithm by the root value.
3 Find the anti-log of the result.
4 This number is the answer.

For example:
$\sqrt[5]{6.538}$
log 6.358 = 0.803320523
log 6.358/5 = 0.803320523/5 = 0.160664104
anti-log 0.160664104 = 1.44765   which is the answer.

Student activity

Work out the following arithmetic using logarithms (check your answer by using normal arithmetic):

(a) 124 × 19.7 × 2,564.387
(b) 132^2 × 0.765 × 1,983.5
(c) $\sqrt[3]{14.32}$

For (**a**) we have:

> log 124   = 2.09342168516
> log 19.7   = 1.29446622616
> log 2564.387 = 3.40898356659

Adding the logs together gives 6.79687147791 and taking the anti-log gives 6,264,284.56357 (compared with the answer using normal arithmetic of 6,264,284.5636).

For (**b**) we have:

> log 132^2 = 2 × log 132 = 2 × 2.12057393121
>   = 4.24114786241
> log 0.765   = −0.11633856484
> log 1983.5 = 3.29743220481

Adding the logs together gives 7.42224150238 and taking the anti-log gives 26,438,785.5604 (compared with an answer of 26,438,785.56).

For (**c**) we have:

> log 14.32 = 1.15594301797
> ÷ 3   = 0.38531433932
> anti-log   = 2.429 (rounded)

OTHER MATHEMATICAL OPERATORS

> ### *Self-assessment 15*
>
> Answer the questions set out below as best as you can. Check your answers against ours on p. 80.
>
> For the variable X which has values 11, 9, 3, 5, 8 calculate:
>
> (**a**) ΣX
>
> (**b**) ΣX^2
>
> (**c**) $(\Sigma X)^2$

We have so far used a number of mathematical operators – things like +, −, ×, ÷, =. In this – the last section – we shall introduce a few more that we will encounter through the text.

Inequality operators

We are used to seeing something like:

$X = 10$

where X equals the number 10. But there are other inequality operators. For example:

$X \leq 10$ (pronounced 'X is less than or equal to 10')

means that X can take any number up to and as high as 10 but not a number which is larger (like 10.00001). Similarly:

$X < 10$ (pronounced 'X less than 10')

means that X can take any value which is less than 10 whilst:

$X \geq 10$ (pronounced 'X greater than or equal to 10')

means that X must take a value which is at least 10 (i.e. 10 or more) whilst:

$X > 10$ (pronounced 'X greater than 10')

means X must take a value greater than 10. Finally:

$X \neq 10$ (pronounced 'X not equal to 10')

means that X can take any value except 10 (it cannot be equal to 10).

Summation

As we shall soon see, we frequently require to determine the total value of a series of numbers. To assist in indicating this arithmetic operation a special symbol is frequently used: Σ (pronounced 'sigma'). This symbol is used to indicate the summation of the relevant variable. Assume the following figures:

5, 8, 9, 12, 15

We can refer to these numbers as variable X and use the Σ symbol to write:

ΣX (pronounced 'sigma X')

rather than say 'add the five numbers together and determine the total'. The result will be found by:

$\Sigma X = 5 + 8 + 9 + 12 + 15 = 49$

More complex operations can be carried out with reference to the Σ term. Thus:

ΣX^2 (pronounced 'sigma X squared')

would indicate to square the X numbers then add them together (giving a result here of 539). Equally, the term:

$$(\Sigma X)^2 \qquad\qquad \text{(pronounced 'sigma } X \text{ all squared')}$$

would refer instead to finding the total of X terms and *then* squaring (giving a result of 2,401).

Student activity

A store has collected data on the following two variables for the last week:

No. of units sold	Price per unit
11	£2.25
5	£2.30
17	£1.67
23	£0.95
14	£1.23

Let 'No. of units sold' be Q and 'Price per unit' P.

Determine the value of the following:

(a) ΣQ

(b) ΣP

(c) $\Sigma(Q \times P)$

What will the answers to part (a) and part (c) actually represent to the store (i.e. what is the manager likely to call these numbers)?

(a) ΣQ will be $11 + 5 + 17 + 23 + 14 = 70$

(b) ΣP will be $2.25 + 2.30 + 1.67 + 0.95 + 1.23 = 8.40$

(c) $\Sigma(Q \times P)$ will be $(11 \times 2.25) + (5 \times 2.30) + (17 \times 1.67) +$
$(23 \times 0.95) + (14 \times 1.23) = 103.71$

As far as the manager is concerned ΣQ (at 70) will be the total number of units sold whilst ΣQP (at £103.71) will be the total income, or revenue, from selling these units.

Factorial

One last mathematical operator that we need to introduce is represented by the character ! (an exclamation mark). This is a symbol referred to as a factorial and is used in conjunction with a whole number or a variable. So we might see, for example:

10! or 4! or 7!

Its meaning is quite straightforward. A factorial is a shorthand way of indicating that we take a sequence of numbers and multiply them together. For example 5! (pronounced '5 factorial') actually stands for:

$$5! = 5 \times 4 \times 3 \times 2 \times 1$$

whilst 10! is:

$$10! = 10 \times 9 \times 8 \times 7 \times 6 \times 5 \times 4 \times 3 \times 2 \times 1$$

This is, a factorial indicates that we take the number shown and multiply it by all the integers less than that number. The result of such multiplication is of course $5! = 120$ whilst $10! = 3,628,800$ (you may actually have a factorial key on your calculator). One special factorial value we must note is 0! which takes a value equal to 1.

SUMMARY

In this chapter we have introduced the basic tools of the trade that, from now on, we assume you can use without any difficulty. If in later chapters you find that you cannot understand some of the arithmetic that is taking place then come back and re-read the appropriate section in this chapter. Good luck!

Solutions to Self-Assessments

Note that we have simply provided the answer to each self-assessment question and not shown how the answer has been arrived at. If you get an answer wrong and don't understand why then you really should read the relevant section of this chapter.

Self-assessment 1
(a) 20
(b) 4
(c) 13

Self-assessment 2
(a) 1
(b) −14
(c) 20
(d) 14

Self-assessment 3
1 (a)   3,873,600
   (b)   3,870,000
2 5 million

Self-assessment 4
(a) 53,000
(b) 5

Self-assessment 5
1 £3
2 £600

Self-assessment 6
1 −£15
2 −35

Self-assessment 7
(a) −50
(b) 50
(c) −50
(d) −2
(e) 2
(f) −2

Self-assessment 8
(a) $\frac{23}{20}$
(b) $\frac{4}{21}$
(c) $\frac{3}{35}$
(d) $-\frac{3}{54}$

Self-assessment 9
(a) 1,673,040
(b) 0.01867

Self-assessment 10
(a) £1.59
(b) 75
(c) 50%

Self-assessment 11
(a) 10,000
(b) 0.0001
(c) 256
(d) 10,400

Self-assessment 12
$T = S − 200 − 0.2S$

Self-assessment 13
(a) 10
(b) 5
(c) 4.046

Self-assessment 14
(a) 2.188366
(b) 0.779524
(c) 2,499.42
(d) 70.513

Self-assessment 15
(a) 36
(b) 300
(c) 1,296

3 DATA COLLECTION AND DATA SOURCES

INTRODUCTION

The next few chapters will be spent analysing data in a number of ways designed to help a manager to identify the key features of a set of data. Before such a process can usually start, however, it is necessary to actually collect the data we want to analyse. This chapter is concerned with the major methods of data collection with particular reference to the various sampling methods which exist. Such data collection exercises are of critical importance to every business organization. We may wish to collect data on customer attitudes to a new product we are considering launching. We may wish to collect data on employee attitudes to some new type of productivity scheme we are thinking of introducing. We may require data to determine the stock levels in an organization. An auditor may collect data on financial transactions listed in the company accounts. Clearly such data collection cannot be seen as an unimportant part of the analysis process – the methods used to collect the data are of critical importance. You may also find it useful to return to this chapter and re-read it when you have worked your way through the rest of the text.

LEARNING OBJECTIVES

By the end of this chapter you should be able to:

- explain the need for a methodical approach to data collection;
- explain each of the stages to be carried out in a data collection exercise;
- explain what is meant by sampling methods;
- describe the main alternative sampling methods available;
- explain the advantages and disadvantages of the alternative methods available.

STAGES IN DATA COLLECTION

We shall illustrate the various stages with reference to a simple scenario. Together with some friends you are thinking of establishing a small restaurant in a local town. The restaurant will specialize in offering value-for-money meals using organic produce only. Naturally, before investing any money into the project, you have decided to collect data on local people's attitudes to the venture, particularly in terms of whether they are likely to be attracted to the restaurant as customers. We shall assume that the data we wish to collect is primary data.

There are a number of logical stages that can be identified in any data collection exercise:

1 Determine the purpose of the exercise.
2 Determine the information to be collected.
3 Determine the method of data collection.
4 Determine the sampling method to be used to select the sample.
5 Carry out a pilot survey.
6 Carry out the main survey.
7 Validate the data and the collection methods.
8 Analyse the data collected.

It is important to realize that the part a manager is usually most interested in – analysing the data and then using it to help make decisions – is the last part of this process. A lot more must be done first – and done properly if the data and any information we extract from it is to be useful and reliable. The principle of 'garbage in – garbage out' is particularly relevant for data collection. If we do not take the time and effort to ensure we collect data in an appropriate and reliable way then any subsequent analysis is, at best, worthless and, at worst, downright dangerous if we base critical decisions on it. We shall look at each of the appropriate stages in turn.

Stage 1: Determine the purpose of the exercise

This is the first question to be raised and it must be adequately answered before proceeding with the subsequent stages of data collection. Any data collection exercise is both time-consuming and expensive and it is essential to know for what purpose the data are to be collected. The declared purpose will have a major effect on the subsequent stages of the exercise, particularly in terms of how much effort and attention we put into the data collection procedure.

Student activity

In our example of collecting data about potential customers why is the data to be collected?

In this example we want the data to help us decide whether a new restaurant in the town would be successful. You can see that this is a particularly important decision. If you take the wrong decision as to whether you think the restaurant will attract enough customers it will have serious consequences so you must ensure as far as possible that we get everything right when collecting data.

In general the data collection exercise could fall into one of two categories:

- it could be part of a regular data collection programme;
- it could be a one-off exercise.

We might also distinguish the ultimate uses to which the data collected could be put:

- for general background information;
- to assist in routine, operational decision-making;
- to assist in strategic decision-making.

Depending on the circumstances, the information may simply be used by management in a general way as part of some overall information process. Equally, the information may be of use in operational decision-making on a day-to-day or regular basis. We might, for example, collect data on employee absenteeism whereby the personnel department – on a regular basis – can monitor absence from work of individual employees or a department. Again, the data may take on a far more important role if it is to be used to assist in strategic, or long-term, decisions.

Student activity

In the example of your collecting data on potential customers, which category and for what type of use is our data collection?

For our data we have a one-off exercise and the data is to be used for making a strategic decision – do we open the new restaurant or not?

Stage 2: Determine the information to be collected

Following on from the first stage it then becomes necessary to determine precisely what information will be collected. At this stage it becomes necessary to balance two conflicting aspects. On the one hand we are likely to wish to collect as much relevant data as possible. On the other, the more data we collect the more expensive and time-consuming the exercise will become. It is important, therefore, to know – from Stage 1 – what the ultimate purpose of the data collection is. This will help us assess the trade-off between the cost of collecting what we would like and what we need.

Student activity

Returning to the example of your survey for a new restaurant, what data would you want to collect?

With the example of a survey to determine potential customers for a new restaurant we might identify the information we would require as:

- personal details (such as age, sex, occupation, income, family size, etc.);
- where in relation to the proposed restaurant they live;
- availability of transport, either their own or public transport;
- current eating-out patterns;
- likely attitude to the new restaurant;
- which features would attract the customer to the new restaurant.

And so on. It is important to realize that, frequently, the data we may wish to obtain and the data we actually obtain may not be the same. For example, it may be considered especially useful to know the income of an individual to determine their likely spending power in the restaurant. People may be very reluctant to reveal such details, however, because they prefer such details to remain private and confidential.

Stage 3: Determine the method of data collection

Having decided on the data we wish to try and collect we must next determine how it is to be collected. Again, this will very much depend on the circumstances surrounding the exercise and the type of data we are trying to collect, but we can generalize two basic situations:

- Is the data likely to be available in some form already?
- Does it look as if we will have to collect the data ourselves?

As we will see later in this chapter a considerable amount of data on many variables likely to be of interest to an organization is already available in one form or another – perhaps through some government data collection exercise at national and local level, perhaps through a market research company, or perhaps internally within our own organization. Many organizations – public and private sector – tend to be data rich but information poor and very often have poor communication systems for letting people within the organization know what data is already available.

In the context of the restaurant scenario we have built up, much data will already have been collected by a variety of organizations. Demographic statistics will be available from the local authority and perhaps through central government on a small area level. The local health authority may have undertaken some research into the eating and dietary habits of local residents. Local transport organizations may have obtained data on levels of car ownership and use of public transport.

Before deciding we need to go out and collect our own data (often at considerable cost in terms of time as well as money), we should consider where relevant data may already be available. Of course, such data will be secondary and there may well be questions as to whether it fits our particular needs and is as reliable as we may want. As ever, this will involve a trade-off between what we would like and what we can reasonably afford to obtain.

However, if we do decide that we need to collect data at first hand then there are a number of alternative approaches to consider. Amongst these will be the following.

Personal interview

This is where a person taking part in the survey is interviewed formally on a face-to-face basis. This method is probably one of the more expensive methods of data collection but it has a high degree of accuracy (although in turn this is very dependent on the skill and experience of the interviewer).

Postal questionnaire

This method is where some form of questionnaire is sent to those taking part in the exercise, completed by them and returned to the organization collecting the data. This is generally less expensive than the first method but considerable effort and skill is required in designing an appropriate questionnaire. Additionally, response rates to postal questionnaires can be quite low (10–15% is normal) and the organization has no way of knowing whether the person completing the questionnaire has properly understood the question and has given the correct response.

Telephone interview

This method tends to be restricted to certain types of survey. It tends to be inexpensive and easy to organize (you only require an interviewer and a telephone) but faces a number of potential problems. Only certain people may have access to a telephone which may introduce bias into the survey. It may also be difficult to extract appropriate information over the phone.

Direct observation

This method is appropriate where we do not require specific information about individuals in the survey. For example, if we are simply counting the number of customers going into a rival restaurant this is easily achieved via direct observation. Similarly, if we wish to check the quality of output on some production line this also can be achieved by direct observation.

The disadvantage of this method is that it does not provide information about the specific characteristics of the members of the sample selected.

Use of computer databases

Increasingly this method of data collection is used. More and more information is stored on computer databases and thereby provides a quick, inexpensive method of extracting data about some sample. Examples would be details of customer accounts, employee records, sales levels, credits and debits, stock levels, quantities ordered and so on. Increasingly, much government data is also available on computer file. The disadvantage is that where such data exists it is of a secondary nature with all the associated potential problems.

Student activity

Which method would you recommend for your restaurant survey?

There is no ideal answer to this question. Much will depend on the time available, the resources available and so on. However, the personal interview is probably to be preferred for this survey. We have already decided that the survey is particularly important because management will use it to help make an important, strategic decision. So, although this type of survey is expensive the information from it will tend to be more reliable and complete.

Stage 4: Determine the sampling method to be used to select the sample

The next stage is to choose an appropriate method for selecting those items in the population which are to form the basis for the sample. These methods are discussed in detail later in the chapter.

Stage 5: Carry out a pilot survey

No matter how well thought out the previous stages it is virtually essential to undertake a pilot – or trial – survey before committing the organization to the trouble and expense of the main survey. Such a pilot survey will allow you to determine whether there are any unforseen problems in any of the previous stages, particularly relating to the data you are trying to collect, questionnaire design and the selection of sample members. It is frequently the case in practice that major changes to the survey methods are made after the pilot survey. In our example, we might design a questionnaire for the personal survey we intend carrying out and then interview, say, 50 people just to see how things work out. If we are happy with the questionnaire then we can carry out the full survey.

Stage 6: Carry out the main survey

Following the pilot survey any necessary amendments can be made to the data collection exercise and the main survey can then be undertaken. It is usually necessary to monitor the progress of the exercise periodically to ensure that it is conforming to the objectives and methods laid down.

Stage 7: Validate the data and the collection methods

Having completed the data collection exercise it is then necessary to validate, or check, both the methods that have been used to collect the data and the data itself. This is particularly important if – as is likely – the data is to be analysed using computer-based methods. This would typically involve checking that some of the basic responses we had obtained were 'sensible' in the context of the survey and that we had obtained the type of sample we had set out to. For example, if we noticed that, say, 90% of the people taking part in our restaurant survey were male then we ought to begin to question both the methods used to select the sample and the potential reliability of any analysis we carried out (unless of course our objective is to attract primarily male customers). Similarly, if we had asked potential customers their annual income (in order to try to assess possible spending patterns) and we found that no one said they had an income less than £50,000 a year we might be concerned about the reliability of the data collected and the methods used to collect it.

Stage 8: Analyse the data collected

Finally, the process of analysing the data to provide the information that was originally required can begin using the techniques that we shall cover in later chapters.

SAMPLING METHODS

You will remember that we said earlier that whenever we have to analyse a sample rather than the population we have to ensure that the sample is representative of the population. The process for selecting a sample from a population to ensure that the sample is properly representative is a particularly specialized and technical area. We shall outline the main methods that can be used in this section.

In general sampling techniques will fall into one of three broad categories:

- *random sampling* where each member of the population has an equal chance of being included in the sample;
- *quasi-random sampling* (semi-random) which is a form of random sampling where the random selection only takes place within certain predefined (i.e. non-random) groups;
- *non-random sampling* which refers to those techniques where the sample is specifically selected rather than chosen at random.

We shall discuss the main techniques falling into these headings in turn. The importance of trying to ensure a representative sample cannot be stressed sufficiently. Failure to ensure this leads to what is known as *bias* in our results – the fact that some part of our statistical population may be under- or over-represented in the sample. This bias in turn may lead to our evaluating the results from the data collection exercise in an inappropriate or misleading way and potentially may lead us to incorrect conclusions about some situation.

Consider a factory assembly line engaged in the mass production of tin cans for the food industry. Naturally, the factory will want to check production periodically. For a variety of reasons it may be impractical to check every single item produced – instead we must sample to check quality. It would clearly be inappropriate to sample production only on every Friday each week, or at 9.00 a.m. each morning. Such a sampling procedure is likely to lead to bias – the sample will not properly represent the statistical population (total production). This may lead management to take inappropriate decisions based on the biased sample data, perhaps shutting down the production line because they think there is a fault, or perhaps *not* shutting down the assembly line when there is a fault but they are unaware of it.

Simple random sampling

This is a method whereby each member of the statistical population has an equal chance of being selected to form the sample. Assume, for illustration, that we had a population consisting of 100 people. The principle of simple random sampling is that we could, for example, write each person's name on a piece of paper, place all the pieces of paper in a box, and choose a piece of paper at random from the box. Each person in the population obviously has the same chance of being selected and the sample that would result would be a true random sample.

Naturally, these days selection of a sample under such conditions could easily be undertaken via a computer program. If we had people's names in a computer file then we could program the computer to randomly select a given number of people for our sample.

The advantage of this method is that:

- the sample selection is unbiased and can be seen to be representative.

The disadvantages are that:

- it is necessary to know each item in the population which, obviously, will not always be the case. In the case of the restaurant survey, for example, we would need to know the name of every person living in the area in order to be able to randomly select from the population;
- not all items in the population will be equally accessible once selected for the sample. In the case of the restaurant survey we might have some people who might be difficult to visit to get them to take part in the survey;
- it is possible that certain parts of the population may be under- or over-represented purely by chance.

Stratified sampling

This is also classed as a random method where we can identify certain groups – or strata – that the population naturally falls into. We can then undertake a random selection within each strata. For example, in the survey on potential customers we may classify potential customers by sex – male or female. If we know, for example, that 55% of the local population are female and 45% male then we can ensure that these proportions are maintained within the sample by ensuring that the two groups – strata – are proportionally represented. The people making up each strata can then be randomly selected from the appropriate part of the population. Such strata might be expressed in terms of sex, age, income level, education, number of children and so on.

Student activity

How would you try and ensure that these proportions were maintained in the sample?

There are a number of different ways you might have suggested. One of them is to keep count of the number of men and the number of women chosen for the sample as it is being conducted. If for example we decided the sample was to contain 100 people then, when we had chosen 55 women for the sample, we would continue to choose only men for the rest.

The advantage of this method is that:

- the sample will generally reflect the major groupings within the population.

The disadvantages are that:

- it is still necessary to know each item in each of the strata of the population;
- detailed information about the size and composition of each strata is needed;
- it may be more expensive to conduct this type of survey than a simple random selection.

Systematic sampling

This is a method of quasi-random sampling and can be used in certain populations which are clearly structured. Returning to our survey of potential customers for the restaurant, let us suppose that we have decided to interview those selected for the sample in their own homes. If we took a street of houses then simple random selection means that we could end up in any of the homes in any order. Systematic sampling, however, operates on the basis that the first item (house) selected is chosen at random. From then on the population is systematically surveyed. If there were, say, 1,000 houses and we wished to interview 100 people then we would select the first house at random. Subsequently we would interview the person at every 10th house afterwards to give the total sample of 100.

The advantage of this method is that:

- this method is particularly easy to conduct for certain types of population.

The disadvantages are that:

- bias can easily occur if there is any pattern to the distribution of items, for example part of one row of houses might only be for the use of retired people;
- the method is not truly random;
- it cannot be applied to all types of population, only those which have a clear structure to them.

Multi-stage sampling

This is a second method of quasi-random sampling and is convenient where the population may be spread over a large geographical area. Under such circumstances simple random sampling may require extensive travelling to the various parts of the area covered. Multi-stage sampling operates by splitting the population into geographically distinct areas, randomly selecting certain of these areas and then selecting a sample (either randomly or systematically or in a stratified way) within these areas only. This means, of course, that certain members of the population have no opportunity of being selected for the sample.

The advantage of this method is that:

- the method saves time and expense.

The disadvantages are that:

- the method may lead to biased results if the stages are not properly selected;
- the method is not truly random;
- the method needs careful thought and design to be properly representative;
- great care must be taken in grouping areas to represent the population.

Quota sampling

The method is generally to stratify the population into groups using appropriate criteria and then to specify the exact number (or quota) required from each group for the sample. So we may classify the population by sex, by age group and by occupation. We would then specify, for example, that the sample must include a quota of 20 people who are female, aged between 20 and 30 and who are clerical workers.

The advantages of this method are:

- the method can lead to highly accurate results;
- the method can save time and expense.

The disadvantages are that:

- the method relies on an accurate identification of appropriate quotas;
- much reliance is placed on the individual interviewer in selecting people to fill the quota which if not properly done might introduce bias into the selection for the quota.

Cluster sampling

This is a method of non-random sampling and is common where the population may be geographically separated. The method involves selecting a certain number of areas and then sampling all members of the population found in that area. Other areas will not be sampled at all. This is not the same as multi-stage sampling where only a sample of items may be selected from each area.

The main advantage of this method is that:

- it is easy and inexpensive as the survey is undertaken in concentrated areas.

The disadvantages are that:

- sampling is not random;
- the cluster areas may not be properly representative of the population.

Judgemental sampling

The last type of method is entirely non-random. This method relies on the person conducting the survey using their knowledge, experience and judgement as to which items to include in the survey. For example, suppose that the head of a company's computer services department wants to find out what other departments think of the services that the computer department offers (in the way of technical support, maintenance, repairs, advice, training and so on). Clearly any of the methods we have described so far could be used. However, the head of the department may use his/her judgement and decide who to include in the survey. Such a decision might be based on those people the head thinks knows most about the services offered, those who would have strong opinions, those who have been with the company some time and are therefore experienced and so on. The key point is that the sample is carefully selected.

The advantages of this method are that:

- experience can be used to ensure a good sample selection;
- it can provide a coherent and focused sample.

The disadvantages are that:

- the method is non-random;
- it is dependent on a 'good' choice by the person exercising judgement in the sample selection.

Sample size

No matter what method is used to collect data about the sample we must also be careful to ensure that the sample contains a sufficient number of the members of the statistical population: that is that the sample size is adequate for the analysis we wish to undertake. Ideally we would like the sample size to be as large as possible since, in principle, the larger the sample size the closer it will represent the population from which it is taken. However, in practice there are frequently limitations to the size of the sample we can select. These limitations might include:

- *costs* since in general the larger the sample we collect the more it will cost us;
- *time* since the larger the sample the longer it will take us and we may have a fixed time scale available;
- *analysis* since we may not have the facilities to analyse large quantities of data for a sample.

In practice the choice of sample size is a compromise between the largest sample size we would like and what the various limitations allow us to do. As an illustration, opinion poll surveys that are frequently reported in the press typically have a sample size of about 1,000.

APPLICATIONS IN BUSINESS AND MANAGEMENT

It is difficult to present a concise summary of the many different types of application of sampling to areas of business and management. The use of such techniques is widespread and the role of 'market research' in most large organizations well established. A few of the indicative areas of use are as follows:

- In the area of auditing where it would not be feasible to check every invoice and payment. Instead a representative sample is chosen and then analysed in detail.
- In the area of mass production it is again infeasible to check every item produced when the number of such items may run into the thousands or millions. Instead a sample is selected and carefully checked against specification.

- In reliability testing where a sample of items is taken and tested to destruction to see how long they will last or what has to happen to cause a failure. It is clearly not possible to test every item in this way.

- In market research which may be conducted amongst customers or employees to obtain information on attitudes and likely behaviour.

DATA SOURCES

Of course, it may not be necessary to collect data at all. We may be able to access data sources which are already available. Increasingly with computer databases, integrated computer networks and the Internet large quantities of data are available which may save an organization from collecting the data first hand (although of course such data is likely to be secondary and may not fit the requirements of the manager perfectly). It is clearly impossible to provide a definitive list of all available data sources. We shall instead outline some of the more readily available public sources of data. You are strongly urged to use your local library to check these out and to become familiar with the type of data they have available.

Guide to Official Statistics

This is published by the UK Central Statistical Office and, whilst not a source of data itself, is an invaluable guide as to where you can find specific sets of data in other UK government publications. The *Guide* provides a detailed index and cross-referencing system of key variables and indicators together with where they are likely to be found in government published sources. So, for example, if you had an interest in trying to locate unemployment figures by age group the *Guide* would indicate (as at 1995) that such data could be found in the *Employment Gazette*; *Regional Trends*; *Scottish Abstract of Statistics*; *Digest of Welsh Statistics*; *Northern Ireland Annual Abstract of Statistics*. As such the *Guide* is an essential first step if you don't know where you are likely to find specific sets of official statistics (or indeed if such statistics are available at all).

Annual Abstract of Statistics

This is published each year and provides detailed summary data on a variety of economic, social, demographic and business variables.

Census of population reports

These are published by the Office of Population Censuses and Surveys (OPCS) for England and Wales and by the General Registrar's Office for Scotland (with the data increasingly available on computer disk as well as in printed form). The reports provide data on population for a variety of geographical areas and are shown in a variety of categories (by age for example) and relating to the ten-year cycle of national censuses that are regularly carried out (the last being in 1991).

Economic Trends

This is a monthly publication detailing the key economic and financial indicators for the UK supported with appropriate graphs and diagrams. Data includes GDP, National Income accounts; personal income and expenditure; prices; earnings, labour force statistics; financial statistics. Also published is the *Economic Trends Annual Supplement* which is a useful source of longer time series sets of data (often covering 20 years or more).

Family Expenditure Survey

This is an annual report of an ongoing survey (started in 1957) of some 7,000 households in the UK which monitors income and expenditure patterns of these households in considerable detail. Typical data illustrates household expenditure for different income groups; expenditure by age; expenditure by socio-economic profile; different categories of expenditure; income by age, occupation and socio-economic characteristics.

Monthly Digest of Statistics

This is published monthly and provides comparable data to that in the *Annual Abstract of Statistics* on national income and expenditure; population; employment; social services; law enforcement; agriculture and industry; energy; transport; retailing; external trade; finance; prices and wages.

Regional Trends

An annual report, this replicates key variables found in other publications but with the data relating to the standard regions of the UK. Data is available on EU comparison; population; education; labour statistics; housing; health; crime and justice; transport; industry and agriculture.

Social Trends

This is another annual publication showing a variety of social and socio-economic indicators of life in the UK. Data typically is available on population; households and families; education; employment; income and wealth; expenditure; health; housing; environment; leisure; crime and justice; and transport.

Europe in Figures

Finally, this is a publication by Eurostat (the Statistical Office of the European Communities) which provides comparative data on all member countries (as well as on major trading partners like the USA and Japan). Data relates to the environment; population; education; the labour market; standard of living; agriculture; energy; industry; finance; international trade.

SUMMARY

It may seem that the area of sampling and data collection is a very complex one. In practice the general principles are very clear – even though the actual mechanics of actually selecting a sample may be complex. We must be clear from the outset, however, what the purposes of the data collection exercise are, to what uses the data will be put once collected and what decisions may be taken based on the data we collect. We must also make every effort to ensure that the sample we collect data for is representative of the statistical population it represents – that it is free from bias.

- A distinction must be carefully drawn between primary and secondary data in terms of its reliability.
- It is usually necessary to base analysis upon some selected sample from the population rather than on the entire population.
- The method of sample selection is critical to the reliability of the data and must be free from bias.
- It is important to determine why the data is being collected. Until we know this we cannot determine the most appropriate way of collecting that data.
- The method chosen for collecting the data will largely depend on why the data is required.
- A variety of sample selection techniques exist, dependent upon the type of population to be dealt with and the type of information to be collected. All have their advantages and disadvantages and a choice will often depend on the particular circumstances surrounding the data collection exercise.

EXAMPLE

In this section we will illustrate the application of some of the concepts and themes introduced in this chapter. The illustration is based around a project in which the author was involved.

Most organizations these days are under considerable pressure to improve 'customer' service and ensure that the products and services that they offer their customers are both meeting the needs of their customers and are felt to be of the appropriate quality and standard.

Whilst we tend to think of such 'quality' pressures in the context of firms which are engaged in the production of physical products – cars, computers, household goods – firms engaged in providing services are not immune from these pressures either. Indeed, one of the noticeable developments over the last few years has been a desire on the part of service organizations in the public sector – hospitals, local authorities, libraries – to improve quality and customer service.

Schools are obviously not immune from these pressures and, indeed, have recently come under the spotlight with the publication of 'league tables' of exam results of their pupils. One school based in the West Country in England decided that it needed detailed information in terms of 'customer' feedback about its current performance and activities.

The school in question was a fee-paying Methodist school offering places to pupils between the ages of 6 and 18 either on a day-attendance basis or on a residential basis. The school is a co-educational boarding and day school with around 700 pupils from 4 years of age up to 18/19 years of age. It is structured into a Pre-Preparatory department for pupils from 4 to 8 years, a Junior School from 8 to 12 years and a Senior School from 12 years upwards. In the Senior School around 40% of pupils are female and approximately the same proportion of all Senior pupils are boarders. The school also attracts a number of overseas pupils and pupils from parents who are in the armed services.

Like many other such public (fee-paying) schools it was facing increasingly difficult times in terms both of trying to control its costs and in terms of maintaining pupil recruitment levels. In 1991 a new headmaster was appointed to the school and together with the chairman of the school's Board of Governors undertook a fundamental review of the school's position and possible futures. Highly committed and professional staff, outstanding exam results, excellent buildings and infrastructure, excellent support staff and facilities and a close rapport between pupils, parents and staff as well as with the wider local community were all identified as key strengths. Nevertheless it was felt appropriate to undertake such an evaluation in order to ensure continuing, future success.

One of the factors stimulating this approach was that the overall environment in which the school was operating (and indeed in which all such schools are operating) was facing considerable change and uncertainty. Some of the factors that needed to be assessed included:

- the effect of demographic changes in the school age population;
- the decline experienced in the independent schools' sector in general in demand for boys' boarding places;
- an unexpected decline in numbers at sixth-form level;
- the impact on demand for places in the independent schools' sector in general following a decade where increases in school fees had outstripped inflation;
- the long-term impact of the economic recession on parents' ability to pay such school fees;
- the impact of the armed services review currently underway by the government which was expected to result in a sizeable decrease in the armed services (and hence in the number of children of parents in the armed forces who would need a place at boarding school);
- the future change of status for Hong Kong (approximately 25% of overseas pupils attending independent schools in the UK are from Hong Kong at present).

In addition at the time, a General Election was imminent giving rise to further uncertainty regarding:

- the potential withdrawal of charity status from independent schools;
- the potential withdrawal of the Assisted Places Scheme whereby the government funds a number of places at independent schools for pupils whose parents are on low incomes;
- the potential of increased direct competition from the state sector with an increase in the number of grant maintained schools – state schools which will be able to opt out of local authority control.

In 1992, as part of the review process, the school commissioned an image research exercise. The purpose of the research was primarily to collect information about parents' perception of the school and about the quality of the services and resources provided. This information could then be consolidated with that available from other sources to help the school review its long-term strategic position. (In terms of our methodology this was to be a one-off exercise to assist in strategic decision-making.)

It was decided to conduct the research through a postal questionnaire that would be distributed to a randomly selected sample of parents who currently had children at the school. Such a random sample was possible since the school had the names and addresses of all pupils/parents. The questionnaire consisted of some 30 questions in total, ranging from questions about how parents initially found out about the school, through to perceptions on the quality of teaching and related support, to a consideration of future changes in services and facilities that parents would like to see. The questionnaire was initially distributed to over 150 parents and generated a response rate of 67%.

To illustrate the type of findings produced and their contribution to decision-making one area will be discussed. This relates to the source of initial contact with the school: how parents first came into contact with the school when considering sending their child to an independent school. Clearly this has important long-term implications as to how the school markets itself in the future. On analysis 77% of parents indicated that the source of initial contact was either that they knew of the school personally or that it had been recommended by a friend, colleague or relative. Clearly such a finding was of considerable interest to the school in a climate of change and uncertainty since it implied that the school had developed a strong and very positive reputation. As any private sector business knows word-of-mouth is a very cost-effective way of attracting new customers.

Overall, many of the findings produced as a result of the research came as little surprise to the school. This, in itself, was reassuring that the research was accurately reflecting views and opinions of parents that had been expressed in other ways (through parents' evenings for example). Equally it implied that staff at the school were, by and large, accurately in touch with parents' views and expectations. However, a number of findings were revealed that the school could use both to improve its operational performance and as part of its longer-term strategic planning.

The research also highlighted some information needs of the school. It had been intended to conduct comparable research amongst parents who had contacted the school regarding a place for their child but who had then subsequently not chosen it. Clearly such research would have been potentially beneficial in terms of providing information as to why some parents chose a 'competitor' instead. However, details of such parents were not currently retained – not really surprising since such data was not up to now seen as important – and this aspect of the research was not attainable. One of the recommendations arising from the research was that the school should retain such data in the future to help it assess why it might be losing potential 'customers' to the competition.

SELF-REVIEW QUESTIONS

1 *Outline the main stages of a data collection exercise.*

2 *What is meant by bias?*

3 *What is the distinction between a random and quasi-random sampling method?*

4 *What are the two main types of quasi-random sampling?*

5 *What are the disadvantages of non-random sampling methods?*

6 *What is the difference between simple random sampling and stratified sampling?*

7 *Why is it necessary for a sample to be properly representative of a population?*

STUDENT EXERCISES

1 In this chapter we have discussed the survey into potential customers who may use a new restaurant. You have been put in charge of the survey to collect this data.

   (a) Draft a report to management outlining each of the main stages in data collection in relation to this survey.

   (b) Explain which method of data collection you feel would be most appropriate.

   (c) Discuss the alternative sample selection methods that could be used and recommend which you feel would be most appropriate.

2 A large international consultancy firm wishes to undertake market research concerned with the services it offers to its many clients. A small task group has been set up and you have been asked to advise on the sampling process that should be used to collect the relevant data. In this context provide a short explanation of each of the following terms in the context of the firm:

(a) simple random sampling;

(b) systematic sample;

(c) quota sampling;

(d) cluster sampling;

(e) bias.

3 A retail outlet selling CDs and cassettes has commissioned a market research firm to undertake a survey into the shop's customers and the shop manager has asked you to explain the following terms contained in the market research firm's proposal:

(a) random sample;

(b) quota sample;

(c) cluster sample.

Explain, in this context, how you might go about trying to obtain a representative sample of the shop's customers.

4 The various police forces in the UK are under pressure from a variety of sources to ensure that the services they provide to the local communities are both appropriate to the needs of that community and are reasonably well thought of. Most forces regularly undertake market research exercises to collect opinions of their 'customers'. Draft a report to the Chief Constable around the following structure.

(a) Explain why an organization like the police needs this type of data/information.

(b) Describe the type of data/information you feel should be collected.

(c) Suggest how the data/information might be collected in a cost-effective manner.

4 TABLES IN BUSINESS

INTRODUCTION

We saw earlier that in most organizations the first task facing a manager when considering some decision is to collect data about the decision situation and then try to make sense of that data: to extract useful information from the data available. Data by itself is worthless in business. This first stage in this process is frequently to present the data in the form of a table. In this chapter we shall introduce a number of common types of table used by managers and see how they can be constructed and how they can be used.

LEARNING OBJECTIVES

By the end of this chapter you should be able to:

- explain why tables are necessary for presenting data;
- explain the key principles of constructing a table;
- construct suitable tables for a data set;
- extract key information from a table;
- construct and interpret a frequency table.

DATA AND INFORMATION

One of the key areas of economic activity for a country relates to its foreign trade – the business it does with other countries. In very simple terms a country sells its products and services to other countries: these are classed as its exports. Similarly it will buy goods and services from other countries: its imports. In 1992 the countries shown below had exports and imports as shown (figures are in millions ECUs):

Germany exports 331,009; Japan imports 179,301; USA imports 409,282; Italy exports 137,581; Japan exports 261,755; UK imports 171,410; USA exports 344,716; Germany imports 315,745; UK exports 144,522; Italy imports 145,777.

Now try to answer the following questions quickly:

Which country had the largest imports?
Which country had the smallest exports?
Which country had the largest difference between exports and imports?

It's not easy, is it?

It takes time to sort through the data, you have to keep looking back through the data to find the answer to each question and you're spending a lot of timing trying to answer the questions. In short, although we have *data* on exports and imports, it is difficult to obtain the *information* we need.

We can think of data as being a simple statement of fact. For example, UK exports in 1992 were 144,522 million ECUs. This is a simple statement – in this case expressed numerically – about some situation that has been observed. For this data to have any real value – to a manager, to an economist, to the government – then typically the data must be processed in some way to provide information. That is, the data must be converted into a form so that it is useful to a manager or decision-maker. The processing of such data into information can take several forms:

- We might compare this data with other data to produce information. For example, here we have compared UK exports both with UK imports and with the imports and exports of other countries.

- We might use this data to perform additional calculations which in turn provide the decision-maker with information. We could have calculated the difference between exports and imports for each country, for example.

- We might examine the data in more detail in terms of its component structure. For a business, for example, which is assessing its future export strategy, we might investigate the UK export data to provide information about which countries the UK exports to (providing information to the company about possible markets overseas) and about the type of goods it exports.

101

- We might examine this data with comparable data over time. For example, looking at UK exports over, say, the last ten years may provide information about longer-term export trends.

The basic distinction between data and information is that information has a value to the decision-maker or user. However, in order to obtain such information we must first obtain and then process the data. It is for this reason that it is often said that data has a cost but only information has a value.

Of course, what is data to one manager may well be information to another and vice versa. This is often the case, for example, with financial data. Many managers are unable to extract any meaningful information from such data but to accountants and other managers with appropriate skills such data can often be transformed into information about the financial health of an organization.

Of course, the skill for the manager lies in knowing *how* to transform data into information: what quantitative techniques to apply. This, in fact, is one of the key purposes of this text: to introduce a variety of common quantitative techniques that allow such a transformation to take place – to those who know what they're doing.

THE USE OF TABLES

To help us obtain information from data a first useful step is often to show the data in the form of a table. There are many different types of table that can be constructed and we shall introduce a number of them. For example, using the data we had earlier on exports and imports we can construct a table showing this data such as that in Table 4.1.

Holiday insurance: shop around for better value						
	Europe		Worldwide		Annual	
	Individual	Family	Individual	Family	Individual	Family
Thomas Cook	30.95	154.75	54.50	272.50	120	250.00
Lunn Polly	30.95	131.53	52.95	225.03	–	–
Post Office	18.20	50.05	43.30	119.08	87.60	175.20
Columbus	11.00	38.50	25.00	87.50	99.00	174.00
Lloyds Bank	22.19	66.62	63.76	191.28	97.38	142.22
Nat West	23.37	81.79	52.58	184.03	88.00	129.00
Whiteleys	16.50	41.25	37.55	93.90	92.25	138.38
General Accident	–	–	–	–	76.88	143.51

Premiums are for two week holiday for either one person under 65, or for a family of five, with three children between the ages of 2 and 15.

 Source: *Financial Times*, 3 June 1995

Table 4.1
Exports and imports for selected countries: 1992
(figures shown are in millions of ECUs)

	Exports	Imports	Difference
USA	344,716	409,282	−64,566
Germany	331,009	315,745	15,264
Japan	261,755	179,301	82,454
UK	144,522	171,410	−26,888
Italy	137,581	145,777	−8,196

Source: Statistical Office of the European Community, *Basic Statistics of the Community, 1994.*

The table contains exactly the same *data* as before but now it is much easier to obtain *information*. We now see that the USA had the largest imports, the UK had the second smallest exports and the USA had the largest difference between exports and imports at −65 billion ECUs (the difference is negative since imports were larger than exports). It is also evident from the table that other information is readily obtained:

- Japan's imports relative to exports are quite low.
- Japan and Germany had a positive difference between exports and imports (they sold more than they bought).
- The USA, UK and Italy had negative differences (they bought more from abroad than they sold).
- Britain and Japan had similar levels of imports.

Some of the reasons why a table allows us to obtain information more readily than the data are as follows:

- The data is easier to read from the table than from the original list.
- It is clear from the table which numbers relate to which country.
- It is easy to compare different countries and the different variables.
- It is clear from the title and headings what the data refers to and where the data has come from.
- We can easily show in a table new data that we have calculated from that originally provided (for example, the difference between exports and imports).
- A table makes it easier to increase the data set and still extract information easily – for example, we could easily add more countries to the table and yet it would still be just as easy to use.

CONSTRUCTING A TABLE

So a table is much easier to use than a set of numbers when we wish to try and pick out the main features of a data set. But how do we go about constructing such a table? The answer is – like many of the topics we shall be covering – that we use a few simple guidelines and a lot of common sense. Whilst there are no strict 'rules' about how such tables should be constructed, there are a number of points which should be followed:

- We should start with a clear idea of exactly what information we are trying to convey. The table must have a clear purpose otherwise there is no use constructing it.
- The table must have an explanatory title. The title should be brief but, at the same time, provide a reasonable description of the contents of the table to other people who may use it.
- The table must indicate the units of measurement of the data.
- We should use rounded numbers in the table. Rounded numbers make a table easier to read (but we must remember the potential loss of accuracy). Here the numbers are already rounded to the nearest million.
- The table should clearly indicate the source of the data used.
- We should use lines to divide the table into sections to help someone using the table to read and use it easily.
- We should not try to include too much data in a single table. It is better to use two simple tables rather than a single complex one.
- Put numbers that you want to compare as close together as possible in the table (which is why we put exports and imports together).
- Try to arrange numbers in columns rather than rows since they are easier for most people to read this way. Obviously we can't always do this for all the data.

All of this sounds very complicated and difficult to remember. But what it boils down to is to try to make the table easy to use whilst, at the same time, representing the data as fairly as possible. Above all when constructing a table we should consider how someone else who might use the table will see it: is it easy to read and understand? In short, it is up to us to use our experience, judgement and common sense in order to present the data in a way that is clear and understandable. When you have completed a table you should always try and look at it as if you were seeing it for the first time and ask yourself whether it is easy to use and understand. If the answer is 'no', then you must try again.

So, let us see how we would go about building up Table 4.1 step by step from the data given.

Step 1

First of all we have to be clear about what we are trying to show. Here we have data on the exports and imports for a particular year for five countries.

So, it seems reasonable to say that we want to show – clearly and in an easily understood way – exports and imports of these countries. But is there anything else we'd like to show in the table? It is frequently the case from data that we are given that we can calculate additional data: sometimes this might be totals, fractions or percentages. In this case we might think about calculating a difference: the difference between exports and imports for each country.

Step 2

We now need to decide on the overall appearance of the table, in particular what we are going to show as the rows of the table and what we are going to show in columns. There is no hard and fast rule for this. We have two categories to show in the table: countries and their exports and imports. We could put countries in the rows and the trade figures in columns or we could reverse this and have the trade figures in rows and the countries in columns. Much of the time deciding what to do is a matter of:

- experience;
- personal preference;
- trial and error.

This last point is particularly important. When constructing tables we have to appreciate that we might need several attempts before we get the table exactly as we want it, even people with considerable experience need to do this from time to time. Fortunately with modern information technology – particularly word processing and spreadsheet facilities – this is quite easy. If you don't have access to such facilities then you should sketch a draft table on paper first before producing the final form of the table.

There are also one or two guidelines that might also help us decide what to put in rows and what in columns. The first of these is that if we have more items in one category than in the other then the larger category is shown in rows. Here we have two categories: countries and trade. For countries we have five items; for trade we have three (exports, imports, difference). So we might try first putting countries in the rows. The second guideline is that most people tend to find it easier to read up and down a column of figures rather than across a row. So, we might have to decide which set of figures people are most likely to want to look at together. Here we could ask: are people likely to want to read, for example, all the export figures together or are they likely to want to read all the trade figures for one country? Of course, the answer is usually that people want to do both so again we might just have to use our judgement to decide which they might want to do first. In this case we might decide that we would want to look at the exports of all of the countries (to see their relative size) so we would decide to put the trade figures in the columns.

Step 3

Construct a draft table from Steps 1 and 2 to see what it looks like. Our draft table might look like Table 4.1 (a). (Notice that the order of countries is different from Table 4.1. We shall explain this shortly.)

Table 4.1 (a)

Germany	331,009	315,745	15,264
Italy	137,581	145,777	−8,196
Japan	261,755	179,301	82,454
UK	144,522	171,410	−26,888
USA	344,716	409,282	−64,566

We can look at this and see whether we might prefer to reverse the rows and columns (that is have the countries across the top of the table. We decide here that we don't want to do this so we carry on to the next step.

Step 4

We need to ensure that someone else looking at the table knows what the rows and columns refer to. In this case it is evident that the rows relate to different countries so we do not need to label this column. The other three columns though do need labelling as in Table 4.1(b).

Table 4.1 (b)

	Exports	*Imports*	*Difference*
Germany	331,009	315,745	15,264
Italy	137,581	145,777	−8,196
Japan	261,755	179,301	82,454
UK	144,522	171,410	−26,888
USA	344,716	409,282	−64,566

Exactly what labels we use is again up to us to decide although we would normally want to keep the column labels short and concise but at the same time descriptive.

Step 5

We also need to ensure that someone using the table knows what units of measurement we are using and it would also be helpful to add a descriptive title so that the user knows at a glance what the table relates to (and so can quickly decide whether the data in the table has any interest or not).

We have also included (in Table 4.1) a line below the table indicating where the data has come from (the source of the data). This is important so that someone using the table both knows the source of the data and, in some cases, can assess the reliability or appropriateness of the data. Declaring the source also enables the user of the table to locate the data themselves if required, perhaps to update the table with the latest information available.

Step 6

If we are now happy with the way the table looks overall we might try to improve its 'readability'. This might include showing certain labels in italics or bold to help them stand out (particularly useful in more complex tables) and we might use lines to help distinguish different columns and rows in the table (this is useful when we might have several subdivisions of the row or column categories we are using or when we have row/column totals that we need to distinguish from the individual data items). Notice that we have decided to try to improve the readability of Table 4.1 by rearranging the order of the countries so that the export and import figures are in descending order down the column.

Student activity

The data referred to below is taken from Social Trends 1993.

In 1971 in the UK there were a total of 13,726,000 males employed. In 1991 the comparable figure was 11,253,000. For females the numbers were 8,413,000 in 1971 and 10,637,000 in 1991.

Construct a suitable table below to show this data. Make one or two comments about the data and what it tells you.

Naturally, there are a number of different ways we could have shown this data in a table. Our version is shown in Table 4.2 but yours might be slightly different. That doesn't matter as long as your table is easy to read, shows the data properly and has a sensible title.

Table 4.2
Employment by sex: United Kingdom 1971 and 1991
(figures are in thousands)

	1971	1991	Change (1991–1971)
Males	13,726	11,592	–2,134
Females	8,413	10,637	2,224
Total	22,139	22,229	90

Source: *Social Trends 1993.*

Notice that we have used lines to help make the table easier to read and to help the reader focus on the two years, 1971 and 1991. Notice also that we have calculated two new sets of data. The first is the change between the two years (with the 1971 number subtracted from the 1991). This allows us to see the change in employment that has occurred over this 20-year period. We have also calculated the total number employed in each year (males plus females).

It is now clear that we can make a number of comments based on the table. First, the number of males employed has decreased (by over 2 million

(2,134 thousand)) whilst the number of females employed has increased by almost the same. We also see from the total figures that the total number employed in each year is almost the same. So, we would conclude that over this period there has been a major switch from employing males to employing females. Of course we have no information as to what has caused such a change: we would need further analysis to investigate such possible causes.

OTHER TYPES OF TABLE

MORTGAGES: by gender of borrower

	Percentages	
	1993	1994
Woman only	8.2	17.2
Man only	17.1	20.2
One woman, one man	73.4	61.3
Two women	0.4	0.6
Two men	0.6	0.4
Other	0.3	0.3
All mortgages (thousands)	**6,846**	**10,410**

Source: Council of Mortgage Lenders

FT Source: *Financial Times*, 9 August 1995

Tables are extremely flexible both in their application and their use. Frequently, we may prefer to show the data in a table not only in absolute figures but also in percentages in order to show relative performance. Very often this enables us to pick out information from the table much more easily. Table 4.3 illustrates an example of this.

Table 4.3 shows the distribution by size of household in Great Britain over the period 1961 to 1991. As with any table we need to spend a little time looking at it to make sure we understand it. We see that the size of households varies from 1 person to 6 people or more. For each year shown the percentage of households who fall into each size category is shown. For example, in 1961 12% of households consisted of one person whereas in 1991 26% of households fell into this category.

Table 4.3
Households by size: percentage distribution
(Great Britain 1961–1991)

	1961	*1971*	*1981*	*1991*
Household size				
1 person	12	18	22	26
2 people	30	32	32	34
3 people	23	19	17	17
4 people	19	17	18	16
5 people	9	8	7	6
6 or more people	7	6	4	2
Number of households (thousands)	16,189	18,317	19,492	9,955

Source: *Social Trends 1993.*
Note: The 1961–1981 No. of household figures are taken from the respective census. The figure for 1991 is based on the General Household Survey and refers to the sample size used to obtain the distribution.

Once again, we can use the table to look for patterns and trends in the data. There are a number of such trends that become apparent on examination:

- The two-person household is the most common size category with about one-third of households in this category.
- The percentage of single-person households has shown a steady increase until it is just over one-quarter of the total by 1991.
- The percentage of two-person households has increased only slightly.
- All the household size categories of 3 or more have shown a decrease in percentage.

We would conclude, based on this data, that over this 30-year period smaller household sizes (one- and two-person) have increased whilst larger household sizes (three or more) have decreased. Again, we do not know the reasons behind such changes from this data. However, we might suggest a number of reasons contributing to such changes:

- an increase in the retired and elderly living alone;
- an increase in the number of teenagers leaving home;
- an increase in family break-ups and an increase in the so-called single-parent family;
- a general reduction in the number of children that couples have.

Clearly, if we were investigating this data in a serious manner we would want to investigate each of these – and other – possible causes in more detail by collecting and analysing related data.

But how were such percentages calculated and – equally important – why do we show such data in percentage terms rather than in terms of the original numbers? The table actually indicates how such percentages were arrived at. We see for each year a figure for 'Number of households'. This indicates the total number of households in each year: 16,189,000, for example, in 1961. Clearly we could produce a table showing the actual number of households in each size category. Instead the table shows the number in each category as a percentage of the total number of households in that year: 9,955,000. The calculation for one-person households in 1991 would be:

$$\frac{\text{Number of households in category}}{\text{Total for year (9,955,000)}} \times 100$$

Each percentage in 1991 would then be calculated by substituting the actual number in that size category into the calculation. For the other years we would repeat these calculations but using the appropriate total for each year.

This also helps explain why the table shows percentages rather than actual numbers. Because the total number of households varies in each year it would be difficult to compare the actual number of households in a size category in one year with that of another year. If the two years had a different number of households in that category we would not know whether this was because of some fundamental change (like the increase in single-parent families) or whether it was simply because the total number of households examined in that year had changed. By taking percentages, however, we cancel out the effect of changing household totals between years, allowing us to examine trends and patterns in the numbers.

It is also worth noting that very often in a percentage table the percentages for a given column do not add up exactly to 100% (as they really should do). For example, in 1991 if we add the percentages together for the different categories we get:

$$26 + 34 + 17 + 16 + 6 + 2 = 101\%$$

The reason this sometimes happens is that in the table we are showing the percentages as rounded figures (in this case to the nearest whole number). By rounding each individual calculation a rounding 'error' occurs in the total. This is nothing to worry about and is quite common. Of course, it would be something to worry about if the column added up to, say, 105% since the rounding error should be quite small. Such a large error would indicate we had made a mistake somewhere in the calculations. In fact this is a useful tip to remember. When constructing a percentage table always make sure that the percentages in a column do add up to 100% (or nearly). This is a good way of checking that you have not made some sort of arithmetic mistake.

Student activity

Table 4.4 shows production of passenger cars by engine size for the UK over the period 1982–1992.

Construct a suitable table below showing relevant percentages and comment on the findings.

Table 4.4
Production of passenger cars by engine size 1982–1992: UK

	1000cc and under	1001cc to 1600cc	1601cc to 2800cc	2801cc and over	Total
1982	197,153	547,676	97,536	45,314	887,679
1987	153,214	718,046	205,067	66,356	1,142,683
1992	22,037	793,307	437,951	38,584	1,291,880

Source: *Monthly Digest of Statistics.*

The first thing we must do when converting any table into percentage format is to think carefully abut what we want to calculate percentages of and what the resulting percentages might allow us to say about patterns and trends. There are a number of possibilities in Table 4.4, some more obvious than others. The two most obvious are:

- showing the production of each engine size group as a percentage of total production in that year;
- showing the percentage *change* in production of each engine size group between each year.

We shall look at the first approach and leave the second until the next section of this chapter. Conveniently, the annual total production for each year is shown in the table. Calculating the percentage of total production that occurred in each size group is then straightforward. To calculate the figure for 1000cc and less in 1982 we have:

$$\frac{197,153}{887,679} \times 100 = 22.2\% \text{ (rounded to 1 decimal place)}$$

This allows us to produce Table 4.5. Notice that we have left the total production figures in this table so that the user of the table can also see how total production has changed over time. We should also make sure that the percentages in each year add up to 100 (or very close to 100) as a method of checking that we have not made any obvious arithmetic errors.

Table 4.5
Production of passenger cars by engine size 1982–1992
(percentage of annual production in reach engine size group)

	1000cc and under	1001cc to 1600cc	1601cc to 2800cc	2801cc and over	Total number
1982	22.2	61.7	11.0	5.1	887,679
1987	13.4	62.8	17.9	5.8	1,142,683
1992	1.7	61.4	33.9	3.0	1,291,880

Source: *Monthly Digest of Statistics.*

Using Table 4.4 and Table 4.5 we can now comment on what the figures appear to tell us. We see from the total production figures that annual production has increased considerably since 1982 (approximately 400,000 increase by 1992). Looking at the percentages we have obtained, however, indicates that this increase in production has not affected production of different engine sizes in the same way. The smallest engine size, 1000cc and under, accounted for almost a quarter (22.2%) of total production in 1982. By 1992 this has fallen to less than 2%! In comparison the engine size group 1601cc to 2800cc had seen a comparable increase from 11% in 1982 to almost 34% in 1992. The engine size group which accounted for most production is 1001cc to 1600cc and we see from Table 4.5 that the percentage of total annual production in this group has really not changed over this period.

Once again, the tables do not tell us why such changes have happened (we need more data to determine that) but careful use of tables does allow us to pick out changes and patterns quite easily.

Percentage change tables

Another common type of table shows percentages in a different way altogether. So far we have considered percentages as showing one number in relation to some total. Sometimes – particularly when we are looking at data over a time period – we may want to show the change between one period

BIG SIX ACCOUNTANCY FIRMS: RESULTS						
Ranking '95 '94	1994–95 income £ m	% change	No. of partners	% change	Other prof'l staff	% change
1 1 Coopers & Lybrand	575.0	+2.7	607	–10.3	6,268	+0.0
2 3 Andersen	539.5	+9.0	389	+3.4	4,873	+3.3
3 2 KPMG	528.4	+6.2	573	–3.5	5,998	–2.9
4 4 Ernst and Young	401.2	+3.3	386	–1.5	4,376	–1.6
5 5 Price Waterhouse	383.2	–0.4	399	–3.8	3,836	–2.1
6 6 Touche Ross	336.8	+1.2	345	+0.9	4,303	+14.4
Source: Big six accountancy firms						

 Source: *Financial Times*, 6 June 1995

and another as a percentage. To illustrate look at Table 4.6(a). This is taken from the *Annual Abstract of Statistics 1993* and shows the production of beer in the UK between 1981 and 1991.

Table 4.6(a)
Beer production: UK 1981–1991
(figures are in thousand hectolitres)

Year	Production
1981	61,721
1982	59,786
1983	60,324
1984	60,105
1985	59,655
1986	59,446
1987	59,906
1988	60,145
1989	60,015
1990	59,653
1991	57,359

Source: *Annual Abstract of Statistics 1993*.

From the table we see that production has fallen somewhat between 1981 and 1991 although in some years it went up again. From the original data it is difficult to pick out any real trends. We could, of course, create a new column showing the change in production from one year to the next (much as we did with imports and exports for each country earlier). However, the difficulty with this is that because the yearly figures are changing it will make comparison of such differences difficult year by year. We can get round this by calculating the difference in each year as a percentage of the production in the previous year. This will make it easier to compare year by year changes in production. Such calculations are straightforward. First we calculate the difference between each year's figures. So, we have:

	Difference	
1981	61,721	
1982	59,786	−1,935 (59,786 − 61,721)

Then we express this difference as a percentage of the number for the first year of the two we are comparing (1981 in this case):

$$\frac{-1,935}{61,721} \times 100 = -3.1 \text{ (rounded to 1 decimal place)}$$

That is, production fell by 3.1% (of its 1981 level) between 1981 and 1982. We can repeat this calculation for each pair of years in the rest of the table.

Student activity

From Table 4.6(a) calculate the difference between each successive pair of years shown and express this as a percentage.

The calculations are as follows:

	Production	*Difference*	*Percentage change*	*Calculation*
1981	61,721			
1982	59,786	−1,935	−3.1	(59,786 − 61,721)/61,721 × 100
1983	60,324	+538	+0.9	(60,324 − 59,786)/59,786 × 100
1984	60,105	−219	−0.4	(60,105 − 60,324)/60,324 × 100
1985	59,655	−450	−0.7	(59,655 − 60,105)/60,105 × 100
1986	59,446	−209	−0.4	(59,446 − 59,655)/59,655 × 100
1987	59,906	+460	+0.8	(59,906 − 59,446)/59,446 × 100
1988	60,145	+239	+0.4	(60,145 − 59,906)/59,906 × 100
1989	60,015	−130	−0.2	(60,015 − 60,145)/60,145 × 100
1990	59,653	−362	−0.6	(59,653 − 60,015)/60,015 × 100
1991	57,359	−2,294	−3.8	(57,359 − 59,653)/59,653 × 100

We see that the largest change (in terms of both absolute value and percentage change) occurred between 1990 and 1991 with a fall in production of 3.8%.

The largest increase occurred between 1982 and 1983 with an increase of 0.9%. Notice that for 1981 we cannot calculate the difference or the percentage change (since we would need the 1980 data for this) so this row is left blank. We could then show the results of the calculations in an appropriate table as in Table 4.6(b).

Table 4.6(b)
Beer production: UK 1981–1991

Year	Production (thousand hectolitres)	Annual percentage change
1981	61,721	
1982	59,786	−3.1
1983	60,324	0.9
1984	60,105	−0.4
1985	59,655	−0.7
1986	59,446	−0.4
1987	59,906	0.8
1988	60,145	0.4
1989	60,015	−0.2
1990	59,653	−0.6
1991	57,359	−3.8

Source: *Annual Abstract of Statistics 1993.*

Index tables

Another common type of table is that which shows data in the form of a simple index. In the last section we saw how to produce a table showing the percentage change from year to year. Sometimes, however, we might want to look at percentage changes over a longer period. For example, from Table 4.6(b) we might want to know: what was the percentage change between 1981 and 1991? or between 1981 and 1986?

Whilst we could use a calculator to determine these figures there is a common way of showing these when we wish to compare the figures over a period of time with reference to a chosen base period. The method is to calculate a simple index (which is really only a type of percentage). In such a series we express each number as a percentage of the number for 1981 (the base period in the series). So, for 1982 the index would be:

$$\frac{59,786}{61,721} \times 100 = 96.9$$

We would interpret this index value as showing that beer production in 1982 was 96.9% of the level of production in 1981 (the base period). Another way of seeing this would be to say that production in 1982 had fallen by 3.1% since the index for 1981 must have a value of 100 (61,721/61,721 × 100).

Similarly for 1983 we would have:

$$\frac{60,324}{61,721} \times 100 = 97.7$$

showing that production between 1981 and 1983 had fallen by 2.3%. The rest of the index values are calculated in the same way.

Student activity

Construct a table showing the index of beer production between 1981 and 1991.

Table 4.6(c) shows the results of the calculations. We see, for example, that production fell by 7.1% between 1981 and 1991. Such an index allows a ready comparison between any given period and the base period.

Table 4.6(c)
Index of beer production: UK 1981–1991

Year	Index of production
1981	100
1982	96.9
1983	97.7
1984	97.4
1985	96.6
1986	96.3
1987	97.1
1988	97.4
1989	97.2
1990	96.6
1991	92.9

Source: Calculated from *Annual Abstract of Statistics 1993.*

One note of caution that we must introduce relates to the choice of base period. Any period in the series can be chosen as the base although it is common to choose the first period for this. Whichever period we do choose as base we must try to make sure that it is a reasonably 'typical' period. For example, if 1981 had been a year where there had been considerable industrial unrest in the beer industry (thereby affecting production) then we should not use this as the base period for the calculations since it could well distort our view of the index over the whole period.

USING COMPLEX TABLES

We have looked at how we construct a table from data that we have. What of the reverse? What about using a table that someone else has produced? This is frequently the case as we often use someone else's tables in our own analysis and research. Consider Table 4.7.

This is a copy of a table from the government publication *Annual Abstract of Statistics 1993*. At first sight the table looks horrendous. It clearly contains (a lot of) complex data and presumably potentially useful information. When confronted with such a table (particularly in an exam) there are a few obvious steps to follow in trying to make sense of it.

Step 1

Don't panic!

With time, attention and care we can always figure out a table, no matter how complex, as long as the person who has produced the table has followed the various rules we have discussed about table construction.

Step 2

Read the title carefully to understand what the table relates to and be sure to check the units of measurement. Here we have a table that provides data on road accidents, on the vehicles involved in road accidents and casualties from road accidents in Great Britain. The data in the table is shown in actual numbers (not 000s or percentages or anything else). Notice also that for this table (and for many which are published by the government) there are a lot of footnotes at the bottom of the table. These relate to particular parts of the table and provide extra information about that part of the table. We shall see this shortly.

Step 3

Look carefully at the row and column labels used to make sure you understand the various categories and sub-categories that are being analysed. In this table the columns are simple: they relate to years between 1981 and 1991.

The rows are more difficult since there are so many of them. But our task has been helped by someone carefully designing the row labels. We see from the way that the rows are laid out that there are seven major row headings (even if we're not yet sure what some of them mean!):

- Road accidents;
- Vehicles involved;
- Vehicles involved per hundred million kilometres travelled;
- Killed;
- Killed and seriously injured;
- All severities;
- Breath tests on car drivers involved in accidents.

Table 4.7
Road accidents, vehicles involved and casualties (Great Britain)

Number

		1981	1982	1983	1984	1985	1986	1987	1988	1989	1990	1991
Road accidents	KKKA	248 276	255 980	242 876	253 183	245 645	247 854	239 063	246 994	260 759	258 441	235 798
Vehicles Involved:												
Pedal cycles	KKKB	26 496	29 428	31 824	32 210	27 953	27 039	27 010	26 561	29 327	27 108	25 424
Motor vehicles	KKKC	390 736	401 460	377 289	396 735	389 473	397 671	387 521	404 571	429 237	427 625	391 769
Two-wheeled motor vehicles	KKKD	70 949	73 033	65 962	65 340	57 822	53 562	47 024	44 279	43 995	40 404	31 702
Cars and taxis	KKKE	265 531	275 507	261 714	279 954	278 517	290 560	287 636	303 693	325 213	330 181	308 007
Light goods vehicles[2]	KKKF	22 106	21 704	19 853	20 911	23 113	23 434	22 651	24 671	25 793	24 052	21 792
Heavy goods vehicles[3]	KKKG	14 554	14 688	13 504	14 197	14 452	14 773	15 107	16 376	17 894	16 524	15 235
Buses and coaches	KKKH	13 083	12 911	12 763	12 302	12 468	12 137	11 766	12 086	12 711	12 200	11 403
Other motor vehicles	KKKI	4 513	3 617	3 493	3 531	3 101	3 205	3 337	3 466	3 631	3 664	3 630
Vehicles Involved per hundred million kilometres travelled:												
Pedal cycles	KKKL	486	460	499	504	462	495	471	508	563	517	435
All two-wheeled motor vehicles	KKKM	799	792	798	805	785	758	701	734	741	725	562
Cars and taxis	KKKN	121	121	113	115	111	110	101	99	98	98	94
Light goods vehicles[2]	KKKO	94	94	86	85	92	88	78	77	73	69	60
Heavy goods vehicles[3]	KKKP	69	71	82	63	63	63	58	59	60	57	54
Total casualties	KKKQ	324 840	334 296	308 584	324 314	317 524	321 451	311 473	322 395	341 592	341 141	311 269
Killed[4]:												
Total	KKKR	5 846	5 934	5 445	5 599	5 165	5 382	5 125	5 052	5 373	5 217	5 568
Pedestrians	KKKS	1 874	1 869	1 914	1 868	1 789	1 841	1 703	1 753	1 706	1 694	1 496
Pedal cycles	KKKT	310	294	323	345	286	271	280	227	294	256	242
All two-wheeled motor vehicles	KKKU	1 131	1 090	963	967	796	762	723	670	683	659	548
Cars and taxis	KKKV	2 287	2 443	2 019	2 179	2 061	2 231	2 206	2 142	2 426	2 371	2 053
Others	KKKW	244	238	226	240	233	277	213	260	264	237	229
Killed and seriously injured[5]:												
By age group[6]												
0–4	KKKY	1 286	1 345	1 403	1 435	1 429	1 289	1 277	1 339	1 342	1 363	1 272
5–9	KKKZ	3 909	3 717	3 586	3 740	3 579	3 254	3 219	3 122	3 094	3 217	2 658
10–14	KKLA	5 162	5 474	5 450	5 541	4 903	4 426	3 988	3 871	3 943	3 832	3 367
15–19	KKLB	21 848	21 413	18 456	18 484	16 582	15 591	13 752	12 866	12 616	11 595	8 749
20–24	KKLC	13 682	14 522	12 575	13 214	13 282	13 058	12 041	11 629	11 512	10 583	8 835
25–29	KKLD	6 466	6 964	6 072	6 549	6 647	6 916	6 854	7 026	7 404	7 240	6 449
30–39	KKLE	8 973	9 366	8 102	8 391	8 276	8 455	8 029	7 999	7 905	7 905	6 974
40–49	KKLF	6 161	6 250	5 441	5 765	5 911	5 698	5 915	5 892	5 873	5 737	5 135
50–59	KKLG	5 771	5 784	4 980	5 027	5 038	4 827	4 566	4 620	4 532	4 425	3 853
60 and over	KKLH	10 399	10 464	10 003	10 512	9 850	10 017	9 081	9 517	9 596	9 113	8 218
By type of road user:												
Child pedestrians[7]	KKLJ	6 547	6 695	6 640	6 823	6 663	5 992	5 472	5 471	5 437	5 545	4 790
Adult pedestrians	KKLK	11 817	12 169	12 139	12 638	12 576	12 880	11 978	12 207	11 859	11 597	10 032
Child pedal cyclists[7]	KKLL	2 096	2 058	2 287	2 269	1 704	1 396	1 458	1 322	1 370	1 295	1 200
Adult pedal cyclists	KKLM	3 393	3 893	4 109	4 326	3 910	3 814	3 638	3 526	3 730	3 270	2 945
Moped riders	KKLN	2 903	3 109	3 241	3 188	2 919	2 571	2 221	1 903	1 729	1 417	989
Motor scooter riders	KKLO	515	608	647	748	715	606	499	380	382	289	226
Motor scooter passengers	KCUU	62	106	95	100	93	66	71	46	44	24	20
Motor cycle riders	KCUV	16 398	16 296	14 260	14 109	12 838	11 819	9 989	9 364	9 414	8 576	6 600
Motor cycle passengers	KCUW	2 400	2 514	2 021	1 805	1 547	1 370	1 086	924	884	783	651
Car and taxi drivers	KCUX	19 149	19 460	15 472	16 530	16 722	17 132	17 167	17 576	17 834	17 403	15 629
Car and taxi passengers	KCUY	14 476	14 525	11 574	12 467	12 385	12 554	11 919	11 770	11 850	11 717	9 764
Users of buses and coaches	KCUZ	961	962	969	929	1 036	859	892	912	835	807	725
Users of goods vehicles	KCVA	2 891	2 797	2 283	2 354	2 454	2 552	2 637	2 485	2 673	2 399	2 122
Users of other vehicles	KCVB	308	312	278	313	254	263	229	255	247	251	229
All severities:												
Total	KCVC	324 840	334 296	308 584	324 314	317 524	321 451	311 473	322 305	341 592	341 141	311 269
Pedestrians	KCVD	60 750	61 419	61 674	63 474	61 390	60 875	57 453	58 843	60 080	60 230	53 992
Vehicle users	KCVE	264 090	272 877	246 910	260 840	256 134	260 576	254 020	263 462	281 512	280 911	257 277
Breath tests on car drivers involved in accidents:												
All drivers	KCVG	265 531	275 507	261 714	279 959	278 517	290 560	287 633	303 693	325 213	330 181	308 007
Tested	KCVH	32 640	34 472	33 769	35 192	36 655	49 559	52 760	60 798	81 771	91 661	90 116
Failed test[8]	KCVI	10 121	11 145	10 200	10 422	10 432	10 014	9 222	8 549	8 508	8 073	7 354

1. Accidents on public roads, involving injury, which are reported to the police.
2. 1.5 tons unladen weight and under.
3. Over 1.5 tons unladen weight.
4. Died within 30 days of accident.

5. Hospital in-patients *plus* casualties with any fracture, internal injury, concussion, crushing, severe general shock, etc, *plus* deaths after 30 days.
6. These figures may not add up to total fatal and serious figures, due to the exclusion of road users whose age was not reported.
7. Age 0–14.
8. Positive result, or refused to provide a specimen.

Source: Social Trends 1993 Central Statistical Office. Crown Copyright 1993. Reproduced by the permission of the Controller of HMSO and the Central Statistical Office.

These major categories stand out because they are shown in **bold** type, the detail immediately below them is indented and each category is separated from the next by blank rows. Under many of these main headings are sub-headings showing further elements of that category.

The first row shows us Road accidents in each year. The next row is labelled Vehicles involved and is shown in bold to indicate it is a main row heading. Underneath – and in lighter type – we see Pedal cycles and Motor vehicles. The lighter type indicates these are sub-categories of the main category of Vehicle involved. We see, therefore, that there are two general types of vehicle involved in road accidents: pedal cycles and motor vehicles. But Motor vehicles itself has a number of sub-categories which are shown indented on the row – Two-wheeled motor vehicles, Cars and taxis and so on. So the authors of the table have done their best to help us read the table properly. For this set of rows the main row heading is in bold, the sub-headings are in light type and sub-sub-headings are indented. Once we realize this it becomes easier to make sense of the rest of the rows (which are also conveniently printed in 'blocks' to help us distinguish between them).

Student activity

Explain the various sub-headings in the category Killed and seriously injured.

For the category Killed and seriously injured we see that there are two main sub-categories (separated by a space row). The first shows the numbers By age group (and this in turn is broken down into ten different age groups). The second sub-category shows the numbers Killed and seriously injured by Type of road user (with 14 different types categorized).

Step 4

Finally, having made sure we understand the rows and columns in the table, we can begin to extract the data from it that we are interested in. For example, we see that in 1981 there were:

- almost 250,000 road accidents in total (from the Road accidents row);
- that just over 13,000 buses and coaches were involved in these accidents (from the Vehicles involved: Buses and coaches row);
- that 1,874 pedestrians were killed in these accidents (from the Killed: Pedestrians row).

Sometimes it will help us obtain data from such a complex table if we use a ruler to ensure we are looking at the correct row (and sometimes column).

Step 5

Having obtained the data we must finally make sure that we understand it properly before using the data for information or before starting to draw conclusions. We see at the bottom of this table that there are a considerable number of footnotes. The number of road accidents shown in the table (at almost 250,000) we must treat with caution since footnote 1 indicates the table relates only to accidents of a certain type:

- on public roads;
- involving injury;
- reported to the police.

There were almost certainly other accidents in 1981 which are not shown in the table since they did not have these characteristics.

Student activity

Using the table answer the following:

(a) *How many road accidents were there in 1990?*

(b) *How many pedal cycles were involved in accidents in 1985?*

(c) *How many pedestrians were killed in 1983?*

(d) *How many motor cycle passengers were killed or seriously injured in 1991?*

(e) *How old does someone have to be to be classed as a child pedal cyclist?*

(f) *How do you explain that in 1990 there were 258,441 road accidents but over 330,000 cars and taxis involved in road accidents?*

(a) In 1990 there were 258,441 road accidents.

(b) In 1985 there were 27,953 pedal cycles involved in accidents.

(c) There were 1,914 pedestrians killed in 1983.

(d) In 1991 there were 651 motor cycle passengers killed or seriously injured.

(e) we see from footnote 7 that a child pedal cyclist is between the ages of 0 and 14.

(f) Although there were 258,441 road accidents in this year it is evident that many of them involved more than one vehicle.

FREQUENCY TABLES

Another common type of table in business is the frequency table which effectively shows the number of data items for some variable that falls into a specific numerical range or category. In fact a number of the tables that we have examined so far in this chapter are frequency tables. Occasionally, however, we will need to be able to construct such a table ourselves from raw data and we shall introduce the principles of this in this section.

Let us develop a simple business scenario. You have decided to set up, with some friends, a small restaurant specializing in organically grown food. As part of your initial business strategy you have decided that such a restaurant is likely to appeal to those who are relatively affluent. You are currently considering two locations for the restaurant, Site A and Site B. As part of the decision process to determine which of the sites you prefer you have decided to take a sample of local residents and ask them what their weekly income is (before tax or any other deduction). Naturally, you need to treat the responses with some caution since not everyone will truthfully reply. However, from the first 20 people surveyed you have obtained the following responses (shown to the nearest £).

500	850	60	418	353	403	343	558	475	443
145	68	395	780	645	148	235	53	65	95

Clearly we need some method for making sense of this data – for turning it into information. We might first show the data in the form of a frequency table as in Table 4.8.

Table 4.8
Gross weekly income

Income £	No. of responses
Up to 99	5
100 up to 199	2
200 up to 299	1
300 up to 399	3
400 up to 499	4
500 up to 599	2
600 up to 699	1
700 up to 799	1
800 or over	1
Total	20

Source: Business survey.

We see from the table that certain income groups have been set out and the number of people (observations) falling into each income group recorded. So, we see that the first income group includes everyone with a gross weekly income up to £99 and that there were 5 people (out of the 20) who fell into this category. Clearly the frequency table is an improvement on the raw data we had earlier because we begin to see the pattern of the distribution of the data. But how do we go about constructing such a table if presented with raw data? As usual there are a number of steps to follow.

Step 1

Determine the lowest and highest values in the data set (the minimum and maximum values). From the original data we were given we find that the minimum is 53 and the maximum is 850.

Step 2

From the minimum and maximum values determine the spread of the data, known as the range. This is given as:

Range = maximum − minimum
= 850 − 53 = 797

or approximately £800. We now know that the classes in the frequency table have to cover a range of about £800.

Step 3

Choose the number of classes or intervals to be used in the table. There is no absolute method of deciding how many classes to have. In practice, it would be a matter of making a first 'best guess', trying this and if it didn't produce what we thought was an appropriate table we would try again. As a general rule we might have between five and 15 intervals in a table, with fewer intervals for small data sets than for large. If there are only a small number of intervals then important details about the data set may be lost as we aggregate the data. On the other hand, with too many intervals the data may be insufficiently aggregated and no obvious patterns in the data will be seen.

One useful tip is that if you're not sure how many intervals to have and you're doing this manually, put more intervals in rather than less. This is because if you later decided you do have too many intervals you can easily add them (and their frequencies) together. On the other hand, if you decided you've too few intervals you can't divide them but have to start again from the beginning.

Step 4

Decide how large each interval should be. Obviously Steps 3 and 4 are usually done at the same time and we must choose interval sizes and the number of intervals together. If possible we should choose intervals which are all the same width as this makes the table easier to read and comparison of interval frequencies is easier. (However, it is not always possible, or desirable, to have equal classes and we shall see the effect of unequal classes later.) In this example we might say: the intervals have to cover a range of about £800 so why don't we try intervals of £100 and that means we need eight of them (we'll see in a moment that this isn't quite right).

Step 5

We now write out the numerical boundaries of the intervals so that they are clear and unambiguous. We see from Table 4.8 that the first interval is up to

£99, the second is from £100 to £199 and so on. By writing them out in this way it also becomes clear that we need nine such intervals and not eight! In fact, we can often use a simple calculation to help us decide how many intervals we do need:

$$\text{No. of intervals} = \frac{\text{Range}}{\text{Size of interval}} + 1$$

or as here:

$$\text{No. of intervals} = \frac{800}{100} + 1 = 8 + 1 = 9$$

In Table 4.8 the intervals are also clearly written so that there is no possible misunderstanding. A common mistake is to express intervals in the form:

£300 to £400

£400 to £500

£500 to £600   and so on.

The problem is that when we come to aggregate the raw data we are uncertain whether to place an observation of, say, £500 in the fifth interval, 400 to 500, or in the sixth interval, 500 to 600. More importantly, other people using your table will be unsure as to how you have grouped the data and may have little confidence in the rest of your analysis.

Notice that in this case we have intervals:

Up to 99

100 up to 199

200 up to 299   and so on.

We could have written these in a different way:

Up to 100

101 up to 200

201 up to 300

301 up to 400

This would have been just as acceptable (since these intervals are just as clear and unambiguous). It is a matter of preference as to which you choose (but remember that the number of observations in some intervals might change as a result). Notice also that we might use special notation in the intervals to denote where they start and/or stop. This notation consists of a number of inequality symbols. For example, rather than write:

100 up to 199

we could write:

$100 < 200$

where the symbol '<' stands for 'less than', so we have an interval between 100 but less than 200 (i.e. 199). This is often a convenient shorthand way of showing the intervals and we shall use it from now on. Other symbols we will come across are:

≤   less than or equal to

So, ≤ 250 means any number less than 250 but also any number equal to 250.

>   greater than

So, >250 means any number greater than 250

≥   greater than or equal to

So, ≥ 250 means any number which is at least 250.

Step 6

Finally, we can work through the data set, counting the frequency of data items in each interval. If we are doing this manually we might use what is known as the tally system. This means that we write down the intervals:

$$
\begin{array}{r}
< 100 \\
100 < 200 \\
200 < 300 \\
300 < 400 \\
400 < 500 \\
500 < 600 \\
600 < 700 \\
700 < 800 \\
\geq 800
\end{array}
$$

and then put a mark, or tally, against an interval each time we have a number in the data set which falls into the interval. In this case, by the time we get half way through the tally (with 10 observations) we would have:

< 100	/
100 < 200	
200 < 300	
300 < 400	/ /
400 < 500	/ / / /
500 < 600	/ /
600 < 700	
700 < 800	
≥ 800	/

Step 7

Having completed the tally we should add up the total of tally marks we have made and check this is the same as the total number of observations. It is quite easy to make a mistake using this manual method and we must check whenever we can that we have not done so.

Step 8

Finally, we can look at the frequency table we have constructed and decide whether we need to start all over again! That is, we can decide whether the table is adequate for our purposes or whether it needs amending – perhaps by changing the number of intervals or perhaps by changing the width of the intervals. Doing this manually is tedious, boring and prone to error. In practice we would want to use computer facilities – perhaps through a spreadsheet – to construct the table for us. Such a method, however, still requires us to choose the number and size of the intervals and make a subjective assessment of the final table.

Student activity

Take the data used to produce Table 4.8. Using intervals:

≤ 100

$101 \leq 200$

$301 \leq 400$ and so on

recalculate the frequency table.

The results would be as shown in Table 4.9. We see that there is a slight change in the distribution figures: the fifth interval now has one more observation and the sixth interval one less. This might seem a trivial difference but once we look at larger and more realistic data sets such differences can become critical.

Table 4.9
Gross weekly income

Income £	No. of responses
≤ 100	5
$101 \leq 200$	2
$201 \leq 300$	1
$301 \leq 400$	3
$401 \leq 500$	5
$501 \leq 600$	1
$601 \leq 700$	1
$701 \leq 800$	1
≥ 801	1
Total	20

Source: Business survey.

Using frequency tables

So far we have looked at constructing a frequency table for only a small amount of data. To illustrate how such tables can be used in decision-making we need to look at larger sets of data. Let us assume that the two surveys have been completed. Around Site A a total of 150 responses were obtained and around Site B a total of 175. The results have been summarized in Table 4.10 (the two full data sets are available for use with the end of chapter computer exercises).

Table 4.10
Gross weekly income: Sites A and B

Income £	Site A No. of responses	Site B No. of responses
< 100	14	0
100 < 200	39	0
200 < 300	32	8
300 < 400	26	28
400 < 500	17	52
500 < 600	9	40
600 < 700	6	31
700 < 800	5	8
800 < 900	2	4
≥ 900	0	4
Total	150	175

Source: Business survey.

We can now use the table to begin to describe the similarities and differences between the two data sets and the two sites.

Student activity

Using Table 4.10 comment on the main similarities and differences between the two sites.

There are a number of comments that we can make. The first is that most of the data observations for Site A are at the lower end of the intervals range (up to £500) whereas for site B most are in the middle of the intervals range (between £300 and £700). This implies that incomes of people around Site B tend to be higher than for people around Site A. This view is reinforced by the fact that Site B has relatively few responses for the lower income intervals with, in fact, no responses in the two lowest intervals. Similarly, Site A has relatively fewer responses at the top of the income intervals. In general, then, we gain an impression from aggregating the data that incomes at Site B tend to be higher than at Site A.

There are one or two notes of caution we must make, however. The first is that we are not implying that everyone near Site B has a higher income than everyone near Site A. There is considerable variability in incomes at both sites. The second point is that we are assuming that the two data sets are properly representative of the populations around the two sites and that people responded truthfully to the question. Third, we must complete further analysis on the data before recommending which site appears to offer the better potential. Nevertheless, such aggregation is a useful first step in making sense of some data set and beginning the comparison of two such sets.

Frequency tables in percentage form

As with most tables a frequency table can also be shown in percentage form, with the percentage of responses in each interval rather than the actual number of responses. This can be particularly useful when, as in this case, we have two data sets with differing total frequencies: 150 and 175 respectively. Table 4.11 shows the percentage frequency distribution where the percentages are expressed in relation to the relevant column total. So, for example, the percentage of responses for Site A with an income $<£100$ is:

$$\frac{14}{150} \times 100 = 9.3\% \text{ (to 1 decimal place)}$$

and for people at Site B with an income $£400 < £500$:

$$\frac{52}{175} \times 100 = 29.7\%$$

Table 4.11
Gross weekly income: Sites A and B

Income £	Site A Percentage of responses	Site B Percentage of responses
< 100	9.3	0
100 < 200	26.0	0
200 < 300	21.3	4.6
300 < 400	17.3	16.0
400 < 500	11.3	29.7
500 < 600	6.0	22.9
600 < 700	4.0	17.7
700 < 800	3.3	4.6
800 < 900	1.3	2.3
≥ 900	0	2.3
Total responses	150	175

Source: Table 4.10.

Using such percentages we see, for example, that although Site B has more responses in the interval £300 < £400 than Site A, the number of responses as a percentage of the total is larger for Site A in this interval.

Percentage frequency tables are particularly useful for comparing two or more sets of data where the sets have different totals. Notice that we should also include somewhere in the table details of how many total frequencies there were.

Cumulative frequency tables

The third type of frequency table is that showing cumulative frequencies (either in terms of the absolute frequencies or in percentage terms). For example, suppose we wanted to know the number of responses with an income of at least £500? We could use Table 4.10 and add up all the frequencies in the appropriate intervals. However, a cumulative frequency table shows this information directly. Table 4.12 shows such a table for the two sites.

Table 4.12
Gross weekly income – cumulative frequencies: Sites A and B

Income £	Site A No. of responses	Site B No. of responses
< 100	14	0
100 < 200	53	0
200 < 300	85	8
300 < 400	111	36
400 < 500	128	88
500 < 600	137	128
600 < 700	143	159
700 < 800	148	167
800 < 900	150	171
≥ 900	150	175

Source: Table 4.10.

You will see that all we have done is to calculate a running total through the table. So, for Site A the frequency for the first interval is 14 (from Table 4.10). For the second interval we have the 14 from the first interval and 39 from the second interval giving a total of 53.

Stop for a moment and think about what this frequency indicates. It tells us that for Site A 53 people had an income less than £200. By implication 97 people (150 − 53) had an income of £200 or more. The rest of the cumulative frequencies are calculated in the same way for the rest of Site A and for Site B. Note that there is no need to show the total frequencies since by default this is shown as the last cumulative frequency.

Student activity

From Table 4.12 construct a cumulative percentage frequency table and comment on the results.

Why do you think we asked you to use Table 4.12 rather than Table 4.11?

Table 4.13 shows the cumulative percentage frequencies obtained simply by adding the individual percentages from Table 4.12. Note that in this case it is useful to retain the total number of frequencies so that the user of the table appreciates how many observations there were in each data set.

Table 4.13
Gross weekly income: cumulative percentage frequencies: Sites A and B

Income £	Site A Percentage of responses	Site B Percentage of responses
< 100	9.3	0
100 < 200	35.3	0
200 < 300	56.7	4.6
300 < 400	74.0	20.6
400 < 500	85.3	50.3
500 < 600	91.3	73.1
600 < 700	95.3	90.9
700 < 800	98.7	95.4
800 < 900	100.0	97.7
≥ 900	100.0	100.0
Total responses	150	175

Source: Table 4.12.

From the table we can now make a few additional comments about the two sites. We see that for income of £600 or more there is not much difference between the two sites: Site A had 4.7% of people with an income of £600 or more (100 − 95.3) compared with 9.1% for Site B (100 − 90.1). The bigger differences are at the bottom of the income intervals and in the middle. For example, 56.7% of people in Site A had an income less than £300 compared with only 4.6% for Site B. Similarly almost 50% of people in Site B had an income of £500 or more (100 − 50.3) compared with only 15% for Site A (100 − 85.3).

Cumulative percentage frequencies, then, can be particularly revealing. You should also have realized that the reason we asked you to use Table 4.12 (the cumulative absolute frequencies) rather than Table 4.11 (the percentage frequencies) is to do with rounding. If we had used Table 4.11 directly (with rounded values) then we would have found the cumulative percentages did not total to 100.0% (try it and see!).

SUMMARY

In this chapter we have begun the process of seeing how we can summarize and describe using data. Tables are a particularly versatile and flexible way of showing data in a concise way. As we have seen they are capable of considerable adaptation to particular circumstances. It is tempting to think that tables are a trivial part of data analysis. They are not. They are frequently a very important first step in such analysis, allowing us to see overall patterns, trends and differences quite easily. For this reason we should ensure that when we produce tables we are rigorous in their construction and presentation so that they present the data as accurately and in as meaningful a way as possible.

Now you have completed this chapter you will understand that:

- tables are essential for presenting data;
- the purpose of a table is to present data in a clear, concise and easy-to-understand way;
- there are no 'rules' as such for constructing tables but there is a set of guidelines to help ensure the table is a useful one;
- there are many different types of table we could construct for a data set. Using appropriate software packages we should experiment with the different types to see which best meets our needs.

EXAMPLE

The level of car sales in the UK is often seen as an important economic indicator – almost a barometer if you like of how the economy is performing. Car sales – in the form of new car registrations – are frequently reported in the media. Table 4.14 shows the level of UK new car registrations for May 1995. Take a few moments to examine the table. Let us assume we have been asked to prepare a short, informal report on the data in the table.

The first thing we must say is that the data only give a snapshot of one month in 1995, compared with the same month in 1994. Nevertheless some important features begin to emerge. The Volume column shows the number of new cars registered in May 1995. We see that this was 152,658 and that almost 89,000 of these were imported (although we have no information in the table as to exactly where these imports came from).

From the second column, % change since May 1994, we see that the total figure has increased by 1.7%. (Note that the table shows the percentage changes with a minus sign (–) and also with a plus sign (+). Normally, we would not bother writing the plus sign in front of a positive number. However, in this case it helps pick out easily from the column those which have experienced an increase and those a decrease. We can also see from this column that Imports experienced a strong rise since May 1994 of over 11% whilst UK produced cars fell by over 9%.

Table 4.14
UK new car registrations May 1995

	Volume May 1995	% change since May 1994	% market share May 1995	% market share May 1994
Total market	152,658	+1.7	100.0	100.0
UK produced	63,714	−9.1	41.7	46.7
Imports	88,944	+11.2	58.3	53.3
Fleet	79,562	+11.0	52.0	48.0
Private	63,787	−7.7	42.0	46.0
BMW	21,797	−6.5	14.3	15.5
Fiat Group	5,989	+26.4	3.9	3.2
Ford Group	36,386	+1.5	23.8	23.9
General Motors	24,990	−1.7	16.4	18.9
Honda	3,344	+7.1	2.2	2.1
Mercedes-Benz	2,644	+11.4	1.7	1.6
Nissan	6,285	+0.3	4.1	4.2
Peugot	15,380	−8.6	10.0	11.2
Renault	9,353	+3.4	6.1	6.0
Toyota	4,240	+18.6	2.8	2.5
Volvo	3,057	+3.5	2.0	2.0
VW Group	10,004	+9.5	6.6	6.1

Source: Society of Motor Manufacturers and Traders.

Columns 3 and 4 are also revealing. Column 3 shows the % market share in 1995 whilst the last column shows the comparable market share in May 1994. We can readily see that Imports account for over half total new car registrations and that their share of the total market is increasing, from 53.3% to 58.3%.

We also see from the table that a distinction is made between registrations to the Private motorist and registrations made in the Fleet business car sector (which is where a company may well buy a large number of cars to provide as company cars to its employees). We see that fleet cars make up 52% of the total market with private at 42% (as an additional exercise you may want to try and find out from published sources what category the missing 6% falls into). We also see that fleet sales have grown by 11% since May 1994 whilst Private has fallen by over 7%. This is clearly mixed news for the car producers. On the one hand with Fleet sales increasing that side of their business is doing better (and indeed the increase in Fleet sales might even be taken as an indicator of business confidence generally). However, cars sold on a Fleet basis are usually quite heavily discounted in terms of price (since a company is often buying a considerable number at one time). Car dealers typically look to achieve a higher profit margin on Private sales and clearly this part of the market shows a considerable decline.

We are also given data on the performance of the major car manufacturers (shown in the table in alphabetic order). A quick look down the May 1995 market share column reveals that Ford has the highest market share at almost one-quarter of the total market. Only three other manufacturers have a market share in double figures: General Motors, BMW and Peugot. Of these only Ford shows an increase in actual sales (of 1.5%) with the other top three showing decreases. Note that although Ford is selling more cars in May 1995 compared with May 1994 its market share has actually decreased by 0.1 percentage points. We can see why this is if we look at the increase across all makes, +1.7%. Although, Ford has increased its sales it has done so at a lower rate than the industry as a whole so its relative increase (and hence its market share) is less. From the % change column we see that Fiat, Mercedes-Benz and Toyota have seen the highest percentage increase in sales over this period.

We should also note that not all car makers are shown in the table. In fact over 9,000 cars in May 1995 are accounted for by 'other' companies (calculated by adding up sales of all the car companies shown and subtracting from total sales). This is almost 6% of total registrations and although this will comprise a number of companies with only a very small market share we might need to watch for any emerging patterns. The South Korean Daewoo company, for example, entered the UK market in April 1995 and registered almost 1,200 cars in May 1995. Potentially, this company may be an emerging threat to the already established car companies.

Finally, we should also note that the table only reflects new car sales. The market for used cars may be showing quite different patterns over this same period.

SELF-REVIEW QUESTIONS

1 *Under what circumstances are percentages more useful in a table than the original figures?*

2 *What are the main items of information that should appear on every table?*

3 *What is the difference between a table showing the percentage change in a variable and one showing the variable as an index?*

4 *What is a frequency table?*

5 *When might it be better to use a percentage change table rather than a table showing the actual values?*

6 *Approximately how many intervals should a frequency table contain?*

STUDENT EXERCISES

1 Using newspapers, business magazines, annual company reports and government publications collect examples of 5–6 tables. From these 2–3 should be examples of good table construction and presentation and the rest should be examples of poor table construction.

Write a short report explaining why each is an example of good or bad.

Table 4.15
Marriages

		1980	1981	1982	1983	1984	1985	1986	1987	1988	1999	1990[2]
United Kingdom												
Marriages	KKAA	418 446	397 846	387 021	389 286	395 797	393 117	393 939	397 937	394 049	392 042	375 410
Persons marrying per 1,000 resident population	KKAB	15.0	14.1	13.4	13.8	14.0	13.9	13.9	14.0	13.8	13.7	13.1
Previous marital status												
Bachelors	KKAC	314 849	297 589	288 408	288 713	293 645	291 171	290 144	296 290	289 493	288 478	276 512
Divorced men	KKAD	87 663	85 141	84 110	86 484	88 691	88 981	91 006	89 814	92 755	92 033	88 199
Widowers	KKAE	15 934	15 116	14 503	14 089	13 461	12 965	12 789	11 833	11 801	11 531	10 699
Spinsters	KKAF	319 088	302 354	293 068	293 554	299 256	296 797	294 564	301 073	293 551	291 516	279 442
Divorced women	KKAG	80 370	80 755	80 148	82 314	83 477	83 921	87 080	85 238	89 066	89 234	85 608
Widows	KKAH	15 982	14 737	13 805	13 418	13 064	12 399	12 295	11 626	11 612	11 294	10 360
First marriage for both partners	KMGH	278 608	263 209	254 868	254 620	258 997	256 594	254 237	260 459	253 150	251 572	240 729
First marriage for one partner	KMGI	76 721	73 525	71 740	73 027	74 913	74 780	76 254	76 445	76 744	76 850	74 496
Remarriage for both partners	KMGJ	63 117	61 112	60 413	61 639	61 890	61 743	63 458	61 033	64 155	63 620	60 185
Males												
Under 21 years	KKAI	52 644	46 197	41 544	37 141	33 447	30 243	25 828	24 269	20 608	19 070	15 930
21–24	KKAJ	141 776	133 522	127 833	127 149	127 351	123 242	119 464	118 355	109 482	102 977	92 270
25–29	KKAK	98 831	96 062	96 194	99 855	105 799	109 896	114 007	119 808	120 939	123 491	122 800
30–34	KKAL	48 104	46 873	45 266	45 794	47 325	47 594	49 287	51 389	53 865	56 442	56 966
35–44	KKAM	39 427	39 366	41 111	43 538	45 955	46 265	48 583	48 598	51 329	51 411	49 984
45–54	KKAN	19 360	18 333	18 286	18 990	19 358	19 652	20 376	19 788	21 544	22 329	21 996
55 and over	KKAO	18 304	17 493	16 787	16 819	16 562	16 225	16 394	15 730	16 282	16 322	15 464
Females												
Under 21 years	KKAP	127 542	11 540	104 642	96 859	90 301	82 209	72 466	68 629	59 284	54 256	45 626
21–24	KKAQ	133 309	129 565	128 446	132 020	136 244	137 437	138 219	140 509	134 122	128 411	119 037
25–29	KKAR	65 818	65 131	66 293	70 284	76 566	80 105	85 316	90 911	95 338	100 531	103 209
30–34	KKAS	34 064	32 786	31 306	32 163	32 998	33 424	35 237	36 643	39 680	41 989	42 794
35–44	KKAT	30 699	30 493	31 795	33 156	34 854	35 380	37 515	36 978	39 534	40 290	38 983
45–54	KKAU	15 011	14 091	13 857	14 325	14 716	14 892	15 414	15 001	16 570	17 172	16 825
55 and over	KKAV	12 003	11 240	10 682	10 479	10 118	9 670	9 772	9 260	9 521	9 393	8 936
England and Wales												
Marriages	KKBA	370 022	351 973	342 166	344 334	349 186	346 389	347 924	351 761	348 492	346 697	331 150
Persons marrying per 1,000 resident population	KKBB	14.9	14.2	13.8	13.9	14.0	13.9	13.9	14.0	13.8	13.7	13.1
Previous marital status												
Bachelors	KKBC	274 140	259 106	250 999	251 845	255 469	253 296	252 953	258 750	252 780	252 230	241 274
Divorced men	KKBD	81 396	79 099	78 040	79 678	81 448	81 370	83 401	82 315	84 991	84 035	80 282
Widowers	KKBE	14 486	113 768	13 127	12 811	12 269	11 723	11 570	10 696	10 721	10 432	9 594
Spinsters	KKBF	277 826	263 368	255 171	256 214	260 359	258 089	256 767	262 958	256 221	254 763	243 825
Divorced women	KKBG	77 595	75 147	74 418	75 909	76 899	77 031	76 964	78 219	81 691	81 702	77 994
Widows	KKBH	14 601	13 458	13 577	12 211	11 928	11 269	11 193	10 584	10 580	10 232	9 331
First marriage for both partners	KMGK	241 001	277 713	220 427	220 949	224 015	221 927	220 372	226 308	219 791	218 904	209 043
First marriage for one partner	KMGL	69 964	67 048	65 316	66 161	67 798	67 531	68 976	69 092	69 419	69 185	67 013
Remarriage for both partners	KMGM	59 057	57 212	56 423	57 224	57 373	56 931	58 576	56 631	59 282	58 606	55 094
Males[1]												
Under 21 years	KKBI	44 062	38 660	34 809	31 216	27 941	25 496	21 758	20 541	17 578	16 312	13 772
21–24	KKBJ	123 080	115 924	110 972	110 537	110 351	106 608	103 651	102 109	95 029	89 263	79 818
25–29	KKBK	88 067	85 391	85 333	88 470	93 227	96 804	100 360	105 458	106 349	108 834	107 784
30–34	KKBL	43 854	42 696	41 084	41 402	42 563	42 532	44 125	46 063	48 112	50 409	50 600
35–44	KKBM	36 323	36 312	37 712	39 882	42 064	42 120	44 309	44 237	46 688	46 549	45 038
45–54	KKBN	17 842	16 862	16 812	17 389	17 790	17 968	18 681	18 055	19 574	20 365	19 991
55 and over	KKBO	16 794	16 128	15 444	15 438	15 250	14 861	15 040	14 500	14 982	14 965	14 147
Females[1]												
Under 21 years	KKBP	110 288	99 246	90 669	84 125	78 026	71 394	62 831	59 705	51 717	47 529	40 022
21–24	KKBQ	116 618	113 149	112 314	115 641	118 928	119 707	120 769	122 999	117 239	112 048	103 653
25–29	KKBR	58 767	58 183	58 932	62 288	67 567	70 495	75 224	80 062	88 833	88 662	90 629
30–34	KKBS	31 259	30 122	28 510	29 194	29 917	30 055	31 658	32 932	35 609	37 452	38 032
35–44	KKBT	28 258	28 011	29 240	30 381	31 969	32 296	34 375	33 818	36 135	36 678	35 315
45–54	KKBU	13 709	12 842	12 596	13 007	13 401	13 549	14 054	13 690	15 173	15 661	15 290
55 and over	KKBV	11 123	10 420	9 905	9 698	9 378	8 893	9 013	8 555	8 786	8 667	8 209

1. The figures for England and Wales include an assumed distribution of 'Age not stated'.
2. 1991 figures not yet available.

Source: Social Trends 1993 Central Statistical Office. Crown Copyright 1993. Reproduced by the permission of HMSO and the Central Statistical Office.

2 Table 4.15 is taken from the *Annual Abstract of Statistics 1993* and shows data on Marriages in the UK between 1980 and 1990.

(a) Using the table answer the following:

    (i) In which year did the largest number of divorced women marry?

    (ii) In which year do you find the largest figure for first marriage for one partner?

    (iii) In which years did the number of males marrying aged 21–24 exceed the number of females in the same age group?

(b) Construct a percentage frequency table for males showing the number of marriages by age group in 1980 and in 1990. Comment on any differences that you observe over this period.

(c) Construct a comparable table for females.

(d) Comment on the age distribution of males marrying in 1980 and 1990 compared with that for females.

3 Table 4.16 is taken from *Social Trends 1993* and shows migration within the UK. Using the table answer the following:

(a) Which region had the largest outward migration?

(b) Which region had the largest inward migration?

(c) Which region experienced the largest net increase in migration?

(d) Which region experienced the largest net decrease in migration?

Table 4.16
Migration[1] within the UK: inter-regional movements, 1991

Thousands

| | Region of origin | | | | | | | | | | | |
	United Kingdom	North	Yorkshire & Humberside	East Midlands	East Anglia	South East	South West	West Midlands	North West	Wales	Scotland	Northern Ireland
Region of destination												
United Kingdom	–	49	85	81	48	265	99	88	100	47	47	9
North	50	–	9	4	2	14	3	3	8	1	5	–
Yorkshire & Humberside	85	9	–	13	4	24	6	7	15	3	4	1
East Midlands	90	4	15	–	6	31	6	12	9	3	3	–
East Anglia	58	2	4	7	–	32	4	3	3	1	2	–
South East	223	14	22	25	23	–	49	26	28	15	17	3
South West	121	3	6	7	4	65	–	13	9	8	4	–
West Midlands	83	3	7	10	3	28	11	–	11	7	3	1
North West	90	7	14	8	3	27	7	11	–	7	6	1
Wales	51	1	2	3	1	17	8	8	9	–	1	–
Scotland	56	6	5	4	2	20	4	3	6	2	–	2
Northern Ireland	12	–	1	1	–	6	1	1	2	–	2	–

1 Data are based on patient movements recorded by the National Health Service Central Registers at Southport and Edinburgh and the Central Services Agency in Belfast.

Source: Social Trends 1993 Central Statistical Office. Crown Copyright 1993. Reproduced by the permission of HMSO and the Central Statistical Office.

4 Table 4.17 shows the age distribution of the UK population in 1901 and in 1991. Draft a short report summarizing the main changes that have occurred over this period.

Table 4.17
Age distribution of the UK population
(figures are in thousands)

Age	1901	1991
Under 5	4,381	3,766
5–14	8,040	6,997
15–29	10,808	12,383
30–44	7,493	11,974
45–64	5,706	12,341
65–74	1,278	5,062
75 and over	531	3,748
Total	38,237	56,467

Source: *Annual Abstract of Statistics 1993.*

5 Table 4.18 shows data on employees in employment in the UK between 1971 and 1981. Construct a table using index numbers and using this draft a short report outlining the major changes that have occurred.

Table 4.18
Employees in employment: by sex and industry
(figures are in thousands and for the UK)

	1971	1981	1991
All industries	22,139	21,892	22,229
of which			
Males	13,726	12,562	11,592
Females	8,413	9,331	10,637
Manufacturing	8,065	6,222	4,793
Services	11,627	13,468	15,744
Other	2,447	2,203	1,692

Source: *Social Trends 1993.*

6 Table 4.19 shows the geographical distribution of the population in England between 1911 and 1991. Using this table, and any other tables you create, comment on the major changes that have occurred over this period.

Table 4.19
Geographical distribution of the enumerated population: standard regions in England
(figures are in thousands)

	1911	1931	1951	1971	1991
England	33,650	37,359	41,159	46,018	46,382
North	2,815	3,038	3,137	3,296	3,019
Yorkshire & Humberside	3,877	4,285	4,522	4,799	4,797
East Midlands	2,263	2,531	2,893	3,390	3,919
East Anglia	1,192	1,232	1,382	1,669	2,018
South East	11,744	13,539	15,127	17,230	16,794
South West	2,687	2,794	3,229	3,781	4,600
West Midlands	3,277	3,743	4,423	5,110	5,089
North West	5,796	6,197	6,447	6,743	6,147

Source: *Annual Abstract of Statistics 1993.*

7 Table 4.20 shows, for England and Wales, the authorized establishment of regular police and the total number of notifiable offences recorded by the police between 1981 and 1991. Using this table and any others you create comment on any trends over this period.

Table 4.20
Authorized establishment of regular police and notifiable offences recorded by the police: England and Wales

	Authorized establishment of regular police	Notifiable offences recorded by the police in thousands
1981	120,008	2,963.8
1982	120,125	3,262.4
1983	120,447	3,247.0
1984	120,679	3,499.1
1985	120,903	3,611.8
1986	121,785	3,847.4
1987	122,648	3,892.2
1988	123,551	3,715.8
1989	124,667	3,870.7
1990	125,646	4,543.6
1991	126,325	5,276.2

Source: *Annual Abstract of Statistics 1993.*

8 A high street shop sells CDs and cassettes and is currently trying to determine its customer profile. As an initial step it has collected data on the ages of a sample of 50 of its customers. These are shown in Table 4.21 (to the nearest year). Construct a suitable frequency table, or tables, and comment on the results.

Table 4.21
Ages of a sample of 50 customers (in years)

12	46	17	13	34	29	19	20	13	16
15	21	22	28	29	42	12	18	23	21
29	13	15	16	22	31	39	11	15	26
23	14	14	15	28	18	17	12	29	18
18	11	18	19	12	24	21	17	14	16

Source: *Business Survey.*

9 Return to Table 4.1 in the chapter which showed exports and imports in 1992 for five countries. Find comparable population figures for these countries for this year. Divide the exports, imports and difference figures by that country's population to obtain what are known as *per capita* figures. Construct an appropriate table and comment on your results.

10 A high street retail organization collects data on its five broad areas of product sales: Food; Electrical Goods; Clothing; Footwear; Furniture. For a five-year period the company has provided data on the profit figures (all measured in £ millions) per area:

Food 1992 £1.07m; Electrical Goods 1990 £4.14m; Clothing 1988 £6.73m.

Footwear 1992 £0.29m; Furniture 1991 £2.04m; Food 1989 £0.99m.

Electrical Goods 1992 £5.62m; Clothing 1992 £10.51m; Furniture 1988 £1.63m.

Electrical Goods 1991 £4.49m; Furniture 1992 £2.12m; Food 1991 £1.19m.

Clothing 1991 £10.05m; Electrical Goods 1988 £2.39m; Food 1988 £1.02m.

Food 1990 £1.01m; Clothing 1990 £8.19m; Footwear 1991 £0.24m;
Furniture 1990 £1.81m; Electrical Goods 1989 £3.29m; Clothing 1989 £7.98m.

Footwear 1990 £0.19m; Furniture 1989 £1.72m; Footwear 1989 £0.21m.

Footwear 1988 £0.20m.

(a) Construct a suitable table to show profits per year per area.

(b) What comments can you make about any trends in profitability over this period?

(c) Construct a suitable table to show profit in each area as a percentage of total profit in that year.

(d) What trends are now apparent in profitability?

COMPUTER EXERCISES

1 File 41.WK1 contains data on the stock of dwellings in the UK shown by region for 1976, 1981, 1986 and 1991 (Source: *Regional Trends 1993*).

(**a**) Construct a suitable table showing the percentage change between years.

(**b**) Construct a table showing the percentage distribution between regions in each year.

(**c**) Construct a table showing stock of dwellings by region as an index. Use 1976 as the base year and then construct a comparable table with 1991 as the base. Which base year would you choose?

In each case comment on the major trends and changes observed.

2 File 42.WK1 shows data on the resident population in the UK shown by region for 1981 and 1991 (Source: *Regional Trends 1993*).
Construct tables comparable to those in exercise 1 above and again comment on the major trends and changes observed.

3 Using both 41.WK1 and 42.WK1 calculate a new set of data showing stock of dwellings per capita (dividing stock by the relevant population figure).
Construct tables comparable to those in exercise 1 above and again comment on the major trends and changes observed.

4 File 43.WK1 contains data on the 100 companies in the Financial Times Share Index (FTSE or the Footsie) in terms of their share price in pence and their market capitalization in £ billion (effectively the market value of the company). Data is shown for a day in February 1993 and a day in May 1993.

(**a**) Construct suitable frequency tables to compare the share prices of these companies in these two periods.

(**b**) Construct suitable frequency tables to compare the market capitalization of these companies in these two periods.

(**c**) Using any newspaper which carries data on daily share prices update the file to show the latest data available and repeat (**a**) and (**b**).
Note that some companies may no longer be in the FTSE and others may have changed their name.

(**d**) In each case comment on the changes revealed by the frequency tables produced.

5 File 44.WK1 shows hypothetical data for last year's profit/loss for 100 high street retail outlets owned by a particular company. Use the data to produce a suitable frequency table of profit/loss and draft a short report commenting on the results.

5 BUSINESS DIAGRAMS

INTRODUCTION

Tables are a useful way of presenting detailed data about some business situation and, as we saw in the last chapter, are particularly versatile and flexible. However, tables are not always the most effective way of presenting business data. Frequently, and typically at the beginning of data analysis, we may want to use an appropriate diagram to present data. In this chapter we shall introduce the more common types of business diagram and see how they are constructed and used.

You will need a supply of graph paper for this chapter.

LEARNING OBJECTIVES

By the end of this chapter you should be able to:

- construct a line, or time series, graph;
- construct simple, multiple and component bar charts;
- construct a pie chart;
- construct a scatter plot;
- explain when and how to use the different types of diagram.

TOOLS OF THE TRADE

Diagrams are a very common way of showing data and providing information from that data. Diagrams are commonly used in the media, on TV and in the press. They are used by advertisers, they are used by businesses and they are even used by politicians! In order to be able to use and construct a variety of diagrams, however, we need to be competent in the principles of diagram construction.

Axes and Coordinates

With almost every diagram – although there are one or two exceptions – we need a point of reference for the numbers we want to show. Such a reference point is known as the origin – shown as 0 (zero) on a graph – and from the origin we can move horizontally – left or right – or vertically – up or down. The horizontal reference line from the origin is known as the horizontal axis and the vertical reference line as the vertical axis, as shown in Fig. 5.1. (The plural of axis is axes, pronounced 'axe-ee's'.)

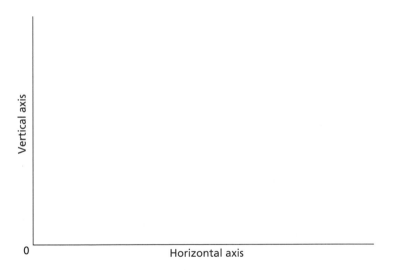

Fig. 5.1 Horizontal and vertical axes

Conventionally, the horizontal axis is referred to as the x axis and the vertical axis as the y axis, since we will often be drawing a graph of two variables, X and Y. The two axes are used to show appropriate numerical scales like those in Fig. 5.2. The exact scales we need will depend on the problem we are looking at.

We are then able to use the axes and the scales to plot any particular point – a pair of X and Y numbers or values – we are given. In order to do this we must make use of what are known as the coordinates of the point. If, for

139

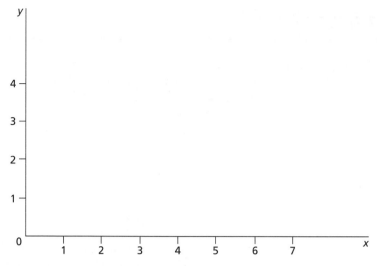

Fig. 5.2 *x* and *y* scales

example, we are told that a particular point has coordinates of $Y = 3$ and $X = 6$ then we can locate this point on the graph quite easily:

- Start from the origin.
- Move across the *x* axis to the right six units (since X is *plus* 6).
- From this point on the *x* axis move up the *y* axis three units (since Y is *plus* 3).
- Mark this point (shown as A in Fig. 5.3).

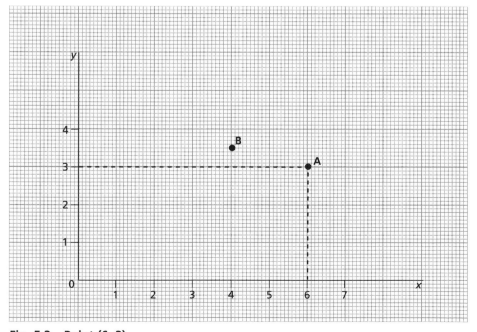

Fig. 5.3   Point (6, 3)

Student activity

From Fig. 5.3 work out the coordinates of point B.

From Fig. 5.3 we can determine that point B is located at coordinates which are 4 on the *x* axis and 3.5 on the *y* axis. Typically, the coordinates for a point may be shown in the form:

Point B (4, 3.5)

rather than specifically showing which coordinate is *x* and which is y. By convention, the *x* coordinate is shown as the first of the pair of numbers in brackets.

Quadrants

So far the coordinates of points have been positive. How would we draw a point which had one, or both, parts of the coordinate negative? The answer is that we would use another *quadrant* of the graph as in Fig. 5.4.

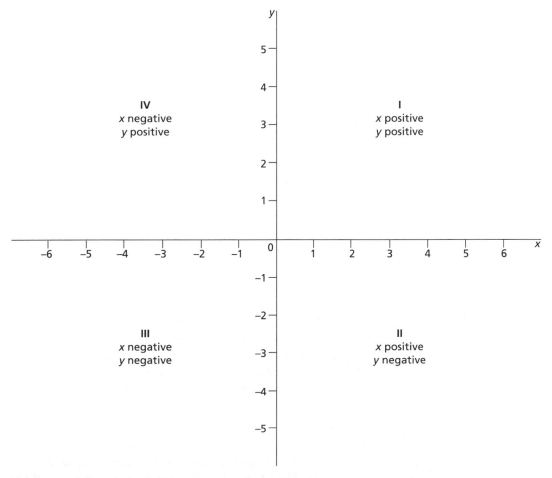

Fig. 5.4   Quadrants

We see that there are effectively four quarters to the graph each with a different combination of *x* and *y* values. The *x* axis has been extended to the left of the origin to include negative values whilst the *y* axis has been extended downwards to include negative values. Quadrant I is now appropriate if both *x* and *y* coordinates are positive; quadrant II if *x* is positive and *y* negative; quadrant III if *x* is negative and *y* is negative; quadrant IV if *x* is negative and *y* positive. For the vast majority of business diagrams we will normally use just quadrant I but occasionally we may use a graph of quadrant I and IV or I and II, and sometimes, for more mathematical analysis, a graph with all four quadrants. Plotting points from coordinates is exactly the same as before but we need to take a little more care over which direction from the origin we move in, depending on whether we have a negative coordinate or a positive.

Student activity

On Fig. 5.4 plot the following points:

A (3, 5)
B (–3, 5)
C (–3, –5)
D (3, –5)

Fig. 5.5 opposite shows the results. Check your own carefully against ours.

Scales on the *x* and *y* axis

So far, the numerical scales on the graphs have been provided for us. However, if we are drawing a graph ourselves it is usually up to us to decide on a suitable numerical scale for the two axes. Often this can be the most difficult part of drawing a graph until we've had a lot of practice. Suppose we were asked to plot the following pairs of points on the same graph:

A: $Y = 220, X = 12$
B: $Y = 140, X = 4$
C: $Y = 50, \quad X = -5$

We now know we have two axes to draw on the graph. Up to now we have always drawn the two axes in the middle of the graph (and the sheet of graph paper). However, this is not always the best place to have them. Depending on the coordinates we have to plot it is sometimes better to move the *x* axis line up or down the paper and sometimes move the *y* axis line to the left or right of the centre. But how do we decide? The answer becomes easier if we follow a number of simple steps.

Step 1

First, we decide which of the four quadrants we need to have in the graph. We see from this problem that all the *Y* values are positive but that we have

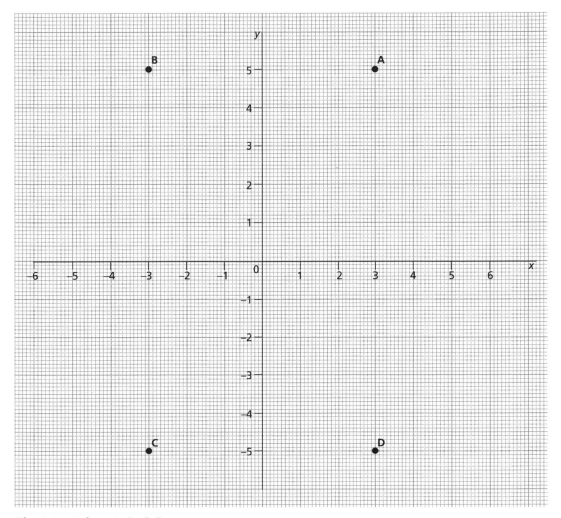

Fig. 5.5 Points A, B, C, D

a mixture of positive and negative values for X. This means that we shall need both quadrants I and IV on the graph.

Step 2

Since we are only using these two quadrants this means the x axis line can be drawn close to the bottom of the sheet since the y axis will only need positive values and can start at the origin (but remembering that we have to leave space on the graph paper for the numerical scale and any titles we want to write in).

Step 3

To help decide whether the y axis needs to be left or right of the centre we can decide on the numerical scales we need for the x axis by looking at the range of coordinates we need to plot. This is important because we need to make best use of the space we have on the graph paper (of course if we're sensibly using a computer package with graphics we don't normally have to worry about this). On the one hand we don't want the graph we have drawn using only a small part of the available space and looking too cramped and small. On the other hand we don't want the graph to cover too much space and to look stretched out. As with tables remember we're trying to convey information to other people in a diagram.

The x coordinates range from –5 to 12. Wherever possible we should try and ensure that scales start and end with numbers that are easy to handle. This usually means 1s, 2s, 5s, 10s and so on. One possibility would be to have the x scale from –5 to 15 and this is perfectly acceptable. However, we would then find when we came to plot the points that one of them was on the very left of the x scale at –5. It is better to leave some space at either end of the scale that we know we will not use so a scale from –10 to 15 might be better.

Step 4

When drawing the scale we also have to decide on how often we mark the scale to indicate the number values. Again, this is often an arbitrary choice but typically between 5 and 10 such 'tick' marks are common, once again using 'sensible' number intervals. We would probably mark the scale at: –10, –5, 0, 5, 10, 15. We could now draw the x axis on the graph as in Fig. 5.6.

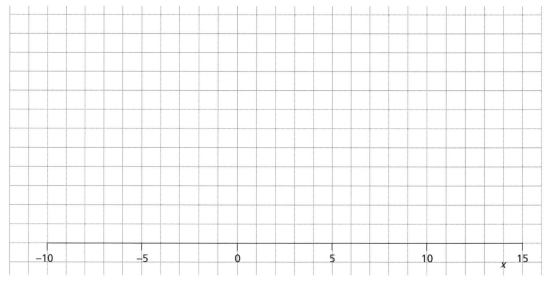

Fig. 5.6 x axis   Scale: 1 square = 1 square centimetre on graph paper

You should leave some space on the graph paper below the x axis line for labels and titles.

Step 5

It is now clear where the y axis line will appear on the paper (since it has to intersect with 0 on the x axis scale). As with the x axis we can decide a suitable scale and markings for the y axis.

Student activity

Suggest a suitable scale for the y axis and a set of 'tick' marks.

The *y* scale ranges from 50 to 220. It is usually better to start a scale from 0 if this is appropriate and to use a scale in multiples of 1s, 5s, 10s, 50s, 100s and so on since these are usually much easier to draw and to read from a scale. So in this case we might decide on a scale from 0 to 250. Here we might suggest marking the scale at 0 (the minimum) and then every 50 so we would show on the scale: 0, 50, 100, 150, 200, 250 as in Fig. 5.7.

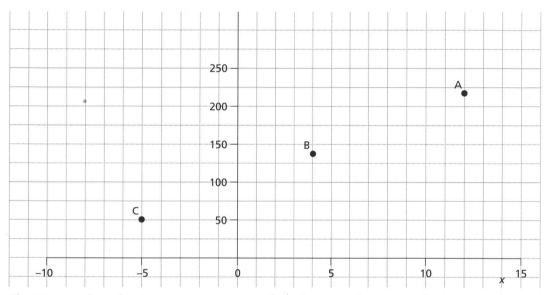

Fig. 5.7   *y* axis and points   Scale: 1 square = 1 square centimetre on graph paper

We could now proceed to plot the points as required by the given co-ordinates and these also are shown in Fig. 5.7. One problem that people often have when starting to draw graphs on graph paper is to decide how long to make the two axis lines – how long to draw them on the graph paper. It can be helpful to use the squares that are already marked on the graph paper. Each major square is usually subdivided into 10 cells horizontally and 10 cells vertically. For the *x* axis we notice that on our paper there are a total of 28 squares available across. The *x* axis has to cover a spread of 25 (–10 to 15) so this suggests we use one square per 1 of the 25 spread that we need. We then have three spare squares and the *x* axis line has to cover a length of 25 of the squares. For the *y* axis the same approach can be taken. On our paper there are 18 squares vertically. Three of these are 'lost' since they are used below the *x* axis for the *X* scale and labels we drew on Fig. 5.6 so we have 15 available to cover a spread of 250. We could use all 15 but we will need some space for the titles at the top of the diagram so if we use 10 this means we will have two squares for every 50 on the scale.

We should also note that it is conventional to draw the scale tick marks below the x axis and to the left of the y axis. The scale numbers should be drawn to coincide with the tick marks as in Fig. 5.7. One last point to note is that sometimes we might decide that we do not need to include 0 in the scale. In our example we might have decided to have a y axis scale from 50 to 250. This is acceptable as long as we make it clear that 0 is not in the Y scale. In Fig. 5.8 we have shown this y axis and indicated with the symbol = drawn across the y axis that the scale from 50 downwards is 'broken', that is the scale does not extend downwards beyond this point. Clearly we cannot do this if the y axis includes both positive and negative values since 0 must then be included.

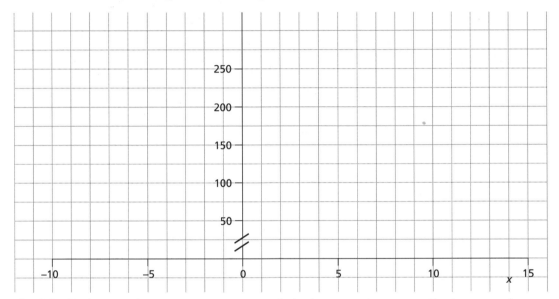

Fig. 5.8   Broken y axis   Scale: 1 square = 1 square centimetre on graph paper

It is also worth thinking about drawing a graph in pencil first just to check you have the scales and axes correct before plotting the points. Particularly in an exam there is nothing worse than seeing a graph where mistakes have been crossed out or blotted out in ink.

Finally, before we turn to examine the use of diagrams in business in detail we should note that we are not always wanting to draw graphs which have number scales on both axes. Sometimes only one of the scales will be numerical with the other representing an attribute variable.

THE NEED FOR DIAGRAMS IN BUSINESS

You will remember that an important part of our approach in this text is to look at different ways of conveying information to the business decision-maker. Tables are all very well but, as we have seen, are often quite complex and can contain considerable data. It is often better to present the data in the form of a diagram rather than a table (although we usually need the table first in order to be able to draw the diagram). Such diagrams are not a substitute for a table but usually allow us to pick out the important characteristics of a data set quickly and easily. This is especially the case when we have access to modern technology which is able to construct such diagrams quickly and accurately as well as providing us with the opportunity of trying different diagrams to see what best suits the business situation we are investigating.

LINE GRAPHS

One of the most common – and simplest – types of diagram in business is the line graph, often referred to as a time series graph. Frequently we will wish to monitor the movement of some variable over a period of time: sales of a product, unemployment, company profits, manpower levels and the like. An easy way of doing this visually is to use the vertical axis to show the numerical value of the variable and the horizontal axis the time period we are examining. Table 5.1 shows data for the number of new registrations of cars in Great Britain over the period 1970–1992 (it also shows other data that we shall be using later in the chapter, but ignore this for the present).

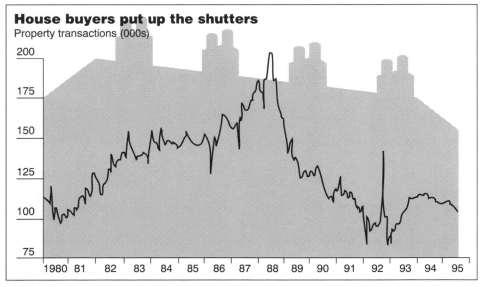

Source: *Financial Times*, 16 June 1995

It is clearly difficult to gain much of a detailed, overall impression of what has happened to this variable over this period. A much better impression is given in Fig. 5.9 which shows the same data graphically. You will see that we have plotted the variable – new car registrations – on the vertical axis and time, in years, on the horizontal. We now have a much clearer picture of how

Table 5.1
New registrations of cars and per capita personal disposable income: Great Britain

	New registrations of cars (000s) (monthly average)	Per capita personal disposable income at 1990 prices (£s)	Consumers' expenditure £ million at 1990 prices		
			Durable goods	Food	Alcoholic drink & tobacco
1970	91.4	3,912	11,865	36,280	26,349
1971	108.5	3,940	14,065	36,312	26,975
1972	177.6	4,256	17,096	36,248	28,882
1973	137.3	4,523	18,029	37,120	31,875
1974	102.8	4,487	15,790	36,470	32,189
1975	98.6	4,514	16,059	36,480	31,576
1976	106.5	4,501	16,850	36,866	31,490
1977	109.4	4,409	15,671	36,547	31,119
1978	131.6	4,734	17,926	37,217	32,000
1979	142.1	4,998	20,221	38,046	32,922
1980	126.6	5,067	19,276	38,095	31,706
1981	124.5	5,025	19,634	37,849	30,222
1982	132.1	5,004	20,652	37,942	28,963
1983	150.5	5,133	24,234	38,582	29,632
1984	146.6	5,309	24,059	37,925	29,695
1985	153.5	5,472	25,192	38,402	29,819
1986	156.9	5,703	27,912	39,610	29,630
1987	168.0	5,882	30,317	40,621	29,976
1988	184.2	6,221	34,950	41,541	30,478
1989	192.1	6,506	36,815	42,281	30,433
1990	167.1	6,621	34,745	41,816	30,272
1991	133.3	6,561	30,472	41,870	29,437
1992	133.3	6,717	30,752	42,380	28,667

Source: *Economic Trends Annual Supplement 1994.*

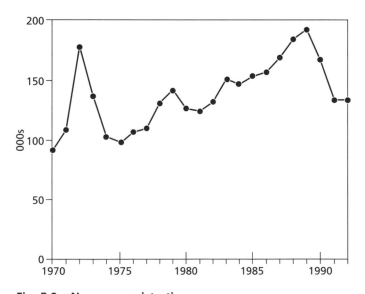

Fig. 5.9   New car registrations
Source: *Table 5.1*

this variable has changed over time. We see that from 1960 to 1989 new car registrations showed a strong upward growth – although this is quite erratic in some years. Since 1989, however, the level of registrations has fallen dramatically. We also note that 1972 appears to show an exceptionally high level of car registrations. It is evident that the diagram does not help us figure out why the variable behaves over time in the way that it does. That is for further investigation and analysis although we might use our knowledge of economics to suggest that the economic recession from 1989 onwards may well have affected demand for new cars. You may wish to try to find out why 1972 was such an exceptional year.

Such a graph is relatively easy to draw if we follow the general principles involved in any graph:

- decide what to show on each axis;
- decide on suitable scales;
- decide on a suitable interval for each scale;
- draw and label the axes;
- plot the values;
- join the points together on the graph;
- provide a suitable title.

Let us look at each step in turn in more details.

- Decide what to show on each of the two axes. For this type of diagram it is conventional to show the numerical values of the variable on the vertical scale and the time on the horizontal.
- Decide on a suitable scale for each of the two axes. For the vertical scale we should determine the minimum and maximum values in the data and from this the range of values that the scale will need to show. Here, the minimum is 91.4 (000) and the maximum 192.1 (000). As always, it is sensible to use a scale to show convenient, rounded maximum and minimum values. Here we might suggest a scale from 0 to 200. It is worth remembering that where it is sensible to do so we should include 0 in the scale, although this is not always appropriate. Here, we could have decided on a scale from 50 to 200, omitting zero. Figure 5.10 shows the same data with this scale.

  It is often a matter of personal judgement as to what the scale should be, although through the use of spreadsheets and computer graphics it is frequently easy to try alternative scales to decide which provides a more appropriate picture of the data. In Fig. 5.11, for example, we might decide that this scale is inappropriate since much of it is unused in the diagram and the time series line is unduly 'flattened' in the process. The scale for the horizontal axis is clearly much easier since this will be determined by the first and last periods we have to show.
- Decide on a suitable interval for each scale. Having determined what we think is a suitable minimum and maximum for the vertical scale we need to decide on a suitable interval to mark the scale on the diagram itself. Typically, somewhere between 5 and 10 such intervals are common

149

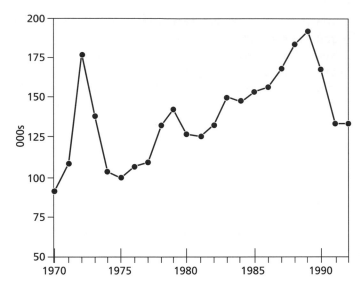

Fig. 5.10   New car registrations: alternative scale
Source: *Economic Trends.*

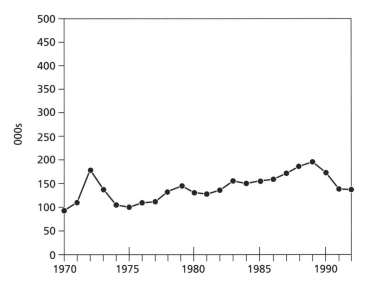

Fig. 5.11   New car registrations: inappropriate scale
Source: *Economic Trends.*

and these will in part be determined by the range we have to cover and
the grid scale on the graph paper we might be using. In this case with
a range of 0 to 200 we might decide on intervals of 25 (0, 25, 50, 75, ...)
or of 50 (0, 50, 100, 150, 200). Once again a choice should be made of
a 'sensible' interval using numbers which are relatively easy to handle:
5s, 10s, 25s, 50s, 100s and so on.

● We should then draw the two axes on the graph and their appropriate
scales and intervals, also making sure that the axes have an appropriate

label or title. We should also ensure that we are making proper use of the appropriate space on the paper.

- We can then simply plot each (year's) value at the appropriate coordinate for the year and the numerical value.
- We can then join these points together using a straight line between each set of points.
- We need to include an appropriate title for the whole diagram and, as with tables, ensure that units of measurement are shown and that the source of the data is given.
- Finally we need to look critically at the diagram we have produced and decide whether it does give a fair, accurate and easily understood picture of the data. If it doesn't then we need to change the diagram until we are satisfied with it.

Student activity

Return to Table 4.7 in Chapter 4. This related to road accident data for Great Britain over the period 1981 to 1991. Look for the data at the bottom of the table which shows the number of drivers involved in accidents who had a breath test. We shall look at the data which shows the number of drivers who failed the test.

For this data construct a suitable time series graph.

Figure 5.12 shows a time series graph for this data, although yours may differ slightly. We have a vertical axis from 0 to 12 (000s) and we see the general

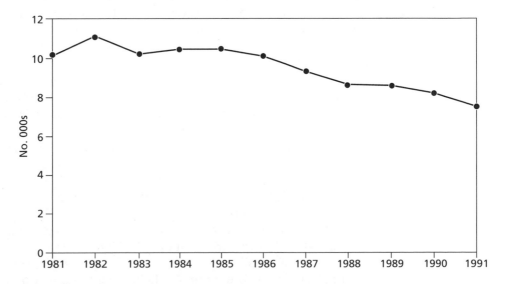

Fig. 5.12   Drivers who failed breath test: Great Britain 1981–91
Source: *Table 4.7.*

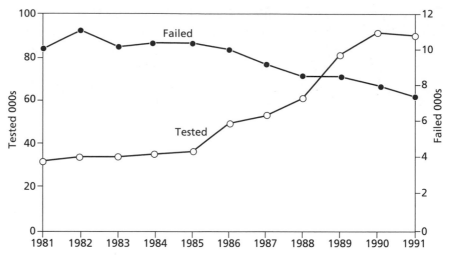

Fig. 5.13   Drivers tested and who failed test: Great Britain 1981–91
Source: *Table 4.7.*

trend in the number of those tested who failed the test over this period. We see that since 1982 the general trend has been for a reduction in the number of those tested who failed the test. Of course, again, we do not know the reasons for this: perhaps better awareness or the impact of government promotion campaigns. Of course this is only one part of the picture. It may be that the numbers failing the test are falling because fewer drivers are being tested.

It would clearly be useful to visually see the number of tests as well as those failing the test. We could, of course, draw two separate time series graphs for each data series. Or perhaps we might think of calculating the number of drivers failing the test as a percentage of those being tested and shown this on a graph. However, we shall illustrate a common type of time series graph which takes the two series and shows them on one graph (not two separate ones). This is shown in Fig. 5.13. Take a few moments to look at the diagram carefully.

You will see that we have shown the two time series on the one diagram but in fact have used two sets of vertical scales: one on the vertical axis on the left and the other on the vertical axis on the right. Checking the diagram carefully we see that the number of drivers tested is shown on the left scale whilst the number of drivers who failed is shown on the right scale. It should be clear why we need two scales: the numbers for the two series are very different and if we tried to draw them on one scale only we would not end up with a useful diagram (try it if you're not sure).

We can now directly compare the two series. We see that the number tested has steadily increased over time whilst the number failing the test has steadily fallen. For example, just over 30,000 drivers were tested in 1981 with just over 10,000 failing the test. By 1991 the number tested had increased to about 90,000 with the number failing falling to just over 7,000.

Whilst this type of line graph using two vertical axes is quite common we must be particularly careful when constructing and using such a

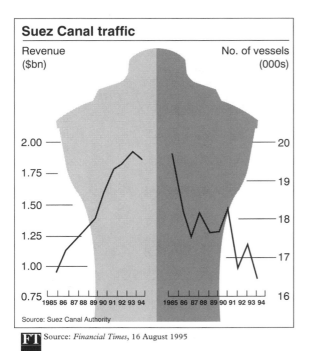

Suez Canal traffic

Revenue ($bn)

No. of vessels (000s)

Source: Suez Canal Authority

Source: *Financial Times*, 16 August 1995

diagram since it is clearly easy to mislead someone using the diagram. We must take particular care that labels are used to distinguish the two series and that it is easy to identify which scale should be used for which series.

Although the time series graphs we have produced in this section all deal with annual data, such graphs are also readily used for data which is non-annual: showing data by quarter, by month, by day and so on. The principles remain unchanged.

BAR CHARTS

A bar chart is one of the more common methods of presenting data in the form of a diagram and can be used in a number of different forms:

- the simple bar chart;
- the multiple bar chart;
- the component bar chart.

Simple bar chart

Consider Table 5.2 which shows unemployment rates in the standard regions of the UK in the first quarter of each year in 1974, 1984 and 1993.

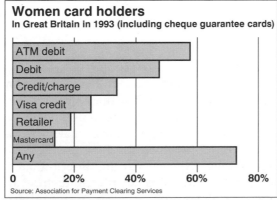

Women card holders
In Great Britain in 1993 (including cheque guarantee cards)

ATM debit
Debit
Credit/charge
Visa credit
Retailer
Mastercard
Any

0   20%   40%   60%   80%

Source: Association for Payment Clearing Services

Source: *Financial Times*, 9 August 1995

There is clearly a lot of data – and possible information – in the table but it is difficult to assess the data quickly. That is, it is not easy from the table to pick out the main features and patterns in the data set. Now consider Fig. 5.14 which shows a simple bar chart for the unemployment rate in each region in 1993. From the

153

Table 5.2
Regional unemployment rates
(figures are percentages, seasonally adjusted, in the first quarter of each year)

	1974	1984	1993
North	4.1	14.7	12.1
Yorkshire & Humberside	2.5	11.3	10.6
East Midlands	1.9	9.5	9.7
East Anglia	1.8	7.8	8.6
South East	1.4	7.5	10.5
South West	2.3	8.7	10.0
West Midlands	2.0	12.6	11.5
North West	3.2	13.5	10.9
Wales	3.3	12.7	10.3
Scotland	3.9	12.4	9.9
Northern Ireland	4.1	15.8	14.7
UK	1.8	10.5	10.6

Source: *Economic Trends Annual Supplement 1994.*

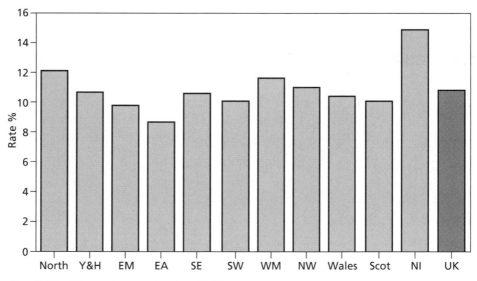

Fig. 5.14   Unemployment rates 1993
Source: ETAS 1994.

diagram we see very quickly the pattern between regions and between each region and the UK. We see that Northern Ireland has the highest unemployment rate and that this is considerably above the UK average. East Anglia has the lowest rate. In fact, we can make the bar chart more useful by rearranging the order in which we show the regions as in Fig. 5.15.

We now have the regions in increasing order – that is the region with the lowest rate on the left and the one with the highest on the right. The UK rate is also shown at its appropriate place in this ordering. This now means that we can readily see which regions have an unemployment rate below the

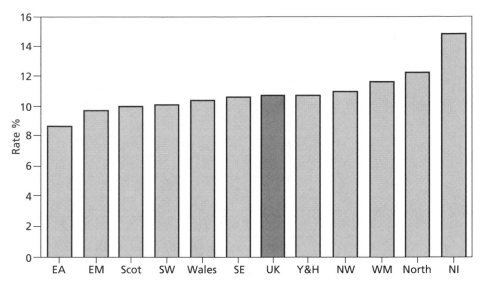

Fig. 5.15   Unemployment rates 1993
Source: ETAS 1994.

UK average and which are above. Whilst we could have reached the same conclusions from the table it would have taken some time.

But how did we construct such a diagram? What 'rules' did we follow?

Constructing a bar chart

Increasingly these days we would use a computer package to draw such a diagram for us, perhaps as part of a spreadsheet or perhaps a specialist graphics package. An appropriate software package offers us the ability to experiment with different forms of data presentation and diagrams until we produce one which we think is suitable for our purposes. Very often the only way to do this is through a process of trial and error – trying different diagrams until we get it right as we did with table construction – and computers are ideal for such an activity. In order to be able to use such software, however, and to be able to answer exam questions we must understand the principles behind drawing a bar chart. Let us look at how to draw a bar chart on a step-by-step basis.

Before we do so it is important always to remember what we are trying to do. We want to present a summary of a set of data that is easy to understand, quick to understand and reasonably accurate. At each stage in drawing a bar chart (or indeed any of the other forms of diagrams we introduce) we must always ensure that what we are doing satisfies these objectives.

Step 1

Given that there are two axes on a graph then we must decide what to put on each axis. In Fig. 5.14 on the horizontal axis we showed the variable we are measuring (unemployment rates). On the vertical axis we showed the frequency of the variable, in this case a percentage. We could just as well have reversed

155

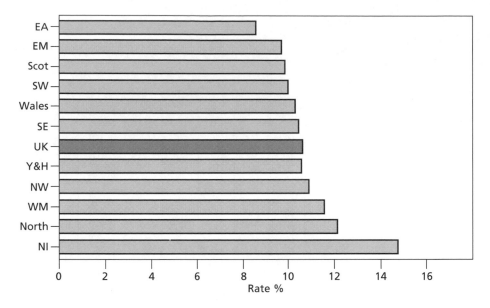

Fig. 5.16   Unemployment rates 1993
Source: ETAS 1994.

the axes as shown in Fig. 5.16 and this is quite a common way of presenting some simple bar charts. We shall stay with the type of bar chart in Fig. 5.14.

Step 2

We now have to decide on a suitable numerical scale for the frequency axis, remembering that the frequency axis shows the height of the bars. Normally, we would want the scale to start at 0 (for reasons we will see shortly) so in the case of unemployment rates in Table 5.2 we need to find the largest value the frequency axis has to deal with. This is 15 for Northern Ireland. It seems sensible then to have a frequency scale running from zero to either 15 or 16.

Step 3

We now decide on a suitable number of intervals for the frequency scale. Again, this is often a matter of personal choice but between 5 and 10 intervals is common and it makes sense to have intervals which are easy to think about (5s, 10s, 100s and so on). If we decide that the scale will go from 0 to 16 then we might decide to have intervals in terms of 0, 2, 4 and so on.

Step 4

If drawing the chart manually we would now draw the vertical and horizontal axes and the numerical scale for the frequency axis. We would need to take care that we were making good use of the graph paper we were using and not having the diagram in just one corner of the sheet. Similarly we would not want the two axes too close to the edges of the paper or we might not have enough space for labels and scales.

Step 5

Next we draw a bar for each element in the variable – each region in this case. The height of each bar is determined by the appropriate frequency. We do, however, need to make sure that:

- the width of the bars is the same;
- the bars are separated from each other by the same space.

Quite a common mistake at this stage is to start drawing the first one or two bars and then find that we aren't going to use all the space on the horizontal scale – or that we don't have enough space to complete the diagram – and so will end up with a diagram that just doesn't look right. We can avoid this by thinking ahead. First we should measure the size of the horizontal scale we have drawn. This may be measured in centimetres or in squares on the graph paper. Let us suppose the scale is 20 cm. On the chart we will have a series of bars and spaces. In fact we will have one more space than bars. So, in this case we will have 12 bars and 13 spaces.

A rule of thumb that usually works is to have the space about half the width of the bar. So this means that we need to have a total of 19 widths (12 + 7 (13/2)). Since we have 20 cm available it seems sensible to let one width equal 1 cm. So, each bar will be 1 cm wide and the space in between will be 0.5 cm wide. This is an easy method of making sure that when we start drawing the bars they will be of about the right size.

Step 6

Having drawn the scales and now the bars we want to make sure that the diagram is properly labelled (like we did with tables). The chart should show:

- a sensible title for the diagram;
- clear labels for the two axes;
- a clear numerical scale on the frequency axis;
- the units of measurement;
- the source of the data.

As with tables we might need to alter the diagram once we see it until we are happy with its appearance. Particularly if using a computer package we might also decide to enhance the appearance of the chart using shading or colours.

Student activity

Return to Table 4.1 in the previous chapter. This showed exports and imports for selected countries. Using the export data construct a suitable bar chart.

The bar chart is shown in Fig. 5.17 although yours may vary slightly from this.

The chart has to deal with values to just under 350,000. The frequency axis – which we have put on the vertical scale – has to be greater than the maximum value of 344,716. So we could put it at 400,000 as we have done (it is often easier to have the scale maximum as an even number rather than an odd one) or perhaps at 500,000. Notice that we have used units of billions of ECUs (a thousand million) rather than the millions in the original table. This allows us to have a scale from 0 to 400 (rather than 400,000) which improves the overall appearance of the diagram. A scale of 400 then is easily divided into units of 50 for the numerical scale. The rest of the chart is then easily constructed using the steps outlined above.

Multiple bar charts

The second type of bar chart to look at is the multiple bar chart, so called because it shows more than a single variable on the diagram. Return to Table 5.2 showing regional unemployment rates for 1974, 1984 and 1993. Now consider Fig. 5.18 which shows a multiple bar chart of the same data.

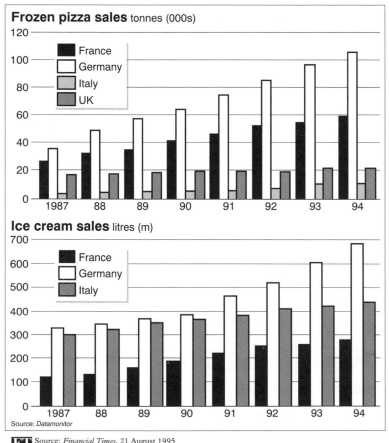

Source: *Financial Times*, 21 August 1995

You will see that we have frequency on the vertical axis as before but we now have three multiple sets of bars, one set for each year, and with each set showing a bar for each of the regions. Notice how the three bars within each region are side by side whilst the bars in different regions have a gap between them. We see that between 1974 and 1984 in every region unemployment rates rose considerably, although with some regional variations. Between 1984 and 1993 the picture is more mixed. Some regions have experienced a fall in the unemployment rate, others a rise. When we are constructing this type of chart we must make sure that the order of the bars in each grouping remains the same. In this case that means that we show the three years in the same order in each region.

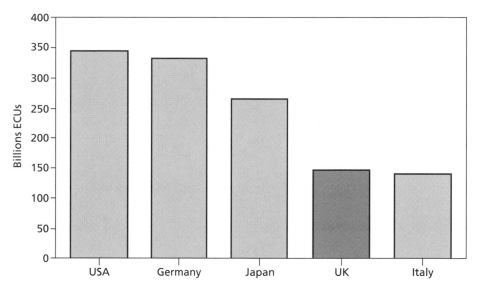

Fig. 5.17   Exports 1992
Source: Table 4.1.

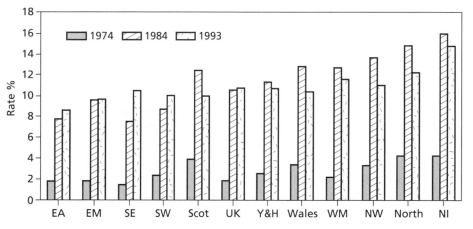

Fig. 5.18   Unemployment rates 1974, 1984, 1993
Source: ETAS 1994.

Student activity

Table 5.3 (on p.160) shows the tenure of dwellings in the UK between 1981 and 1991. Construct a multiple bar chart to show this data.

Table 5.3
Tenure of dwellings UK
(figures are percentages of total dwelling stock)

	1981	*1986*	*1991*
Owner occupied	57	63	68
Rented from local authority	31	26	22
Rented from private landlord	11	9	7
Rented from housing association	2	3	3

Source: *Regional Tends 1993.*

The multiple bar chart using this data is shown in Fig. 5.19 and Fig. 5.20, depending on whether we want to compare across the years or across the dwelling types. We could examine the changes over time within each tenure type or we could examine changes over time between tenure groups.

From Figs 5.19 and 5.20 we see that we have a frequency scale of 100. This is logical since we are measuring a percentage variable. Whilst we could have chosen a different maximum value for the scale, say 80%, showing 100 reinforces the fact that we have a percentage variable. The four types of tenure are then shown in decreasing order (that is with the largest type first, then the second largest and so on) in Fig. 5.19 and over time in Fig. 5.20. From the diagrams we see that owner occupied is by far the largest tenure type and over this period has showed a steady increase in percentage terms: that is, this type of tenure is becoming more important. The second largest type is rented from LA (local authority) but, together with the third largest, rented from private, we see that both of these types of tenure have shown a

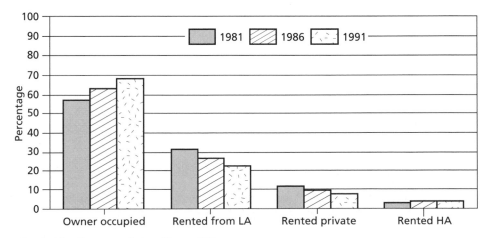

Fig. 5.19   Tenure of dwellings: UK
(Percentage of total dwelling stock by tenure type)

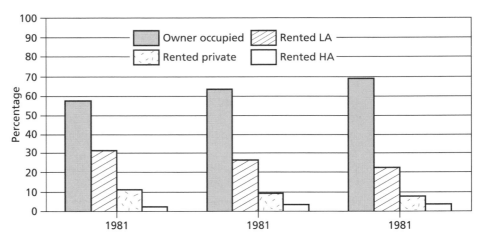

Fig. 5.20 Tenure of dwellings: UK
(Percentage of total dwelling stock by year)

steady decrease over the period. Finally, the smallest type is rented from housing association which has also shown a steady increase.

We must, as ever, be careful about interpreting such percentage figures. It is tempting to conclude that fewer people are renting houses from local authorities or from the private sector. This may well be the case but we cannot determine this from the data given. All that we can say from the data given is that these two types are decreasing in terms of relative importance. For example, it could well be that more people are renting from these two types (i.e. there is an increase in absolute terms) but that this increase is less than that for the other two sectors. Without further data we must limit our conclusions to those supported directly by the data available.

Component bar chart

The final type of bar chart we will look at is known as the component bar chart. It gets its name from the fact that we use a single bar to represent a variable and the bar itself is broken into segments, or components, to show subdivisions of the variable. Let us look at Table 5.4 showing the breakdown of UK energy consumption. The component bar chart is shown in Fig. 5.21.

You will see how the component bar chart has been constructed. We draw one bar for each year showing the total energy consumption in that year. We then divide the bar into its component elements (fuel type in this case). The easiest way to do this is to calculate cumulative consumption by type. The order in which we add the components is really up to us.

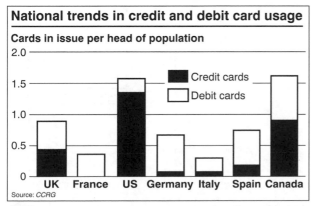

Source: *Financial Times*, 15 September 1995

161

Sometimes we might start with the largest component, sometimes with one which changes relatively little between the different bars in the chart. Here, we shall start with petroleum since it is relatively stable over time. Figure 5.21 shows the component bar charts in terms of actual consumption (in thousand million therms) whilst Fig. 5.22 shows a percentage component bar chart, with consumption by fuel type as a percentage of total consumption.

Table 5.4
Total inland energy consumption by final users: UK
(heat supplied basis: million therms)

	1971	1981	1991
Solid fuel	14,816	7,310	5,416
Gas	7,714	16,895	20,208
Electricity	6,757	7,521	9,590
Petroleum	27,617	23,197	25,235
Total	56,904	54,917	60,449

Source: Adapted from *Annual Abstract of Statistics.*

Bar charts are a common and useful method of showing variables. However, there are a few points we should watch for when drawing such charts:

- The bar widths must all be the same. Using different widths may well distort our interpretation of the diagram.
- The spaces between bars should all be the same width.
- We should be careful to ensure the height of each bar accurately represents the numerical value of that variable/category.
- We should ensure that the numerical scale includes 0.
- We should not use a broken numerical scale.

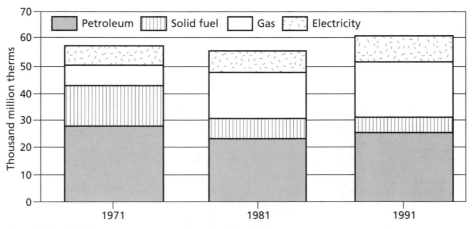

Fig. 5.21   UK energy consumption by fuel type
Source: Adapted from Annual Abstract of Statistics.

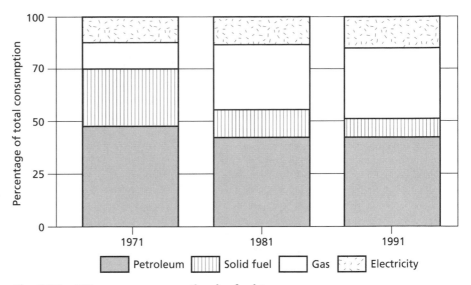

Fig. 5.22 UK energy consumption by fuel type
Source: Adapted from Annual Abstract of Statistics.

- We should ensure that the numerical axis is properly drawn and labelled.
- If using a multiple or component bar we should ensure the ordering of the bars is the same for each part of the diagram.
- If using a multiple or stacked bar we should ensure that there are appropriate labels to identify the component elements of the bars.

PIE CHARTS

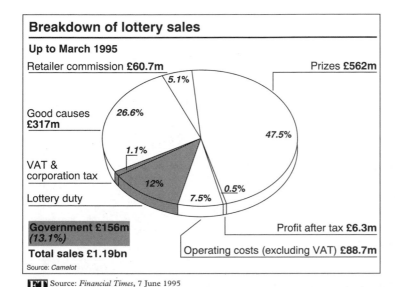

Bar charts are not the only way to represent data with a diagram. Another very common type of diagram used in business presentation is the pie chart which can be useful at showing the component parts of some variable (similar to the component bar chart). Look at Fig. 5.23. This shows manpower in the regional and district health authorities for the UK in 1991 by category of staff.

The diagram also explains why this type of figure is known as a pie chart because it has been drawn to look like a pie which has been 'cut' into sections or 'slices' (use your imagination a little!). We can see at a glance which 'slice' of the

163

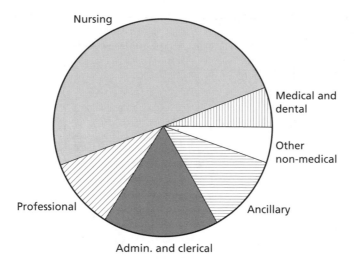

Fig. 5.23   Health authority manpower 1981 and 1991
Source: *Social Trends 1993.*

pie is largest and how the various 'slices' compare to each other. Drawing a pie chart manually is quite awkward and time-consuming and we will assume that you will typically be using a computer package. However, we will explain the manual method since it will help you understand the principles. A pie chart consists of a circle which is used to represent the total of whatever variable we are looking at. The circle is then divided into segments where each segment represents one component element of the variable total. The first step is to calculate each component as a percentage of the total. This has already been done for the data in Table 5.5.

Table 5.5
Health service staff: UK 1991

	Number (000's)	Percentage of total
Medical and dental	57.8	5.7
Nursery and midwifery	501.3	49.8
Professional and technical	106.5	10.6
Administrative and clerical	172.7	17.2
Ancillary	115.1	11.4
Other non-medical	53.2	5.3
Total	1,006.6	

Source: *Social Trends 1993.*

Second, we draw a circle. This represents the total for the data. Third, we need to divide the circle into segments with each segment showing a component in relation to its relative (percentage) size. You may remember from your

Industry uses less energy

Energy consumption

By final user (%)   **1960**   **1994**

Domestic 29 ⎯⎯⎯⎯   Domestic 29

Industry 42 ⎯⎯⎯⎯   Industry 25

Other 12 ⎯⎯⎯⎯   Other 13

Transport 17 ⎯⎯⎯⎯   Transport 33

Source: *Digest of UK Energy Statistics 1995*

Recent government figures illustrate how industry's share of energy consumption in the UK has fallen sharply in the past three decades. The contraction of many large, energy-intensive industries such as iron and steel means that industry now uses less energy than the domestic sector.

The other big change in energy consumption has been the strong growth in the transport segment, partly caused by wider car ownership and the growing use of road transport to move goods. Domestic energy use has been remarkably consistent, although its share fell as low as 24 per cent in the intervening years.   *Robert Corzine*

Digest of United Kingdom Energy Statistics 1995, HMSO

FT   Source: *Financial Times*, 22 August 1995

geometry that a circle is defined as having 360° (° stands for degrees). So, our first segment – Medical and dental comprises 5.7% of the total. If we work this out then 5.7% of 360° is 21° (rounded). In other words, the portion of the diagram representing this group of staff will cover 21° of the circle which has a total of 360°. Next, we divide the circle we have drawn such that one portion covers 21°, as in Fig. 5.24. (You would actually need an instrument called a protractor to enable you to do this.)

Finally, to complete the pie chart we divide the rest of the circle into segments corresponding to the proportions of the other sectors:

Medical and dental	21°
Nursery and midwifery	179°
Professional and technical	38°
Administrative and clerical	62°
Ancillary	41°
Other non-medical	19°

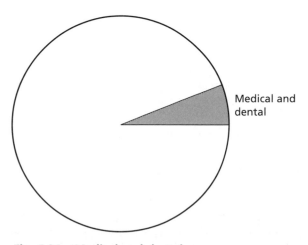

Fig. 5.24   Medical and dental

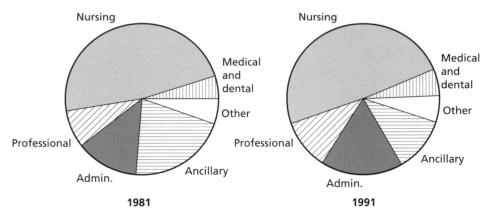

Fig. 5.25   Health authority manpower 1981 and 1991

The use of pie charts in presenting such business information is widespread and it is easy to see why. They give an immediate picture of the data and have an instant impact on the person looking at them. In addition, many computer packages offer the facility for constructing pie charts directly so avoiding the tedious manual method. From a practical viewpoint, though, their use is extremely limited. Not only are they difficult to construct (as you've just found out!), it is also difficult to compare different pie charts directly. Such diagrams are inappropriate for detailed statistical analysis. This is illustrated in Fig. 5.25 which shows health service manpower by category for 1981 and for 1991. It is difficult to assess the changes that have taken place by examining the pie diagram. About the only obvious change that is evident is the reduction in the ancillary category between 1981 and 1991. It is not evident from the diagram (as it is from the data) that the professional category has increased by almost 33% over this period.

SCATTER DIAGRAMS

The last type of diagram we look at in this chapter is the scatter diagram (or scatter plot). The diagrams we have introduced are usually concerned with showing one variable (although time series graphs may show more than this). Frequently in business we may know – or think – that two variables are related to each other in some way. Examples might include personal income and spending, costs and production levels, profits and sales. A scatter diagram is a useful visual way of assessing whether there is some connection between two variables.

Consider the data shown earlier in Table 5.1. The first variable is new registrations of cars as a monthly average in each year. The second is per capita personal disposable income (PDI). We could show each variable as a time series, perhaps on the same graph if we used two separate axes. Figure 5.26 shows this but it doesn't really help a lot. The PDI series is generally rising indicating increasing per capita disposable income (although there are a few years where it falls). New registration of cars is more erratic.

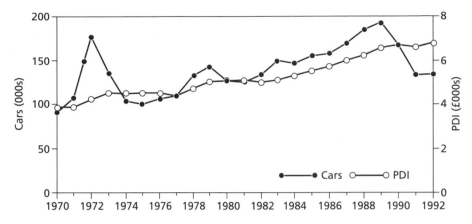

Fig. 5.26　Car registrations and personal disposable income
Source: ETAS 1994.

A little bit of thought and we might be surprised at the lack of any obvious pattern between the two variables. After all, it seems sensible to assume that people's ability to afford a new car will depend to a large extent on their income. If across the whole economy, people's incomes are rising we might expect new car registrations (an indication of sales) to rise and vice versa. It is in this type of situation – where we think that there might be a relationship between two variables – that the use of a scatter plot (sometimes known as an XY graph) comes in. Look at Fig. 5.27. This shows a scatter plot of the data we have just been looking at (you see how the diagram gets its name, from the scatter of points).

Let us explain the diagram. On the vertical y axis we have car registrations. On the horizontal x axis we have PDI. Unlike most of the other diagrams we have looked at, it is important on a scatter diagram to decide which variable

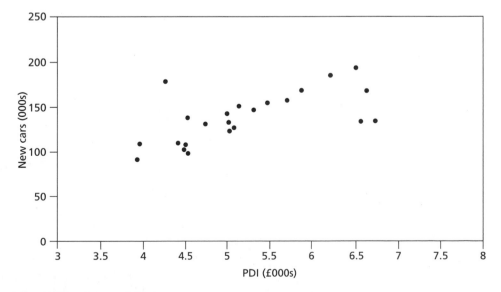

Fig. 5.27　Cars and income
Source: ETAS 1994.

to show on which axis. We are proposing a relationship between cars and PDI in such a way that PDI influences cars (i.e. as income changes so does the new registration of cars). In scatter diagram terminology cars is the dependent or *y* variable (since its value will in part depend on the PDI variable). The PDI variable is known as the independent, or explanatory, variable (*x*).

Once we have decided which variable goes on which axis we use the principles we developed earlier in the chapter to plot the coordinates of the points, where each point represents the combination of cars and PDI for a given year. Notice that the *x* scale does not start at the origin (since this would not allow us to use most of the graph) but at 3,000.

What we now see is evidence of a relationship between the two variables that was not evident from the time series graph. With one or two exceptions the points lie reasonably close together in a line that starts from about (4, 100) and goes to (6.5, 200). The cluster of points is around this line and the line itself moves upwards as we look at it from left to right. This implies that as PDI increases (moves to the right) cars increase also (move upwards). This relationship is not absolute – since the points do not form a line exactly. This suggests that there may be other variables affecting decisions to buy new cars other than simply income but there does appear to be evidence of a reasonable relationship.

There are also one or two notable exceptions to this cluster. These are marked on Fig. 5.28. Point 1, on inspection of Table 5.1, relates to 1972 when for reasons not apparent from the data car registrations were abnormally high given the level of income. Conversely Point 2 shows 1991 and 1992 where car registrations were considerably below the norm given income levels.

A scatter diagram is particularly useful at helping identify relationships between variables although it does not explain by itself why the relationship exists. For that we must use our knowledge of business and economics. It is also impor-

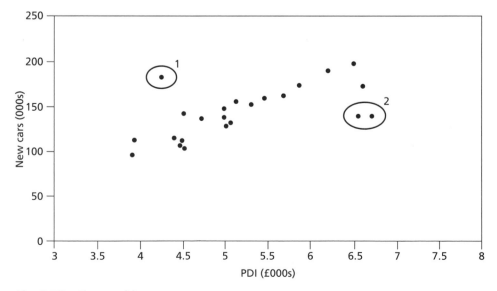

Fig. 5.28   Cars and income
Source: ETAS 1994.

tant to realize that a scatter diagram may also show that there is no evidence of a relationship between two variables, perhaps when we expected one.

Student activity

Table 5.1 shows data on PDI and a number of component categories of consumers' expenditure in the UK. For consumption on durable goods produce a scatter diagram with PDI and comment on the results.

Figure 5.29 shows the result. Durable goods is the *y* variable and PDI again the *x* variable. Once again we have a scatter plot where there is a reasonable clustering of points around a (imaginary) line and once again this line moves upwards. This implies that consumption on durable goods (TVs, videos, hi fi equipment and the like) increases as personal disposable income increases. And again, 1991 and 1992 shows consumption of durable goods which is slightly lower than we might expect given the PDI level.

USING THE DIFFERENT DIAGRAMS

As we said at the beginning of this chapter there are often no right or wrong choices in terms of which type of diagram to use to represent a set of data. Much of the choice will be the result of trial and error: trying one type of diagram and seeing how it looks. Fortunately these days modern technology means that a manager can experiment with different diagrams quickly and

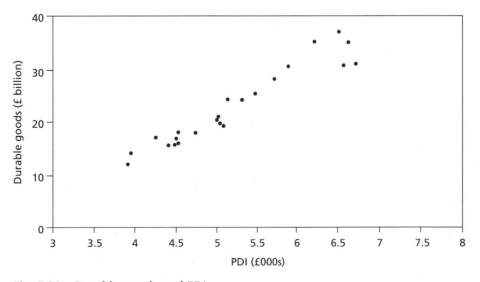

Fig. 5.29   Durable goods and PDI
Source: ETAS 1994.

easily. The important point to remember, though, is that the diagram we choose should present a picture of the data in a form which:

- is easy for others to understand;
- shows the data reasonably accurately;
- does not give a distorted view of the situation.

The advantages and disadvantages of each type of diagram we have introduced are summarized in Table 5.6.

Table 5.6
Advantages and disadvantages of the different diagrams

Diagram	Advantages	Disadvantages
Simple bar	• Easy to produce • Easy to understand • Adaptable to different situations	• Limited to one variable • Comparison of diagrams can be difficult
Multiple bar	• Useful for comparing different components of a variable • Flexible • Easy to produce	• Difficult to see what is happening to the group total • Only useful if there are a small number of components • Can look messy if components are changing in importance over time
Component bar	• Useful where group total needs to be shown • Can show either total or percentages	• Less easy to produce • Not easy to interpret if group totals are changing • Not easy to compare components between bars
Pie	• Popular • Easy to understand • Useful for variables with a small number of groups • Useful where one or two groups form a large part of the total	• Difficult to produce manually • Looks messy with more than five or six 'slices' • Difficult to pick out detail • Comparison between pie charts is difficult
Line diagram/ Time series diagram	• Easy to construct • Easy to understand • Useful where we have a variable changing over time	• Limited to two variables • Easy to distort by altering the scale used • Difficult to read off precise values
Scatter plot	• Useful where we assume there is a relationship between two variables	• Limited to two variables

SUMMARY

In this chapter we have introduced a number of diagrams commonly used in business presentation and analysis. Diagrams offer a flexible and 'user-friendly' way of presenting an overall picture of a set of data. Often, it may be the case that we could use several of the diagrams introduced with one set of data. We must use our judgement and experience – and some trial and error – to choose the diagram that best shows the data. We must remember that the purpose of a diagram is to present a summary picture of a set of data in an easy-to-understand form but which at the same time is reasonably accurate and not misleading.

Now you have completed this chapter you will appreciate that:

- The purpose of both tabular and graphical methods of data presentation is to provide a clear, concise and reasonably accurate description of a data set.
- Tables provide a considerable amount of detailed information but are frequently too complex to provide information quickly.
- Time series graphs are useful for identifying trends in one or more variables over a period of time.
- Bar charts are probably one of the most useful methods of graphical presentation since they are easy to construct and easy to interpret.
- Care should be taken with all diagrammatic forms of representing data to ensure definitions are clear and unambiguous and that scales used are not misleading.

EXAMPLE

The following example is based on a real set of data that a high street music company collected and analysed. The data relates to an 18-month period during which the company sold an album produced by a particular pop group. From its EPoS system the company was able to monitor the sales of this album in both CD and cassette format on a week-by-week basis for all its stores across the country. The firm was particularly interested in assessing the impact that a number of key events had had on sales and on trying to determine how long to stock other albums for. Clearly, albums stocked in the stores take up space and if the album is not selling particularly well this space could be better utilized for other albums from other artists. On the other hand, removing the album from display too soon could result in lost sales.

Figure 5.30 shows a time series graph of weekly sales of the album. Notice that three specific weeks have been marked on the graph. The first marked the launch of a special promotion of this group by the store nationwide in the run up to the Christmas period. It can be seen that the promotion appears to have been very successful with sales climbing to a particularly high level. The second period coincided with a single being taken from the

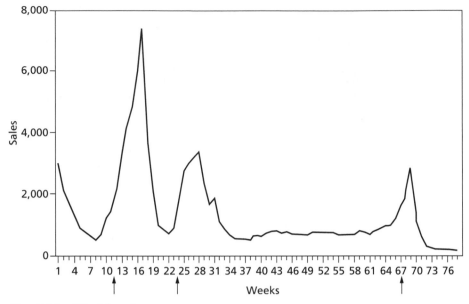

Fig. 5.30   Weekly sales

album by the record company. This had some chart success with spin-offs for sales of the album. The third was the Christmas period in the second year. Figure 5.31 shows the album sales split by format: CD and cassette.

Figure 5.32 shows the cumulative percentage sales of the album. This has been calculated in the following way. Weekly sales were added together on a cumulative (or running total basis) and then the cumulative weekly sales calcu-

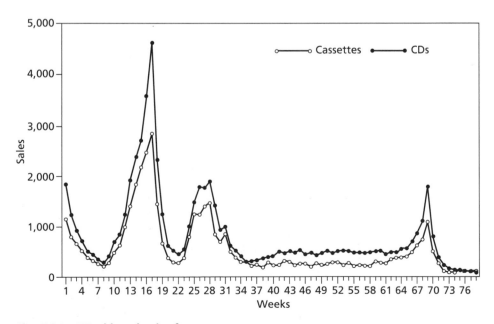

Fig. 5.31   Weekly sales by format

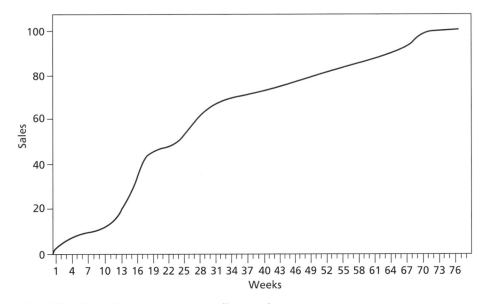

Fig. 5.32   Cumulative percentage album sales

lated as a percentage of total sales over the entire period. So, for example, in week 40 the cumulative percentage sales were just over 70%. This means that 70% of all sales the store was going to make had been achieved by week 40. It can be seen from the graph that after week 70 cumulative sales follow a very 'flat' pattern implying that additional weekly sales will be very low (and in fact by week 70 98% of total sales had been achieved).

Potentially this is of some help to the manager who is trying to decide which albums to display in the limited floorspace available in the stores. A decision not to stock the album after week 70 would cost the company very little in terms of lost sales and potentially could be used to promote faster selling albums (thereby generating much more sales revenue). The company was also able to calculate that 60% of its total sales were in CD format and 40% in cassette. This is also potentially useful in terms of helping decide how much floorspace to allocate to the two different formats for all albums and also in terms of ordering the two formats from the record company.

SELF-REVIEW QUESTIONS

1 *What are the benefits in constructing a diagram rather than showing data in a table?*

2 *What are the disadvantages of a pie chart?*

3 *Why is it usually better to use a percentage component bar chart rather than a component bar chart of the original figures?*

4 *What are the main items of information that should appear on every table or diagram?*

5 *How do you work out the size of each section in a pie chart?*

6 *How do you decide which variable to put on the vertical axis in a scatter diagram?*

STUDENT EXERCISES

The data for each of these exercises is contained in a file on the accompanying data disk. Where possible you should use computer spreadsheet or graphics facilities to produce the diagrams required although most of the exercises can be completed manually.

1 Return to Table 4.1 showing exports and imports for selected countries. Produce suitable diagrams to illustrate this data.

2 Return to Table 4.18 showing employees in employment by sex and industry between 1971 and 1991. Construct suitable diagrams to illustrate this data.

3 Return to Table 4.19 showing the geographical distribution of the enumerated population in England between 1911 and 1991. Construct suitable diagrams to illustrate this data.

4 Return to Table 4.20 showing establishment of police and notifiable offences recorded. Produce a scatter plot of this data and comment on the results.

5 Return to Table 5.1. Produce scatter diagrams using PDI and consumers' expenditure on food and on alcoholic drink and tobacco. Compare these two diagrams with that for durable goods. How do you explain the differences in the relationship as evidenced by each scatter diagram between PDI and each of the component expenditures?

6 Table 5.6 shows prison service manpower for Great Britain between 1971 and 1991. Produce suitable diagrams to illustrate this data.

Table 5.6
Prison service manpower: Great Britain

	1971	*1981*	*1991*
Prison officer class	13,087	19,441	26,762
Governor class	532	614	928
Other non-industrial staff	3,027	4,358	5,047
Industrial staff	1,825	2,426	2,497
Total	18,471	26,839	35,234

Source: *Regional Trends 1993.*

7 Table 5.7 shows UK consumers' expenditure by component categories in 1952 and in 1992. Use suitable diagrams to illustrate the data and comment on your findings.

Table 5.7
UK consumers' expenditure by component categories
(£ million, 1990 prices)

Category	Year	
	1952	*1992*
Durable goods	3,479	30,752
Food	27,336	42,380
Alcoholic drink and tobacco	17,597	28,667
Clothing and footwear	5,658	20,629
Energy products	8,108	22,977
Other goods	8,971	38,873
Rent, rates and water charges	17,712	39,682
Other services	37,875	115,981
Total	121,088	339,941

Source: *Economic Trends Annual Abstract 1994.*

8 Using the data in Table 5.8 compare and contrast the situation in 1981 with that in 1991 through the use of diagrams.

Table 5.8
Health service staff: UK 1981 and 1991
(thousands)

	1981	*1991*
Medical and dental	49.7	57.8
Nursery and midwifery	429.8	501.3
Professional and technical	80.2	106.5
Administrative and clerical	133.3	172.7
Ancillary	220.1	115.1
Other non-medical	56.2	53.2
Total	1,032.2	1,006.6

Source: *Social Trends 1993.*

6 BUSINESS DIAGRAMS: HISTOGRAMS

INTRODUCTION

We looked at a number of common business diagrams in the previous chapter. In this chapter we shall focus our attention on a special class of business diagram – the histogram – and its variants. We have already introduced the method of tabulating data into the form of a frequency table. The graphical presentation of such a table in the form of a histogram and the use of cumulative frequencies allowing us to begin the process of quantifying the key elements of a data set are detailed in this chapter. Such methods provide a link between the purely descriptive approach to examining data and the numerical analysis of such data that we shall be introducing as we progress through the next few chapters.

LEARNING OBJECTIVES

By the end of this chapter you should be able to:

- construct a histogram from a frequency table;
- deal with open-ended and unequal intervals;
- construct and use a frequency polygon;
- construct and use an ogive;
- explain and use percentiles.

HISTOGRAMS

To illustrate the construction and use of histograms we shall return to Table 4.10 in Chapter 4, reproduced here as Table 6.1. You will remember that we had established a scenario whereby you had decided to set up a small restaurant specializing in organically grown food. You are currently considering two locations for the restaurant, Site A and Site B. As part of the decision process to determine which of the sites you prefer you took a sample of local residents and asked them what their weekly income is (before tax or any other deduction). Figure 6.1 shows the comparable histogram of the data for Site A.

Table 6.1
Gross weekly income: Sites A and B

Income £	Site A No. of responses	Site B No. of responses
< 100	14	0
100 < 200	39	0
200 < 300	32	8
300 < 400	26	28
400 < 500	17	52
500 < 600	9	40
600 < 700	6	31
700 < 800	5	8
800 < 900	2	4
≥ 900	0	4
Total	150	175

Source: Business survey.

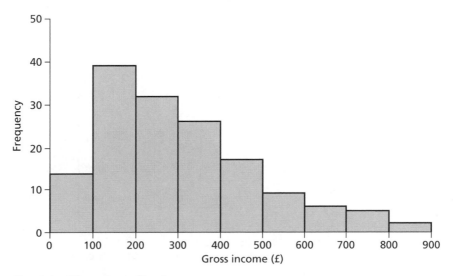

Fig. 6.1   Histogram: Site A
Source: Table 6.1.

At first sight the histogram looks very much like the bar charts we were looking at in the previous chapter. However, there is one critical difference. You will see that the bars in the histogram do not have spaces between them – they form a continuous block of bars. The reason for this is that histograms are used with data which is continuous rather than discrete (where we would use a bar chart). Here the data is technically continuous – it could take any value between £0 and £900 so a histogram is appropriate. We see from the histogram that we obtain a clear and immediate picture of the gross income distribution in Site A. We have a number of people with income in the <£100 group but the highest number of people occur in the next group £100<£200. After this group there is a gradual falling away of the height of the bars indicating fewer and fewer people in the higher income groups.

Drawing a histogram is much the same as drawing a bar chart (although there are one or two differences that we will discuss shortly). One thing we should note is that the frequency is always shown on the vertical axis in a histogram (unlike a bar chart where we could use either).

Student activity

From Table 6.1 construct a histogram for Site B and compare it with that for Site A.

Figure 6.2 shows the histogram for Site B. Notice that we have included the first two intervals <£100 and £100<£200 even though there are no observations for Site B in these intervals. The reason for this is that we want to

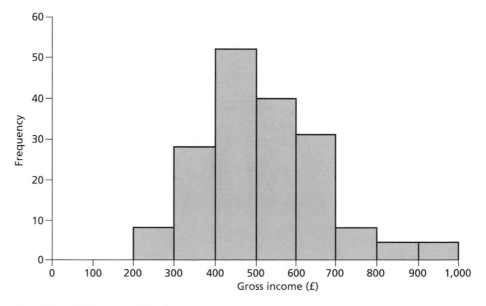

Fig. 6.2   Histogram: Site B
Source: Table 6.1.

compare this histogram with that for Site A so we need to keep the scales as similar as possible. The one thing you might have had difficulty with is the last interval – £900 or more. All the other intervals have clear upper and lower limits but this one only has a lower limit and is technically known as an *open-ended interval*. They are quite common in frequency tables and can cause problems when drawing a corresponding histogram. What we must do is to close off this interval by making a choice about what the upper numerical limit should be. One common approach for dealing with an open-ended interval is to set the width of the interval to the same as most of the other intervals in the frequency table. In this case all the other intervals have a width of £100 so if we give this last interval the same width it will have an upper limit of £1,000.

Drawing the histogram, then, is straightforward. Comparing the two histograms we notice a number of major differences. Site B is more concentrated around the middle of the income values whereas Site A has a considerable 'tail' off to the right. The bulk of Site B values are around the £300 to £700 range whereas for Site A the higher frequency bars are £100–£400. Finally, Site B incomes start in the third interval and there is no one with an income of <£200.

Student activity

Based only on this data would you suggest Site A or Site B for your restaurant?

Overall, we might conclude that Site B has more people in the higher income groups than Site A. Given that we had said that we wanted to aim the restaurant at the relatively affluent target market then it appears – based on this data only – that Site B would be preferable. Note that we are not saying that everyone on Site B has a higher income than everyone in Site A. There is clearly some variation in both sites and some individuals in Site A have relatively high incomes. However, overall Site B has a higher income profile.

It is also worth noting that, although in this example we produced a histogram of the frequencies, we could have also produced a histogram showing the percentage frequencies. This is often useful when we have two sets of data – as in this case – where the total number of observations is different. The construction of such a histogram would be exactly the same.

HISTOGRAMS WITH UNEQUAL INTERVALS

Conveniently, the frequency table we have used for our histograms had intervals which are all the same width. This is not always the case, however, as many frequency tables – particularly those from secondary sources – will have unequal intervals. When this happens we must take care when constructing the histogram. To illustrate this, let us suppose for Site A in Table 6.1 we decided to put the interval £700<£800 and £800<£900 together as there are only a few observations in both intervals. This would give an interval £700<£900 which would have seven observations in it. When it came to drawing the histogram we might produce something like that in Fig. 6.3. The histogram is the same as Fig. 6.1 with the exception of the last bar. This now covers a £200 interval and we have drawn it with a frequency of 7. However, doing this seems to give a distorted view of the relative size of this interval. The bar for this interval looks almost as large – and as important – as that for £400<£500 (which has a frequency of 17). The problem is caused because the interval is larger than all the others – twice as large.

To avoid giving a distorted picture of the size of this interval – in terms of the frequency – we must adjust it. To do so we follow a simple rule. Since the interval is twice the normal size then we must halve the frequency used to plot a bar for that interval. In other words we should have drawn a bar which had a height of 3.5 and not 7. This would have avoided the distortion in Fig. 6.3.

We can generalize this rule as follows:

- If an interval is larger than normal then we divide the frequency by the ratio of that interval width to the normal interval width. Here, the ratio would be 200/100, or 2, and we would divide 7 by 2 to give 3.5.

- If an interval is smaller than normal then we multiply the frequency by the ratio of the normal interval width to the actual interval width.

If the interval had covered, say, £700<£750 the ratio would be 100/50 or 2 and we would multiply the frequency of 7 by 2 to give a frequency of 14 that we would plot on the histogram. The reason for this is that the interval is

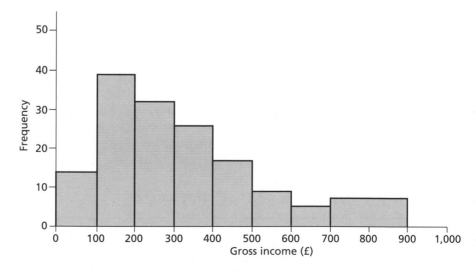

Fig. 6.3   Histogram: Site A – unequal intervals
Source: Table 6.1.

now smaller than normal so we must adjust the frequency upwards when drawing the histogram.

If we can, however, we should avoid having to do any of this by constructing frequency tales with equal intervals (although this is not always possible with every data set).

Student activity

Table 6.2 shows population data for the UK for 1901 and 1991 by age group. Construct a histogram for the 1991 data.

Table 6.2
Age distribution of the enumerated population
(census figures UK: figures are in thousands)

Age group Years	1901	1991
Under 5	4,381	3,766
5–14	8,040	6,997
15–29	10,808	12,383
30–44	7,493	11,974
45–59	4,639	9,448
60–74	2,345	7,955
75 and over	531	3,748
Total	38,237	56,467

Note: The data may not sum to the totals shown because of rounding error.
Source: *Annual Abstract of Statistics 1993.*

Figure 6.4 shows the histogram for this data. Check your version carefully against ours, particularly the first two bars and the last one. Most of the intervals cover 15 years. The first two do not: they cover five years and ten years respectively. Since these intervals have a smaller width than normal we apply the second of our two rules:

Under 5: Actual width 5; Normal width 15
Ratio 15/5 = 3
Actual frequency: 3,766
Adjusted frequency: $3,766 \times 3 = 7,532$

5–14: Actual width 10; Normal width 15
Ratio 15/10 = 1.5
Actual frequency: 6,997
Adjusted frequency: $6,997 \times 1.5 = 10,495.5$

So, these first two intervals must be plotted with a height of 7,532 and 10,495.5 respectively. Make sure you actually did this (as well as you could given the limitations of being this accurate on a graph). The last interval on

181

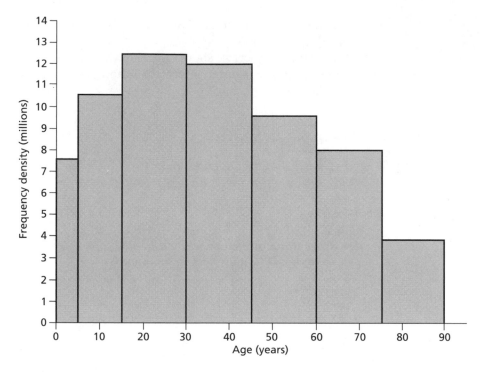

Fig. 6.4   UK age distribution 1991
Source: Table 6.2.

your diagram might also be different. We decided to close the interval at 89 to give it the same width as normal so no adjustment to the frequency is necessary. However, if you closed the interval at 99 (or 100) then you would need to adjust the width. If you had:

> 75–99: Actual width 25; Normal width 15
> Ratio 25/15 = 1.67
> Actual frequency: 3,748
> Adjusted frequency: 3,748/1.67 = 2,244.3

You may also have noticed that we have labelled the vertical axis slightly differently. Technically we are now measuring what is known as the *frequency density* rather than the actual frequencies and it is appropriate to label the diagram accordingly. In this way we, and other users of the diagram, recognize that adjusted frequencies have been used to construct bars for unequal intervals. Notice how different the first two bars would have been had we drawn them using the original (and unadjusted) frequencies. It is also important to realize – perhaps some of you have just found out – that many spreadsheet and graphics packages cannot easily deal with unequal interval widths when drawing a histogram. You should check any software you are using very carefully.

FREQUENCY POLYGONS

Histograms provide us with a good perspective on the distribution of the values within a data set. However, as we began to see earlier, it is difficult to use histograms to compare one data set with another. For this reason we might want to use instead something called a frequency polygon. These are based on the same data as a histogram but rather than plot the height of each interval as a bar a frequency polygon plots the height as a single point. Further this single point is plotted at the midpoint of each interval.

Figure 6.5 shows a frequency polygon for the data for Site A. At the midpoint of each interval and the corresponding height for the frequency we have plotted a single point, marked with a ●. These points have then been joined to their immediate neighbours with straight lines. This then forms the frequency polygon. However, there are a few points we should note about the diagram.

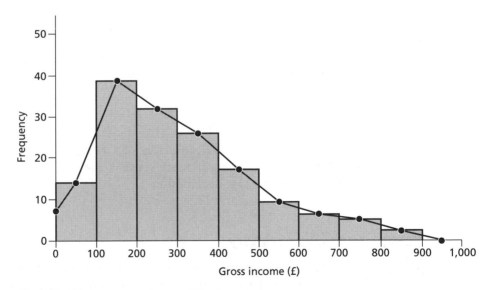

Fig. 6.5   Frequency polygon: Site A

The first is that we would not normally draw *both* the histogram bars and the frequency polygon. We have done so here to illustrate the process. In practice we would draw the frequency polygon directly from the data in the frequency table. The second point relates to the two ends of the frequency polygon. You will notice from Fig. 6.5 that the right-hand end of the polygon has been drawn down to the *x* axis. This is conventional and we do this by plotting a final midpoint on the next interval along (which of course has a zero frequency). We would normally do this at both ends of the polygon. However, in this case, it makes no sense to do this at the left-hand end. The next (zero frequency) interval would actually be from £0 to –£100 which doesn't make sense in people's incomes (which after all is what we are measuring). Instead we close the frequency polygon by plotting a point on the *y* axis which is the midpoint of the height of the bar (and which is effectively a point equal to half of the frequency of this interval).

Figure 6.6 shows what the polygon would look like if we drew it straight from the data. The shape of the distribution is now quite clear. We could now go on to add the frequency polygon for Site B to the same graph to facili-

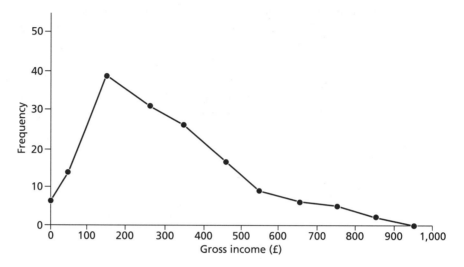

Fig. 6.6   Frequency polygon: Site A

tate comparison. However, since the size of the two samples for the two sites are different it would make more sense to compare percentage distributions rather than frequency distributions.

Student activity

Using the percentages from Table 4.11 construct the percentage frequency polygon for Site A and Site B on the same diagram.

Figure 6.7 shows the polygons. Notice that this time we can close the polygon at Site B at both ends by extending it down to the *x* axis. It also becomes clear that we can now use the polygons to compare the two sites directly. Both sites have a reasonably similar distribution (in terms of their overall shape). But there are one or two key differences. The first is that the polygon for Site B is shifted over to the right compared with Site A. This implies that generally incomes at Site B are higher. Site B also has a smaller 'tail' at the top end of the income scale implying that the data values are less spread out (at least in this part of the distribution) compared with Site A.

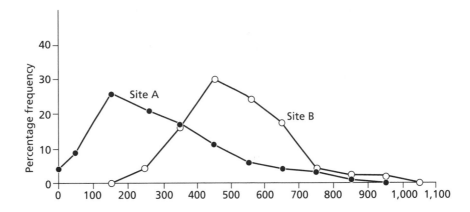

Fig. 6.7 Percentage frequency polygons: Sites A and B
Source: Table 4.11.

Frequency polygons for data with unequal intervals

When we're drawing a frequency polygon for a distribution which has unequal intervals we need to be a little more careful. For intervals which are unequal we cannot use the midpoint values to plot the points. The reason for this can be explained by reference back to Fig. 6.5. You will see that by drawing lines which join midpoints together we are keeping the total area under the polygon line exactly the same as the area of all the bars we drew. We 'lose' part of each bar by drawing the polygon line but the polygon line 'gains' us an area above each bar in recompense. So, the total area stays the same. For unequal intervals, however, this would not work (try it if you're not sure). What we have to do is adapt the method slightly.

Consider Fig. 6.8 which shows a histogram that we might have drawn. The first three intervals are of normal width and we have used the midpoints as usual to draw the polygon lines. The next two intervals are unequal so we must change our approach to ensure the total area remains the same. We do this by finding the midpoint between points A and B and use this to continue the polygon line from the last proper midpoint of the third bar. You will see that the midpoint between A and B is halfway between the frequency for the third bar and the fourth bar. We extend this line downwards until it intersects with the top of the next bar (the frequency) and repeat the process for a point midway between C and D and then E and F. This sounds complicated but in practice is straightforward. Note that we wouldn't normally use both a solid and a dotted line for the polygon. We've done that here just to help you distinguish what is happening.

Student activity

Return to Table 6.2 which showed the age distribution for the UK in 1901 and 1991. Draw a frequency polygon for both years on the same diagram. Do this in stages: calculate the adjusted percentages for the unequal intervals; then draw the polygons.

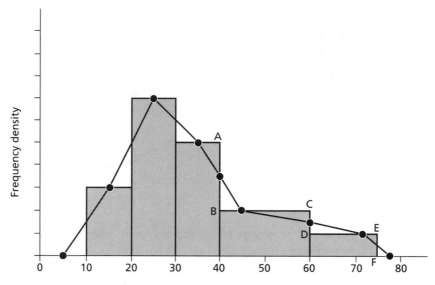

Fig. 6.8   Polygon for unequal intervals

Table 6.3 shows the relevant calculations and also the coordinates that we need to use to draw the polygon for each of the two years in Fig. 6.9. The coordinates for your polygons for the last interval 75 and over may be slightly different from ours if you had a different closing point than 89. Notice also that both polygons come down to the x axis at an age of 97.5. We see from the polygons that the age distributions in the two years were quite different. It is evident that, relatively, in 1901 there were more people in the younger age groups (<25) and that after this the number of people in older age groups

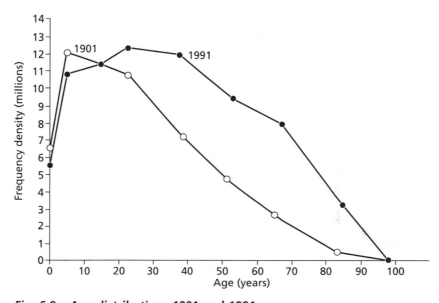

Fig. 6.9   Age distributions 1901 and 1991

tailed off quite quickly. It is also evident that in 1991 there were considerably more in the older age groups (50+ in particular) and the 'tail-off' effect did not really begin until the 70+ age group. We must be particularly careful about using such polygons, however, for unequal interval widths, and not make the mistake of assuming that the actual frequencies can be read directly from the polygon diagram.

Table 6.3
Age distribution of the enumerated population: calculations for the polygons

Age group Years	1901	Adjusted frequency	1991	Adjusted frequency
Under 5	4,381	13,143	3,766	11,298
5–14	8,040	12,060	6,997	10,466
15–29	10,808	10,808	12,383	12,383
30–44	7,493	7,493	11,974	11,974
45–59	4,639	4,639	9,448	9,448
60–74	2,345	2,345	7,955	7,955
75 and over	531	531	3,748	3,748
Total	38,237			56,467

Coordinates of points to be plotted:

1901:
0, 6,572; 5, 12,602; 15, 11,434; 22.5,10,808; 37.5, 7,493; 52.5, 4,639;
67.5, 2,345; 82.5, 531; 97.5, 0

1991:
0, 5,649; 5, 10,882; 15, 11,425; 22.5, 12,383; 37.5, 11,974; 52.5, 9,448;
67.5, 7,955; 82.5, 3,748; 97.5, 0

OGIVES

The final diagram we introduce is the *ogive* (pronounced 'oh-jive') which is actually a cumulative frequency distribution. We saw in Chapter 4 that it is occasionally useful to show frequencies not just in terms of how many observations occur in a given interval but also in terms of the cumulative number of observations up to that point. It is these cumulative frequencies that the ogive shows.

Table 6.4 shows the cumulative frequencies for the income data on the two potential restaurant sites (and is a replica of Table 4.12 in Chapter 4). Rather than plot actual frequencies as in a histogram we can plot the cumulative frequencies. Those for Site A are shown in Fig. 6.10. You will see that we have drawn a bar in each interval with a height which now corresponds with the cumulative frequency rather than the individual frequency. You will see also that we have drawn a line on the diagram. The line joins together the points which show the cumulative frequency at the upper class boundary of each interval. It is this line which is the ogive and as with the frequency polygon we would normally draw it straight onto the diagram without drawing the bars first.

Table 6.4
Gross weekly income: cumulative frequencies – Sites A and B

Income £	Site A No. of responses	Site B No. of responses
< 100	14	0
100 < 200	53	0
200 < 300	85	8
300 < 400	111	36
400 < 500	128	88
500 < 600	137	128
600 < 700	143	159
700 < 800	148	167
800 < 900	150	171
≥ 900	150	175

Source: Table 4.10.

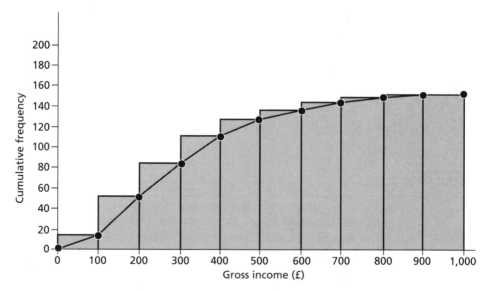

Fig. 6.10   Cumulative frequencies: Site A
Source: Table 6.4.

The same ogive is shown in Fig. 6.11. Notice that the ogive starts at a frequency of 0 and ends at 150, which is the total number of frequencies in the distribution. Clearly, as with the frequency polygon, the ogive is most useful for comparing two or more distributions: Site A with Site B, for example.

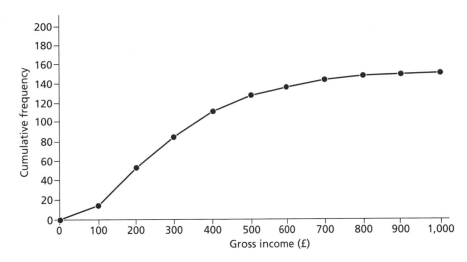

Fig. 6.11   Ogive: Site A

As with the frequency polygon it usually makes more sense to construct ogives for percentage frequencies rather than actual when the data sets are of different size.

Student activity

Construct an ogive relating to cumulative percentage frequencies for Site A and Site B on the same diagram. The data is shown in Table 6.5 (reproduced from Table 4.13).

Table 6.5
Gross weekly income: cumulative percentage frequencies – Sites A and B

Income £	Site A Percentage of responses	Site B Percentage of responses
< 100	9.3	0
100 < 200	35.3	0
200 < 300	56.7	4.6
300 < 400	74.0	20.6
400 < 500	85.3	50.3
500 < 600	91.3	73.1
600 < 700	95.3	90.9
700 < 800	98.7	95.4
800 < 900	100.0	97.7
≥ 900	100.0	100.0
Total	150	175

Source: Table 4.12.

189

Figure 6.12 shows the results. Notice that since both ogives are in percentage form they both start from 0 and end at 100. Notice also how the ogive for Site B starts from (200, 0) since there is a zero frequency in the first two intervals. We can use the ogives to compare the two sites. We see that the ogives are relatively similar at the top income range – from about £700 onwards the two ogive lines are quite close. Below this, however, there is a considerable difference. For example, we see that around 35% of people in Site A have an income less than £200 whereas everyone in Site B has at least this income. The differences in income levels are clearly evident from the ogives.

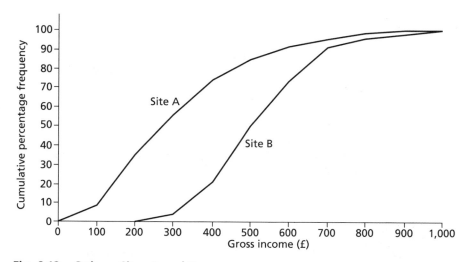

Fig. 6.12   Ogives: Sites A and B

PERCENTILES

In fact we can use the ogives to obtain what are referred to as the *percentiles* of the distribution. For example, suppose we wanted to find the income level that the richest 10% of people in both sites received. This would translate, in statistical jargon, to saying that we wanted to find the 90th percentile (or the income level that divided the bottom 90% of the distribution from the top 10%). It is clear that this would correspond with the 90% point on the vertical scale since our scale measures percentages. Figure 6.13 shows that by extending a line from this point along to both ogives and then down to the income axis we can estimate the corresponding income levels.

For Site A the 90th percentile is approximately £580, and approximately £695 for Site B. This implies that in Site A the highest 10% have an income of at least £580 whilst in Site B the corresponding group have an income of at least £695. Correspondingly of course 90% of people in Site A have an income lower than £580. There was no particular reason for choosing the 90th percentile. We would in practice choose a percentile which had some relevance for the problem. Figure 6.13 also shows the 25th percentile at £160 and £415 for Sites A and B respectively.

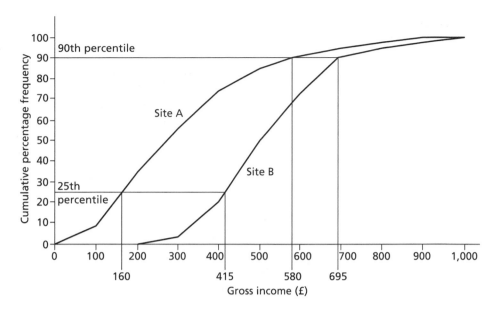

Fig. 6.13   Percentiles

Student activity

From your version of Figure 6.13 estimate:

(**a**) *the 75th percentile*
(**b**) *the 50th percentile*

The estimated results (and how close you are to our numbers will depend on the accuracy and scales on your own graph) are:

		Site A	*Site B*
(**a**)	75th percentile	£410	£610
(**b**)	50th percentile	£220	£500

In fact these percentiles – together with the 25th – are more frequently known as *quartiles* since they divide the distribution into four quarters (where each quarter contains the same percentage of observations). The quartiles are often used to compare distributions. Site A for example, has one-quarter of people with an income higher than £410 but also one-quarter with an income less than £160. By simple definition it must have one half of the people with an income *between* £160 and £410. For Site B the 50th percentile tells us that one half of the people have an income less than £500 (and therefore one half must have an income more than this). By using the quartiles we reinforce the view we have already developed that Site B is a higher income site than Site A. From the quartiles, for example, we see that one-quarter of those in Site B have an income less than £415 whereas for Site A only one-quarter have an income *above* £410.

SUMMARY

In this chapter the techniques relating to frequency tables have been introduced. Such a table is a useful way of aggregating raw data and can be developed in a number of useful ways to construct histograms, frequency polygons and curves, calculate cumulative frequencies and examine percentiles.

Now you have completed this chapter you will appreciate that:

- Frequency tables are a useful means of aggregating a mass of raw data. Such tables are relatively straightforward to construct and easy to interpret. Percentage frequency tables are particularly useful when dealing with data sets of unequal sizes.

- A histogram is a graphical representation of a frequency table and is constructed along the same lines as a simple bar chart. Care must be taken when dealing with unequal intervals to ensure the areas of intervals are comparable.

- An ogive shows cumulative frequencies graphically and is particularly useful for identifying specific percentile values of the distribution.

- Quartiles and percentiles break the distribution into equal parts: quartiles into quarters and percentiles into percentages.

- A frequency polygon is constructed from the histogram and may show more clearly the shape of the distribution.

EXAMPLE

In this example we shall examine how histograms and related diagrams can be used to assist management decision-making. The example is again based on a real organization – a retail company with a number of small supermarkets operating mostly in medium-sized towns. Traditionally, the company's supermarket in a particular town has been the only major shopping outlet for groceries and related products. Lately, however, the company has found itself losing customers and market share to larger out-of-town retail hypermarkets and superstores located in nearby large towns and cities. In one of the company's stores in a particular market town, the company had recently refurbished the delicatessen counter. Such counters were seen as a critical element of the stores' operations – offering a range of fresh meats, fish and cheeses – and market research generally had indicated that customers saw such counters as an indicator of the 'freshness' of a company's products in general. Not only did such a counter generate sales itself but it also acted as a catalyst by encouraging customers to increase their purchases of other products in the store as well as countering the competitive threat of larger superstores.

For the store in question, adverse customer comments about the original deli counter had been forthcoming over the last few years and the counter itself looked somewhat old-fashioned and offered only a limited and somewhat traditional range of fresh deli products. Company management felt that a refurbishment would have a beneficial impact on the store's performance generally and a relatively expensive refurbishment was undertaken at the end of 1994. The company now wished to assess the impact that the refurbishment had had on deli counter sales both to assess whether the investment appeared to have been worthwhile in a strict financial sense and also to assess whether such refurbishment should be undertaken in other stores. Through the company's EPoS system it was possible to collect (secondary) data on daily sales of the deli counter for a four month period at the start of 1995 and also for the comparable four month period at the start of 1994. This then provided a set of sales data after the refurbishment and before the refurbishment.

Figure 6.14 shows the frequency polygons of daily sales before and after the refurbishment. The profile of daily sales before the refurbishment is considerably and noticeably different from that after. The before profile is a much more concentrated one and at generally lower daily sales levels than the after situation, with daily sales spread fairly equally over the sales range £37.50 to £177.50. The after profile is quite different with most day's sales

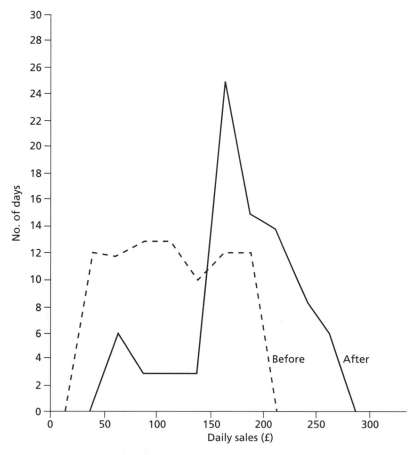

Fig. 6.14 Daily sales: polygons

in the region of £175 to £250, although we note the mini-peak on the left of the polygon in the interval £50<£75.

Figure 6.15 shows the same data but in the form of a cumulative percentage ogive, again before and after the refurbishment. We note that the before ogive is to the left of the after ogive, implying that daily sales before the refurbishment were consistently below those after. As an indicator, the figure shows the 50th percentile at approximately £107 before refurbishment and approximately £178 after. These figures imply that before refurbishment daily sales were below £107 50% of the time whereas after refurbishment daily sales were above £178 50% of the time (and from the before ogive we can also estimate that only 14% of daily sales were above £178 – found by extending the dotted line from £178 upwards to the before ogive and then across to the vertical axis). Again, we have confirmation that daily deli sales after refurbishment are higher than those before.

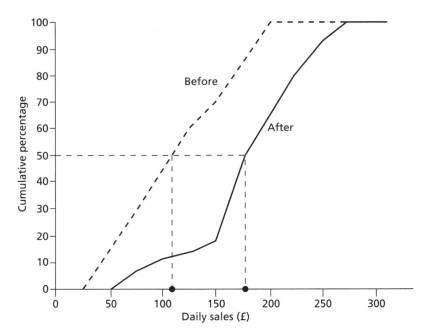

Fig. 6.15   Daily sales: ogives

Finally, Fig. 6.16 shows the average sales before and after refurbishment for each day of the week in the form of a bar chart (and just because we used bar charts in the previous chapter doesn't mean we can't use them as part of our analysis in this one!). We see quite clearly that average daily sales are greater for the after refurbishment situation for every day of the week. This is quite an important finding, since without this piece of analysis we would know that daily sales were generally higher but not that they were consistently higher on every day of the week. Notice also that the weekly profile of sales has not changed since refurbishment. That is, in the before situation Sunday saw the lowest average daily sales figure followed by an increase on Monday,

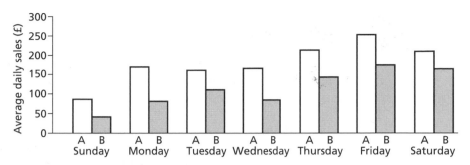

Fig. 6.16   Average daily sales before and after refurbishment

a further increase on Tuesday, a slight fall on Wednesday (although the supermarket was open all day on Wednesday many of the neighbouring small shops in the town centre closed for half a day with a subsequent knock-on effect on the supermarket's takings). Following this, average daily sales increased through Thursday, peaked on Friday and dropped again on Saturday. The after situation is virtually the same in terms of this pattern implying that customers' general shopping patterns as a result of the refurbishment have not really altered, simply the about they buy from the deli counter (which has increased).

The company concluded that the refurbishment had generally given rise to an increase in daily sales on the deli counter and further, using statistics we introduce in the next chapter, were able to quantify this increase in financial terms. This then enabled them to assess whether the cost of the refurbishment was 'profitable' in terms of generating additional sales (they concluded that it was profitable and that a further series of refurbishment in other supermarkets was not only financially justified but would also strengthen the company's competitive position).

 ## SELF-REVIEW QUESTIONS

1 *Approximately how many intervals should a frequency table contain?*

2 *What are the two main problems encountered when constructing frequency tables?*

3 *What is an ogive?*

4 *Into how many parts do the quartiles divide the distribution?*

5 *What is the difference between a histogram and a frequency polygon?*

6 *Under what circumstances would it be better to show a histogram in percentage terms rather than in absolute frequencies?*

7 *Which diagram would use the midpoints: an ogive or a frequency polygon?*

8 *How are unequal intervals treated when constructing a histogram?*

STUDENT EXERCISES

1 Return to Table 4.4 in Chapter 4. Using the diagrams introduced in this chapter compare car production in 1982 with that for 1992.

2 Table 6.6 shows data relating to the age at marriage of males and females in the UK in 1980 and in 1990. Using diagrams and percentiles compare and contrast the data between the sexes and between the years.

Table 6.6
Marriages: UK
(figures shown are numbers)

Age at marriage (years)	1980		1990	
	Males	Females	Males	Females
Under 21	52,644	127,542	15,930	45,626
21–24	141,776	133,309	92,270	119,037
25–29	98,831	65,818	122,800	103,209
30–34	48,104	34,064	56,966	42,794
35–44	39,427	30,699	49,984	38,983
45–54	19,360	15,011	21,996	16,825
55 and over	18,304	12,003	15,464	8,936

Source: *Annual Abstract of Statistics 1993.*

3 Table 6.7 shows unemployment by age and by sex in January 1993. Using diagrams and percentiles compare males and females. Update the table with the latest published data available and, using appropriate diagrams, assess the changes that have occurred since January 1993.

Table 6.7
Unemployment by age and sex January 1993
(figures show the percentage in each age group and refer to the UK)

Age	Males	Females
Under 20 years	6.9	13.0
20–29	37.3	39.8
30–39	23.3	17.0
40–49	16.3	16.2
50–59	13.9	14.0
60 or over	2.3	0.1
Total number	2,353,826	1,959,245

Source: *Regional Trends 1994.*

4 Table 6.8 shows the size of manufacturing units in the UK in 1992. Using diagrams and percentiles comment on the data.

Collect comparable data for an earlier year and compare changes between the two years.

Table 6.8
Size of manufacturing units in 1992: analysis by number of employees

No. of employees	No. of manufacturing units
1–9	99,767
10–19	18,994
20–49	17,389
50–99	7,563
100–199	4,690
200–499	3,165
500–999	873
1,000 or over	383
Total	152,824

Source: *Annual Abstract of Statistic 1993.*

5 Table 6.9 shows data on the duration of marriage for those couples divorcing in 1971 and those divorcing in 1990. Compare the changes over this period.

Table 6.9
Divorce by duration of marriage: Great Britain
(figures shown are percentages)

Duration of marriage (years)	1971	1990
0–2	1.2	9.5
3–4	12.2	13.7
5–9	30.5	27.5
10–14	19.4	17.9
15–19	12.6	12.9
20–24	9.5	9.3
25–29	5.8	4.9
30 or over	8.9	4.1
Total number (000s)	79.2	165.7

Source: *Social Trends 1994.*

6 A company is currently undertaking negotiations with a trade union representing the sales staff who work in the company's stores throughout the
country. The trade union is submitting a claim for increased wages for the sales
staff and is basing part of its argument around the fact that clerical and admin-
istrative staff in the company are much better paid than the sales staff and that
this differential should be reduced by giving the sales staff a pay increase.

The head of the accounts department has taken two samples of data from
the payroll file held on the computer at head office. In both cases the sample
was of 50 employees selected at random and shows their typical weekly salary.

Weekly salary of 50 clerical/admin. staff, measured in £s:

119.00	184.82	146.41	137.22	190.42
147.60	134.40	153.58	164.40	98.80
153.60	151.62	140.82	147.21	98.80
123.60	144.86	118.80	137.93	92.41
118.40	158.00	166.50	136.00	104.81
129.62	111.20	101.22	187.62	154.00
140.29	172.71	161.62	124.02	155.62
152.42	173.22	101.20	130.82	176.82
139.62	166.82	164.82	122.82	128.40
160.71	172.00	150.82	145.43	148.42

Weekly salary of 50 sales staff, measured in £s:

100.29	123.58	117.22	90.42	106.82
119.62	140.82	94.40	126.00	138.00
116.71	98.80	97.21	98.80	145.60
114.40	96.55	137.93	88.88	128.40
121.62	101.22	136.00	92.41	108.41
104.86	161.62	124.02	104.81	88.81
128.00	101.20	130.82	154.00	95.61
111.20	83.62	133.60	155.62	106.81
116.82	164.82	122.82	152.41	103.21
106.41	110.82	145.43	115.38	148.42

(a) Using the data in the above tables construct suitable frequency tables for
the two sets of data.

(b) Draw a histogram for each frequency table.

(c) Construct a frequency polygon for each histogram.

(d) Using the frequency tables, histograms and frequency polygons as appropriate compare the two distributions for similarities and differences.

(e) Do you think the trade union is correct to argue that sales staff are paid
less than clerical/admin. staff?

7 Using the same data as in exercise **6** above construct suitable ogives for the two distributions.

(**a**) What proportion of sales staff earn less than £100 per week?

(**b**) What is the corresponding proportion of clerical/admin. staff?

(**c**) What does a comparison of these two percentages reveal about the comparative pay levels of the two groups?

(**d**) What proportion of sales staff earn more than £175 per week?

(**e**) What is the corresponding figure for clerical/admin. staff?

7 MANAGEMENT STATISTICS

INTRODUCTION

So far we have looked at a number of ways of providing a general description of a set of data in which we have some interest. We have seen how tables, diagrams and some simple arithmetic involving percentages can help us develop an overview of a set of data. What we now require to do is to move away from the description of data to its analysis and this is where we need to start developing statistical and mathematical skills that can be applied in business. In this chapter we introduce a number of common management statistics.

LEARNING OBJECTIVES

By the end of this chapter you should be able to:

- calculate the mean and median for both raw and grouped data;
- calculate the standard deviation for raw and grouped data;
- calculate the coefficient of variation and the coefficient of skewness;
- calculate index numbers;
- use index numbers to deflate a time series;
- apply such statistics to common business situations.

THE NEED FOR STATISTICS

Tables and diagrams are all very well at presenting an overview of a set of data. However, they provide us with little detailed numerical information about a set of data – they rely after all on a visual presentation of that data. It is numerical – or statistical – data that we will often require to help us reach some decision. There are two specific statistical measures that we will often need:

- a measure of an average value in a data set;
- a measure of variability around the average.

Consider the following scenario. You have been successful at a job interview and a post of trainee business analyst in a national bank is on offer. The starting salary on offer is quite low but with an eye to the future you think that the chance of promotion – and future high salary – might make the job worth taking. You ask the personnel manager: 'How much do business analysts in the bank earn per annum once they are past the trainee stage?' Back comes the reply that the average annual salary of business analysts is £30,000. That's sufficiently encouraging to make you take the job. A couple of months after starting, however, you're concerned to realize after talking to the other business analysts that their salary levels are considerably below this £30,000 figure. Eventually you realize that for the nine other analysts working with you their salary levels are as shown in Table 7.1 It is evident that two senior people in the section have very high salaries but everyone else is considerably below the £30,000 average figure that was quoted.

Table 7.1
Gross annual salary: business analysis section (£)

70,000	65,000	18,000	17,000	19,000
19,000	21,000	20,000	21,000	

Statistics has a very mixed reputation. As we have seen from this simple example statistics can be used to inform or to mislead – either deliberately or accidentally. Before using the statistic we were given to make a decision we should have been more careful in evaluating that statistic – identifying what it told us about the situation and equally what it did not tell us. Through the rest of this chapter we shall look at a number of common management statistics and assess how they are calculated and what they tell us about some data set.

AVERAGES

We used the term 'average' earlier without bothering to define precisely what we mean by average. Everyone uses the term: average salary, average age, average height, average time unemployed and so on. In fact, just about everyone already knows how to calculate an average.

House sales average 22 weeks

Time to move

Average number of weeks to sell a home

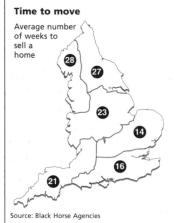

Source: Black Horse Agencies

It takes 22 weeks on average to sell a home in England, according to an analysis by Black Horse Agencies, the estate agency chain owned by Lloyds Bank. However, homes in north-west England take twice as long to sell as those in the eastern counties. The national average is for a sale to be agreed at about 92 per cent of the original asking price after nine potential buyers have viewed the property. In the south-east up to 13 potential buyers view a property before a sale is agreed.

Properties in the south-east and eastern counties sell for 94 per cent of the asking price on average, compared with 88 per cent in the north-west.

Simon London

 Source: *Financial Times*, 17 August 1995

Student activity

Return to Table 7.1. From the individual salary figures given calculate the average salary.

The method you probably adopted was to add together the nine individual salary figures and then divide by 9 (since there are nine people). This would give:

£270,000/9 = £30,000

(confirming the personnel officer didn't actually lie to us). In fact, this average is technically known as the arithmetic mean.

The arithmetic mean

For a set of data like that in Table 7.1 the arithmetic mean is calculated as:

$$\text{Mean} = \frac{\Sigma x}{n}$$

where x refers to the individual numbers in the data set and n is the number of data items in the data set. The symbol Σ indicates that we are to sum all the x values (refer back to Chapter 2 if you are unsure about the Σ symbol). Here we would have:

$$\Sigma x = 270,000$$
$$n = 9$$
$$\text{and } \Sigma x/n = 270,000/9$$
$$= £30,000$$

So the formula for the arithmetic mean is simply a shorthand way of telling us how to calculate the statistic.

However, as we saw with this example, the mean – as an average – is not really typical of this data set. Two items in the data set are way above the mean value – £70,000 and £65,000 – whilst the rest are considerably below. In fact, no one in this analyst's section actually has a salary of £30,000. It is for this reason that a statistic like the mean should be used with extreme caution in reaching any conclusions about the data set. We should only use such a statistic if we are sure it is a typical value for the data.

We might be able to check this by looking at the raw data directly – as in Table 7.1 – to see whether the mean does appear to be typical or not ('eyeballing the data' as it is often referred to). However, it is clear that with a large data set this becomes quite impractical. We could not readily tell just from visual inspection of the original data whether the mean was typical if the data set consisted of 50, 500 or 5,000 individual data items. For this reason we must try to assess the mean value by using other statistics which might help us assess how typical it is for the data set we are looking at.

The median

One way we might do this is to calculate a second measure of average known as the median. The median is a measure of average which represents the middle value of a data set which has been ordered (that is, has been ranked from lowest value to highest). For the salary example we can obtain the median by:

● ranking the data;
● counting along until we get to the data item in the middle.

This item will be the median value.

Student activity

Determine the median for Table 7.1.

If we rank the data we have:

17,000 18,000 19,000 19,000 20,000 21,000 21,000 65,000 70,000

Median

and counting along until we get to the middle item, we see that the median is £20,000. We could genuinely refer to this as the average salary for this group which is why we should use the terms mean and median to distinguish between our two averages.

The median has one useful feature that the mean does not. The median always divides the data set into two equal parts: one part falls below the median and one part falls above. That is, four people have a salary below the median and four a salary above. We can say this even if we have not seen the raw data in Table 7.1 because the median always divides a data set up in this way. For the mean we have no way of knowing how many data items fall either side other than by checking the raw data in the original data set. We also see that, in this case, the median might be a 'better' measure of average than the mean since much of the data is closer to the median value than to the mean value.

However, with larger data sets – where we may not have seen the actual individual data items – comparing the mean and median values might be useful. We see that in this case the mean value, at £30,000, is higher than the median, at £20,000. What can we infer from this (assuming we had not seen the raw data)? We know that the mean includes all the data in its calculation – including any extreme values (high or low). The median, however, simply counts along the ordered data until it gets to the middle: extreme high values beyond that are effectively ignored. Since the mean is above the median and since the mean includes all the data it can be inferred that there must be some extreme high values in the data pulling the mean value above the median and above much of the data set. The reverse would be true if the mean were below the median – this would imply that there were some extreme low values in the data set.

Student activity

The analyst who is currently on a salary of £70,000 has just received a pay increase putting that person on £90,000. Without doing any calculations, what would you expect to happen to the mean value of £30,000 and to the median of £20,000?

We would expect the mean to increase since there will be an increase of £20,000 in the total used to calculate the mean (and we might mentally estimate that the mean will increase by just over £2,000 (20,000/9)). We would not expect the median to change at all, however, since the middle value will remain unaltered.

VARIABILITY

It has also become clear that in addition to calculating an average for a data set we also want some statistical measure of how variable the individual data items are around the average (whether it is the mean or median we are using). After all, we could have two data sets both with a mean of £30,000 but with very different variability around that mean within the individual data items. We might have one data set with considerable variability as in Table 7.1 and another data set with the same mean but where more of the people in that group earned a salary close to the mean. Table 7.2 shows another section in the bank where nine people also have a mean salary of

£30,000 but we see that the individual salaries are much closer to the mean. Variability around the mean in this case would be more or less zero.

There are a number of measures of variability that we can use and we shall introduce them in term. You should also note that such variability is also referred to as *dispersion*.

Table 7.2
Annual salaries

29,000	32,000	28,000	30,500	31,000
29,900	29,000	31,100	29,500	

The range

The simplest measure is known as the *range* which is the difference between the highest value in that data set and the lowest and is a simple measure of the overall spread of the data. From Table 7.1 we find that the highest value is £70,000 and the lowest is £17,000 so the range is given by:

Range: Highest − Lowest = 70,000 − 17,000 = £53,000

That is, £53,000 separates the lowest salary from the highest.

Student activity

Determine the range for Table 7.2 and compare it with that for Table 7.1.

From Table 7.2 the range is:

Range: 32,000 − 28,000 = £4,000

That is, only £4,000 separates the highest and lowest salaries. Compare this with the £53,000 for Table 7.1 and it is clear that there is a much wider range of salaries in Table 7.1 than Table 7.2.

The range is quite useful as a quick measure of variability. However, it only uses two numbers: the highest and lowest and provides no indication of the variability of all the items in the data set.

Standard deviation

One statistic which does use all the data in its calculation of the variability of a data set is the *standard deviation*. This is a commonly used statistic and is important in more advanced statistical analysis. The standard deviation provides us with a statistic which measures the variability of all the items in the data set from the mean. For a small data set the calculations are straight-forward although for a larger data set we would use typically either a spreadsheet or a specialist statistics package.

Table 7.3
Deviation from the mean

Actual salary x	Mean $\bar{X}$	Deviation $(x - \bar{X})$
70,000	30,000	+40,000
65,000	30,000	+35,000
18,000	30,000	−12,000
17,000	30,000	−13,000
19,000	30,000	−11,000
19,000	30,000	−11,000
21,000	30,000	−9,000
20,000	30,000	−10,000
21,000	30,000	−9,000

We wish to measure, for the data set as a whole, by how much salaries vary from the mean. A logical first step, then, is to find the difference between each salary and the mean that we calculated. This is shown in Table 7.3. The first column, x, shows the individual salaries. The second column shows the mean salary and we denote this with the symbol, $\bar{X}$ (pronounced 'x bar').

The difference between each individual salary and the mean is then easily calculated as $(x - \bar{X})$. We see that some deviations are positive (implying the actual salary is above the mean) and some are negative (implying that the actual salary is below the mean). Similarly, some deviations are relatively small whilst others are quite large. Remember what we are trying to do. We are trying to calculate a statistic which shows variability from the mean, not just for any one salary (data item) but for the data set as a whole. It seems as if we could now simply total all the individual deviations and divide by 9 to give an average deviation from the mean.

Student activity

Sum the individual deviations. What total did you get? Why?

By summing the individual totals we get a result of 0 (and clearly the average deviation would be zero also). On reflection, the reason for this must be that since the mean is an average of all the individual salaries the deviations around the mean must cancel each other out (since some will be higher and some lower). In fact, you will realize that this total must always be 0 for any data set (and is a useful check that we've not made an arithmetic mistake in our calculations).

So how do we proceed to get a statistic to show variability for the whole data set? One approach is as follows. What we are actually intent upon is the size of the deviations from the mean and we're not really interested in whether the individual deviations are positive or negative. One way of removing the cancelling effect of positive and negative signs is to square each number (remembering that multiplying two minuses makes a plus). This is shown in Table 7.4. You will see that we have taken each individual deviation and squared it (don't worry that we've got ridiculously large numbers to work with for the moment). This gives a total of 3,642,000,000 which we can now average over the data set by dividing by 9 to give 404,666,666.7 as an average squared deviation for the data.

Table 7.4
Squared deviations from the mean

Actual salary x	Mean $\overline{X}$	Deviation $(x - \overline{X})$	Squared deviation $(x - \overline{X})^2$
70,000	30,000	40,000	1,600,000,000
65,000	30,000	35,000	1,225,000,000
18,000	30,000	−12,000	144,000,000
17,000	30,000	−13,000	169,000,000
19,000	30,000	−11,000	121,000,000
19,000	30,000	−11,000	121,000,000
21,000	30,000	−9,000	81,000,000
20,000	30,000	−10,000	100,000,000
21,000	30,000	−9,000	81,000,000
Total		0	3,642,000,000

Given that we squared the original deviations we need to reverse that process in order to get back to sensible units of measurement. That is we need to take the square root of this number:

$$\sqrt{404,666,666.7} = 20,116.33$$

This number is the standard deviation and is measured in the same units as the mean, that is the standard deviation for this data is £20,116.33

Remember how the statistic was calculated to help you understand what it means. It is an indication of the deviation of the individual items in the data set from the mean of that data set. Other things being equal a high standard deviation implies considerable variation within the data set from the mean. A small standard deviation implies relatively little variability. If you think about it you will realize that the smallest possible value for the standard deviation would be zero implying that every single item in the data set was exactly the same as the mean. Technically, there is no upper limit as to what the standard deviation could be – the higher it is then the more variability in the data set around the mean value.

Student activity

Calculate the standard deviation for Table 7.2 and compare it with that for Table 7.1.

The calculations are shown in Table 7.5 to give a standard deviation of:

Table 7.5
Squared deviations from the mean

Actual salary x	Mean $\bar{X}$	Deviation $(x - \bar{X})$	Squared deviation $(x - \bar{X})^2$
29,000	30,000	−1,000	1,000,000
32,000	30,000	2,000	4,000,000
28,000	30,000	−2,000	4,000,000
30,500	30,000	500	250,000
31,000	30,000	1,000	1,000,000
29,900	30,000	−100	10,000
29,000	30,000	−1,000	1,000,000
31,100	30,000	1,100	1,210,000
29,500	30,000	−500	250,000
Total		0	12,720,000

$$\sqrt{12,720,000/9} = \sqrt{1,413,333.3} = £1,188.84$$

We see that the standard deviation for the second group is much lower than that of the first and we would conclude that variability around the mean of the second group was lower than variability around the first.

We can generalize the formula for the calculation of the standard deviation as:

$$\text{Standard deviation} = \sqrt{\frac{\Sigma (x - \bar{X})^2}{n}}$$

Coefficient of variation

In our example, both sets of data had the same mean. Frequently this will not be the case and if the means of two groups differ it can be difficult to compare their standard deviations (which after all use the mean in the calculations).

To help us compare two, or more, standard deviations, particularly when the means of data sets differ, we can use something known as the *coefficient of variation*. This is given as:

$$CV = \frac{SD}{\text{Mean}} \times 100$$

That is, the coefficient of variation (CV) is simply the ratio of the standard deviation (SD) to the mean expressed as a percentage. For the data set referring to business analysts this would be:

$$CV = \frac{20,116.33}{30,000} \times 100 = 67.1\%$$

and indicates that in this data set the standard deviation takes a value which is 67.1% of the mean value. Again, other things being equal, a higher CV implies more variability in the data set relative to the mean. For the second data set we have:

$$CV = \frac{1,188.84}{30,000} \times 100 = 3.9\%$$

confirming the considerably lower level of variability in this data set. We shall see shortly that such coefficients are useful for comparing relative dispersion between two or more data sets.

Quartiles

The standard deviation is a common measure of variability but it measures variability around the mean. What about variability around the other average – the median?

Such variability is often measured using something known as the *interquartile range* or IQR. The IQR is given as:

$$IQR = Q_3 - Q_1$$

where Q_3 is the upper quartile and Q_1 is the lower quartile. You will remember that we introduced quartiles in the previous chapter. The upper quartile is the value that divides the data set so that one-quarter of the data takes a higher numerical value and three-quarters less whilst the lower quartile divides the data so that three-quarters takes a higher value and one-quarter less. (The median is often shown as Q_2.) The IQR is then simply the difference between these two quartiles.

This sounds straightforward but the implications are important as illustrated in Fig. 7.1. The IQR – the difference between the upper and lower quartiles – contains the central 50% of the data, as illustrated in the diagram. It is important to realize,

---

Pay increases hold steady

Settlement trends

% increase in basic rates
(based on a rolling analysis)

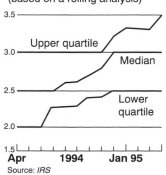

Source: *IRS*

There are no signs of an upsurge in the level of wages in the current pay round, in spite of a falling trend in unemployment. The latest evidence from Industrial Relations Services is that median pay awards are steady at around 3 per cent, while incomes Data Services points to a growing number slipping over the 3 per cent level. Even the overall rise in earnings is climbing only at an annual rate of 3.5 per cent, not much above the 3.3 per cent retail prices index for April. IRS points out that the median-level figure has been the same for five consecutive months. However, a wage gap does appear to be growing between a public sector held in check by a government pay bill freeze at a 2.5 per cent median level while private sector deals are running at 3 per cent.   *Robert Taylor*

Source: *Financial Times*, 6 June 1995

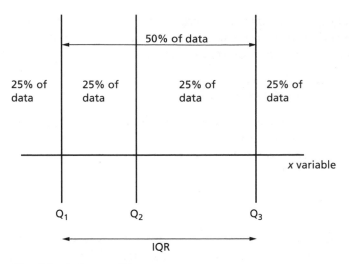

Fig. 7.1   Interquartile range

however, that Q_1 and Q_3 may not be equidistant from Q_2, the median. That is, the gap between Q_1 and Q_2 and between Q_2 and Q_3 may be different depending on the shape of the distribution (the shape of the frequency polygon). As we shall soon see a difference in these two gaps can be used to infer the shape of the frequency polygon.

In our simple examples there is little point in actually calculating the quartiles and the IQR as the data set is so small. We shall see their use in a larger example shortly. In practice, to obtain the lower quartile we would proceed as we did for the median:

- Order the data from lowest to highest.
- Count along until we are one-quarter through the data set.
- This item then gives the Q_1 value.

For the upper quartile we would proceed in exactly the same way but count along until we were three-quarters of the way through the data set.

SKEWNESS

The final statistic we need to introduce before we can put all of them to use in analysis of business data is the *coefficient of skewness*. Given that we are trying to use various statistics which provide us with a reliable description of a set of data, the one aspect that is missing is a statistic which provides us with a picture of the overall shape of the distribution of the data. We could of course construct a histogram or frequency polygon but a quick statistical summary would frequently be useful. This is provided by the coefficient of skewness which is given by:

$$Sk = \frac{3(\text{Mean} - \text{Median})}{\text{Standard deviation}}$$

In general the numerical value of the coefficient will fall into one of three categories:

- negative;
- zero;
- positive.

To understand the implications of this consider the distributions shown in Figs 7.2–7.4. Figure 7.2 shows the distribution of some data set which is relatively symmetrical. It has no extreme high or low values. In such a case the mean and the median will take similar or identical numerical values. If this is the case then the skewness formula will also take a value of zero (since Mean – Median will be zero and the whole formula then becomes zero).

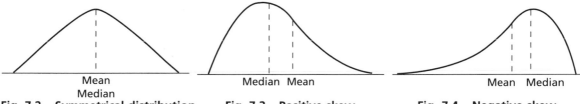

| Fig. 7.2 **Symmetrical distribution** | Fig. 7.3 **Positive skew** | Fig. 7.4 **Negative skew** |

In Fig. 7.3, however, we have a few extreme high values in the data set. As we saw earlier in this chapter this will tend to pull the mean value higher than the median. In the skewness formula the term (Mean – Median) will be positive and since the standard deviation must always be non-negative (since we square all values) the skewness coefficient must be positive also. In other words, if we are told that the coefficient of skewness for a data set is positive we know the distribution will be similar to that in Fig. 7.3. Moreover, the more extreme the high values the higher the coefficient value will be. This type of distribution is described as having a positive skew.

The opposite situation takes place in Fig. 7.4 where we have a few extreme low values in the data set. This will now pull the mean below the median and the skewness coefficient will take a negative value. By knowing the coefficient of skewness for a data set we can infer the general shape of the distribution.

USING THE STATISTICS

We are now in a position to apply the various statistics we have introduced to help us describe and analyse a data set. In practice, we would be likely to use all the statistics we have looked at together rather than one at a time. To illustrate this we shall use the statistics provided in Table 7.6. This shows the output from a specialist statistical package which has analysed the data we have looked at before regarding Site A and Site B for a restaurant. You will recollect that we had collected data on a sample of people's gross income.

Table 7.6
Statistical analysis of Site A and Site B

	Site A	Site B
Observations	150	175
Minimum	52.5	217
Maximum	871	950.25
Range	818.5	733.25
Mean	303.36	522.56
Standard deviation	184.304	143.595
Lower quartile	155	435.75
Median	260	497
Upper quartile	402.5	610.75
Interquartile range	247.5	175
Coeff. of variation	60.75	27.48
Skewness	0.9	0.6

Student activity

Using the statistics in Table 7.6 compare income distributions in the two sites.

There is actually quite a lot of information in the statistical analysis provided. We note first of all that Site B has a higher mean income than Site A – £523 and £303 respectively, a difference of over £200. From the data on the range we see that this difference appears to occur mostly at the bottom end of the income range. Maximum income in Site A is £871 and £950 in Site B – not a very large difference at all. At the bottom of the income groups, however, there is much more of a difference. Minimum income in Site A is just over £50 whilst it is just over £200 in Site B.

Site A appears to have not just a lower mean income but also more variability around this mean. This is confirmed by both the standard deviation and the coefficient of variation. The standard deviation is higher in Site A and the coefficient of variation is considerably higher – 61% compared with 27%.

So, we know that mean income is some £220 higher in Site B but how representative is the mean income? We see that for both sets of data the median is below the mean at £260 for Site A and £497 for Site B. The skewness coefficient indicates that both distributions are positively skewed implying a small number of extreme high incomes. The skewness is more pronounced in Site A: 0.9 compared with 0.6.

We can also use the data on quartiles and the interquartile range. First of all the IQR for Site B is lower: £175 compared with £247.5. Again, this confirms our view that variability in Site B incomes is generally lower. A smaller IQR contains the middle 50% of incomes. Looking at the quartiles we can also extract some useful information. First, we see that one-quarter of Site A have an income above £402.5 (the upper quartile) whilst three-quarters of Site B have an income above £435.75 (the lower quartile). We confirm the impression that overall Site B has a higher income group and that variability of incomes in Site B is less than in Site A.

We can also use the quartiles to confirm that the disparity of incomes between the two sites exists at all income levels. The difference between the two lower quartiles is some £280 implying that someone who is at the lower quartile income point on Site B has an income this much higher than their counterpart in Site A. For the median person this difference is about £240 and for the person at the upper quartile point the difference is some £210. At all these points on the distribution income levels on Site B are over £200 higher than at Site A.

In conclusion, you should not underestimate what we have just done. We have been able to build up a detailed and reasonably accurate picture of two sets of data by using only a handful of statistics. If we understand what the statistics reveal and can interpret them in the specific context of a business situation we have a very powerful source of information.

Salaries, Bonuses and Car Allowances in City of London Finance

Position	Lower quartile £	Median salary £	Upper quartile £	Average salary £	Average bonus %	Car provision % with	Car or allowance £ value	Car or allowance £ year
Corporate finance head	100,000	112,500	156,000	127,363	59.5	100	24,543	8,195
Capital markets head	137,500	145,000	165,500	149,333	83.7	100	30,333	9,540
Bond sales head	85,000	97,375	105,000	98,344	36.3	87	20,039	7,908
Fund m'ment director	108,000	125,000	146,500	126,968	44.4	100	26,083	9,340
Eurobond trading head	82,000	110,000	133,895	114,945	45.4	91	19,060	8,008
Equity trading head	85,000	100,000	143,750	111,500	70.0	100	19,250	8,089
Private banking head	82,151	95,001	105,000	93,576	18.7	100	25,000	8,417
Head of research	85,000	101,035	130,000	101,717	41.8	88	19,537	7,075
Financial director	66,700	77,152	90,000	88,408	23.2	83	21,753	7,494
Chief fx dealer	62,502	80,850	92,754	81,978	23.9	73	19,341	6,657
Legal services head	58,000	70,000	80,000	69,867	20.5	85	20,472	6,916
Personnel director	58,500	68,000	82,500	73,444	22.8	89	19,813	7,224
Money markets head	57,020	65,635	75,000	68,306	30.9	87	17,643	5,673
D–P director	55,907	67,000	85,000	70,729	28.1	86	16,732	6,670
Credit manager	35,000	45,000	50,500	43,228	10.8	68	15,263	5,459
Customer services head	26,430	31,500	39,300	32,289	8.7	37	12,374	4,692

Source: Day Associates, Suite 2.31, 75 Whitechapel Rd, London E1 1DU: tel 0171 375 1397, fax 0171 375 1723

Source: *Financial Times*, 9 August 1995

STATISTICS FOR AGGREGATED DATA

So far, we have seen how we can calculate a range of statistics for raw data. We are frequently in the position of analysing aggregated – or grouped – data that comes from a secondary source. We need to be able to calculate comparable statistics for such data where we do not have access to the individual values in the data set. We shall illustrate the various calculations with reference to the aggregated income data for Site A and Site B in Table 7.7.

Table 7.7
Gross weekly income: Sites A and B

Income £	Site A No. of responses	Site B No. of responses
< 100	14	0
100 < 200	39	0
200 < 300	32	8
300 < 400	26	28
400 < 500	17	52
500 < 600	9	40
600 < 700	6	31
700 < 800	5	8
800 < 900	2	4
≥ 900	0	4
Total	150	175

Source: Table 4.10.

Arithmetic mean

To calculate the mean for raw data we add together the individual data items and divide by n, the number of data items. For aggregated data like that in Table 7.7 we cannot do this since we do not have the individual data items. We see from Table 7.7, for example, that there are 14 people in Site A with an income of less than £100 but we do not know the exact values of these 14 items.

To calculate the mean we must make an assumption: that items within an interval all take the same value – that of the midpoint of that interval. So, for the 14 people in the <£100 interval the midpoint would be £50 and we assume that all 14 have this income level. To sum the items in this interval we can then simply multiply the frequency (14) by the midpoint (50). We then repeat this for all the intervals in the data set as in Table 7.8.

Table 7.8
Calculations for the mean: Site A

Interval	Midpoint (m)	Frequency (f)	(fm)
< 100	50	14	700
100 < 200	150	39	5,850
200 < 300	250	32	8,000
300 < 400	350	26	9,100
400 < 500	450	17	7,650
500 < 600	550	9	4,950
600 < 700	650	6	3,900
700 < 800	750	5	3,750
800 < 900	850	2	1,700
≥ 900	950	0	0
		150	45,600

Each interval midpoint (m) has been multiplied by its frequency (f) and these totals (fm) have been summed to give 45,600 (our estimate of the total income of those 150 people). Since we have 150 data items the mean is then:

$$\frac{\Sigma fm}{\Sigma f} = \frac{45,600}{150} = £304$$

giving an estimate of the mean from the aggregated data of £304.

Student activity

Calculate the mean for Site B from Table 7.7.

Why are the two means from the aggregated data different from those calculated for the raw data in Table 7.6?

The relevant calculations are shown in Table 7.9. The mean for Site B is then estimated as:

$$\frac{\Sigma fm}{\Sigma f} = \frac{90,550}{175} = £517.43$$

Table 7.9
Calculations for the mean: Site B

Interval	Midpoint (m)	Frequency (f)	(fm)
< 100	50	0	0
100 < 200	150	0	0
200 < 300	250	8	2,000
300 < 400	350	28	9,800
400 < 500	450	52	23,400
500 < 600	550	40	22,000
600 < 700	650	31	20,150
700 < 800	750	8	6,000
800 < 900	850	4	3,400
≥ 900	950	4	3,800
		175	90,550

The reason these calculations give slightly different results for the means compared with the raw data results in Table 7.6 relates to the assumption we had to make in order to calculate the means for the aggregated data. We had to assume that all the items in an interval took the midpoint value. Clearly, this assumption will not be entirely accurate so some discrepancy between the raw data mean and the aggregate data mean appears. It is for this reason that we have been careful to refer to the mean from the aggregated data as an estimate only. In practice of course we would not calculate the mean from a frequency table if we had the raw data available. We have done so in this case to illustrate the numerical differences that can occur.

Two additional points to note about the grouped mean are:

- It will be influenced by the intervals – and therefore the midpoints – that have been chosen. A different choice of intervals will tend to lead to a slightly different mean value.

- It will be influenced by any assumptions made about any open-ended intervals in the frequency table. Different assumptions will lead to a different calculated value for the mean.

You will remember from the previous chapter when we looked at the construction of histograms that we had to make assumptions about the limits for any open-ended interval in the frequency table. These assumptions that we make will affect the midpoint values also and so will also affect the mean we calculate for aggregated data that has open-ended intervals.

The standard deviation

Having calculated the mean we can also calculate the standard deviation for aggregated data using the formula:

$$\sqrt{\frac{\Sigma fm^2}{\Sigma f} - \left(\frac{\Sigma fm}{\Sigma f}\right)^2}$$

The formula looks complicated but simply requires us to square the midpoint (m^2) and multiply by the frequency and then substitute values into the formula. Because the formula is more complex than most we have seen so far we should take extra care in its calculation to avoid arithmetic errors. Note that the second part of the expression (to be subtracted) is simply the mean value squared. Table 7.10 shows the calculations for Site A.

Table 7.10
Calculations for the standard deviation: Site A

Intervals	Midpoint (m)	(f)	(fm)	(m²)	(fm²)
< 100	50	14	700	2,500	35,000
100 < 200	150	39	5,850	22,500	877,500
200 < 300	250	32	8,000	62,500	2,000,000
300 < 400	350	26	9,100	122,500	3,185,000
400 < 500	450	17	7,650	202,500	3,442,500
500 < 600	550	9	4,950	302,500	2,722,500
600 < 700	650	6	3,900	422,500	2,535,000
700 < 800	750	5	3,750	562,500	2,812,500
800 < 900	850	2	1,700	722,500	1,445,000
≥ 900	950	0	0	902,500	0
Totals		150	45,600		19,055,000

Notice that in the expression Σfm^2 the order of calculation is:

- square the midpoints;
- multiply this by the frequency;
- sum these over all the intervals.

The rest of the calculation is then:

$$\sqrt{\frac{\Sigma fm^2}{\Sigma f} - (\frac{\Sigma fm}{\Sigma f})^2} = \sqrt{\frac{19,055,000}{150} - (\frac{45,600}{150})^2}$$
$$= \sqrt{127,033.33 - 92,416}$$
$$= \sqrt{34,617.33}$$
$$= 186.06$$

giving a standard deviation of £186.06. Once again, notice that the standard deviation from aggregated data may be less accurate than that from the raw data (as in Table 7.6). You should be especially careful in performing the arithmetic on the formula. One common problem is that students sometimes end up with a negative number in the last square root expression because of arithmetic errors they have made. If this is the case you know for certain that you have made a mistake and should go back and check your calculations.

Student activity

Calculate the standard deviation for the aggregated data for Site B.

The result gives a standard deviation of £147.44. The calculations are in Table 7.11. Again, we should note that the statistics based on aggregated data is slightly different from that based on the raw data and as such should be treated as an estimate only:

$$\sqrt{\frac{\Sigma fm^2}{\Sigma f} - \left(\frac{\Sigma fm}{\Sigma f}\right)^2} = \sqrt{\frac{50,657,500}{175} - \left(\frac{90,550}{175}\right)^2}$$

$$= \sqrt{289,471.43 - 267,732.33}$$

$$= \sqrt{21,739.10}$$

$$= 147.44$$

Table 7.11
Calculations for the standard deviation: Site B

Intervals	Midpoint (m)	(f)	(fm)	(m²)	(fm²)
< 100	50	0	0	2,500	0
100 < 200	150	0	0	22,500	0
200 < 300	250	8	2,000	62,500	500,000
300 < 400	350	28	9,800	122,500	3,430,000
400 < 500	450	52	23,400	202,500	10,530,000
500 < 600	550	40	22,000	302,500	12,100,000
600 < 700	650	31	20,150	422,500	13,097,500
700 < 800	750	8	6,000	562,500	4,500,000
800 < 900	850	4	3,400	722,500	2,890,000
≥ 900	950	4	3,800	902,500	3,610,000
Totals		175	90,550		50,657,500

Median and quartiles

We can also calculate the median and the two quartiles from aggregated data. To do so we follow a sequence of calculations:

- From the frequency table calculate the cumulative frequencies.
- Calculate which item is the median item from $(n + 1)/2$.
- Using the cumulative frequencies determine which interval this median item falls into.
- Use the median estimation formula:

$$\text{Median} = \text{LCL} + (\text{MI} - \text{CF})\frac{\text{CW}}{\text{F}}$$

where:

LCL is the lower class limit of the interval in which the median item occurs;

MI is the median item;

CF is the cumulative frequency up to the median item interval;

CW is the width of the median item interval;

F is the frequency of observations in the median item interval.

This looks horrendous but is actually quite easy to calculate. Again we will illustrate with reference to the Site A data. Table 7.12 shows the frequencies and cumulative frequencies for this data. Following our sequence we then have:

Table 7.12
Calculations for the median: Site A gross weekly income

Income £	No. of responses	Cumulative no. of responses
< 100	14	14
100 < 200	39	53
200 < 300	32	85
300 < 400	26	111
400 < 500	17	128
500 < 600	9	137
600 < 700	6	143
700 < 800	5	148
800 < 900	2	150
≥ 900	0	150
Total	150	

- The median item is given by $(n + 1)/2$ or $(150 + 1)/2 = 75.5$. This item is the median item in the distribution (in this case actually midway between item number 75 and item number 76 since we have an even number of items).

- From the cumulative frequencies we know that the median item must be in the interval £200 < £300. There are 53 items up to this interval and 85 including this interval. So the median value must be somewhere between £200 but less than £300.

- We now use the formula. We have:

LCL	£200
MI	75.5
CF	53
CW	£100
F	32

and substituting (carefully) into the equation we have:

$$\text{Median} = \text{LCL} + (\text{MI} - \text{CF}) \frac{\text{CW}}{\text{F}}.$$

$$= 200 + (75.5 - 53) \frac{100}{32}$$

$$= 200 + (22.5)3.125$$

$$= 200 + 70.31$$

$$= £270.31$$

So the median value for Site A is estimated at £270.31. It isn't necessary to explain in detail why the formula is the right one to use but you may be able to puzzle it out. We know that the median must be at least £200 (since this is the lower limit of the interval which contains the median item). We know that there are 32 items within this interval and we make an assumption (as we had to with the mean) that these items are spread equally through this interval of £100 (and are actually assumed to be £3.125 apart). We also know that the median item is 75.5 so effectively we can count along 22.5 items from £200 to estimate the median value.

Student activity

Estimate the median for Site B from the data in Table 7.7.

The median for Site B is estimated at £500.

Again, following step by step we have the cumulative frequencies as in Table 7.13 and the calculation as follows:

Table 7.13
Gross weekly income: Site B

Income £	No. of responses	Cumulative no. of responses
< 100	0	0
100 < 200	0	0
200 < 300	8	8
300 < 400	28	36
400 < 500	52	88
500 < 600	40	128
600 < 700	31	159
700 < 800	8	167
800 < 900	4	171
≥ 900	4	175
Total	175	175

- The median item is (175+1)/2 = 88.

- The median item is in the interval £400 < £500. (You may have realized at this stage that the median value must be £500 and the rest of the calculation is unnecessary.)
- We now use the formula. We have:

LCL	£400
MI	88
CF	36
CW	£100
F	52

and substituting into the equation we have:

$$\text{Median} = \text{LCL} + (\text{MI} - \text{CF})\frac{\text{CW}}{\text{F}}$$

$$= 400 + (88 - 36)\frac{100}{52}$$

$$= 400 + (52)1.923$$

$$= 400 + 99.996$$

$$= £500$$

A point to help you check that you have the right answer (but often forgotten by students) is that your calculated answer must have a value somewhere within the interval the median falls into. It is easy to make an arithmetic error in the calculation. However, if you calculate a median value less than the lower limit of the interval or above the upper limit you should realize something is wrong. Another aspect that can be confusing is the difference between the median item and the median value. The median item is simply telling us which item (out of the total) is the median. We must then calculate the value corresponding to that item to find the median value.

The lower and upper quartiles can also be estimated using this same approach. The only difference is that rather than finding the median item as one of our steps we find the corresponding quartile items. These are:

Lower quartile item = $(n + 1)/3$
Upper quartile item = $3(n + 1)/4$

Returning to Table 7.12 for Site A we have:

Lower quartile:

- Lower quartile item is $(150 + 1)/4 = 37.75$.
- This item occurs in the interval £100 < £200.
- The formula is:

$$Q_1 = \text{LCL} + (\text{LQI} - \text{CF})\frac{\text{CW}}{\text{F}}$$

$$= 100 + (37.75 - 14)\frac{100}{39}$$

$$= 100 + (23.75)2.564$$

$$= 100 + 60.895$$

$$= £160.90$$

Upper quartile:
- Upper quartile item is 3(150 + 1)/4 = 113.25.
- This item occurs in the interval £400 < £500.
- The formula is:

$$Q_3 = LCL + (LQI - CF)\frac{CW}{F}$$

$$= 400 + (113.25 - 111)\frac{100}{17}$$

$$= 400 + (2.25)5.882$$
$$= 400 + 13.23$$
$$= £413.23$$

Student activity

Estimate the quartiles for Site B.

From Table 7.13 we have:

Lower quartile:
- Lower quartile item is (175 + 1)/4 = 44.
- This item occurs in the interval £400 < £500.
- The formula is:

$$Q_1 = LCL + (LQI - CF)\frac{CW}{F}$$

$$= 400 + (44 - 36)\frac{100}{52}$$

$$= 400 + (8)1.923$$
$$= 400 + 15.384$$
$$= £415.38$$

Upper quartile:
- Upper quartile item is 3(175 + 1)/4 = 132.
- This item occurs in the interval £600 < £700.
- The formula is:

$$Q_3 = LCL + (LQI - CF)\frac{CW}{F}$$

$$= 600 + (132 - 128)\frac{100}{40}$$

$$= 600 + (4)2.5$$
$$= 600 + 10$$
$$= £610$$

POPULATIONS AND SAMPLES

Having introduced the array of statistics commonly used in business analysis, we must now make the distinction between analysing a set of data which represents some statistical population and a set of data which represents only a sample from that population. A statistical population refers to the entire set of data which is of interest to us. A sample is a representative part of that population. For a variety of reasons – time, cost, availability of data – we frequently have to resort to collecting data on a sample in a business situation. There are important implications of this which we shall explore in more detail in Chapter 9. For the present, there is a critical factor that we should note in terms of how we calculate the standard deviation.

We developed the formula for calculating the standard deviation for raw data as:

$$\sqrt{\frac{\Sigma(x - \overline{X})^2}{n}}$$

This is technically only correct if we are convinced that the data relates to a population. If the data instead represents a sample then the formula becomes:

$$\sqrt{\frac{\Sigma(x - \overline{X})^2}{n - 1}}$$

and for aggregated data:

$$\sqrt{\frac{\Sigma fm^2}{\Sigma f - 1} - \left(\frac{\Sigma fm}{\Sigma f - 1}\right)^2}$$

One further point relating to this is that you should check any computer software you are using to analyse sample data. Many spreadsheet packages have a built-in function for calculating the standard deviation given a set of raw data. However, not all software distinguishes between a sample and a population and you may find that the package you are using applies the population standard deviation formula. This will lead to some arithmetic difference in the standard deviation result.

WEIGHTED AVERAGES

There is one particular type of average which is also worth detailing. This is the weighted average. Consider the data in Table 7.14 which shows annual salaries for different types of employee in a company.

Table 7.14
Annual salaries

Employee category	Annual salary £
Senior managers	48,000
Middle managers	27,000
Administrative	18,000
Clerical	15,000
Manual skilled	17,500
Manual unskilled	11,500

Source: Payroll section.

Student activity

Calculate the mean salary for the company. Is this the right way to work out the mean in this example?

At first sight the mean is easily calculated. We simply add up the salary figures and divide by 6, the number of employee groups we have. This would give:

$$\frac{137,000}{6} = £22,833$$

as the mean salary. However, there is one thing in particular that should concern us about using this statistic and that is it assumes there are the same number of people in each employee class. If there are not then the statistic will be biased in terms of representing the mean salary.

Suppose the numbers employed in each group were as shown in Table 7.15. We see that there is considerable variation in the numbers employed in each group. By simply averaging the salaries it is clear that we are treating, for example, the senior manager group as of equal importance in the calculation as manual unskilled.

Table 7.15
Annual salaries and employees

Employee category	Annual salary £	No. of employees
Senior managers	48,000	8
Middle managers	27,000	56
Administrative	18,000	87
Clerical	15,000	102
Manual skilled	17,500	187
Manual unskilled	11,500	349
Total		789

Source: Payroll section.

To get round this problem we should calculate a weighted average. This literally weights each salary according to its relative importance – in this case relative importance as measured by number of employees. Simply, we can attach a weight to each salary where the weight is the number of employees in that category. The calculations are shown in Table 7.16. We have multiplied the salary in each group by the number of employees in that group. If we now take this total and divide by the number of employees we will have a weighted average salary (technically a weighted mean salary):

$$\frac{12,278,000}{789} = £15,561.47$$

Table 7.16
Weighted average

Employee category	Annual salary £	No. of employees	Weighted salary £
Senior managers	48,000	8	384,000
Middle managers	27,000	56	1,512,000
Administrative	18,000	87	1,566,000
Clerical	15,000	102	1,530,000
Manual skilled	17,500	187	3,272,500
Manual unskilled	11,500	349	4,013,500
Total		789	12,278,000

Source: Payroll section.

In general, denoting the variable for which we require an average as x and the weights to be used as w we have:

$$\text{Weighted mean} = \frac{\Sigma wx}{\Sigma w}$$

INDEX NUMBERS

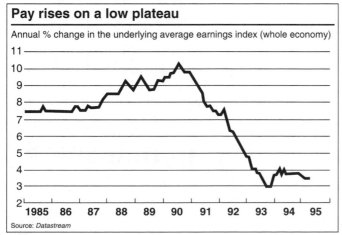

Pay rises on a low plateau

Annual % change in the underlying average earnings index (whole economy)

Source: Datastream

FT Source: *Financial Times*, 15 June 1995

Finally in this chapter we turn to the statistics generally known as index numbers. The term index number can refer to two different types of statistics. The first type – the simple index number – is a method of expressing changes in a single variable over time. In fact, we looked at this in Chapter 4 where we looked at the example of annual beer production and saw how this could be expressed in simple index number form.

It is the second type of index number that we want to look at in this section – the aggregate or composite index. In fact you are probably already aware of some common aggregate indices (the

225

Economy: Summer heat has caused a surge in the cost of some foods

Soaring potato price affects inflation rate

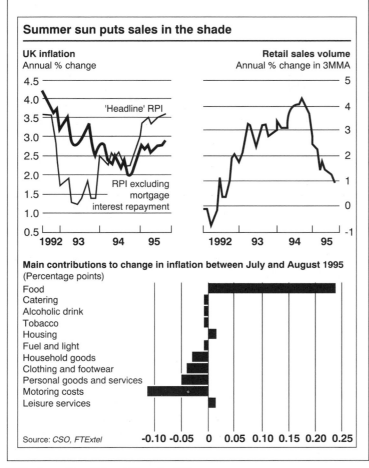

Summer sun puts sales in the shade

UK inflation
Annual % change

'Headline' RPI

RPI excluding mortgage interest repayment

1992 93 94 95

Retail sales volume
Annual % change in 3MMA

1992 93 94 95

Main contributions to change in inflation between July and August 1995
(Percentage points)

Food
Catering
Alcoholic drink
Tobacco
Housing
Fuel and light
Household goods
Clothing and footwear
Personal goods and services
Motoring costs
Leisure services

-0.10 -0.05 0 0.05 0.10 0.15 0.20 0.25

Source: *CSO, FTExtel*

FT Source: *Financial Times*, 15 September 1995

plural of index): the Retail Price Index (RPI), the FT share price index (the Footsie as it is known), the Dow Jones index (showing US share prices), the index of industrial production. All these are well-known and well-publicized examples of an aggregate index (although most people who refer to these indices probably don't know that they are in fact an aggregate index). An aggregate index for some variable – like retail prices – is effectively a form of a weighted average.

To see what this means – and more importantly to see how such a statistic can be used – we shall use the Retail Price Index (RPI) as an example. Table 7.17 shows the RPI for January 1993 to September 1994 (in case you're wondering why we stopped at September 1994 it's because that was the latest available when we were writing this book). In September 1994, for example, the RPI was 145.0, January 1987 = 100. To understand what this means we have to remember that any index has a base period – the time period when the index was set to the value of 100. So, the RPI in 1994 had a base of January 1987. This helps us to determine quite easily that from January 1987 to September 1994 retail prices had risen by 45% (145 – 100).

Inflation soars

Table 7.17
General Index of Retail Prices (January 1987 = 100)

Month	Index	
	1993	1994
January	137.9	141.3
February	138.8	142.1
March	139.3	142.5
April	140.6	144.2
May	141.1	144.7
June	141.0	144.7
July	140.7	144.0
August	141.3	144.7
September	141.9	145.0
October	141.8	
November	141.6	
December	141.9	

Source: *Monthly Digest of Statistics.*

The RPI, then, allows us to see readily the change in retail prices between a given month and the base period (1987). It can also be used with some simple arithmetic to calculate the change in retail prices between any two months. For example, suppose we wanted to calculate the change in retail prices over the last year (i.e. between September 1993 and September 1994). We can now use the index numbers for the two months and work out the percentage change between them:

$$\frac{\text{September } 1994 - \text{September } 1993}{\text{September } 1993} \times 100$$

$$= \frac{145.0 - 141.9}{141.9} \times 100$$

$$= 2.2\%$$

That is, retail prices rose by 2.2% over the period September 1993 to September 1994.

Student activity

Calculate the percentage change in retail prices for each month between 1993 and 1994.

Performing the same arithmetic we would have the results shown in Table 7.18. In fact, this is often a source of misunderstanding and confusion to people. The RPI is generally accepted as showing the level of inflation in the economy. We see from the calculations in Table 7.18 that inflation in 1994 was between 2.2% and 2.6%. In every case, however, the figure is positive implying that, looking back over the last 12 months from any given month in 1994, prices were higher than they were in 1993.

Table 7.18
General Index of Retail Prices and change over the previous 12 months

Month	Index (January 1987 = 100)		Annual change %
	1993	1994	
January	137.9	141.3	2.5
February	138.8	142.1	2.4
March	139.3	142.5	2.3
April	140.6	144.2	2.6
May	141.1	144.7	2.6
June	141.0	144.7	2.6
July	140.7	144.0	2.3
August	141.3	144.7	2.4
September	141.9	145.0	2.2
October	141.8		
November	141.6		
December	141.9		

Source: Table 7.17.

However, economic and business commentators (and frequently politicians) will often refer to the *trend in the RPI*. We see that during 1994 the trend in RPI was downwards from January to March, upwards to June and then fluctuating to September. A typical economic comment in April 1994 (when the March figures would have been published) would be to state that 'the general trend in inflation during the first part of 1994 is downwards'. This is quite correct since we see that the change (on a year-by-year basis) has fallen from 2.5% to 2.3%. The level of inflation – the rate by which prices are increasing – has fallen. Such a statement, however, is often misunderstood by many as implying that *prices* have fallen. Clearly they have not (the RPI is higher every month in 1994). It is the *rate* at which prices are increasing that has fallen, not prices themselves which have fallen. You must make sure that you clearly understand the implications of such figures and such statements.

But what does the RPI actually measure (and how)? The Central Statistical Office's explanation of the RPI is:

> The retail prices index measures the change from month to month in the average level of prices of goods and services purchased by most households in the United Kingdom ... The index covers a large and representative selection of more than 600 separate goods and services, for which price movements are regularly measured in 180 towns throughout the country.

What the RPI tries to do is to measure the change in the prices of a 'basket' of over 600 goods and services. This 'basket' has been put together to be representative of most households and is based on the *Family Expenditure Survey*. This survey collects detailed data on expenditure patterns of a sample of families across the country. Once the 'basket' of goods and services has been identified then the prices of these items are monitored on a regular basis in different towns which again are taken to be largely representative of the country.

Approximately 150,000 price details are used to compile the RPI. Although the RPI is based on over 600 separate goods and services it is clear that we could not simply add up the price changes in each of these and average over the 600. The reason for this is that the different goods and services will have a different degree of importance in the overall 'basket' of goods and services bought. We could not add together, for example, the price change of a tin of beans with that of a family saloon car. What this effectively means is that the RPI has to be calculated along the lines of a weighted average where prices is the variable for which we require an average and the weights used are the 'basket' of goods and services identified.

Table 7.19 shows the 1994 weights of the groups comprising the 'basket' of goods and services. We see that the total of all the weights used is 1,000 and that each group – Food, Catering, Alcoholic drink, etc. – has a weight reflecting its relative importance. Food, for example, has a weight of 142 implying that food prices make up some 14.2% of the RPI. These weights, as mentioned earlier, are derived from the *Family Expenditure Survey*. Within each group are sub-groups and individual items. The Alcoholic drink group, for example, actually consists of two sub-groups – Beer (with a weight of 44) and Wines and spirits (with a weight of 32). Each sub-group is made up of on-sales and off-sales (drink bought for consumption on licensed premises or bought for consumption off licensed premises. Weights are respectively for the Beer items 38 and 6 and for Wines and spirits 11 and 21.

Table 7.19
Group weights for 1994

All items	1,000
Food	142
Catering	45
Alcoholic drink	76
Tobacco	35
Housing	158
Fuel and light	45
Household goods	76
Household services	47
Clothing and footwear	58
Personal goods and services	37
Motoring expenditure	142
Fares and other travel costs	20
Leisure goods	48
Leisure services	71

Source: *Monthly Digest of Statistics*.

Student activity

Consider the weights of the items in the Beer sub-group and the Wines and spirits sub-group. What do they imply about people's drinking habits?

For Beer we see that the weight for on-sales is considerably higher than for off-sales whereas for Wines and spirits this is reversed. This implies that consumption of beer largely takes place where it is bought (i.e. in the pub). Consumption of wines and spirits largely takes place somewhere other than where they are bought (e.g. people may buy wine in a local supermarket for consumption at home).

The weights, then, are used to attach differing degrees of importance to the price changes of the 600-plus items used in the composition of the RPI. However, it is also important to realize that the weights themselves change over time (reflecting people's changing preferences and purchases). In fact the weights used to calculate the RPI are updated each year with the new expenditure patterns revealed by the *Family Expenditure Survey*. Table 7.20 illustrates the changes that have been evidenced over time in some of the weight groups.

Table 7.20
Weights for selected groups in selected years

Group	Weights in year:		
	1952	1974	1994
Food	399	253	142
Alcoholic drink	78	70	76
Tobacco	90	43	35
Housing	72	124	158
Fuel and light	66	52	45
Clothing and footwear	98	91	58

Source: *Monthly Digest of Statistics.*

Using the RPI to deflate a series

The RPI is used as a measure of general inflation in the economy and is seen as an important economic indicator. It has another important use, however, which is to deflate financial time series.

Consider Table 7.21 which shows average gross weekly earnings for full-time employees in Great Britain for selected years. Notice that the figures relate to April in each year. Looking at the All employees data it is tempting to conclude that average earnings have consistently risen over this period. The average is some £30 higher per week in 1993 than in 1986.

Table 7.21
Average gross weekly earnings for full-time employees in Great Britain
(figures in £s at April each year)

Year	All employees	Males	Females
1986	181.1	203.6	134.7
1987	195.3	220.1	145.5
1988	214.7	241.6	161.6
1989	235.3	264.5	179.3
1990	258.5	290.3	198.6
1991	280.8	314.2	220.0
1992	301.1	335.7	238.8
1993	313.3	349.3	250.0

Source: *Monthly Digest of Statistics.*

However, these figures clearly ignore inflation – the eroding effect of rising prices on money income. Clearly if inflation had been high over this same period then, although employees might have received more money, they may have needed this extra income simply to pay higher prices. The quantity of goods and services they could afford may not have changed – indeed it may have gone down.

For this reason we frequently want – with financial data – to be able to distinguish between money income and real income. The former is the physical amount of money received. The latter represents what that money would buy, in terms of goods and services. Fundamentally, we want to use money income figures to answer the question: are we better off in 1993 compared with 1986? Better off, not in terms of money income but in terms of what we could afford to buy with that income.

One approach would be to compare the percentage change in earnings with the percentage change in inflation over the same period. The relevant calculations are shown in Table 7.22. For the All employees earnings data we have calculated the percentage change in each year since 1986. By 1993, for example, average earnings had increased by 73%. Also shown is the RPI in April of each year and again we have calculated the percentage change in the RPI since 1986. We see that by 1993 retail prices had risen by 43.9%. So we can conclude that the increase in average earnings has been higher than the general increase in retail prices. This implies – for the 'average' employee – that their gross earnings have increased at a faster rate than prices and, other things being equal, they would be better off in 1993 than in 1986 in terms of what their earnings would actually buy.

Table 7.22
Average gross weekly earnings for full-time employees in Great Britain
(figures in £s at April each year; RPI is for April in each year)

Year	All employees	Percentage change since 1986	RPI Jan. 1987 = 100	Percentage change since 1986
1986	181.1		97.7	
1987	195.3	7.8	101.8	4.2
1988	214.7	18.6	105.8	8.3
1989	235.3	29.9	114.3	17.0
1990	258.5	42.7	125.1	28.0
1991	280.8	55.1	133.1	36.2
1992	301.1	66.3	138.8	42.1
1993	313.3	73.0	140.6	43.9

Source: *Monthly Digest of Statistics.*

But this is quite a clumsy approach to the problem. Comparison between years becomes very difficult as do comparisons between different groups – such as comparing males and females. A different approach – but using the same principles – is known as deflating the series. Effectively what this means is that we want to deflate – remove the effects of inflation – from the earnings data. This will provide data which is more amenable to comparison.

Deflating is performed through some simple arithmetic:

$$\text{Real value in period } t = \text{Money value } t \times \frac{100}{\text{Price index } t}$$

That is we multiply the money value figure in a given time period, t, by a ratio of 100 (since this is the RPI in the base period) to the RPI in that period. The calculation for 1993, for example, would be:

$$\text{Real value} = 313.3 \times \frac{100}{140.6}$$
$$= 228.8$$

That is the real value of average earnings in 1993 was £228.8, base January 1987.

What does this mean? It tells us that the money earnings of £313.3 were actually worth only £228.8 once we had taken inflation into account between January 1987 (the base period) and April 1993 (the period we are calculating a real earnings value for). The difference between the money earnings and the real earnings figures (313.3 – 228.8 = £84.5) represents the extra money we would have to spend in 1993 to pay for the increased prices in our 'basket' of goods and services.

The figure of £228.8 may be referred to in different – but identical – ways:

- as the real average earnings in 1993;
- as the average earnings in 1993 at January 1987 prices;
- as the average earnings in 1993 at constant (January 1987) prices.

Student activity

Calculate the real earnings figures for each of the other years in Table 7.22.

Why is the real earnings figure for 1986 higher than the money figure?

Table 7.23 shows the real earnings series and we now see the benefits of deflating a series since direct comparison is possible between different years. Each real figure has had the effects of inflation – as measured by the RPI – removed. We see that since 1986 real average earnings have consistently risen (although by far less than it appears when looking at the money earnings series). In real terms – i.e. in terms of what money will actually buy us once we have taken inflation into account – average earnings have risen by £37.4 between 1993 and 1986.

Table 7.23
Average gross weekly earnings for full-time employees in Great Britain at constant prices
(figures in £s at April each year)

Year	All employees	
	Current prices	Constant prices
1986	181.1	185.4
1987	195.3	191.8
1988	214.7	202.9
1989	235.3	205.9
1990	258.5	206.6
1991	280.8	211.0
1992	301.1	216.9
1993	313.3	222.8

Source: Table 7.22.

The reason why the 1986 real figure is higher than the money figure is explained by the fact that the base period was 1987 (a year later) and that in 1986 the RPI was lower than in January 1987. This means that our money in 1986 was worth more – in terms of what it would buy – than the equivalent money sum in January 1987. The real income figure for 1986 is accordingly higher than the money figure to reflect this.

It is worth commenting that the RPI is not the only price index available. Clearly the RPI is meant to reflect what is happening to the prices of goods and services bought by a 'typical' household. Those households which are not typical – i.e. have a different expenditure pattern than that reflected in the weights used to calculate the RPI – may experience a different level of inflation. For example, the RPI is calculated to include an item for mortgage interest payments (with a weight in 1994 of 44). If interest rates rise then by default mortgage interest payments rise and so does the RPI. However, if you belong to a household which does not have mortgage interest payments – perhaps because your income is too low to afford a mortgage, perhaps because you prefer to rent, perhaps because you cannot get a mortgage, perhaps because your mortgage was paid off when you retired – then to some lesser or greater extent the RPI will not accurately measure the inflation that affects your consumption.

To try to minimize this problem the Central Statistical Office produces a variety of price indices. Some of these are special cases of the RPI, others are price indices in their own right. They include:

- RPI all items;
- RPI all items except seasonal food;
- RPI all items except food;
- RPI all items except housing;
- RPI all non-food items;
- Pensioner price index – one-person household;
- Pensioner price index – two-person household.

Table 7.24 shows how different these can be. It is also worth noting that many time series published by the government come in two formats: in money terms (often referred to as current prices) and in real terms (adjusted by the RPI). The adjustment is undertaken by the CSO and both real and money values are often shown.

Table 7.24
Comparison of price indices

Year:	1962	1972	1982	1992
RPI all items	14.2	23.0	85.9	146.4
RPI total food	14.0	23.3	89.0	135.0
RPI total non-food	14.4	23.1	85.1	148.7
Pensioner index – one-person household	13.9	22.8	86.9	137.6
Pensioner index – two-person household	14.0	22.8	86.7	138.7

Source: ETAS 1994.

Rebasing an index

Frequently when using a published index we find that, part way through a series, the index has been rebased: that is, the base year used has been changed. This makes it difficult to use the index over a lengthy time period.

Let us examine Table 7.25. This is a copy of a table in *Economic Trends Annual Supplement 1994* and shows the RPI from 1962 to September 1994. You will notice that from 1962 to 1973 the base period was January 1962, from 1974 to 1986 the base period was January 1974 and since 1987 the base period has been January 1987.

Table 7.25
General Index of Retail Prices (all items)[1]

	Annual Average	Jan	Feb	Mar	Apr	May	Jun	Jul	Aug	Sep	Oct	Nov	Dec
January 1962 = 100													
1962	101.6	100.0	100.1	100.5	101.9	102.2	102.9	102.5	101.6	101.5	101.4	101.8	102.3
1963	103.6	102.7	103.6	103.7	104.0	103.9	103.8	103.9	103.0	103.3	103.7	104.0	104.2
1964	107.0	104.7	104.8	105.2	106.1	107.0	107.4	107.4	107.8	107.8	107.9	108.8	109.2
1965	112.1	109.5	109.5	109.9	112.0	112.4	112.7	112.7	112.9	113.0	113.1	113.6	114.1
1966	116.5	114.3	114.4	114.6	116.0	116.8	117.1	116.6	117.3	117.1	117.4	118.1	118.3
1967	119.4	118.5	118.6	118.6	119.5	119.4	119.9	119.2	118.9	118.8	119.7	120.4	121.2
1968	125.0	121.6	122.2	122.6	124.8	124.9	125.4	125.5	125.7	125.8	126.4	126.7	126.4
1969	131.8	129.1	129.8	130.3	131.7	131.5	132.1	132.1	131.8	132.2	133.2	133.5	134.4
1970	140.2	135.5	136.2	137.0	139.1	139.5	139.9	140.9	140.8	141.5	143.0	144.0	145.0
1971	153.4	147.0	147.8	149.0	152.2	153.2	154.3	155.2	155.3	155.5	156.4	157.3	158.1
1972	164.3	159.0	159.8	160.3	161.8	162.6	163.7	164.2	165.5	166.4	168.7	169.3	170.2
1973	179.4	171.2	172.4	173.4	176.7	178.0	178.9	179.7	180.2	181.8	185.4	186.8	188.2
1974	..	191.8	..	..	..	..	..	..	..	..	..	..	..
January 1974 = 100													
1974	108.5	100.0	101.7	102.6	106.1	107.6	108.7	109.7	109.8	111.0	113.2	115.2	116.9
1975	134.8	119.9	121.9	124.3	129.1	134.5	137.1	138.5	139.3	140.5	142.5	144.2	146.0
1976	157.1	147.9	149.8	150.6	153.5	155.2	156.0	156.3	158.5	160.6	163.5	165.8	168.0
1977	182.0	172.4	174.1	175.8	180.3	181.7	183.6	183.8	184.7	185.7	186.5	187.4	188.4
1978	197.1	189.5	190.6	191.8	194.6	195.7	197.2	198.1	199.4	200.2	201.1	202.5	204.2
1979	223.5	207.2	208.9	210.6	214.2	215.9	219.6	229.1	230.9	233.2	235.6	237.7	239.4
1980	263.7	245.3	248.8	252.2	260.8	263.2	265.7	267.9	268.5	270.2	271.9	274.1	275.6
1981	295.0	277.3	279.8	284.0	292.2	294.1	295.8	297.1	299.3	301.0	303.7	306.9	308.8
1982	320.4	310.6	310.7	313.4	319.7	322.0	322.9	323.0	323.1	322.9	324.5	326.1	325.5
1983	335.1	325.9	327.3	327.9	332.5	333.9	334.7	336.5	338.0	339.5	340.7	341.9	342.8
1984	351.8	342.6	344.0	345.1	349.7	351.0	351.9	351.5	354.8	355.5	357.7	358.8	358.5
1985	373.2	359.8	362.7	366.1	373.9	375.6	376.4	375.7	376.7	376.5	377.1	378.4	378.9
1986	385.9	379.7	381.1	381.6	385.3	386.0	385.8	384.7	385.9	387.8	388.4	391.7	393.0
1987	..	394.5	..	..	..	..	..	..	..	..	..	..	..
January 1987 = 100													
1987	101.9	100.0	100.4	100.6	101.8	101.9	101.9	101.8	102.1	102.4	102.9	103.4	103.3
1988	106.9	103.3	103.7	104.1	105.8	106.2	106.6	106.7	107.9	108.4	109.5	110.0	110.3
1989	115.2	111.0	111.8	112.3	114.3	115.0	115.4	115.5	115.8	116.6	117.5	118.5	118.8
1990	126.1	119.5	120.2	121.4	125.1	126.2	126.7	126.8	128.1	129.3	130.3	130.0	129.9
1991	133.5	130.2	130.9	131.4	133.1	133.5	134.1	133.8	134.1	134.6	135.1	135.6	135.7
1992	138.5	135.6	136.3	136.7	138.8	139.3	139.3	138.8	138.9	139.4	139.9	139.7	139.2
1993	140.7	137.9	138.8	139.3	140.6	141.1	141.0	140.7	141.3	141.9	141.8	141.6	141.9
1994	..	141.3	142.1	142.5	144.2	144.7	144.7	144.0	144.7	145.0	..	..	..

1 Further historical information is available in the HMSO publication *Retail Prices 1914 to 1990*, ISBN 0116204990.
Source: Social Trends 1993 Central Statistical Office. Crown Copyright 1993. Reproduced by the permission of the Controller of HMSO and the Central Statistical Office.

Suppose we wished to use (as we did in the previous section) RPI data which covers more than one base period – for example the RPI from 1984 to 1994? Clearly we cannot mix the two sets of RPI (1984–1986 and 1987–1994) since they have two different base periods. What we must do is to rebase the index (also known as chaining).

The key to this is given in the table: look carefully at the year 1987. You will see this appears twice. First of all – but for January only – we have an index base 1974 of 394.5. We also have a full set of indices for 1987 base 1987, with the January figure (naturally) at 100.0. The figure of 394.5 for January 1987 (base 1972) has effectively been converted into 100 at January 1987 by dividing through by 394.5 and multiplying by 100.

We can replicate this for the other base 1972 indices:

$$1984 \text{ index (base 1987)} = 351.8 \times \frac{100}{394.5}$$
$$= 89.2$$
$$1985 \text{ index (base 1987)} = 373.2 \times \frac{100}{394.5}$$
$$= 94.6$$

Student activity

Calculate the index for 1986, base 1987.

$$1986 \text{ index (base 1987)} = 385.9 \times \frac{100}{394.5}$$
$$= 97.8$$

giving an RPI series base 1987 as shown in Table 7.26. Notice that we chose to rebase the index for 1987. We could equally have chosen to reuse the values from 1987 to the 1974 base using the same principles. This is left as an end of chapter exercise.

Table 7.26
Rebased RPI index, Janaury 1987 = 100

	RPI Annual average
1984	89,2
1985	94.6
1986	97.8
1987	101.9
1988	106.9
1989	115.2
1990	126.1
1991	133.5
1992	138.5
1993	140.7

SUMMARY

The statistics we have introduced in this chapter allow us to begin the process of describing a data set without having to resort to the raw data, the frequency table or the histogram. With these statistics alone we can identify many of the key features of a data set. As such they are a valuable aid to the manager and decision-maker in presenting a concise summary of a large set of data without the need for tables and diagrams. It is frequently the case, in business analysis, that such descriptive statistics are all the information that is provided. Using what we have learned about the different measures provides us with a powerful means of describing the full set of data.

Now that you have completed this chapter you will appreciate that:

- There are two common measures of average, the arithmetic mean and the median.
- The mean is found by averaging the sum total of the numbers in the data set over the number of items. The mean is easily distorted by a few extreme values in the data set which can make it unrepresentative of the majority of data items.
- The median is the item in the middle of the ordered data set. There are always an equal number of items above the median as below. The median is particularly useful in data sets where the mean may not represent a typical value.
- Measures of dispersion or variability are based around the mean or around the median.
- The standard deviation measures dispersion around the arithmetic mean.
- The coefficient of variation is a measure of relative dispersion expressing the standard deviation as a percentage of the arithmetic mean.
- The interquartile range measures dispersion around the median value and is the difference between the upper and lower quartiles.
- The coefficient of skewness is an indication of the general shape of the data distribution.
- Statistics based on the raw data are more accurate than those based on grouped data.
- Weighted averages may be useful where a simple average would be misleading.
- Price index numbers are useful for assessing the movement in some monetary variable after the effects of inflation are removed.

EXAMPLE

The UK National Lottery was launched towards the end of 1994 in a blaze of publicity and promotion. At that time the lottery worked along straightforward lines. For the sum of £1 anyone over the age of 16 was able to purchase a lottery ticket from any of the authorized outlets up and down the country and to choose any six numbers between 1 and 49. On prime-time TV on a Saturday evening six numbers were selected mechanically and at random. Anyone whose six numbers matched those six chosen was entitled to a share in the weekly jackpot prize (of around £6 million when the lottery started and about £8 million per week during 1995). There are a variety of smaller prizes for those who match five out of six numbers or four out of six and so on.

For the lottery to take place at all, however, considerable effort had to be invested in setting up the national network of authorized lottery ticket agents – places where you can buy a lottery ticket – and installing appropriate computer links from each outlet to the lottery organizers so that lottery ticket sales and the numbers chosen can be centrally registered. Understandably, for the lottery to be 'successful' in terms of ensuring a sufficient number of tickets were bought each week, then an adequate network of ticket agents was needed. The lottery company – Camelot – was relatively selective in its approach to authorizing such outlets with a view to ensuring that outlets chosen – typically retail outlets of some description – had a sufficiently high number of customers passing through that outlet in terms of their normal business. Understandably, the company did not want to have a chain of outlets which normally only attracted a few customers since this would be unlikely to generate much in the way of lottery ticket sales.

From the perspective of the retail outlets which were interested in trying to have themselves chosen as lottery outlets, not only would lottery ticket sales generate income in the form of commission but there was also the anticipation that customers would be attracted to the outlet to buy a lottery ticket and might then also buy other products. One such organization operated a chain of almost 250 small grocery/supermarket shops. Typically, these were located in out-of-town centres in housing estate areas and relied largely on convenience shopping from local residents. The shops typically would have a limited range of food products, alcoholic drinks, a small frozen food section, newspapers and magazines, tobacco and confectionery. Some 129 of their outlets had been awarded lottery outlet status by Camelot whilst 112 outlets had not (on the basis that their weekly turnover and customer numbers did not justify them being a lottery ticket agent). The layout of most of these shops was much the same, with a small counter at the front of the shop with the cash till, a rack of newspapers and magazines, tobacco products and confectionery. Other products, notably food and drink, were in the main body of the shop. Lottery tickets were also available from this counter enabling customers to purchase a ticket when they had completed the rest of their shopping or simply to buy a ticket by itself. The finance director of the company was keen to establish fairly quickly after the launch of the lottery whether there was any 'knock-on' effect in terms of customers buying lottery tickets who also bought items which they might not otherwise have bought. Given the store layout, such 'impulse' purchases were likely to be newspapers and magazines, tobacco products and confectionery (NTC products). Purchases of non-NTC products – food, drink, etc. – were unlikely to show any increase it was thought.

Some relatively straightforward statistical analysis was undertaken although the methodology adopted was particularly important. One approach would have been for the company to look at average (mean) weekly sales of the 129 lottery outlets before the introduction of the lottery and then again after its introduction. It might then be thought that any increase in NTC mean sales could be implied to relate to the introduction of the lottery and the fact that lottery ticket purchasers were 'impulse' buying. However, the problem with such an approach lies in the concept of something known as seasonality (something we look at in detail in Chapter 13). Briefly, the sales of many items – like ice-cream, sun-tan lotion, umbrellas – rises at certain times of the year and falls at others – simply because of the time of year and not because of any other factors. Ice-cream sales, for example, are likely to increase in the summer and decrease in the winter. So, simply comparing mean weekly sales of the lottery outlet shops before and after the introduction of the lottery might have been misleading if sales were affected by such a seasonal effect.

The approach adopted was to compare mean weekly sales of NTC and non-NTC products before and after the introduction of the lottery but between shops which were lottery outlets and those which were not. Since it seems reasonable to assume that the same seasonal effects (if any) would affect both lottery outlet and non-lottery outlet shops in the same way, then seeing what changes in mean weekly sales had occurred in both types of shop might give a clearer picture of the impact of the lottery on such 'impulse' sales.

Table 7.27 shows the statistics calculated. The table is quite complex and will need some explanation. First, the table splits the company's shops into two categories: those authorized to act as lottery outlets and those which are not. Weekly sales are then shown for each group of shops for a period of four weeks immediately before the introduction of the lottery and a period of four weeks one month after the introduction. Weekly sales are further divided between sales of NTC products and non-NTC products. So, for example, we see that lottery outlet shops had mean weekly sales of £2,296 of NTC products before the introduction of the lottery and mean weekly sales of NTC products of £2,781 after the introduction. (The standard deviation of each mean is also shown.) It is tempting to conclude, based on these figures alone, that customers on average are increasing their purchases of NTC products in these lottery outlet shops. However, as we commented earlier, this increase of £485 per shop per week could have arisen for a number of other reasons, most notably the fact that the two periods are at different times of the year (some three months apart) and sales potentially could have increased because of the seasonal effect noted earlier. This is where the other statistics are helpful.

First we note that mean weekly sales of NTC products in non-lottery outlet shops have also increased from £1,544 to £1,557 – but an increase of only £13. Since the only major difference between the two types of shop is whether they sell lottery tickets or not this does tend to support the view that customers coming to buy lottery tickets were increasing their purchases of items on display immediately around the lottery ticket stand (the NTC products).

Table 7.27
Weekly sales per shop

	Before introduction of National Lottery £	After introduction of National Lottery £
Lottery outlet shops (*n* = 129)		
NTC products:		
Mean sales	2,296	2,781
Std. dev.	701	1,045
Non-NTC products:		
Mean sales	1,348	1,346
Std. dev.	427	403
Non-Lottery outlet shops (*n* = 112)		
NTC products:		
Mean sales	1,544	1,557
Std. dev.	540	539
Non-NTC products:		
Mean sales	1,218	1,214
Std. dev.	429	415

This view is further supported if we examine mean weekly sales of non-NTC products. In the case of both types of shop these have remained virtually unchanged: about £1,350 for lottery outlet shops and about £1,220 for non-lottery outlet shops. Looking at the statistics together, it is clear that it is only the mean weekly sales of NTC products in lottery outlet shops that have changed since the introduction of the lottery.

The finance director was equally convinced of this apparent effect of the lottery in terms of an average increase in weekly sales per shop of almost £500 – although of course there was no guarantee that this effect would continue longer-term (since it might relate simply to the novelty effect of the new lottery). It also had to be pointed out to the finance director that variability of weekly sales of NTC products in lottery outlet stores had also increased – from a standard deviation of £701 to one of £1,045. It is evident that not all outlets are experiencing the same impact on NTC sales (although analysis of the full data set did reveal that all shops did experience an increase, although of different amounts) and indeed the relative variability around the mean, as measured by the coefficient of variation, has increased from about 30% to about 38%.

The company quite rightly decided that regular three-monthly monitoring of these stores would be undertaken to keep an eye on any developing trends.

Self-review questions

1 Why are statistics based on the raw data more accurate than those based on aggregated data?

2 Why will the calculation of the mean be affected by open-ended intervals whilst the median will not?

3 Under what conditions will the mean take a higher value than the median?

4 Under what conditions would you prefer to use the median rather than the mean as the measure of average?

5 What would you conclude about the distribution of data in a data set if the mean and median were the same?

6 Does the standard deviation measure dispersion around the mean or the median?

7 What statistic is used to compare two or more standard deviations?

8 Does a positive skew distribution lean to the left or to the right?

9 Why will dispersion statistics based on aggregated data be inaccurate?

Student exercises

1 A large national retail organization is currently reviewing its long-term strategy. The organization operates a number of small to medium-size food stores in different parts of the country, organized on a regional basis. Table 7.28 shows the summary statistics for stores in two regions, Northern and Eastern, in terms of profitability in 1994. Comment on profitability between the two regions.

Table 7.28
Profits for stores in Northern Region and in Eastern Region
(Figures in £s)

	Northern	Eastern
Sample size	113	121
Minimum	–13,070	–4,130
Maximum	93,050	98,800
Range	106,120	102,920
Mean	12,981.2	16,882.2
Median	6,840	9,580
Standard deviation	17,476.3	18,804.7
Coefficient of variation	134.6%	111.4%
Lower quartile	3,530	3,930
Upper quartile	15,170	25,310
Interquartile range	11,640	21,380
Skewness	2.3	1.8

Source: Finance department.

241

2 Table 6.2 in Chapter 6 showed the age distribution of the UK population in 1901 and in 1991. Using the statistics introduced in this chapter compare the two age distributions.

3 Table 6.6 in Chapter 6 showed data relating to the age at marriage of males and females in the UK in 1980 and in 1990. Outline the main changes that have taken place over this period.

4 Table 6.7 shows unemployment by age and by sex in January 1993. Compare males and females unemployed in terms of their age distributions.

5 Table 6.8 shows the size of manufacturing units in 1992. Comment on the data using the statistics introduced in this chapter. Collect comparable data for an earlier year and compare changes between the two years.

6 Table 6.9 shows data on the duration of marriage for those divorcing in 1971 and in 1990. Compare the changes over this period.

7 Table 7.29 shows data on the distribution of household income 1990–91 for the UK as a whole and for two regions. Compare the regional distributions with that for the UK using the statistics introduced in this chapter. Compare your relevant statistics with that shown in the table under the heading 'Average gross weekly income per household'.

Table 7.29
Distribution of household income 1990–91

Percentage of households in each weekly income group	UK	Yorkshire & Humberside	South East
Under 80	12.2	14.6	8.8
80 < 125	11.3	12.5	8.8
125 < 175	8.9	9.5	7.1
175 < 275	15.5	19.1	13.5
275 < 375	15.4	15.1	14.1
375 < 475	12.5	11.1	13.1
475 < 650	12.9	11.3	15.6
650 or over	11.4	6.7	18.9
Average gross weekly income per household (£)	350.1	295.5	434.1

Source: *Regional Tends 1993.*

8 Return to Table 4.7 in Chapter 4 which provided data on road accidents in Great Britain. From the table find the data on those killed and seriously injured by age group in 1981 and 1991.
    Compare the two age distributions. What factors could you suggest as to why the two distributions differ?

9 Return to Table 7.21 showing average earnings by employee and sex. Calculate a real average earnings series for each sex and comment on the findings.

10 Return to Table 7.25 showing the RPI from 1962 to 1994. Produce a rebased series to cover this entire period:

(a) using 1962 as the base;

(b) using 1974 as the base;

(c) using 1987 as the base.

11 Table 7.30 shows, for England and Wales from 1980/81 to 1991/92, the standard maintenance grant for full-time students and the real value of this grant deflated by both the RPI and the average earnings index. You have been asked to prepare a short report to your Student Union president commenting on this data. You have also been asked to advise on which of these two deflators (RPI or average earnings), or others you might suggest, is the more appropriate.

Table 7.30
Student awards – real value and parental contributions: England & Wales
(£s and percentages)

	Standard maintenance grant[1] (£)	Real value (£) at 1991–92 prices deflated by		Average assessed contribution by parents[2] (percentages)	Student loans[3] (£) (maximum)
		Retail prices index	Average earnings index		
1980/81	1,430	2,811	3,481	13	..
1981/82	1,535	2,708	3,362	14	..
1982/83	1,595	2,623	3,211	19	..
1983/84	1,660	2,597	3,146	20	..
1984/85	1,775	2,652	3,130	25	..
1985/86	1,830	2,581	2,979	30	..
1986/87	1,901	2,603	2,886	30	..
1987/88	1,972	2,592	2,751	31	..
1988/89	2,050	2,545	2,614	31	..
1989/90	2,155	2,488	2,520	31	..
1990/91	2,265	2,358	2,438	..	420
1991/92	2,265	2,265	2,265	..	580

1 Excludes those studying in London and those studying elsewhere living in the parental home. Prior to 1982/83 Oxford and Cambridge were also excluded. Since 1984/85 the grant has included an additional travel allowance of £50.

2 Assuming full payment of parental and other contributions including a notional assessment in respect of students for whom fees only were paid by LEAs.

3 At current prices. The amounts quoted are for students studying outside London and living away from home. Different amounts are payable in the final year.

Source: *Social Trends 1993.*

8 DEALING WITH UNCERTAINTY IN BUSINESS

INTRODUCTION

In this chapter we examine how businesses can try to deal with uncertainties surrounding decisions they have to take. We examine the basics of probability and the role that probability plays in helping to deal with uncertainty and we introduce two common and useful probability distributions.

Up to this point we have – implicitly – assumed that the data and information we have about some business situation is *certain*. In practice in business the data we have may well reflect some degree of uncertainty. A business may launch a new product: it will not know for certain what next year's sales will be. A personnel manager is about to negotiate next year's pay and conditions with trade union representatives: the manager cannot know for certain what their reaction to the company's offer will be. Many situations which require a decision have some degree of uncertainty associated with them.

Probability allows us to try to measure such uncertainty and to assess how to take it into account in the decision-making process. Many of the more advanced – and useful – quantitative methods developed for business decision-making rely on probability: market research, quality control, business forecasting, statistical inference and statistical modelling are examples.

LEARNING OBJECTIVES

By the end of this chapter you should be able to:

- explain the principles of probability;
- use the multiplication and addition rules;
- explain the principle of expected value;
- use the Binomial distribution;
- use the Normal distribution.

PROBABILITY AND ITS TERMINOLOGY

Although probability is essential for more advanced applications of quantitative methods in business its principles are readily understood and applied. We shall look at the basic ideas behind probability and the language used with probability with some insultingly simple examples. Once the basic ideas have been explored we shall move on to look at more realistic business applications.

(*Note:* Gramatically, dice refers to the singular whilst the plural is die. However, we shall use the word 'dice' to refer to one or more.)

Student activity

Assume you have an ordinary six-sided dice which, as normal, has a different number between one and six on each face. You roll the dice across the table. What is the chance that:

(a) *the dice shows a six?*
(b) *the dice shows an even number?*
(c) *the dice shows a number between one and six?*
(d) *the dice shows the number seven?*

What assumptions have you made?

Basic probability is not much more than applied common sense and a little logic. With six different numbers on the dice it seems logical that the chance of any one of them being thrown is 1 in 6, or $\frac{1}{6}$ as a fraction, so this must be the chance that we throw a six. The chance of throwing an even number must be 3/6 or 1/2 since three out of the six possible numbers are even (2, 4, 6). The third part might seem an odd question but we are certain of throwing a number between one and six. It might be a bit of a puzzle as to how we actually write this numerically though. The last one is also straightforward: the answer must be zero – there is no chance of throwing the number seven since it doesn't appear anywhere on the sides of the dice.

And what about assumptions that we have made? This is actually an important question because when we are using probability – particularly in business – there are always assumptions behind the probability calculations. It is important that we make such assumptions explicit – particularly to others who might be using the results of our calculations to make a decision. In this case the critical assumption is that the dice is a 'fair' one – it has not been tampered with in any way to affect the chance of any one number being thrown.

This simple example actually introduces many of the probability concepts that we will build on. First of all, it is conventional to express the probability of something happening as a number between 0 and 1 (either as a fraction or as a decimal, it doesn't matter which) with 0 implying that something can never happen and 1 implying that something is certain to happen. It will also be helpful at this stage to introduce some of the terminology or jargon that surrounds probability. Some of the terms we shall be using from now on include the following:

Experiment

An experiment is some activity or action that takes place – like throwing the dice.

Outcomes

Outcomes are the results of the experiment. In the case of the dice there are six possible outcomes – each being one of the six numbers.

Events

An event is the specific outcome(s) that we are interested in from the experiment. Notice that we can define different events from exactly the same experiment with the same outcomes. One event might be the dice showing a six. A different event might be the dice showing an even number.

We said, quite rightly, that the probability of throwing a six was $\frac{1}{6}$ and the way we can formalize this is to say that:

$$\text{Probability of an event} = \frac{\text{number of ways the event could occur}}{\text{total number of outcomes}}$$

We would normally write 'probability of an event' as P(E), where E stands for event. So in the case of the event being a 6 we have:

$$P(6) = \frac{1}{6}$$

since there are six different outcomes but only one of them meets our definition of the event. Similarly:

$$P(\text{Even}) = \frac{3}{6} = 0$$

$$P(1 \text{ to } 6) = \frac{6}{6} = 1 \text{ (implying that this event \textit{must} happen)}$$

$$P(7) = \frac{0}{6} = 0 \text{ (implying the event can \textit{never} happen)}$$

A few more bits of terminology that we will find useful are as follows:

Mutually exclusive events

Two events are said to be mutually exclusive if they cannot occur simultaneously. If we define event E_1 as the dice showing a six and event E_2 as the dice showing an odd number then, by definition, E_1 and E_2 are mutually exclusive and:

$$P(E_1 \text{ and } E_2) = 0$$

That is the probability of both events occurring together is zero. Clearly not all events are mutually exclusive.

Independent and conditional events

Two events are said to be independent if the probability of one event occurring does not affect the probability of the other event occurring. Consider two events: E_1 is that you pass your exam in quantitative methods; E_2 is that you have red hair. There is no reason to assume that the two events are in any way connected and we would class them as independent: the probability of your passing the exam is in no way affected by the probability of your having red hair.

However, some events may not be independent: one event may be conditional or dependent on another. Let E_1 stay the same. Let E_2 be the probability that you have carefully studied this book and completed all the exercises before the exam. It now seems reasonable to say that the probability of E_1 will depend on E_2 (although notice that we're carefully not saying whether the probability of E_1 will go up or go down!). We shall see shortly that it is important to distinguish between events which are conditional and events which are independent.

Collectively exhaustive events

A group of events is said to be collectively exhaustive if they include all possible outcomes from the experiment (like showing a number between one and six).

Complement of an event

If two events are collectively exhaustive and independent then we can use the probability of the first event to deduce the probability of the second. Let E_1 be that the dice shows a six. Let E_2 be that the dice shows one to five. These two events are independent and collectively exhaustive and one is the complement of the other. This means that:

$$P(E_1) = \frac{1}{6} \text{ (as we already know)}$$

But since $P(E_1 \text{ and } E_2) = 1$ (by definition since they are collectively exhaustive) then:

$$P(E_2) = 1 - P(E_1) = 1 - \frac{1}{6} = \frac{5}{6}$$

In more complex applications of probability it can often be easier to determine the probability of something *not* happening and then use the complement principle to deduce the probability of something happening.

MEASURING PROBABILITY

Although it might sound strange there are in fact three different ways in which we might consider actually measuring or quantifying the probability of some event. Before we explore these different ways it will be instructive to consider what a probability actually does measure.

Student activity

As we have seen the probability of each number showing on any one throw is 1/6. Do you think each of the six numbers will appear once and once only if we throw the dice six times? Explain why you think this will, or will not, happen.

It seems highly unlikely (although still possible) that on throwing the dice six times each of the six numbers appears once and once only. The reasoning behind this is to do with what the 1/6 probability figure actually means (and equally what it does not). The figure does not mean that a given number will appear exactly one time out of six. Rather it is a measure of a long run average. If we throw the dice a sufficient number of times then – on average – each number will appear 1/6th of the time. It is important when dealing with probability situations that we remember that probability is a long-run average and not a guarantee that something will – or will not – occur. With this is mind we can detail the three approaches to measuring probability.

A priori approach

The first of these is known as the *a priori* (pronounced 'a pry-or-eye') approach, or the theoretical approach. This approach assumes that *before* the experiment takes place we can quantify the probabilities of different events. Throwing a dice and assessing the probability of a six being thrown is an example of this. Before we actually throw the dice we can assess the probability of the event as $\frac{1}{6}$.

Empirical approach

We are not always in a position, however, to assess probability prior to an experiment using theory or logic. Consider the following example. A company manufactures compact discs (CDs). Some of these contain a minor fault which means they shouldn't be sold as they will not play properly.

Student activity

If we choose one of the CDs at random what is the probability that it will be faulty?

The answer is: we don't know! And there is no way of assessing this probability on an *a priori* basis. What we would have to do is assess the empirical probability. We could take a sample of CDs – say 1,000 – and carefully check each one. If we found, for example, that five of these were faulty then we would assess the empirical probability of a CD being faulty as:

P(Faulty) = 5/1,000 = 0.005

Subjective approach

The third approach is to provide a personal, subjective assessment of probability.

Student activity

What is the probability of your passing the quantitative methods exam?

Clearly, the *a priori* approach cannot be used since there is no theoretical way of quantifying this. We might use the empirical approach to see how many people in the past have passed the exam and use this as the probability. The problem with this is that it doesn't relate to you personally. Subjectively you might feel you have a better (or worse) chance of passing than this long-run average. So, in some circumstances, we might just use a personal view about the likelihood of something occurring.

Student activity

We're back to the dice problem.

You've rolled the dice 100 times. Every time the dice has shown a number between one and five but never six.

You throw the dice one more time. What is the probability that a six will appear this time?

The answer is: it depends which approach you use. On an *a priori* basis the answer is 1/6 since, theoretically, a six has the same chance of occurring as the other numbers. Using the empirical approach you might argue the probability is 0, since it has not happened in the past 100 throws. Subjectively you might say the probability was 1 – it must happen since a six is long overdue given the long-run average concept of probability. This is why – as we commented earlier – that when applying probability for real it is critically important to make any assumptions about the situation quite explicit.

LAWS OF PROBABILITY

When dealing with simple probability problems we can use the approach developed to quantify the probability of an event occurring. For more complex problems, however, we need to be more formal in our approach and it is useful to use the two basic laws for dealing with probability.

The multiplication law

Consider a simple experiment. We throw our six-sided dice and note the number that is thrown. We then throw the dice a second time.

Student activity

What is the probability that on both occasions we throw a six?

The approach is fairly straightforward. Let us use the terminology we have developed. Let E_1 be that the first dice shows a six. Let E_2 be that the second dice shows a six. We then require:

$P(E_1 \text{ and } E_2)$

that is, the probability that *both* events occurred. It seems logical to say that:

$P(E_1) = 1/6$
$P(E_2) = 1/6$

so:

$P(E_1 \text{ and } E_2) = P(E_1) \times P(E_2) = 1/6 \times 1/6 = 1/36$

That is, there is a probability of 1/36 that we will throw two sixes. For obvious reasons this is known as the multiplication law. When we are dealing with situations where we require *both* events to occur then the multiplication law can be used. The law is easily extended to cover more events:

$P(E_1 \text{ and } E_2 \text{ and } E_3) = P(E_1) \times P(E_2) \times P(E_3)$

and so on.

Student activity

A firm manufactures a product which has three small electrical components (A, B, C) in it. The firm offers a money-back guarantee if any of these three components fails within 12 months. In the past it has found that 98% of component A lasts at least 12 months, 99% of component B and 95% of component C.

Calculate the probability for a product chosen at random that:

(a) *all three components will last at least 12 months;*

(b) *the product will be returned by the customer within 12 months as faulty.*

What assumptions have you made?

If we denote the probabilities of the three components as not developing a fault within 12 months as:

$$P(A) = 0.98$$
$$P(B) = 0.99$$
$$P(C) = 0.95$$

then for part (**a**) we require the probability that none develop a fault within 12 months:

$$P(A \text{ and } B \text{ and } C) = P(A) \times P(B) \times P(C)$$
$$= 0.98 \times 0.99 \times 0.95$$
$$= 0.92169$$

that is, there is a probability of just over 92% that a product chosen at random will not develop a fault within 12 months.

For part (**b**) we use the complement principle:

$$P(\text{No fault}) + P(\text{Some fault}) = 1$$

That is, the probability that a product does not develop a fault plus the probability that a product develops some fault must equal 1. This then gives:

$$P(\text{Some fault}) = 1 - P(\text{No fault})$$
$$= 1 - 0.92169$$
$$= 0.07831$$

as the probability that a product chosen at random will develop some fault in the next 12 months. Notice that it would have been quite difficult to work out P(Some fault) directly since there are a number of different ways this could happen (e.g. A is faulty but B and C are not; B is faulty but A and C are not and so on).

The question about assumptions is again a critical one. There are two key assumptions that we might have made. The first is that the (empirical) probabilities we have observed in the past about faulty components will continue to apply in the future. The second assumption is to do with the fact that these three events (A, B, C being faulty/not faulty) are independent of each other. In other words, we are implicitly assuming that the probability of B being faulty is not affected by whether A or C was faulty. For the multiplication law this is a critical assumption because the law as we have it only works if the events we are dealing with are independent.

But what if events are not independent – what if they are conditional? Then we must amend the law to take this into account. Let us illustrate with a different experiment. We take a pack of ordinary playing cards: there are 52 cards in the pack, and 26 are black and 26 are red. What is the probability of choosing two cards at random and that both cards are red?

Student activity

Determine the probability that both cards are red.

At first sight we have another application of the multiplication law since we have a *both/and* situation. Let us define the two events as:

E_1 : the first card is red
E_2 : the second card is red

We require:

$P(E_1$ and $E_2)$

But a little thought reveals that the two events are *not* independent: the probability of E_2 will be affected by E_1.

$P(E_1) = 26/52 = 0.5$

$P(E_2)$, however, will not be 0.5 but will depend on E_1. If E_1 was red then:

$P(E_2) = 25/51$

since there are now 25 red cards in the remaining 51. If E_2 was *not* red then:

$P(E_2) = 26/51$

since there are still 26 red cards from the 51 remaining.
    When dealing with conditional events we must amend the law such that:

$P(E_1$ and $E_2) = P(E_1) \times P(E_2 | E_1)$

where $P(E_2 | E_1)$ is known as the conditional probability of E_2 *given that* E_1 has occurred (the symbol | is read as 'given that'). Here we have:

$P(E_2 | E_1) = 25/51$

so:

$$P(E_1 \text{ and } E_2) = P(E_1) \times P(E_2 | E_1)$$
$$= 26/52 \times 25/51$$
$$= 0.2451 \text{ (to 4 decimal places)}$$

Student activity

In a pack of cards there are four different suits each comprising 13 cards: hearts, clubs, diamonds, spades. Hearts and diamonds are red suits, clubs and spades are black.

If we choose two cards at random what is the probability that:

(a) *both will be clubs?*
(b) *the first will be a heart and the second a diamond?*
(c) *the first will be black and the second will be a heart?*

For part (**a**) we have:

E_1 : the first card is a club
E_2 : the second card is a club
$$P(E_1 \text{ and } E_2) = P(E_1) \times P(E_2 | E_1)$$
$$= 13/52 \times 12/51$$
$$= 0.0588$$

For part (**b**) we have:

E$_1$: the first card is a heart
E$_2$: the second card is a diamond

$$P(E_1 \text{ and } E_2) = P(E_1) \times P(E_2|E_1)$$
$$= 13/52 \times 13/51$$
$$= 0.0637$$

For part (**c**) we have:

E$_1$: the first card is black
E$_2$: the second card is a heart

$$P(E_1 \text{ and } E_2) = P(E_1) \times P(E_2|E_1)$$
$$= 26/52 \times 13/51$$
$$= 0.1275$$

It is worth noting that if:

$$P(E_2|E_1) = P(E_2)$$

then the two events E$_1$ and E$_2$ are independent.

Addition law

The second law of probability is the addition law. Where the multiplication law is concerned with situations where two (or more) events *both* occur, the addition law is concerned with those situations where *either* of two events occur.

Consider the following example. We return to the pack of cards and we wish to calculate the probability that, on choosing one card at random, the card chosen is either an ace or a king. If we use the following notation:

E$_1$: card is an ace
E$_2$: card is a king

then we require:

$$P(E_1 \text{ or } E_2) \text{ which is given by } P(E_1) + P(E_2)$$

In this example:

$$P(E_1) = 4/52$$
$$P(E_2) = 4/52$$

so:

$$P(E_1 \text{ or } E_2) = P(E_1) + P(E_2)$$
$$= 4/52 + 4/52$$
$$= 8/52 = 0.1538$$

which we can confirm is correct since there are eight cards out of 52 which are either aces or kings.

Student activity

Using the rule determine the probability that a card chosen at random is either an ace or a heart.

Is there any reason for thinking your answer using the rule might be incorrect?

If we apply the rule to find the probability that a card is either an ace or a heart we have:

E_1: card is an ace
E_2: card is a heart

$P(E_1) = 4/52$
$P(E_2) = 13/52$

so:

$$P(E_1 \text{ or } E_2) = P(E_1) + P(E_2)$$
$$= 4/52 + 13/52$$
$$= 17/52$$

But on reflection this doesn't seem right. We are actually counting one card twice – the ace of hearts – which is both an ace and a heart so the 17/52 result is incorrect. The reason for this is that the basic law only works where two events are mutually exclusive. If they are not – as in the ace/heart example – then the rule must be amended:

$$P(E_1 \text{ or } E_2) = P(E_1) + P(E_2) - P(E_1 \text{ and } E_2)$$

where we subtract the probability that the card is both an ace and a heart. (You might have realized that the probability given by $P(E_1 \text{ and } E_2)$ is determined using the multiplication law.) In this case $P(E_1 \text{ and } E_2) = 1/52$ so we now have:

$$P(E_1 \text{ or } E_2) = P(E_1) + P(E_2) - P(E_1 \text{ and } E_2)$$
$$= 4/52 + 13/52 - 1/52$$
$$= 16/52$$

as the correct answer.

The two laws we have developed in this section form the basis for complex problem-solving involving probability.

SOME BUSINESS EXAMPLES

Having looked at how probability can be used for cards and dice let us look at a number of illustrative business examples. Since the best way to understand how probability can be applied is to practise we have set up a number of examples each followed by a Student activity exercise and a discussion of the solution.

Example 1

Your company is trying to decide which credit or bank account debit cards to accept when customers are purchasing products. The company has collected data on a random sample of 2,125 of its customers and found that the number of customers with the following credit/debit cards is:

Card type	No. of customers
American Express	1,360
Access	1,466
Visa	1,679
Switch	567
Storecard	1,211

Student activity

(a) If 2,083 customers have at least one card what is the probability that a customer does not have any cards?

(b) What is the probability that a customer has a Visa card?

(c) Independent research shows that 58% of people have both an Access and a Visa card. What is the probability that a customer has either of these?

(d) Looking at the data I conclude that at least 38% of customers hold both a Visa card and a Storecard. Am I right or wrong?

The answer to each part of the question is as follows.

For part (**a**) we know that:

$$P(\text{No cards}) = 1 - P(\text{At least one card})$$

So, since we are told that 2,083 customers have at least one card, we then know that:

$$P(\text{No cards}) = 1 - 2,083/2,125 = 0.02$$

For part (**b**) the answer can be obtained directly from the information given:

$$P(\text{Visa}) = 1,679/2,125 = 0.79$$

For part (**c**) we must use the addition law in the form:

$$P(A \text{ or } V) = P(A) + P(V) - P(A \text{ and } V)$$

since events A and V are not mutually exclusive (some people have both cards). So:

$$P(A \text{ or } V) = 1,466/2,125 + 1,679/2,125 - (0.58)$$
$$= 0.90$$

For part (**d**) we know that a total of 2,890 customers hold Visa or a Storecard. We are told that 2,083 customers have at least one card so at least 807 customers (2,890–2,083) must have both these cards. This is 38% of the total sample so I am right in my statement.

Example 2

A company operates 30-day terms for all its customers meaning that customers are expected to pay their bills/invoices within 30 days of receipt. Experience has shown that 80% of all customer accounts are paid within one month and 70% of the remainder are settled during the second month. Of those accounts still unpaid after two months 50% are settled during the third month after a final demand has been sent. The company is trying to incorporate such uncertainty into its cash flow projection for the next three months.

Student activity

(**a**) What is the probability for any particular account that payment is received by the end of the second month?

(**b**) What is the probability for any particular account that payment is received by the end of the third month?

(**c**) What proportion of payments for all accounts can the firm expect to have received by the end of the third month?

We use the following notation:

S_n = account settled in month n
NS_n = account not settled in month n

We are given:

$P(S_1) = 0.80$ hence $P(NS_1) = 0.20$
$P(S_2) = 0.70$ hence $P(NS_2) = 0.30$
$P(S_3) = 0.50$ hence $P(NS_3) = 0.50$

For part (**a**) we require $P(S_2 | NS_1)$ – the probability that an account is settled during the second month given that it was not settled during the first month. This is given by:

$P(NS_1) \times P(S_2) = 0.20 \times 0.70 = 0.14$

For part (**b**) we require $P(S_3 | NS_1 \text{ and } NS_2)$ – the probability that an account is settled during the third month given that it was not settled either during the first or second month. This is given by:

$P(NS_1) \times P(NS_2) \times P(S_3) = 0.20 \times 0.30 \times 0.50 = 0.03$

For part (**c**) we know will have 80% of all accounts settled in month one; 14% of all accounts settled in month two; 3% of all accounts settled in month three. Hence 97% of all accounts will be settled by the end of month three.

Example 3

Two local construction firms are in competition when bidding for work. In the recent past, of 20 contracts for which they have competed, ten were awarded to company A, six to company B and the remainder to other companies. Three new contracts have been offered for tender.

Student activity

What is the probability that:

(**a**) *A will win all three contracts?*

(**b**) *B will obtain at least one contract?*

We have:

> P(A wins) = 0.5
>
> P(B wins) = 0.3
>
> P(Neither) = 0.2

For part (**a**) we use the multiplication law and if we assume the events are independent then:

> P(A wins all 3) = P(A) × P(A) × P(A)
> = 0.5 × 0.5 × 0.5
> = 0.125

For part (**b**) we require:

> P(B wins at least one) = 1 – P(B wins none)
>
> P(B fails to win any one contract) = 1 – 0.3 = 0.7

Hence:

P(B wins at least one) = 1 – (0.7 × 0.7 × 0.7)
> = 1 – 0.343
> = 0.657

Example 4

A company purchases two machines, X and Y. It is estimated that machine X has an 80% chance of lasting three years and machine Y a 75% chance.

Student activity

What is the probability that:

(a) *both machines last three years?*

(b) *neither machine lasts three years?*

(c) *at least one machine lasts three years?*

We have:

X: machine X lasts three years
Y: machine Y lasts three years

P(X) = 0.8
P(Y) = 0.75

For part (**a**) we require, assuming the two events are independent:

P(X) × P(Y) = 0.8 × 0.75 = 0.6

That is, there is a 60% probability that both machines will last three years.
For part (**b**) we have:

P(X does not last three years) = 1 − 0.8 = 0.2

P(Y does not last three years) = 1 − 0.75 = 0.25

Hence:

P(neither lasts three years) = 0.2 × 0.25 = 0.05

Finally for part (**c**) we require:

1 − P(neither machine lasts) = 1 − 0.05 = 0.95

PROBABILITY TREES

For more complex problems it can be difficult to make sure you fully understand all the possible outcomes from that situation – as you may have found out in some of the last section's activities. One approach that can be quite useful is to construct what is known as a *probability tree* for a problem. This tries to ensure that we have all outcomes properly identified and can be useful in determining the probabilities of events. It can also be useful at illustrating a complex problem to someone who has little grasp of probability.

Figures 8.1 to 8.4 show the construction of a probability tree for Example 2 in the previous section. The purpose of a tree is to show diagrammatically all the outcomes from some experiment and their respective probabilities. From Fig. 8.1 we see that, in Month 1, there are two possible outcomes: the invoice is paid or it is not. Starting from the left we draw two 'branches' to represent each of the outcomes. Obviously in Month 2 we are faced with two

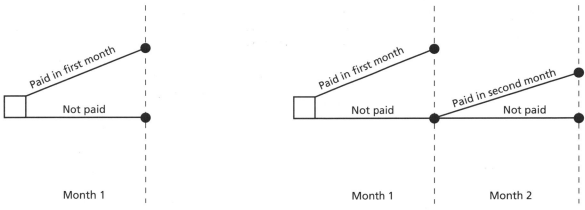

Fig. 8.1 **Probability tree: Stage I**

Fig. 8.2 **Probability tree: Stage II**

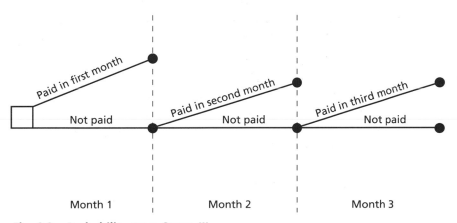

Fig. 8.3 **Probability tree: Stage III**

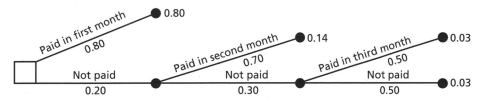

Fig. 8.4 **Completed probability tree**

comparable outcomes. However, these two branches are only relevant to (i.e. are conditional upon) the Not paid branch for Month 1 and are drawn accordingly. Similarly for Month 3 we add two more branches. Finally in Figure 8.4 we complete the tree by adding the probability of each outcome. We can also calculate the probabilities of each sequence of outcomes putting these as we have done at the very end of each branch.

A probability tree is quite easy to draw for a problem but can prove very useful in helping us understand a probability situation and allowing us to assess whether we have calculated a probability correctly.

Two points in particular are worthy of note and will help us check that we have drawn a tree correctly. The first is that the probabilities for each set of branches (for Months 1, 2, 3) must total to 1 since each of the branches is collectively exhaustive and mutually exclusive. The second point is that the probabilities shown at the right-hand tip of each branch must also total to 1 for the same reasons (0.80 + 0.14 + 0.07 + 0.03).

Student activity

A manufacturing firm is keen to try to improve the quality of its product. At present it is estimated that about 2% of its current output is substandard in some way and is classed as a reject. However, output is not checked before it is sold to customers. If a customer buys a substandard item then they are expected to return it to the company for a full refund. Not only is this costly but it also adversely affects the company's reputation.

The firm is thinking of investing in an automatic quality testing piece of equipment which will check each item after it is produced. However, this equipment is not 100% reliable. It may identify an item as a reject when in fact it is not. Similarly, it may pass an item as satisfactory when in fact it is substandard. The probability of an item being classed as a reject when it is not is 0.01 and the probability of not being classed as a reject when it is substandard is 0.003.

(a) *What is the probability of an item being substandard but passed as OK?*

(b) *What is the probability of an item not being rejected and not being substandard?*

Use a probability tree.

The probability tree is given in Fig. 8.5. Output will either be substandard or satisfactory (although without testing we do not know which category any individual item will fall into). We are told that 2% of current output is substandard so the probability of an item being satisfactory is 1 − 0.02 or 0.98. If we assume that all output will be tested (since we will not know in advance whether an item is substandard or not) then for both satisfactory and substandard output there are two branches: output will be tested and rejected or tested and accepted. We are told that the probability of an item being classed as a reject when it is not is 1%. This will be the third branch from the top: output which is actually satisfactory but which has been – incorrectly – rejected after testing. We then know that the bottom branch must have a probability of 0.99 (1 − 0.01). Similar logic applies to the top two branches. The probability of a substandard item not being classed after testing as a reject is 0.003 so the probability of a substandard item correctly

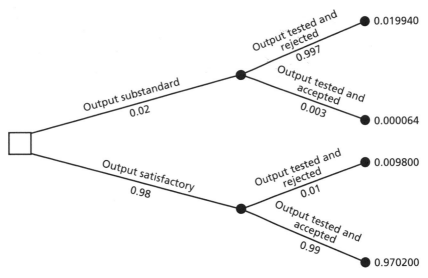

Fig. 8.5 Probability tree

being classed as a reject is 0.997 (1 − 0.003).

For the two questions set we then have:

(a) 0.02 × 0.003 = 0.00006

(b) 0.98 × 0.99 = 0.9702

We can also see from the tree that if we install the testing equipment then overall it will classify 99.014% of all output correctly (0.01994 + 0.9702).

Whenever we have drawn a tree for a problem we should always go back through the problem to check that we have the logic correct – that is the tree matches the probability and outcome information contained in the problem. It is very easy in more complex problems to draw part of the tree incorrectly and you need to check for this.

EXPECTED VALUE

One addition to using probability to help decision-making involves the use of what is known as *expected value*. The principles of expected value are easily illustrated.

Student activity

A friend has asked you to engage in a bet. On the throw of an ordinary dice if the dice shows a six your friend wins the bet and you pay him £5. If it doesn't show a six your friend will pay you £2.50.

Would you take the bet (assuming your friend was honest)?

Our logic might run as follows. I have a 1/6 chance of losing £5. I have a 5/6 chance of winning £2.50. In the long run (if I were to get involved in this bet a large number of times) then 1/6 of the time I would expect to lose and 5/6th of the time I'd expect to win. This means that:

Probability	Financial outcome
1/6	−£5
5/6	+£2.50

So the long-run outcome would be:

$$(1/6 \times -5) + (5/6 \times 2.50) = £1.25$$

That is, on average and in the long run I would expect to be £1.25 in profit for each bet that took place. It seems too good to turn down and I'd accept the bet (assuming I didn't think my friend might have tampered with the dice in some way).

Of course, this calculation does not guarantee that if we play the bet only once I won't be out of pocket (having had to pay £5 if I lost). But what we have done is to use both the probability information together with the financial outcomes to assess whether the long-term net outcome would be favourable to us or not. Effectively, we have used this information to help make a decision.

In fact, what we have calculated is the *expected value* of a decision. We did this quite easily simply by taking each outcome in turn, multiplying the probability of that outcome by its financial consequences and adding all of these multiplications together. As a formula we have:

$$\text{Expected value (EV)} = \Sigma pv$$

where p is the probability of an outcome and v is the monetary value of that outcome.

For such a simple calculation the potential as an aid to decision-making is large. We must remember, however, that the EV is not a guaranteed outcome – rather it is an indication of a long-run outcome were we to repeat the situation and the decision a large number of times. As such expected value can help us reach a decision, taking into account both the financial consequences of different outcomes and their probability.

To illustrate the business use of expected value let us return to the previous problem for which we constructed a decision tree. You will remember that the firm producing some item is thinking about installing testing equipment to check production before it goes to the customer. Suppose annual output of this item is 1 million a year. If the firm sells an item which is later found to be substandard this costs the company £15 (since the item has to be replaced free of charge to the customer). An item rejected by the testing equipment but not actually substandard costs the firm £9.50 (since production costs on that item have been incurred and now an additional item will have to be manufactured). A part which is substandard and is rejected costs the firm £5 (since some production costs have been incurred). How much should the firm be willing to pay for the testing equipment?

This is clearly an important question to the company. What is the value of this testing equipment? We can first of all calculate the expected value of *not* buying the equipment. We know from the original problem that at present all output is sold without testing and any substandard output returned by the customer for a refund. Each time this happens it costs the company £15. The EV of the current situation then is given by:

Outcome	Probability	Financial outcome
Satisfactory output	0.98	0
Substandard output	0.02	−£15

giving an EV of:

$$EV = (0.98 \times 0) + (0.02 \times -15) = -£0.30$$

But annual output is 1 million so the annual EV will be:

$$EV = 1,000,000 \times -£0.30 = -£300,000$$

That is the expected annual cost of substandard output being returned is £300,000. This is the current situation. We know from the earlier probability tree that the testing equipment will improve the situation in terms of less substandard output being sold. From the tree we see that if we install the testing equipment then there are four outcomes:

(**a**) output is substandard and is tested and rejected;

(**b**) output is substandard and is tested and accepted;

(**c**) output is satisfactory and is tested and rejected;

(**d**) output is satisfactory and is tested and accepted.

Student activity

For each of the outcomes determine the relevant probability and the relevant financial outcome. Calculate the EV for these outcomes.

We can summarize the situation as:

Outcomes	Probability	Financial outcome
(**a**) Output substandard/rejected	0.01994	−£5
(**b**) Output substandard/accepted	0.00006	−£15
(**c**) Output satisfactory/rejected	0.0098	−£9.50
(**d**) Output satisfactory/accepted	0.9702	£0
	1.00000	

The probabilities can be taken directly from the tree and we are given the cost consequences of each of the outcomes. Using the EV formula we have:

$$EV = (0.01994 \times -5) + (0.00006 \times -15) + (0.0098 \times -9.50) \\ + (0.9702 \times 0)$$
$$= -0.0997 - 0.0009 - 0.0931 + 0$$
$$= -0.1937$$

as the expected cost per item. Again, given that annual output is 1 million the annual expected cost is:

$$EV = 1,000,000 \times -0.1937 = -£193,700$$

So, without the testing equipment the expected annual cost of substandard production is £300,000. With the testing equipment this expected annual cost falls to £193,700 – an expected cost saving each year of £106,300.

We now have another piece of information to help the company's management decide what to do. If the annual cost of obtaining the testing equipment is less than £106,300 (the savings the equipment is expected to make each year) then the equipment will be worth obtaining. If the annual cost of the equipment is more than this then, based on this information, the equipment will not be cost-effective.

Expected value calculations will not indicate – by themselves – what decision to take in any given situation. However, they do provide additional information to help the decision-maker take outcomes and their relative probabilities into account.

PROBABILITY DISTRIBUTIONS

So far we have looked at the probability of a specific event occurring. We now move on to look at the *probability distribution* – the distribution of probabilities for all events from some experiment.

Consider a simple experiment where we have two ordinary coins. One side of each coin is labelled heads, the other side tails. We throw both coins in the air and note whether each coin shows heads or tails.

Student activity

What are the different possible outcomes from this experiment?
What is the probability of each outcome?

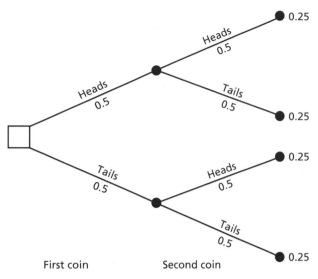

Fig. 8.6   Probability tree for two coins

Although not strictly necessary we have drawn a simple probability tree to show all the outcomes from this experiment and their respective probabilities in Fig. 8.6. There are a total of four outcomes each with a probability of 0.25. However, we can simplify this by showing the number of heads showing on the two coins (since if a coin is not showing heads it must show tails):

No. of heads	No. of ways no. of heads can occur	Probability
0	1	0.25
1	2	0.50
2	1	0.25
Total	4	1.00

So the probability of no heads (2 tails) is 0.25, the probability of 1 head is 0.5 (since this could occur in two ways) and the probability of 2 heads (no tails) is 0.25. What we have produced is the probability distribution for this experiment.

Clearly this distribution is an *a priori* distribution. We can also produce an empirical probability distribution in any given situation. Consider Table 8.1 which replicates the frequency table for the two surveys we conducted earlier into income levels at two sites we were considering for a new restaurant. We can transform these frequency distributions into probability distributions simply by dividing the frequency in each interval by the total number of frequencies for that site. So, for example, for the first interval for Site A, <£100, the relevant probability would be:

Table 8.1
Gross weekly income: Sites A and B

Income £	Site A No. of responses	Site B No. of responses
< 100	14	0
100 < 200	39	0
200 < 300	32	8
300 < 400	26	28
400 < 500	17	52
500 < 600	9	40
600 < 700	6	31
700 < 800	5	8
800 < 900	2	4
≥ 900	0	4
Total	150	175

Source: Table 4.10.

$$\frac{14}{150} = 0.093$$

That is, if we chose someone at random from Site A there is a probability of 0.093 that that person would have an income of less than £100.

Student activity

Produce the probability distributions for Site A and Site B.

Table 8.2 shows the two probability distributions. Note that the totals must now equal 1.

Table 8.2
Gross weekly income Sites A and B: probability distribution

Income £	Site A No. of responses	Site B No. of responses
< 100	0.093	0
100 < 200	0.26	0
200 < 300	0.213	0.046
300 < 400	0.173	0.16
400 < 500	0.113	0.297
500 < 600	0.06	0.229
600 < 700	0.04	0.177
700 < 800	0.033	0.046
800 < 900	0.013	0.023
≥ 900	0	0.023
Total	1	1

Source: Table 8.1.

As with any distribution we could draw an appropriate histogram. This is shown for Site A in Fig. 8.7 where the vertical axis now measures probability rather than frequency. It is also worth noting that, rather than reading probabilities directly from the table, we could now use the diagram as an alternative. Given that the total area of all the bars on the probability histogram must total to 1 then we could, for example, obtain the probability that a person's income would be £600 or more simply by calculating the area of the relevant bars on the probability histogram (shown marked in Fig. 8.7). This approach of finding the area on such a diagram to represent probability of an event is an important one to which we shall return later in this chapter.

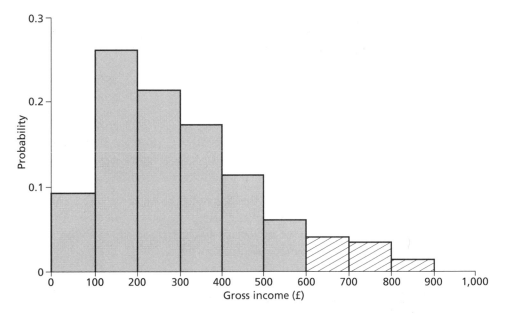

Fig. 8.7   Probability distribution: Site A

THE BINOMIAL DISTRIBUTION

In business statistics there are a number of theoretical probability distributions that are particularly important. In the rest of this chapter we shall look at two of these in particular. The first is the *binomial distribution*.

Consider the following situation. A large retail store has recently launched its own in-store credit card. Customers can obtain such a card and use it in the store to purchase items. Once each month a customer will then receive a statement showing how much they have purchased in the store that month. The store expects payment in full from the customer within two weeks of receipt of the statement.

The finance manager is concerned about the impact that late payment (or non-payment) might have on the store's cash flow situation and has organized a small research project. It has been found that at any one time 5% of the store's customers who have such a card are late with their payment. Suppose we chose two customers who have a card at random.

Student activity

Determine the probability distribution consisting of:

(a) *neither customer being late with their payment;*

(b) *one customer being late;*

(c) *both customers being late.*

This isn't very difficult and is similar to the coin tossing example we had earlier. We would have:

Outcome (no. of late payers)	Probability	
0	0.9025	(0.95×0.95)
1	0.0950	$(0.95 \times 0.05) + (0.05 \times 0.95)$
2	0.0025	(0.05×0.05)
Total	1.0000	

The only part of the distribution we have to be careful about is the probability that we have one late payer since this can occur in two different ways.

Suppose we now wish to determine the relevant distribution if we choose three customers at random.

Student activity

Calculate the probability distribution in terms of number of late payers if we now choose three customers.

Although this is a little more complex the principles are the same.

Outcome (no. of late payers)	Probability	
0	0.857375	$(0.95 \times 0.95 \times 0.95)$
1	0.135375	$(0.95 \times 0.95 \times 0.05) + (0.95 \times 0.05 \times 0.95) + (0.05 \times 0.95 \times 0.95)$
2	0.007125	$(0.95 \times 0.05 \times 0.05) + (0.05 \times 0.95 \times 0.05) + (0.05 \times 0.05 \times 0.95)$
3	0.000125	$(0.05 \times 0.05 \times 0.05)$
Total	1.0000	

The two parts which might need explanation are 1 and 2 late payers. Each of these can occur in three different ways (depending which of the three customers is a late payer or not) and we must take care that we have included all three ways in the distribution (we can always check of course, by seeing that the total equals 1).

Naturally we could extend this approach to cover four customers or 40 or 400. However, as we're sure you'll agree the more customers we include the more complex the calculations become. It would be useful to have some general method for deriving such a probability distribution and this is exactly what the binomial distribution does.

We can identify the key features of the experiment we have just described (choosing customers at random and checking to see if they are late payers):

- the experiment consisted of a number of *trials* (choosing three customers in our example);
- two outcomes were possible in each trial (late payer, not a late payer);
- the probability of the outcomes in each trial do not change;
- the trials are independent.

If these factors apply then we have what is known as a binomial experiment. Under such conditions we can the use the binomial formula to calculate directly the probabilities we have determined using (tedious) logic. The formula can be expressed as:

$$^nC_r \, p^r \, q^{(n-r)}$$

where:

^nC_r is the term for determining the number of different ways the event can occur;

p is the probability of the outcome from the trial under investigation;

q is $(1 - p)$, the probability of the specified outcome from the trial not occurring;

n is the number of trials;

r is the specified number of outcomes we are looking for.

This undoubtedly looks and sounds very complex but is in fact no more than we have done already. In our example we would have:

$p = 0.05$ (the probability of a customer being a late payer);

$q = 1 - 0.05 = 0.95$ (the probability of a customer not being a late payer);

$n =$ the number of trials, 3;

$r =$ the number of late payers out of n (0, 1, 2, 3).

The only term still to explain is the ^nC_r term. This is a shorthand way of referring to the number of ways an event can occur. It is calculated as:

$$^nC_r = \frac{n!}{r!(n-r)!}$$

where ! is a factorial (which we introduced in Chapter 2).

If we specify $r = 1$ (we want the number of ways we can obtain one late payer from three customers) then we calculate:

$$^nC_r = \frac{n!}{r!(n-r)!}$$

$$= \frac{3!}{1!(3-1)!} = \frac{6}{2} = 3$$

That is, there are three different ways of having one late payer from a sample of three customers. The calculation of the probability would then be:

$$P(1 \text{ late payer}) = {}^nC_r \, p^r \, q^{(n-r)}$$

$$= (3)(0.05)^1(0.95)^2$$

$$= 0.135375$$

Student activity

Use the formula to determine the probability of two late payers out of the three customers.

Here we have $r = 2$ so:

$$P(2 \text{ late payers}) = {}^nC_r \, p^r \, q^{(n-r)}$$

$$^nC_r = \frac{n!}{r!(n-r)!}$$

$$= \frac{3!}{2!(3-2)!} = \frac{6}{2} = 3$$

$$= (3)(0.05)^2(0.95)^1$$

$$= 0.007125$$

So, the formula is simply a convenient – and generalized – method of calculating probabilities in a binomial situation. We begin to see its usefulness when n and r take larger values. Suppose we now took a sample of 10 customers.

Student activity

Determine the probability distribution of late payers with a sample of ten customers.

Without the formula it would be very difficult to determine the number of ways in which we could have three (or four or five or ...) customers who were late payers. With the formula it becomes straightforward.

0 late payers:

$n = 10, r = 0$

$${}^{n}C_{r} = \frac{10!}{0!10!} = 1$$

(since $0! = 1$ and $10!/10!$ must also equal 1).

Then ${}^{n}C_{r}\, p^{r}\, q^{(n-r)} = 1(0.05)^{0}(0.95)^{10} = 0.5987$

1 late payer:

$n = 10, r = 1$

$${}^{n}C_{r} = \frac{10!}{1!9!} = 10$$

Then ${}^{n}C_{r}\, p^{r}\, q^{(n-r)} = 10(0.05)^{1}(0.95)^{9} = 0.3151$

2 late payers:

$n = 10, r = 2$

$${}^{n}C_{r} = \frac{10!}{2!8!} = 45$$

Then ${}^{n}C_{r}\, p^{r}\, q^{(n-r)} = 45(0.05)^{2}(0.95)^{8} = 0.0746$

3 late payers:

$n = 10, r = 3$

$${}^{n}C_{r} = \frac{10!}{3!7!} = 120$$

Then ${}^{n}C_{r}\, p^{r}\, q^{(n-r)} = 120(0.05)^{3}(0.95)^{7} = 0.0105$

4 late payers:

$n = 10, r = 4$

$${}^{n}C_{r} = \frac{10!}{4!6!} = 210$$

Then ${}^{n}C_{r}\, p^{r}\, q^{(n-r)} = 210(0.05)^{4}(0.95)^{6} = 0.00096$

5 late payers:

$n = 10, r = 5$

$${}^{n}C_{r} = \frac{10!}{5!5!} = 252$$

Then ${}^{n}C_{r}\, p^{r}\, q^{(n-r)} = 252(0.05)^{5}(0.95)^{5} = 0.00006$

It is evident that as r increases so the probability decreases and that after $r = 5$ the probability will (to 4 decimal places) effectively equal zero. We do not need therefore to work out the remaining probabilities since they will be zero. Summarizing this we have:

Outcome (no. of late payers)	Probability
0	0.5987
1	0.3151
2	0.0746
3	0.0105
4	0.00096
5	0.00006
6	0
7	0
8	0
9	0
10	0
Total	1

Mean and standard deviation of a binomial distribution

We might also ask the reasonable question: if we have a sample of ten customers how many on average will be late payers? This actually implies that we require the mean number of late payers in a sample of ten (and since we want the mean we should also want the standard deviation).

Given that the probability distribution we have just derived is the same in principle as a frequency distribution we could use the formula we developed in Chapter 7 to calculate these two statistics. Fortunately the mean and standard deviation of a binomial distribution can be derived directly.

Without proof we state that for a binomial distribution:

Mean = np

Standard deviation = $\sqrt{npq}$

So here we would have:

Mean = $10(0.05) = 0.5$

That is, the mean number of customers who would be late payers in a total of 10 customers would be 0.5. Similarly we would have:

Standard deviation = $\sqrt{10(0.05)(0.95)} = 0.6892$

Student activity

If we took a sample of 100 customers what would the mean number of late payers be, and what would be the standard deviation?

With $n = 100$ we then have:

Mean = $100(0.05) = 5$

Standard deviation = $\sqrt{100(0.05)(0.95)} = 2.1794$

We might also be able to incorporate such calculations in management information. For example, if we were told that the average amount owed per customer was £89 then we can readily determine that for every 100 customers £445 of this (5 × £89) will not have been paid and will be a debt to the store.

Binomial tables

You probably heaved a huge sigh of relief in the last Student activity exercise when we *didn't* ask you to work out the relevant probability distribution for $n = 100$! It is clear that even using the formula the calculations can be quite time-consuming. For this reason sets of pre-calculated binomial probabilities are available and one set is shown in Appendix 2. You will see that the tables cover several pages and correspond to different combinations of n and p – p values are shown across the top of each table (0.01, 0.02, 0.03 and so on) whilst different n values are shown down the side of the table ($n = 2$, $n = 5$, $n = 10$). If we are faced with a binomial problem then it may be that the specific combination of n and p appears in the tables and we can use this as a shortcut to determining the relevant probabilities. However, not all combinations of n and p will be covered in the tables which is why you do need to be able to use the formula as well.

Let us return to our example of 10 customers with a relevant p value of 0.05 (representing late payment). This combination does appear and the relevant extract from the table appears below:

		$p = 0.05$
$n = 10$	$r \geq 0$	1.0000
	1	0.4013
	2	0.0861
	3	0.0115
	4	0.0010
	5	0.0001
	6	

Notice that r only goes as far as 6 since, as we know, the probabilities rapidly tail off to zero. But how do we use the table?

The first thing to note is that the tables show cumulative probabilities and not individual probabilities. That is, the figures represent the probability that r is greater than or equal to the numerical value shown. So, for example, from the table we have:

$r \geq 0$ 1.0000

That is, the probability that r is greater than or equal to zero is 1 (by definition) and that:

$r \geq 1$ 0.4013

is the probability that r is greater than or equal to 1.

If we require an individual probability then we can use two cumulative probabilities. For example:

$$P(r \geq 0) - P(r \geq 1) = P(r = 0)$$

or:

$$1.000 - 0.4013 = 0.5987$$

which is the probability that none of the customers would be a late payer. Referring back to the earlier calculations (using the formula) you can confirm that this is the same probability.

Student activity

Suppose we took a sample of 50 customers. What is the probability that six of them would be late payers?

From the tables we require $p = 0.05$ and $n = 50$. We also require:

$$P(r \geq 5) \text{ and } P(r \geq 6)$$

which are read from the tables as 0.1036 and 0.0378 respectively. We then require:

$$P(r = 6) = P(r \geq 5) - P(r \geq 6) = 0.1036 - 0.0378 = 0.0658$$

as the solution.

THE NORMAL DISTRIBUTION

The second of the probability distributions that we will look at is the normal distribution. Whereas the binomial distribution looked at variables which were discrete in value the normal looks at variables which are continuous.

The general shape of a normal distribution is as shown in Fig. 8.8 and the distribution is often referred to as a bell-shaped curve. We see that the distribution is symmetrical about the mean (both halves are identical); the mean and the median take the same value (hence the distribution has zero skew); the total area under the curve is equal to 1; technically the curve extends to plus and minus infinity on the x axis (the curve never touches the x axis). Any variable which is normally distributed will follow this general pattern – a feature which will be useful shortly. What distinguishes one normally distributed variable from another is not the shape of the distribution but two specific statistical parameters:

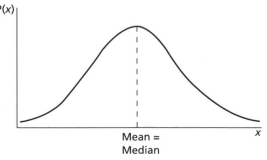

Fig. 8.8 The normal distribution

- the mean of that distribution;
- the standard deviation.

It is these two statistics that differentiate one variable from another when both are normally distributed.

With the binomial distribution we could use the formula or pre-calculated tables to obtain the relevant probabilities. For the normal distribution the only feasible approach is to use pre-calculated tables. We see why if we examine the relevant formula for normal probability:

$$P(x) = \frac{1}{\sqrt{2\pi}\sigma} e^{-\frac{(x-\mu)^2}{2\sigma^2}}$$

where: μ is the mean of the variable
σ is the standard deviation
$\pi = 3.14159$
$e = 2.71828$

and x the value for which we require a probability. The prospect of trying to use this formula (like we did for the binomial) to work out a probability is not a pleasant one.

However, there is a problem in using pre-calculated tables. We saw with the binomial that – even though it dealt only with discrete variables – not all combinations of n and p were included in such tables (and if they were not then we could always go back to the formula). The normal distribution deals with continuous variables and the combinations of mean and standard deviation that we would need our tables to cover would be almost limitless. To get round this problem statisticians have devised the concept of the *standardized normal distribution*.

Standardized normal distribution

To illustrate the principle of the standardized normal distribution and to see how we can use pre-calculated tables to obtain a normal probability we shall use a simple example.

A company specializes in packing breakfast cereal for a national chain of supermarkets under the supermarket's own brand name. The company operates two packing lines where automatic machines pack cereal into two sizes of carton. Machine A is calibrated to pack a mean of 500 grams into a carton whilst Machine B is calibrated to pack a mean of 1,000 grams. However, the packing machines are not 100% reliable and some variation in the mean weight packed arises. For Machine A the variability as measured by the standard deviation is 10 g whilst for Machine B it is 15 g. It is also known that the weight packed by each machine follows the normal distribution. However, the supermarket chain has recently been complaining because they think that too many of the cereal boxes are underweight. You have been asked to provide some information. Specifically you have been asked to find out:

What is the probability that:

- Machine A will produce a pack weighing less than 490 g?
- Machine B will produce a pack weighing more than 1,015 g?

We can summarize what we know about the two machines:

Machine A: mean amount 500 g, SD 10 g

Machine B: mean amount 1,000 g, SD 15 g

Both weight distributions are normally distributed. We know that we have two normal distributions but also that the two distributions differ from each other both in their mean and their standard deviation. To derive the relevant probabilities it might seem as if we need two individual probability tables – one for the mean and standard deviation of Machine A and another for Machine B. However, we can transform both distributions from *absolute* to *relative values*. As we shall see the benefit of doing this is that both individual distributions will then be standardized to a common format and once this is done we can easily use pre-calculated tables.

For Machine A we can determine a number of possible values for the amount packed into a cereal box:

Amount packed (g)	470	480	490	500	510	520	530
Difference from mean (g)	−30	−20	−10	0	+10	+20	+30
SDs from mean	−3	−2	−1	0	+1	+2	+3

We have taken certain (arbitrary) amounts that Machine A could pack into a box: 470 grams, 480 grams and so on. We can then see how different each of these amounts are from the mean amount (500 grams). Finally we can express this difference in term of how many standard deviations away from the mean this amount is: 470 grams, for example, is 30 grams below the mean and this represents a point 3 standard deviations below the mean. We can perform similar arithmetic on Machine B.

Student activity

Derive a comparable table for Machine B by using the same last row as in the table for Machine A (SDs from the mean). Work out what the differences from the mean would be to correspond to these SDs and then derive the corresponding amounts packed.

For Machine B we derive:

Amount packed (g)	955	970	985	1,000	1,015	1,030	1,045
Difference from mean (g)	−45	−30	−15	0	+15	+30	+45
SDs from mean	−3	−2	−1	0	+1	+2	+3

Let us now put these two tables together:

Amount packed: Machine A (g)	470	480	490	500	510	520	530
SDs from mean	−3	−2	−1	0	+1	+2	+3
Amount packed: Machine B (g)	955	970	985	1,000	1,015	1,030	1,045

What we now see is that although the two distributions differ in terms of their means and standard deviations we can convert both of them into a comparable format by expressing each distribution in terms of the number of standard deviations away from its own mean. But why bother?

The answer goes back to what we are trying to do. We are trying to resolve the problem of needing a different pre-calculated table of probabilities for every different normal distribution – each with its own, different mean and its own, different standard deviation. Instead of dealing with each normal distribution in its own right we can convert each one into a standardized scale – expressed in terms of SDs away from the mean of that distribution. We can now see, for example, that a weight of 470 grams from Machine A and 955 grams from Machine B are effectively the same – when expressed in this standardized format (see Fig. 8.9).

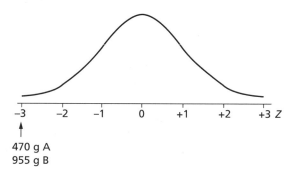

Fig. 8.9 Standardized normal distribution

Because they are the same we can use one set – and one set only – of pre-calculated normal probability tables. These are shown in Appendix 3. What someone has kindly done (and this was in pre-pocket calculator days let alone pre-computer days) is to calculate the relevant probabilities for a normal distribution which has a mean of zero and a standard deviation of 1 by using the horrendous formula that we saw earlier. This means that as long as we transform – or standardize – our specific normal distribution into a form where it also has a mean of 0 and a standard deviation of 1 then we can use these tables directly.

We should note that we would not normally work out a whole series of values for the problem as we have done here (470 g, 480 g and so on). Instead we would take the specific numerical value that we were trying to find a probability for, X, and use a simple formula to obtain what is known as a Z score:

$$Z = \frac{X - \text{Mean}}{\text{SD}}$$

where X is the specific numerical value for which we require a probability, Mean is the mean of the normal distribution that X comes from and SD is the standard deviation.

Remember for Machine A we were asked to find the probability that Machine A will process a pack weighing less than 490 g. We now see that 490 g is effectively a Z score of -1:

$$Z = \frac{X - \text{Mean}}{\text{SD}} = \frac{490 - 500}{10} = -1$$

Student activity

Find the Z score for a weight of 1,015 g for Machine B.

For Machine B the Z score would be:

$$Z = \frac{X - \text{Mean}}{\text{SD}} = \frac{1,015 - 1,000}{15} = +1$$

Using normal probability tables

We can now use the normal probability table to answer the questions that were set. Recollect that for Machine B the equipment was calibrated to fill the box with a mean of 1,000 g, SD 15 g, and we now wish to determine the probability that any one box will contain more than 1,015 g. We already have the relevant Z score ($Z = 1$).

Referring to Appendix 3 we see that the table of probabilities is shown by row and by column. Both row and column actually refer to the Z score value. The rows refer to the first decimal digit of the calculated Z score – ranging from 0.0 through to 3.0. The columns across the top of the table refer to the second decimal digit. So, looking at the first row (0.0) and then moving across the columns we effectively have Z scores of 0.00, 0.01, 0.02 and so on. Conventionally Z scores are calculated to two decimal places. Our score for Machine B is $Z = 1.00$ and we read a value from the table of 0.1587.

To understand what this shows consider Fig. 8.10. This shows the standardized normal distribution together with the Z score of 1.00. The area to the right of the Z score is the area we are seeking (to represent the proportion of all boxes which have contents more than 1,015 g).

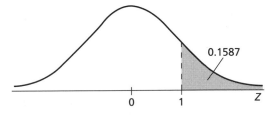

Fig. 8.10   Z = +1

This is also what the figures in the table show – the area under the curve to the right of the Z score value (referred to as the area in the tail of the distribution). So, the figure of 0.1587 implies that some 15.9% of all boxes will contain more than 1,015 g.

Used in this way the normal distribution tables allow us to calculate the proportion of the distribution that falls in any given area under the curve.

Student activity

Determine the probability that Machine A packs a box with less than 490 g.

We already know for Machine A that 490 g equates with a Z score of -1.0. Referring to the table we seem to have a problem since negative Z scores do not appear. Recollect, however, that the normal distribution is symmetrical around its mean – the two halves of the distribution are identical. This means that the probability associated with $Z = -1.0$ must be exactly the same as the probability associated with $Z = 1.0$:

$$P(Z < -1) = P(Z > 1)$$

and this is illustrated in Fig. 8.11. We know therefore that 15.9% of boxes from Machine A will weigh less the 490 g.

The use of the normal distribution and the associated table is quite straightforward although the one difficulty that some people have initially is in making sure that they are finding the probability of the correct area under the curve. Practice as always is the best way of making sure you have it right. It can also be useful for more complex applications to sketch the distribution and mark the area that you are actually asked

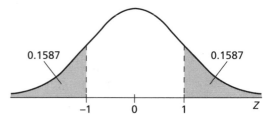

Fig. 8.11   Negative Z scores

to find a probability for (as we did in Figs 8.10 and 8.11). We shall work through some more examples to reinforce the use of the tables.

Having worked out the required probability for Machine A we have been asked to provide more:

The probability that for Machine A a box will weigh:

(**a**) less than 525 g;
(**b**) more than 480 g;
(**c**) more than 520 g but less than 525 g;
(**d**) more than 480 g but less than 510 g.

Let us examine each in turn. The first thing we must do is to transform each weight, or weights, into a Z score. Then we should sketch the curve and the area that we require. Finally we should use the table to find the relevant probability.

(**a**) The Z score is:

$$\frac{525 - 500}{10} = 2.5$$

Figure 8.12 sketches the area that we require. Notice that the area under the curve we require is to the *left* of $Z = 2.5$ since we require the probability that a box will weigh *less than* 525 g. This reinforces the benefits of sketching the curve to make sure we know exactly which area we require. From the table we find that for $Z = 2.5$ we have a probability of 0.0062. However, the probability that we require will be given by:

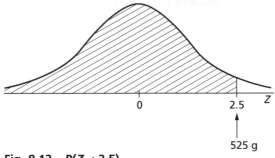

Fig. 8.12 **P(Z < 2.5)**

$$P(Z < 2.5) = 1 - 0.0062 = 0.9938$$

since the total area under the curve must equal 1. We find that 99.38% of boxes from Machine A will weigh less than 525 g.

(**b**) We require the probability that a box will weigh more than 480 g. This equates to a Z score of:

$$\frac{480 - 500}{10} = -2.0$$

The sketch is shown in Fig. 8.13 with the area that we require to the right of $Z = -2.0$. From the table we see a probability of 0.0228 which gives:

$$P(Z > -2.0) = 1 - 0.0228 = 0.9772$$

(**c**) Our third calculation requires the probability that a box will weigh more than 520 g but less than 525 g. We now require two Z scores:

$$Z_1 = \frac{520 - 500}{10} = +2.0$$

$$Z_2 = +2.5 \text{ (from part (a))}$$

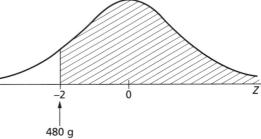

Fig. 8.13 **P(Z > –2.0)**

The sketch is in Fig. 8.14. From the tables we can find the relevant probabilities:

$$P(Z_1 > 2.0) = 0.0228$$

$$P(Z_2 > 2.5) = 0.0062$$

But we need to be careful about how we actually find the answer we require. The figure of 0.0228 is the probability that Z_1 is greater

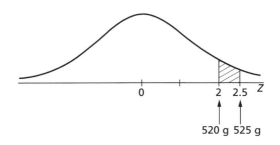

Fig. 8.14 **P(Z > 2 and Z < 2.5)**

than 2.0 (i.e. is the whole of the area to the right of $Z = 2.0$. Similarly the figure of 0.0062 is the whole of the area to the right of $Z = 2.5$. It follows then that if we perform the arithmetic such that:

$$0.0228 - 0.0062 = 0.0166$$

this must be the area we have shaded in Fig. 8.14. That is, the probability that a box will weigh more than 520 g and less than 525 g is 0.0166.

(**d**) Finally, we require the probability that a box will weigh more than 480 g but less than 510 g. Again we require two Z scores (although we have them from the earlier problems):

$$Z_1 = -2.0$$
$$Z_2 = +1.0$$

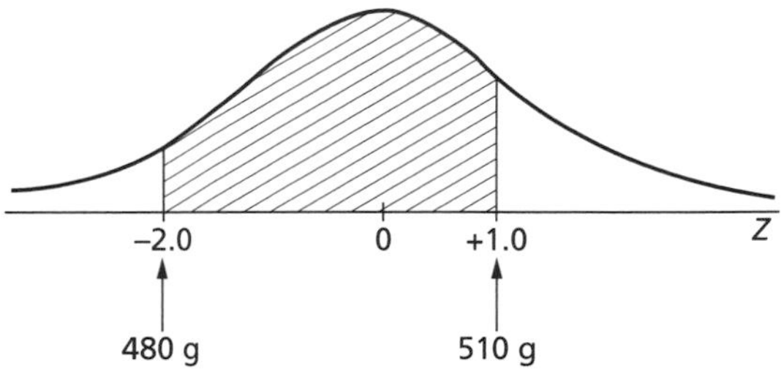

Fig. 8.15 $P(Z > -2.0 \text{ and } Z < 1.0)$

The sketch is shown in Fig. 8.15. Again, the probabilities relating to the Z scores are easily read from the table although finding the answer to our problem is a little more difficult. We have:

$$Z_1: 0.0228$$
$$Z_2: 0.1587$$

Recollect that the probabilities refer to the area in the tail of the distribution which is not what we require. However, we know the area (probability) to the left of $Z = -2.0$ is 0.0228. It follows then that the area to the right of $Z = -2.0$ up to $Z = 0$ must be:

$$0.5 - 0.0228 = 0.4772$$

since the area to the left of $Z = 0$ must be 0.5 (half of the area under the curve). Applying similar logic to the right-hand side we have:

$$0.5 - 0.1587 = 0.3413$$

as the area between $Z = 0$ and $Z = 1.0$. The area that we require (shaded in Fig. 8.15) must then be:

$$0.4772 + 0.3413 = 0.8185$$

Using normal tables to derive probabilities for complex problems is not difficult as long as you are clear which area you actually require and understand what the probabilities in the table refer to.

Student activity

For Machine B find the probability that a box will weigh more than 970 g but less than 975 g.

Using the same principles the Z scores are:

$$Z_1: \frac{970 - 1,000}{15} = -2.0$$

$$Z_2: \frac{975 - 1,000}{15} = -1.67 \text{ (to 2 decimal places)}$$

and the sketch is as in Fig. 8.16. For Z_1 the corresponding probability is 0.0228 and for Z_2 0.0485 (check carefully that you have read the table properly as this is the first time we have used two decimal places in the Z score). The relevant probability is then:

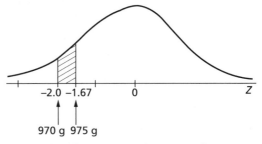

Fig. 8.16   P($Z > -2.0$ and $Z < -1.67$)

$$0.0485 - 0.0228 = 0.0257$$

So far we have found the probability for a problem where we are given a weight. We can also use the tables in the reverse way: finding a weight if we are given a probability. Consider the following. For Machine A we have been asked to determine the box weights around the mean between which 95% of all output will occur. That is,

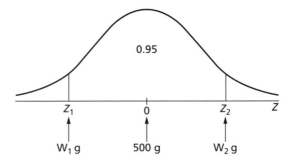

Fig. 8.17   Central 95% area

we want a lower weight, W_1, and an upper weight, W_2, such that 95% of boxes will have a weight between these two limits. Figure 8.17 sketches what we seek. We want to calculate what W_1 and W_2 will be in grams (and these are equidistant from the mean weight of 500 g) so that 95% of output falls in the central part of the distribution.

In terms of our standardized normal distribution this means that we need to find two Z scores, Z_1 and Z_2 which contain the central 95% of the area under the curve. We see that the two Z scores will be equal (since they are equi-distant from the mean of zero) except that one will be positive and one negative. We also know that the area in the two tails of the distribution must equal 5% of the total area (0.05). Since the two tails will also be equal this means that each tail will represent 0.025 of the area. So the problem comes down to saying: what must the Z score be (Z_2) to give an area in the tail of 0.025?

If we look at the normal table we can search through it looking for a probability figure of 0.025 (or as close as possible to this) and read off the corresponding Z score. If we do this we see a Z score of 1.96. Referring back to the sketch this means that 95% of the area under the curve will lie between $\pm$ 1.96 standard deviations from the mean (since this is all a Z score is). To transform the Z score of 1.96 back into a weight we see that:

$$Z = \frac{X - \text{Mean}}{\text{SD}} \qquad \text{and here} \qquad Z = 1.96 = \frac{X - 500}{10}$$

Rearranging gives:

$$1.96 = \frac{X - 500}{10} \qquad \text{Multiply both sides by 10}$$

$$19.6 = X - 500 \qquad \text{Add 500 to both sides}$$

$$519.6 = X$$

That is, a weight of 519.6 g will have a Z score of 1.96. On the left of the mean the comparable figure will be 480.4 g (500 – 19.6). So we know that the central 95% of boxes from Machine A will have a weight between 480.4 g and 519.6 g (or $\pm$1.96 SDs around the mean).

Student activity

For Machine B find the weights equi-distant from the mean which will contain the central 99% of boxes.

For Machine B the areas in the two tails will now be 0.01, or 0.005 each. Searching through the table we find that this is a Z score of either 2.57 (0.0051) or 2.58 (0.0049). If we choose 2.58 as the Z score then we have:

$$Z = \frac{X - \text{Mean}}{\text{SD}} \qquad \text{and here} \qquad Z = 2.58 = \frac{X - 1,000}{15}$$

Rearranging gives:

$$2.58 = \frac{X - 1,000}{15} \qquad \text{Multiply both sides by 15}$$

$$38.7 = X - 1,000 \qquad \text{Add 1,000 to both sides}$$

$$1,038.7 = X$$

and to find the lower weight we subtract 38.7 from 100 to give 961.3 and 1,038.7 as the weights between which the central 99% of output from Machine B will fall. We will find out in the next chapter that the combinations of:

$Z = \pm$ 1.96 SDs and the central 95% of the distribution

$Z = \pm$ 2.58 SDs and the central 99% of the distribution

have a special use in statistics.

Finally, there is one last illustration of the use of normal probabilities that we can illustrate. We know for Machine A that it has a calibration setting for a mean weight of 500 g, SD 10 g. The company manager now has a decision to make regarding the advertised weight printed on the boxes. How much should we say the box contains? Clearly we cannot say 500 g since we know that half of the boxes will weigh less than this (although half will weigh more) and we may well get into trouble with trading standards departments and consumer rights organizations.

Suppose that current legislation says that no more than 1% of output can fall below the advertised weight. How can we decide what advertised weight to print on the boxes? If we apply what we now know about the normal distribution we can say that the area in the left-hand tail of the distribution must be no more than 1% (0.01) of the total area under the curve. If we find the equivalent Z score for this area we can then find what weight this Z score equates to for Machine A (but remember we are looking at the area only in *one* tail of the distribution, not in *both* tails as we were in the last example).

From the table we see that a probability value of 0.01 equates most closely to a Z score of 2.33 (but remember this is actually –2.33 since we are looking at the left-hand tail only). This means that:

$$Z = -2.33 = \frac{X - 500}{10}$$

which if we rearrange to solve gives 476.7 g. That is, if we advertise the weight of boxes as 476.7 g then no more than 1% of them will be underweight.

Student activity

Find the comparable weight for Machine B.

For Machine B we require:

$$Z = -2.33 = \frac{X - 1,000}{15}$$

which gives a weight of 965.05 g. So, if we advertise the weight of boxes as 965 g no more than 1% will be underweight.

SUMMARY

In this chapter we have considered the impact of uncertainty in the context of business decision-making and seen how, potentially, probability can help in such a situation. Probability is useful in a business context for helping managers assess the likelihood that a decision will have a particular outcome. Probability also allows a business organization to choose between alternative decisions in terms of expected outcomes. This can be particularly useful when combined with financial information in the form of an expected value.

Decision trees are a useful method of presenting combined information on probabilities and financial outcomes and are useful in complex, sequential decision-making.

The concept of a probability distribution is also of considerable use in business and two such theoretical distributions – the binomial and the normal – are particularly useful. We shall develop the use of the normal distribution in the next chapter.

Now that you have completed this chapter you will appreciate that:

- An event is a defined outcome of an experiment.
- An experiment is a process which generates specified outcomes.
- Independent events are events which have no influence on each other.
- Conditional events are events which in some way affect each other's likelihood.
- Mutually exclusive events are events which cannot occur together.
- Probability indicates the likelihood that an event will occur.
- The addition rule is used for situations where a probability in the form P(A <u>or</u> B) is required.
- The multiplication rule is used for situations where a probability in the form P(A <u>and</u> B) is required.
- An expected value is the sum of a series of possible outcomes and their associated probabilities.
- A decision tree is a diagram that can be used to represent more complex problems and to show the related probabilities, outcomes and expected values.
- The binomial distribution is useful for dealing with situations which can be summarized as trials where two defined outcomes are possible in each trial.
- The normal distribution takes the familiar symmetrical or bell-shape and is characterized by its mean and standard deviation.
- The normal probabilities relate to the probability that some value in the distribution has (or has not) been exceeded.
- To use the normal probability tables the variable under investigation must be 'standardized'.

EXAMPLE

In the previous chapter example we looked at the impact of the launch of the National Lottery in the UK on a company's product sales. In this example we shall look at the Lottery from a different perspective and use it to illustrate how probability can be applied in decision situations.

Following the successful launch of the National Lottery in 1994, the company responsible, Camelot Group PLC, decided to launch an instant scratch card in 1995. Unlike the main lottery tickets – where a purchaser chooses six lottery numbers and waits to see whether these match the jackpot numbers chosen at random on a weekly basis – the scratch cards provide an instant outcome in terms of whether you have won a prize or not. The scratch cards are available for £1 each. On the card are 6 'banknote' symbols which have to be scratched off with a coin. When scratched each symbol reveals a prize amount and if there are three identical amounts revealed then the card wins that amount of prize money. Of course, if there are not three identical amounts revealed then there is no prize. Naturally, the quantity of cards available is pre-printed and determined by Camelot. However, in the related publicity and information material the company indicates that with this card:

> 'You've got a 1 in 4.98 overall chance of winning any prize each time you play.'

and, helpfully shows both the prize amounts, the prizes available and the odds of winning each prize. The table below shows this information:

Prize £	No. of prizes available	Approximate odds of winning (1 in:)
1	10,324,813	10
2	7,227,099	14
5	1,549,195	67
10	1,290,741	80
20	258,015	400
50	86,121	1,200
200	4,349	24,000
25,000	39	2,650,000

Let us consider the information made available by the company. Overall we are told our chance of winning a prize is approximately 1 in 5. This implies a probability of winning a prize of 0.2. However, the prize could range from £1 up to £25,000 and we see the odds of winning a prize of £1 are 1 in 10 – a probability of 0.1 whilst that of winning the top prize is somewhat smaller at 0.0000004 (1/2,650,000)! It seems appropriate to use the principles of expected value to provide an indication of the likely overall financial outcome of buying such cards. Clearly, we already have the range of possible financial outcomes – the prizes we could win – and if we multiply these by the probability of winning each particular prize we have the expected value result.

Whilst there are different approaches we could take let us derive the full set of probabilities by estimating how many such cards are available in total (that is, the population of cards from which prize winning cards could be chosen). We have no direct information on the total number of cards printed. However, we see from the above table that there are a total of 20,740,372 winning cards (the sum of the number of prizes of each value). Since we are told that we have a 1 in 4.98 chance of winning this implies that there are approximately 103,287,053 cards printed (since 20,740,372/103,287,053 = 1 in 4.98, or 0.2008). However, it seems unlikely that the company would have printed precisely this number of cards as it is clear that the odds figures are rounded for convenience. In fact, if we use the odds figures for each prize amount to estimate the number of cards printed we get a total cards figure ranging from 101,179,386 for the £2 prize to 104,376,000 for the £200 prize. We shall actually use as the total the figure of 103,350,000 which is calculated from the odds of the top prize. This means that we now have a distribution which looks like:

Prize £	No. of cards
0	82,609,628
1	10,324,813
2	7,227,099
5	1,549,195
10	1,290,741
20	258,015
50	86,121
200	4,349
25,000	39
Total	103,350,000

Note that we have now included in the distribution the prize of £0 (i.e. you win nothing) and by subtracting all the prize cards from the total number of 103,350,000 we deduce that just over 82 million cards will not win a prize. From this we can then determine the probability of each prize:

Prize £	No. of cards	Probability	Prize × Prob.
0	82,609,628	0.7993190905	0
1	10,324,813	0.099901432	0.099901432
2	7,227,099	0.069928389	0.1398567779
5	1,549,195	0.014989792	0.0749489598
10	1,290,741	0.0124890276	0.1248902758
20	258,015	0.0024965167	0.0499303338
50	86,121	0.0008332946	0.0416647315
200	4,349	0.0000420803	0.0084160619
25,000	39	0.0000003774	0.0094339623
Total	103,350,000	1.0	0.5490425351

Note that we have to use a considerable number of decimal places for the probabilities since some of these are quite small. The probabilities are determined by taking the ratio of the number of cards associated with each prize to the total number of cards (so for a prize of £0 we have 82,609,628/103,350,000 = 0.7993190905) and then multiply each probability by its associated prize value. If we then sum these figures we obtain an expected value of £0.549, or effectively 55p. This is the expected financial outcome of the scratch card from the purchaser's perspective. Given that each card costs £1 then the net expected value would actually be negative: −£0.45 (£1 − £0.549) implying that this situation has an expected loss associated with it. On a purely rational basis it does not make sense to purchase a card since its associated expected value is negative. But then you could just get lucky!

From the company's perspective, the information can also be used to estimate the amount of income the cards will generate and the gross profit. A total income of £103,350,000 will be generated (assuming all the cards printed are sold). From this total prize money will have to be paid out of £56,743,546 (calculated by multiplying each amount of prize money by the number of winning cards: for example, £975,000 will be paid in total to the 39 cards winning £25,000 each). Again, this assumes that all winning cards will be paid out. This will give the company a gross profit (before any other costs are deducted such as printing, distribution, publicity) of £46,606,454 (£103,350,000 − £56,743,546), although the company is committed to giving at least a quarter of total ticket sales to the five nominated national charity boards for distribution to good causes.

SELF-REVIEW QUESTIONS

1 *How would you know that something was wrong if you were told that P(x) = 1.4?*

2 *What is the general form of the addition rule?*

3 *What type of events is the addition rule used for?*

4 *What is the general form of the multiplication rule?*

5 *What type of events is the multiplication rule used for?*

6 *What is meant by 'expected value'?*

7 *What is meant by P(X) = 0.3?*

8 *Explain what P(X/Y) means.*

9 *What is a probability distribution?*

10 *What is a Z score?*

11 *What are the main features of the normal distribution?*

12 *Why do we need to standardize a normally distributed variable?*

STUDENT EXERCISES

1   In the section on the binomial distribution we have a formula for calculating the mean and standard deviation of the distribution. Return to the distribution we derived for the number of late payers out of a total of 10 customers. Using the formula we introduced in Chapter 7 calculate the mean and standard deviation for this distribution and compare them against the results obtained using the binomial mean and standard deviation formulae.

2   A lottery system works as follows. You choose six different numbers between 1 and 50. The lottery computer then chooses six different numbers between 1 and 50 at random. If your numbers are the same as those chosen by the computer you win (the order of the numbers does not matter).
      What chance have you of winning?

3 My local football team lost their last match 2–4. I've not seen any details of the match but I'm sure the score at some point must have been 2–2.
  What is the probability of this?

4 A small builder's merchant buys 50 kilo bags of cement from the wholesaler in multiples of 100 (i.e. 100 bags, 200 bags, 300 bags, etc.). The cement has a short shelf life of one month. The merchant buys the cement at £8 per bag and sells it at £10. However, if a bag is not sold in the first month it is returned to the wholesaler for a refund of £2 per bag.
  From past experience monthly demand has been:

Monthly demand	0	100	200	300
Probability	0.05	0.3	0.45	0.2

  (a) How many bags a month should the merchant buy? (Determine the financial consequences of all the combinations of bags bought and bags sold.)

  (b) A smart-alec student comes along and says that she can predict next month's sales with 100% accuracy. Assuming she is right how much should the merchant be willing to pay for such a forecast?

5 An auditor is checking invoices that have been paid to see if they contain any errors. Historically around 6% of all invoices are expected to contain some error. The auditor takes a random batch of 10 invoices.
  Calculate the probability distribution of errors for this batch of 10. What assumptions have you made?

6 An enterprising graduate who has been unable to find gainful employment has taken to visiting an office block in town each lunchtime with an array of freshly made sandwiches for sale. The graduate reckons that he has a 90% chance of selling a sandwich to any of the people working in the office block. He visits one office with 12 employees.

  (a) Calculate the probability distribution of sandwich sales.

  (b) Calculate the mean number of sales.

  (c) How might the graduate use this information to improve the profitability of his activities?

7 A firm is involved in manufacturing high quality electrical equipment. Each item produced costs £6,000 and total annual output is 500 items. At the end of the production process each item is individually tested for quality and safety. If the item is defective in any way it is scrapped at a complete loss to the firm since it has been found not cost-effective to repair such items. Historically 1 item in a 1,000 is found to be faulty in some way.

  (a) Determine the probability that the firm will produce zero faulty items in a year.

(**b**) Determine the probability that the firm will produce no more than three faulty items in a year.

(**c**) The firm is considering employing a quality inspector at an additional cost of £1,000 per year. The inspector, however, will be able to prevent any item from being defective. Suggest how the firm might evaluate whether employing the inspector would be cost-effective.

8 On average last year a local leisure centre had 230 customers per day, standard deviation 27, and the distribution of customers was found to be normal. Determine the probability that on any one day the centre has:

(**a**) more than 270 customers;

(**b**) less than 210 customers;

(**c**) between 225 and 250 customers.

9 A supermarket sells one particular item in its store on a regular basis. It currently has 750 units of this item in stock and no deliveries are expected until next week. The manager knows that average weekly sales of this item are 625, standard deviation of 55, and that sales are normally distributed. Calculate the probability that the firm will not have enough stock to meet sales.

10 The Finance Department of a large organization has responsibility for monitoring costs in other departments of the organization. A photocopier facility is available for one department's use and data has been collected which reveals that the number of photocopies made on the machine on a daily basis follows the normal distribution; the mean of the distribution is 380 copies per day with a standard deviation of 35. The cost per copy is estimated at 6p.

(**a**) Determine the probability that daily costs incurred on the photocopier machine will be:
   (i)   more than £25;
   (ii) less than £22.50;
   (iii) between £24 and £26.

(**b**) Explain the basis of your calculations in a short memo to the Finance Director.

11 A firm has recently introduced a new domestic gas central heating system on to the market and is keen to collect and analyse information relating to the efficiency of the system in terms of gas used. The firm has contacted 500 customers and monitored the energy consumption of their heating systems.

Therms used	No. of customers
970 < 975	4
975 < 980	7
980 < 985	22
985 < 990	46
990 < 995	75
995 < 1,000	96
1,000 < 1,005	95
1,005 < 1,010	76
1,010 < 1,015	45
1,015 < 1,020	22
1,020 < 1,025	9
1,025 < 1,030	3

(a) Calculate the mean, median, standard deviation and coefficient of skewness for this data. Comment on the shape of the distribution.

(b) Obtain the probability distribution for this data.

(c) Using the probability distribution determine the probability that a customer chosen at random will use:

(i)   more than 1,020 therms;
(ii) less than 985 therms;
(iii) between 980 and 1,000 therms;
(iv) between 995 and 1,010 therms.

(d) Using normal probability tables determine the probabilities in (c) above. Why are there differences in the two sets of probabilities?

The following two questions will require you to undertake some research to collect relevant data. You may wish to undertake these questions as part of a small group rather than by yourself.

12 In the UK in 1994 the National Lottery was launched. The publicity at the time claimed that the chance of winning the jackpot prize in the Lottery was 1 in 14 million.

Find out if this figure is correct.

13 You are the recipient of some sad news. Your favourite grannie has just passed away at the age of 96.

However, you have also heard that she has left you £1,000 in her will. The problem is that she was all too well aware of your spendthrift habits. Accordingly, her instructions in the will are that you cannot get your hands on the cash for the next five years. You can, however, decide whether the money should be invested in a building society account for five years or whether it should be used to purchase £1,000 of premium bonds in your name (she disapproved of the National Lottery as gambling).

Which would you choose and why (and what assumptions have you made)?

9 THE PRINCIPLES OF MARKET RESEARCH AND STATISTICAL INFERENCE

INTRODUCTION

Over the last two chapters we have begun to develop a number of statistical methods and some basic statistical concepts. In this chapter we apply these to a particularly important area for many organizations – that of market research and statistical inference. Most organizations these days regularly engage in some form of market research or undertake surveys: to assess customers' reactions to new products and services, to seek employees' attitudes before changing organizational structures, to ascertain citizens' views of public sector services, to assess the quality of items produced in factory and so on.

Manufacturing survey shows US economic growth

Optimism falls in financial sector

Business optimism in the financial services sector fell by the biggest amount for three years in the third quarter of this year, according to a survey published today.

The decline, which was particularly marked among banks, general insurers and venture capitalists, was the steepest since the UK's forced exit from the European exchange rate mechanism in September 1992, the survey shows.

 Source: *Financial Times*, 9 October 1995

London tops business location poll

London has been voted Europe's top business location for the fifth year in succession, says a survey of directors from 500 leading European companies.

The survey, by international property consultants Healey & Baker, asked business people to rank cities according to access to markets and customers, domestic and international transport links, cost and availability of staff, quality of communication as well as property costs.

The survey confirmed London's pre-eminent position with Paris in second place, Frankfurt third, Brussels fourth and Amsterdam fifth. The only other British cities to be ranked in the survey of the top 30 locations were Manchester (13) and Glasgow (18).

 Source: *Financial Times*, 9 October 1995

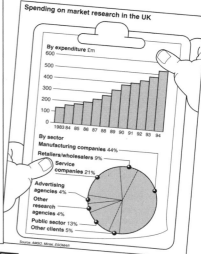

 Source: *Financial Times*, 29 June 1995

Such surveys and market research are typically based on a sample set of data and we need some statistical approach to help us assess such sample information in the context of decision-making.

LEARNING OBJECTIVES

By the end of this chapter you should be able to:

- explain the principles of statistical inference;
- explain the meaning of the standard error;
- describe the properties of the Central Limit Theorem;
- calculate and explain a confidence interval around a sample mean and a sample percentage;
- apply a variety of common hypothesis tests to business problems.

SAMPLES AND POPULATIONS

We have already discussed – in Chapter 3 – the need for business organizations to collect data about some sample rather than about the defined statistical population. Because of the cost, the time involved and the effort involved in collecting data on an entire statistical population most organizations collect data on a representative sub-set of that population – from a sample. However, there are inherent difficulties in making decisions based only on a sample set of data. The first is that we must assume that the sample is properly representative of the population it is meant to represent. We examined ways of trying to ensure that this was the case in Chapter 3. More fundamental, however, is the problem of using sample data to make conclusions about the population. No matter how representative our sample it does – by its very nature – only tell us about the statistical characteristics of that sample and *not* about the population. Yet it is the population characteristics that we are actually interested in.

In this chapter we shall look at how we can use sample information to help us make decisions about some statistical population, even when we have no direct information about that population. Let us illustrate with the example we have used before.

You will recollect that in earlier chapters we introduced the scenario of establishing a small restaurant. Given that the restaurant was aiming to attract relatively affluent customers it investigated two possible sites for the restaurant in terms of the income profile of local residents. We saw in Chapters 5 and 6 that Site B was preferable in this context since it appeared to have people with a higher level of income. However, you will also recollect that we came to this conclusion based only on limited, sample data which revealed, amongst other things, that:

For Site B:
Mean income   £522.56
Standard deviation   £143.60
Sample size   175

Assume that our financial analysis into the viability of the restaurant has revealed that we need a customer base with a mean income of at least £500 in order for the new venture to be successful. We are faced with a fundamental problem as we seek to make a business decision using this sample information. We see that these 175 people have a relatively high mean income – at £522.56 – and this meets our criterion of a mean income of at least £500. But this is, after all, only 175 of the several thousand people who form the catchment area for the restaurant. What we actually want to know is the mean income of the entire (statistical) population. Is this at least £500? Yet this is unobtainable (otherwise we would not have bothered with a sample). We are faced with taking a decision based only on limited sample data when what we would like is population data.

This is a very common problem in business decision-making and one which this chapter seeks to discuss. We wish to take some decision relating to some statistical population but the key characteristics of that population are unknown: instead we must take our decision based only on the limited sample information we have collected. There is, of course, one easy solution to the problem that we know the sample mean but do not know the population mean. We could simply say that the population mean is the same value as the sample mean and that, therefore, the population mean income exceeds the critical threshold of £500 that we have said is the minimum we require if the restaurant venture is to have a good chance of being successful.

Student activity

How likely do you think it is that the population mean takes exactly the same value as the sample mean?

The answer is we really don't know but it does seem unlikely that the two will be *exactly* equal. After all the sample mean is based on only 175 people so we might expect some arithmetic difference between the population mean and the mean from only a sample. So, if the sample mean and the population mean are unlikely to be exactly the same could we try to determine how close they are to each other? In other words, is there any way in which we could say that, for example, the sample mean is within £5 of the population mean (or within £10 or some other specific number)? Whilst this would not be as good as knowing the value of the population mean precisely at least we would know the value of the population mean within a few pounds which would be a big help in trying to decide whether to set up the restaurant at Site B.

In fact, using the principles of what is known as *statistical inference* that we shall develop in this chapter, it is possible to do exactly that: to estimate within a given numerical range what value the population mean takes and to do this based only on limited sample information. In statistical jargon we would say that we are trying to *infer* a value for the population mean based on the sample results.

THE SAMPLING DISTRIBUTION

In order to do this we have to develop one or two more statistical concepts. The first of these is that of a *sampling distribution*. To try to identify the mean income of residents of Site B we took a sample of 175 people. We assume (as we always must in statistical inference) that the sample is properly representative of the population. Nevertheless it is only one sample. In principle, we could take a second sample of 175 people from this same statistical population and calculate the mean of this sample. We could take a third sample and then a fourth and so on. Each of these samples would have a mean.

Whilst we would expect these sample means to be similar we would not necessarily expect them all to be exactly the same. After all, one of our samples might have included the 175 people in Site B with the lowest incomes. Another might have included the 175 people with the highest incomes. Most of the samples, however, we would expect to contain a mixture of incomes.

Suppose we had taken five samples, each of 175 people, and found the following:

Sample no.	Sample mean
1	£522.56
2	£518.32
3	£525.61
4	£532.18
5	£498.39

Although we see that the sample means are arithmetically slightly different we also see that they are reasonably similar (we don't have a mean of £42.75 for example) as we would expect since they are all from the same statistical population. Given that we have a set of data we could construct a frequency distribution. Although it doesn't make much sense to do this for only five numbers we can imagine that if we had more we might have a frequency table such that:

Interval	No. of sample means
£490 < £500	1
£500 < £510	0
£510 < £520	1
£520 < £530	2
£530 < £540	1
£540 < £550	0

and clearly we could build up a frequency distribution of sample means if we were to continue taking samples of 175 from the population (although remember that we wouldn't actually do this in practice – we are using this approach to illustrate some important principles). So, we can actually treat this set of sample means as a distribution in its own right.

You will be able to see what we are suggesting. In principle we could take repeated samples from the population and for each sample calculate the sample mean. If we were to do this then we could build up a picture of the frequency distribution of all the sample results and then produce a histogram of the sample means. This histogram would show the distribution, not of the original data – individual customers' income – but of the mean income calculated from each sample.

Because of its special nature we refer to this as the *sampling distribution of sample means* (usually abbreviated just to the sampling distribution). This is a distribution of the means of different samples taken from the statistical population. It is usually only a theoretical distribution since it consists of the means of every possible sample that we could take from a population (which we would not normally be able to do, let alone want to). Given that only one person out of the 175 has to be different to give a technically different sample we see that the number of possible samples that we could take even from a small population is extremely large. (In fact, for a statistical population consisting of only 100 items there are over 29 billion billion billion billion different samples of 30 items that could be taken.)

So, in theory, we could take repeated samples from a population and calculate the mean of each sample. We could then construct a frequency table for these sample means and from the frequency table draw a histogram. We could also calculate the mean and standard deviation from the frequency table.

Student activity

Suppose we were to calculate the mean and standard deviation for the data making up this frequency table. How would you explain what the mean and standard deviation actually measured?

We need to give this some thought because there are a lot of different means floating around. The mean of this frequency table will actually be the mean of all the sample means – the 'grand' mean if you like, or the average of all the sample means. The standard deviation will be a measure of the variability of the sample means from this grand mean – that is, an indication by how much on average a sample mean will differ from this grand mean. However, although in practice we could never obtain this sampling distribution (either as a frequency table or histogram) since it is only theoretical, it has a number of characteristics that can be predicted from statistical theory. These predictions are generated by what is known as the Central Limit Theorem which states that:

> If we take random samples of size n from a statistical population then the distribution of sample means will approximate that of the normal probability distribution. This approximation will come closer the larger is n, the size of the sample.
>
> Moreover, the mean of the sampling distribution will be equal to the population mean and the standard deviation of the sampling distribution will be given by $\sigma/\sqrt{n}$, where σ is the standard deviation of the population.

This statement of the Central Limit Theorem (CLT) contains a number of important implications we need to be clear about:

- The first is that – no matter what shape the original distribution – the sampling distribution will approximate to the normal if we take samples of a sufficiently large size. The term 'sufficiently large samples' is usually taken to mean a sample size of at least 30. We shall see the importance of this tendency for the sampling distribution to be normally distributed in a short while. In the context of our restaurant example we have no idea of what the population income distribution looks like (although we might suspect that like most it will be skewed). However, the CLT says that the sampling distribution of sample *mean* incomes will approximate to the normal distribution.

- The second implication is that the mean of the sampling distribution will be identical to that of the population. Whilst we cannot 'prove' this without advanced statistics it does seem intuitively likely. After all, the sampling distribution comprises all the means of all the samples we could take from a population. If we were then to calculate the mean of this distribution – the grand mean of all the sample means if you like – it seems sensible to conclude that it must equal the population mean since we are using all the population data in the sampling distribution.

- The third implication is that the sampling distribution has a standard deviation given by $\sigma/\sqrt{n}$. It can be seen that the value of this standard deviation will decrease as we increase the sample size. Given that this standard deviation measures the variability of the sample means around the population mean, again this seems intuitively sensible. If we take larger samples (i.e. we include more of the population in the sample) then it seems reasonable to say that the variability of the sample means around the population mean will decrease. In practice, we would not normally know the value of σ and would replace it by s, the sample standard deviation to give $s/\sqrt{n}$. The standard deviation of the sampling distribution is more usually referred to as the *standard error* and we shall call it this from now on.

We now have three groups of data: the population, the sample and the distribution of sample means (often called the sampling distribution). Each of these will have a mean and a standard deviation. We can denote each with the following symbols:

	Mean	*Standard deviation*
Population	μ	σ
Sample	$\overline{X}$	s
Sampling distribution	μ	$s/\sqrt{n}$

The mean of the population is denoted by the symbol μ, pronounced 'mew', and the standard deviation as σ, sigma, the sample mean by $\overline{X}$ with s as the standard deviation, and the sampling distribution by μ with $s/\sqrt{n}$ as the standard deviation. This last standard deviation is more usually referred to as the standard error, as noted above. From now on we shall be using these symbols and it is important that you remember what each one refers to, particularly in terms of whether it relates to the sample, the population or the sampling distribution.

At this stage we have simply told you what results mathematics predicts we would get from such repeated sampling. We are now going to get you to do a small experiment which will help you understand these predictions even if we cannot 'prove' them mathematically.

The experiment

Suppose we take four small pieces of card. We make sure the pieces are all the same size and shape. On each piece we write one each of the numbers 1, 2, 3, 4 so that we have four pieces with four different numbers. We will call this our population.

Student activity

Calculate the mean of this population and its standard deviation.

The mean is easily worked out. We have:

$$\frac{\Sigma x}{n} = \frac{(1 + 2 + 3 + 4)}{4} = \frac{10}{4} = 2.5$$

The standard deviation will then be:

X	Mean	Deviation	Deviation²
1	2.5	−1.5	2.25
2	2.5	−0.5	0.25
3	2.5	+0.5	0.25
4	2.5	+1.5	2.25
Total			5.00

giving:

$$\sqrt{(5/4)} = 1.118034$$

We now know the mean, 2.5, and standard deviation, 1.118034, of this population. But let us suppose for a moment that we did not know these (as would normally be the case for our customer population). We could take a sample from this population and calculate its mean. This sample mean will then give us an estimate of the population mean.

Suppose we now put the four pieces of card into a small bag or box. Without looking we choose one piece, look at the number on it, put it back into the bag/box, shake it and choose a second piece. That is, we choose a sample of two numbers. For this sample we could obviously work out the sample mean. If the two numbers chosen had been 1 and 2 for example then the mean would have been 1.5 ((1 + 2)/2).

Now, in this example, because the population is so small it is actually possible to identify what *all* the different samples (and their means) might be and so to obtain the sampling distribution. If we are logical we see that the sample could have been:

First number chosen	Second number chosen	Sample mean
1	1	1

or it could have been:

First number	Second number	Sample mean
1	2	1.5

and so on. In other words it is possible to calculate the mean of every possible sample we could have taken from this population. There are 16 possible samples and their means are then:

First number	Second number	Sample mean
1	1	1
1	2	1.5
1	3	2
1	4	2.5
2	1	1.5
2	2	2
2	3	2.5
2	4	3
3	1	2
3	2	2.5
3	3	3
3	4	3.5
4	1	2.5
4	2	3
4	3	3.5
4	4	4

giving a frequency distribution:

Sample mean	No. of samples
1	1
1.5	2
2	3
2.5	4
3	3
3.5	2
4	1
Total	16

The histogram for this distribution is shown in Fig. 9.1(b).

You probably realized that the distribution of sample means looks fairly symmetrical and is beginning to look like the normal distribution. This distribution is obviously different in shape from that of the population, which would have been 'flat' since each number (1–4) has the same frequency (of 1).

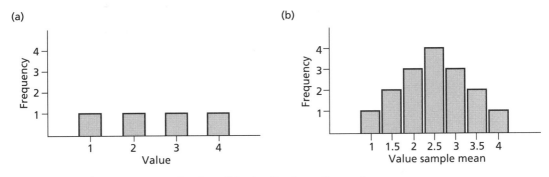

Fig. 9.1 **(a) Population distribution. (b) Distribution of sample means**

Student activity

Calculate the mean and standard deviation of the frequency table. Compare these with those from the population.

We can easily work out the mean of the distribution of sample means. This would be:

$$\frac{(1 \times 1) + (1.5 \times 2) + (2 \times 3) + (2.5 \times 4) + (3 \times 3) + (3.5 \times 2) + (4 \times 1)}{16}$$

Mean = 2.5

which is exactly the same as the population mean! That is, the mean of the sampling distribution is exactly the same as the mean of the population from which the samples were taken and as predicted by the Central Limit Theorem.

We can also work out the standard deviation of the sampling distribution (just as we can with any form of distribution). The calculations are:

Sample mean	No. of samples (frequency)	Mean	Deviation	Deviation²	Frequency × deviation²
1	1	2.5	−1.5	2.25	2.25
1.5	2	2.5	−1	1	2
2	3	2.5	−0.5	0.25	0.75
2.5	4	2.5	0	0	0
3	3	2.5	0.5	0.25	0.75
3.5	2	2.5	1	1	2
4	1	2.5	1.5	2.25	2.25
Total	16			7.00	10.00

giving:

Standard error = $\sqrt{10/16}$ = 0.7905694

That is, the sampling distribution has a standard error of 0.7905694.

301

But how does this relate to the standard deviation of the population which we calculated earlier as 1.118034? Take the standard deviation of the population and divide it by the square root of the size of the sample (2) that we took. This gives:

$$\frac{1.118034}{\sqrt{2}} = 0.7905694$$

which is the standard error!

So, there is a clear link between the statistical characteristics of the population – the mean and standard deviation – and those of the sampling distribution. For the mean the link is a direct one: the two means are identical. For the standard error the link is indirect – through the square root of the sample size.

Student activity

Suppose we had taken samples of three cards rather than two.
What would the mean and standard error of the sampling distribution
have been? What about a sample size of four?

For a sample size of three the mean would be the same. The standard error would have been:

$$\frac{1.118034}{\sqrt{3}} = 0.645497$$

and for a sample of size 4 the standard error would be:

$$\frac{1.118034}{\sqrt{4}} = 0.559017$$

You will realize that as we take larger sample sizes then the standard error decreases. You will remember that any standard deviation shows the variability of the data around the mean. So, the standard error must show the same. However, in this case we are referring to the sampling distribution. This shows the distribution of sample means around the population mean. So, as the standard error gets smaller it indicates that there is less variability in the data – the sample means are closer to the population mean.

To reinforce these ideas further, and before we move on to look how these ideas help us make a decision about locating the restaurant, let us look at another illustration, this time output from a computer-based simulation. In Computer Exercise 5 in Chapter 4 we had a set of data which showed the annual profit/loss made by 100 retail outlets of a company. Let us define this as the population.

Figure 9.2 shows the histogram for the statistical population of 100 data items. From the diagram we see that the distribution of the data is quite

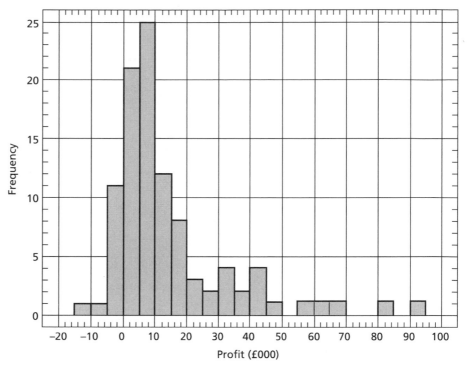

Fig. 9.2   Population distribution

skewed. The data set has a mean value of £13,979.40 and a standard deviation of £18,195.60.

Suppose we were to now take a large number of samples from this population, for each sample to calculate the mean, and then obtain the distribution of these sample means. Clearly, this would be the sampling distribution and we know from the Central Limit Theorem what this ought to look like. Figure 9.3 shows the simulated sampling distribution (using a computer program on the data disk that accompanies this text) after several hundred samples where we take samples of size 10, 30, 50 and 70 from the population.

Even though the CLT says that samples should be of 30 or above we already begin to see with a sample size of only 10 that the sampling distribution is starting to take the normal shape. The distribution becomes closer to the normal the larger the sample size.

Note also that with a larger sample size the variability within each distribution gets less. That is, the data is more centralized and less spread out along the horizontal axis. This implies that the sample means (which form the distributions in Fig. 9.3) are getting closer to the mean of the sampling distribution and that the standard error (which is the standard deviation of these distributions) is getting smaller as the sample size increases. (Note that the simulated distributions are not perfectly symmetrical since we took only several hundred samples from the population and not all samples as would be required to give the real sampling distribution.)

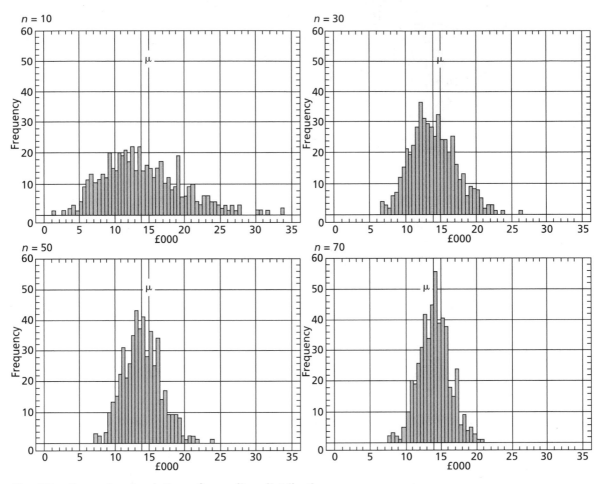

Fig. 9.3   Computer simulation of sampling distributions

CONFIDENCE INTERVALS

This is all very well, you might be saying, but how does it help in trying to decide whether to set up the restaurant in Site B? You will remember that what we were wanting to do was to infer (or estimate) a value for the population mean income based only on sample data. The Central Limit Theorem predicts the characteristics of the sampling distribution which is made up of all the different sample means we could have taken from this population. But we only have *one* sample mean – £522.56 – so what can we say about μ, the value of the population mean we are trying to estimate?

Consider Fig. 9.4 which shows the sampling distribution as predicted by the Central Limit Theorem. This distribution is normal and has a mean identical to the (unknown) population mean. It is also important to keep reminding yourself that this distribution is made up not of the population data (people's income) but of sample means, $\bar{X}$s. We have one sample mean: that for the 175 people we included in the sample we took and which gave a sample mean of £522.56.

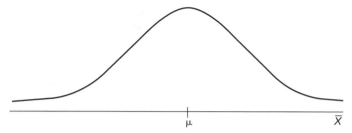

Fig. 9.4   Sampling distribution of sample means

Student activity

Whereabouts on the x axis scale would you put the value for our sample mean of £522.56?

The answer is: we've absolutely no idea! We simply don't know whereabouts our sample mean value of £522.56 is in relation to μ – which after all is completely unknown. Our sample mean could be below μ, above μ or for all we know exactly equal to μ. So in our search to try to infer a value for μ based on $\bar{X}$ we seem to be stuck. However, although we do not know *for certain* how close $\bar{X}$ and μ might be to each other we can take an educated guess – or, in the terminology of the previous chapter, we can attach a probability as to where in this distribution $\bar{X}$ occurs and how close $\bar{X}$ and μ are to each other.

The way in which we do this is to calculate what is known as a *confidence interval*: this is a numerical interval (a given range of values around the known sample mean) which we are confident (but not certain) contains μ the population mean. We approach this with the help of Fig. 9.5. This shows the sampling distribution on which we have imposed two arbitrary Z scores to correspond to the central 95% of the distribution.

We know from the work on the normal distribution in the previous chapter that for any variable which is normally distributed the central 95% of the distribution will lie between a Z score of –1.96 and +1.96 (go back and re-read about Z scores in Chapter 8 if you don't know where these numbers came from). Recollect that the Z scores are in fact only showing how many standard deviations a given point is away from the mean of the distribution. Recollect also that the distribution we are examining is the sampling distribution and its

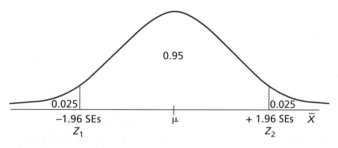

Fig. 9.5   Confidence interval

standard deviation is measured by the standard error, $s/\sqrt{n}$. In fact, we actually know the numerical value of each of these values from the sample that we took.

Student activity

Calculate the standard error for Site B. How would you interpret the result?

For Site B we have:

$$s = 143.6$$
$$n = 175$$
$$SE = s/\sqrt{n} = 143.6/\sqrt{175} = 10.86$$

That is, the standard error is £10.86. Remember that the standard error is only the standard deviation of the sampling distribution and is a measure of the variability of the sample means from the population mean (which is also the mean of the sampling distribution).

Given that we can calculate the SE for the sampling distribution this means that we can also calculate the comparable values for the two Z scores of −1.96 and +1.96.

Student activity

Calculate the comparable values for −1.96 SE and +1.96 SE. How do you think we could use this information to infer about the value of the population mean?

The Z scores are calculated as:

$$-1.96 \text{ SE} = -1.96 \times 10.86 = -£21.29$$
$$+1.96 \text{ SE} = +1.96 \times 10.86 = +£21.29$$

Referring back to Fig. 9.5 we now know that this central interval goes from £21.29 below μ to £21.29 above μ. But how does this help us infer what value μ itself might take?

Student activity

Return to the sample that we took for Site B. What is the probability that $\bar{X}$, at £522.56, falls in this central 95% interval?

We said earlier that we simply did not know where $\bar{X}$, at £522.56, occurred in this distribution. This is correct but not quite the full picture. While we do not know *for certain* where it occurs we can say that there is a probability of 0.95 that it falls in this central area (since by definition this area must contain 95% of all possible sample means). We can rephrase this to say that there is a 95% chance that $\bar{x}$ is no further away from μ than £21.29 (or that the population mean and the sample mean are within £21.29 of each other).

This is an important statement and is worth looking at more closely. We know that there is a 95% chance that our sample mean falls in this central area. If it does so then the maximum difference between the sample mean and the (unknown) population mean must be £21.29 (equal to 1.96 SEs). Since we know – with a 95% probability – the maximum difference between $\bar{x}$ and μ and since we know what value $\bar{x}$ takes this implies that we can now calculate a range of values within which we think the population mean must lie. This interval is calculated as:

$$\bar{x} - 1.96 \ s/\sqrt{n} \text{ to } \bar{x} + 1.96 \ s/\sqrt{n}$$

often shown as $\bar{x} \pm 1.96 \ s/\sqrt{n}$.

In this example this works out at:

$$£522.56 \pm £21.29$$

or an interval between £501.27 and £543.85. That is, we are 95% confident that the population mean lies in the range £501.27 to £543.85.

This is a major achievement and should not be underestimated. Based only on limited sample data (a sample size of 175) we are able to infer a value for the population mean which otherwise would be completely unknown. We would conclude, based on this limited sample information and the principles of statistical inference, that the mean income of the population was above £500. We have reached this conclusion because we have been able to estimate how close together the (unknown) population mean is likely to be to a (known) sample mean.

However, it is important to realize that we are only 95% confident that the population mean will fall in this interval. There is a 5% chance that it will occur either below £501.27 or above £543.85. Figure 9.6 illustrates the logic of this confidence interval.

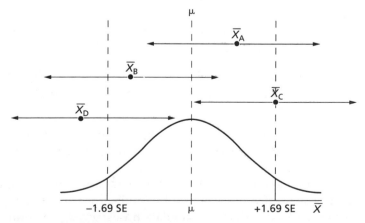

Fig. 9.6   Confidence interval

Let us suppose that the sample mean actually fell in the sampling distribution at the point represented by $\bar{X}_A$. The size of the confidence interval either side of this value is exactly the same as ± 1.96 SEs (£42.58 in the context of our problem). We see that this interval includes μ, the population mean. So, if $\bar{X}$ occurs at point A it must include the population mean value in its range. The same is true if $\bar{X}$ occurs at point B. Similarly, at point C although this time the interval only just includes μ. Only if the sample mean falls in part of the distribution which is outside this central 95% area will the interval *not* include μ (as in $\bar{X}_D$) and the chance of this happening is only 5%. So, although we do not have a guaranteed numerical value for μ, we do have a fairly narrow range of values which we are 95% certain μ will occur in.

Student activity

For Site A we took a sample of 150 people and found the sample mean to be £303.36 with a standard deviation of £184.30.

Calculate a 95% confidence interval and comment on how you would interpret the result.

For Site A we have:

$$SE = s/\sqrt{n} = 184.30/\sqrt{150} = 15.05$$

Confidence interval:

$$\bar{X} \pm 1.96 \, s/\sqrt{n}$$
$$303.36 \pm 1.96(15.05) = 303.36 \pm 29.50$$

giving an interval from £274.10 to £332.86. We would conclude that we are 95% confident that the population mean income in Site A would be between £274.10 and £332.86.

Although we have taken a lot of time and effort to develop the principles and concepts of the confidence interval, we see from the last activity that the calculation and interpretation is actually quite quick and easy in practice as long as we have understood what to do and why. It is also worth commenting that the confidence interval only has reliability if:

- the sample data is properly representative of the statistical population;
- we are sure that the information collected in the sample is reliable and accurate.

It is also important to realize that through the use of a confidence interval we are not offering a guaranteed conclusion but rather one which has a probability level attached to it.

In summary, the use of confidence intervals and statistical inference offers a very cost-effective way to all organizations of assessing statistical characteristics of some defined population based only on limited sample data.

Other confidence intervals

You may have asked yourself: why did we choose 95% as the appropriate value for the calculation of the confidence interval? The answer is that a 95% confidence interval is one of the conventionally accepted intervals to calculate. The other is a 99% interval where we would be 99% certain that the population mean occurred within a calculated interval. A 99% interval would be given by:

$$\bar{X} \pm 2.58 \, s/\sqrt{n}$$

where the appropriate Z score to enclose the central 99% of the sampling distribution is now ±2.58 rather than ±1.96.

Student activity

Calculate a 99% confidence interval for Site A and Site B. Why has the interval got larger compared with the 95% interval?

We have:

Site A:
$$\bar{X} \pm 2.58 \, s/\sqrt{n}$$
$$303.36 \pm 2.58(15.05) = 303.36 \pm 38.83$$

giving an interval from £264.53 to £342.19.

Site B:
$$\bar{X} \pm 2.58 \, s/\sqrt{n}$$
$$522.56 \pm 2.58(10.86) = 522.56 \pm 28.02$$

giving an interval from £494.54 to £550.58.

You will see that for both sites the size of the interval has increased. The reason for this is logical, as long as we understand the principles of a confidence interval. In order to be more certain that μ falls within the calculated range then we must increase the size of the interval. This is comparable to trying to throw a piece of paper into a waste paper basket. If we want to increase the chance of throwing the paper into the basket then one way to do this is to increase the size of the basket we're throwing at.

You will also see for Site B that we are now facing a rather tricky situation regarding our decision as to whether Site B meets the criterion of having a population mean income exceeding £500. With a probability of 95% we were confident that Site B's population had a mean income level which exceeded our criterion of £500. However, at the 99% level we see that the mean income could actually be lower than this (since the lower value of the interval is £494.54).

This is not uncommon and illustrates that we would not take critical decisions based simply on such statistical analysis. In this case, given the seriousness of the decision as to whether to open the restaurant or not, we might justifiably argue that we should take a larger sample of people's incomes in Site B since, through the SE calculation, a larger sample will, other things being equal, give us a smaller standard error and a more precise estimate of the population mean.

Student activity

A large national company employs a number of its staff as sales representatives who tour the country trying to persuade customers to buy the company's products. Company cars are provided to employees and the company is considering replacing some of these (which are several years old) with the latest models to decrease running costs. One particular factor of concern to the company is the fuel consumption of these new cars. For the past few months a sample of 75 cars has been closely monitored and their mean fuel consumption found to be 47 miles per gallon (mpg), standard deviation 15 mpg.

Calculate a confidence interval for this data and comment on how the confidence interval might be used by management.

It is always helpful to summarize the data we are given with this type of problem:

$\bar{X}$ = 47 mpg

s = 15 mpg

n = 75

We are not told whether to calculate a 95% or a 99% confidence interval. A 95% interval would give us a smaller numerical range but a 99% interval would increase the chance of the interval containing μ. Given that the company might be wanting to use such data for important decisions we might decide a 99% interval was 'safer' since we have a higher probability that the interval contains the population value. We then have:

$\bar{X} \pm 2.58 \; s/\sqrt{n}$

$47 \pm 2.58 \; (15/\sqrt{75}) = 47 \pm 2.58 \; (1.73)$

47 ± 4.46

That is, we are 99% certain that the population mean fuel consumption would be between 42.54 mpg and 51.46 mpg.

We are now confident that we know the population mean fuel consumption to within almost 5 mpg (precisely to within 4.46 mpg). This would be of considerable help to management in trying to quantify the potential cost savings – in reduced fuel consumption – by replacing existing vehicles with the latest models. We could report to management that we are 99% confident that the mean mpg is no lower than 42.54 and we could use such figures in our calculations relating to potential cost savings of the new models.

Sample size and the confidence interval

It will be clear that the size of the confidence interval depends, in part, on the size of the sample we have used. As the sample size increases, other things being equal, so the size of the standard error will decrease and so will the size of the confidence interval. However, the relationship between the size of the confidence interval and the size of the sample is not a direct one: doubling the sample size, for example, will not lead to a halving of the size of the confidence interval.

Student activity

Return to the sample of 175 that we had for Site B. Suppose we doubled this to 350 and the sample mean and standard deviation remained unchanged. What would be the 95% confidence interval now?

What would the sample size have to be if we wanted the 95% confidence interval to be half that when n = 175?

Assuming that the sample mean and standard deviation remain unchanged the 95% confidence interval is:

$$\bar{X} \pm 1.96 \ s/\sqrt{n} = 522.56 \pm 1.96 \ (143.6/\sqrt{350})$$
$$= 522.56 \pm 1.96 \ (7.68)$$
$$= 522.56 \pm 15.05$$

compared with ±£21.29 with a sample size of 175. A doubling of the sample size (and possibly a doubling of the cost of collecting and analysing the sample data) has led to a decrease in the size of the interval of only 29%.

If we did require a reduction in the size of the interval by half then we can determine what the sample size would have to be:

Interval with $n = 175$ is ±21.29

We require an interval of ±10.65 (half of the current one, at 21.29). The interval is then given by:

1.96 $s/\sqrt{n}$ which we require to equal 10.65

Rearranging gives:

1.96 $s/\sqrt{n}$ = 10.65

dividing by 1.96:

$s/\sqrt{n}$ = 10.65/1.96 = 5.43

multiplying through by $\sqrt{n}$:

$$s = 5.43\sqrt{n}$$

dividing by 5.43:

$$s/5.43 = \sqrt{n}$$

and finally squaring both sides (since $(\sqrt{n})^2 = n$):

$$(s/5.43)^2 = n$$

and, since we know $s = 143.6$, we can calculate:

$$n = (s/5.43)^2 = (143.6/5.43)^2 = 699.4$$

That is, we would need a sample of 700 to reduce the size of the confidence interval by half.

It is important to realize that there is a trade-off between the size of the sample we require and the decrease in the size of the confidence interval. If we require a smaller confidence interval (a smaller numerical range around the sample mean) then we must increase the size of the sample considerably. Management must decide whether this will be cost-effective.

CONFIDENCE INTERVALS WITH PERCENTAGES

We have been able to calculate a confidence interval based on a sample mean. In many cases some survey or market research may not provide a mean value but rather a percentage or proportion response.

Consider the manager of a supermarket who is thinking of replacing an existing product with a new brand. The manager wants to try and ensure that the new product will be popular with customers before actually making the change so a small research exercise is conducted to ask customers whether they would purchase the new product if it were available. Customers will typically respond either 'Yes' or 'No'. At the end of the exercise suppose we find that 53% of 1,250 customers responded that yes, they would buy the new product if it were available.

This result is not a mean in the sense of our last example but rather a percentage response. Since it is not a mean it makes no sense to talk of its standard deviation and with no standard deviation how do we calculate a confidence interval around the sample result?

The answer is that we use a different formula for the standard error when dealing with this type of percentage response, although all other aspects of the confidence interval calculation remain the same. The formula is:

$$\text{SE} = \sqrt{\frac{P(100 - P)}{n}}$$

where P is the percentage result from the sample and n the sample size. Apart from this, the calculation of the confidence interval, and its interpretation, is exactly as before.

Student activity

Calculate a 95% confidence interval for this problem and comment on the result.

The calculations are:

$$SE = \sqrt{\frac{P(100 - P)}{n}}$$

$$= \sqrt{\frac{53(47)}{1,250}}$$

$$= 1.417$$

and the interval then:

$$53\% \pm 1.96(1.417) = 53\% \pm 2.78\%$$
$$= 50.2\% \text{ to } 55.8\%$$

That is we are 95% confident that the sample result and the population result are within 2.78% of each other. We estimate the population result to be between 50.2% and 55.8% – that is, if we were able to survey the whole population we are 95% confident that we would get a result between 50% and 56% (rounded).

Notice that one feature of sample results in such a percentage form is that the size of the confidence interval is typically quite large. It may well be necessary for this type of survey result to use larger sample sizes.

AN INTRODUCTION TO HYPOTHESIS TESTING

Confidence intervals are a useful way of assessing a likely value for the population value. There are times, however, when we wish to be more rigorous and assess the sample result against a specific population value.

Consider the last example. In the market research we found in the sample of 1,250 customers that 53% indicated they would buy the new product if it were available. Assume that for the product line to be viable more than 50% of customers would have to buy the product if it were to be introduced. Clearly it is not easy to decide based on the sample result whether this criterion would be met. On the face of it the sample result of 53% exceeds the minimum 50% required for the product to be viable. However, we also realize that this is only a sample. We now know, based on the sampling distribution, that this is only one of many possible samples for this population. We could argue that another sample of 1,250 customers might indicate a result less than the required 50%.

The confidence interval we calculated earlier indicates the population value could be anywhere between 50.2% and 55.8% which does not really help the manager make a decision. It is in circumstances like this, where we wish to compare the sample result against *one* specific population value, that the process of a hypothesis test comes in useful.

Consider our problem. We have a population (of customers) and we wish to know whether more than 50% of them would buy the new product. The information we have relates only to a sample of 1,250 members of the population. To undertake a test we set up a hypothetical (hence the term hypothesis test) scenario.

Let us assume for the moment that in the population more than 50% *would* buy the new product. Clearly this is just speculation, or a hypothesis, at the moment. The only evidence that we have to help us assess whether this hypothesis is true or not is the sample result: 53% said 'Yes'. So, we need to try to use this sample result to assess the likelihood, or probability, of our hypothesis actually being correct. The purpose of the exercise is to try to determine whether the hypothesis is likely to be correct or is likely to be incorrect. This will then help us decide whether we should or should not introduce the new product.

The general principles of the test are very similar to that of the confidence interval but take a slightly different approach. We establish a sampling distribution with a mean equal to the hypothesized value. Based on the sample information we can calculate the standard error for the distribution. Using the standard error and the hypothesized mean we can predict, in probability terms, where the result of a sample taken from such a population should occur if the hypothesis is correct. For example, we know that, based on an assumed population mean, 95% of all sample means *should* fall within 1.96 SEs of the population mean. This approach allows us to establish a limit within which a sample result should occur if the assumed population mean is correct. We can then proceed to calculate exactly where in this assumed sampling distribution the sample result actually does occur. If it lies within the predetermined limit then it seems reasonable to conclude the hypothesis is likely to be correct. If it falls outside this predetermined limit then it seems more likely the hypothesis about the population mean is incorrect.

All of this probably sounds very complicated but can actually be summarized into a straightforward and logical process (as long as we understand the principles behind what we are doing). Such an approach allows us to assess a sample result against some specific value for the population. To help us make a decision we can apply the process of a formal hypothesis test. The process follows a number of predetermined stages:

- Formulate two hypotheses verbally.
- Formulate two hypotheses numerically.
- Choose a level of probability which we can attach to the conclusion we reach.
- Calculate what is known as a critical statistic.
- Calculate what is known as a test statistic.
- Make a choice between the two hypotheses.

Finally ensure that you can explain what you have done and which hypothesis you have chosen in the context of the problem.

We examine these stages in more detail below.

Formulate two hypotheses verbally

Although the process involves assessing statistics it is frequently useful to verbalize what we are trying to do. Verbally we might say: one hypothesis is that we would *not* find more than 50% of customers buying the new product; the other hypothesis is that we would. Clearly our two (verbal) hypotheses are, in hypothesis test jargon, mutually exclusive and collectively exhaustive. That is, the two hypotheses are quite distinct from each other and by accepting one hypothesis we must automatically reject the other. Both hypotheses together cover all possible situations (they are collectively exhaustive): there are no other possibilities other than the two hypotheses we have formulated.

Formulate two hypotheses numerically

The next stage is to formulate numerically the two hypotheses. There is a standard way of writing two hypotheses for a test and we must ensure we can use it.

Numerically we would show the first hypothesis as:

$$H_0: \pi \leq 50\%$$

where, H_0, is known as the null hypothesis and the symbol π, pi, denotes the critical population value (just as we used μ to denote the population mean). The null hypothesis simply indicates that π is not greater than 50%.

The alternative hypothesis would then be:

$$H_1: \pi > 50\%$$

i.e. that π is greater than 50%. The term H_0 is always used for the null hypotheses and H_1 for the alternative. The two hypotheses indicate that:

H_0: the population value does not exceed 50%

H_1: the population value does exceed 50%

At the end of the test we must choose between one of these two. The null hypothesis is formulated on the assumption that the evidence does not support going ahead with the new product. This may seem odd but it is up to us to prove our case. Until we do so the assumption is that more than 50% of customers would *not* buy the product. That is, until we provide sufficient statistical evidence we cannot reject H_0. This principle of sticking with H_0 unless we have evidence to the contrary is an important one. Before rejecting H_0 we must bring sufficient statistical evidence to bear. If we do not do this then we must not reject H_0 no matter what else we might think.

It is also worth noting that the formulation of the two hypotheses is where many students initially make mistakes. These might include:

- getting H_0 and H_1 the wrong way round;
- not including all possibilities in the two hypotheses – for example writing H_0 $\pi < 50$ and $H_1 > 50$. This is technically incorrect since we have ignored the possibility of $\pi = 50$ and would not know which hypothesis to go for if we got such a result.

Always check the hypotheses produced against the question set very carefully.

Choose a level of probability for the test

The next stage in the test is to choose a level of probability that we can attach to our conclusion. We can never be 100% certain about our decision (given we are dealing with one sample from a sampling distribution). We might decide we wish to be 95% or 99% confident that our decision is the appropriate one given the available evidence. Conventionally we denote this level with the symbol α, alpha. If we want to undertake the test at the 99% level we would then write:

H_0: $\pi \le 50\%$
H_1: $\pi > 50\%$

$\alpha = 0.01$

with α calculated as 100 minus the confidence level divided by 100, in this case $(100 - 99)/100 = 0.01$

Calculate a critical statistic

The fourth stage is to determine what is known as a critical statistic. This is actually just finding a Z score from the appropriate normal table. It can be very helpful to sketch the sampling distribution that relates to our problem as this will often help us make sure we have the right Z score for this stage. Figure 9.7 shows such a sketch for our problem.

We have a normal sampling distribution (courtesy of the CLT) with a hypothesized value of 50% in the middle. The level of probability associated with the test is actually simply the critical area that we have marked in the

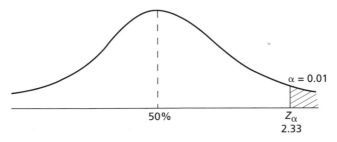

Fig. 9.7   Critical statistic

right-hand tail of the distribution. Effectively this area corresponds to 0.01 (or 1% of the total area). We now require a Z score (Z_α) which will give such a tail area. In this case the Z score relating to $\alpha = 0.01$ (i.e. 99%) would be $Z = 2.33$. The test statistic is denoted as Z_α since it relates directly to the chosen significance level.

It is important to appreciate what Z_α represents. We are hypothesizing, H_0, that the population has a value which is *not* more than the 50% required. This population has a normally shaped sampling distribution (courtesy of the Central Limit Theorem). This distribution is made up of different sample results, including the one we have of 53%. *If* the null hypothesis is correct then we would not expect, with a 99% probability, a sample result to exceed the null hypothesis value of 50% by more than 2.33 SEs. In other words, we would expect the observed sample value to be no higher than 2.33 SEs above the hypothesized population value. Z_α is simply the maximum difference between π and the sample statistic actually calculated *if* H_0 is not to be rejected.

We would then have:

H_0: $\pi \leq 50\%$
H_1: $\pi > 50\%$
$\alpha = 0.01$
$Z_\alpha = 2.33$

If we found that the observed sample value was more than 2.33 SEs above the hypothesized population value then we would have to conclude with a 99% probability that our assumption in the null hypothesis was inappropriate. Given that we know the sample result to be a fact, and the null hypothesis is just an assumption, then it seems unlikely based on the evidence that the assumption is valid. The logic behind this is that if the assumption were valid we would not expect to obtain a sample result so far away from the (assumed) population value.

Calculate the test statistic

Having obtained a critical statistic we now calculate a test statistic for Z, usually labelled Z_C. That is, we now calculate how many SEs away from the assumed population value the sample value *actually* is.

You should be able to see where we are going with this. If we find that the sample value is more than 2.33 SEs above the population value this tends to suggest our assumption about the population value, as expressed in the null hypothesis, is unlikely. If we find that the sample value is *not* more than 2.33 SEs above then we have no reason to reject the null hypothesis. That is, we have failed to provide sufficient evidence to reject it.

The statistic is calculated using the Z score formula:

$$Z_C = \frac{\text{Sample value} - \text{Assumed population value}}{\text{Standard deviation}}$$

Recollect that in our sample we obtained a sample result of 53% based on a sample size of 1,250. The standard deviation is the standard error of the sampling distribution. Since we are assuming the population value is 50% the standard error for the test is:

$$SE = \sqrt{\frac{50(100 - 50)}{1,250}}$$
$$= 1.414$$

This gives:

$$Z = \frac{53 - 50}{1.414} = 2.12$$

This value indicates how many SEs above the assumed population value of 50% the observed sample value of 53% actually is. That is, the sample result is 2.12 SEs above the assumed population value of 50%.

How does this help us decide whether to bring in the new product? Look at Fig. 9.8 which shows both statistics. Recollect that we were looking for evidence that more than 50% of customers would buy the new product. The survey revealed that 53% of customers surveyed indicated they would buy. However, we set up a hypothesis that indicated we would have to bring sufficient evidence before we decided that more than 50% of the *population* fell into this category based on the sample evidence. In order for this evidence to be sufficient we decide that the sample result would have to be more than 2.33 SEs above the assumed population value.

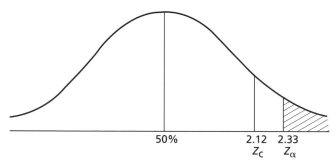

Fig. 9.8   Critical and test statistics

Clearly we have now calculated that the sample result is *not* more than 2.33 SEs above. We do not have sufficient evidence to reject the null hypothesis. We do not have sufficient evidence to conclude, based on this sample, that more than 50% of all customers would buy the new product. We cannot recommend the introduction of the product based on this evidence.

Consider what we might say to someone who commented that, after all, the sample result was 53% – above the criterion we had set for introducing the new product of more than 50%. The answer to this comment lies in the logic of the sampling distribution. We would say that any sample is not a 100% reflection of the population but an estimate only. Through what we can refer to as sampling variation we would expect a numerical difference between a sample value and the (unknown) population value. Using statistics we can quantify what such variation should be. In this case the difference between 50% and 53% is within the range of the variation we would expect. We would conclude that even though we found a sample result of 53% this is still consistent with the population value being 50% or less.

Summary of the test procedure

It may seem that the test we have conducted has been both complex and time-consuming. Part of the reason for this has been the need to explain what we are doing at each stage and why. In practice, and with practice, such tests can be conducted in a matter of seconds (and are often built in to statistical software packages).

We can summarize the procedure as follows:

- Formulate the null and alternative hypotheses. The alternative should be phrased in terms of the critical population value you wish to test against.
- Choose a value for α, the significance level.
- Obtain the critical value for Z based on α.
- Calculate a Z_C score for the sample.
- Compare Z_C with Z_α. If the calculated score is greater than the critical value reject H_0. If it is not then you cannot reject H_0 based on the sample evidence available.
- Finally, check the logic of your conclusion from the test in the context of the problem. Particularly when you first start doing these tests it can be easy to lose your way (particularly in terms of formulating the hypotheses). Always check your statistical conclusion with the original problem to see if it looks 'sensible' in context.

The use of a sketch diagram can be very helpful in checking that you have reached the right conclusion based on the test you have conducted.

OTHER ASPECTS OF TESTS

There are one or two other aspects to such tests to bring to your attention at this stage.

One- and two-tail tests

We can generalize the way that the two hypotheses should look depending on whether they are what are known as one- or two-tail tests. For a two-tail test we will always have:

H_0: population value $= X$
H_1: population value $\neq X$

where X is the numerical value we are testing.
For one-tail tests we may have one of:

H_0: population value $\leq X$ or population value $\geq X$
H_1: population value $> X$ or population value $< X$

Clearly, the test we conducted was a one-tail test since the critical area is literally in one tail only of the sampling distribution. Sometimes, the critical area may lie in both tails (hence a two-tail test) as in Fig. 9.9.

Usually there will be an indication in the problem you are given as to whether you should be doing a one-tail or a two-tail test. A one-tail test has key words associated with it like *at least, no more than, greater than, less than, lower than,* all implying a one-way test.

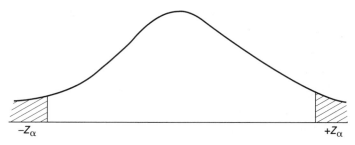

Fig. 9.9   Two-tail test

Value of α

The value of α is generally set at 0.01 or 0.05, corresponding to 99% and 95% significance levels. The choice is to some extent arbitrary but the more important the decision then the more logic there is to choosing $\alpha = 0.01$ rather than 0.05.

Critical Z values

Assuming a choice of α of either 0.01 or 0.05 then the critical Z values will be:

	$\alpha = 0.01$	$\alpha = 0.05$
One-tail test	Z: 2.33	Z: 1.64
Two-tail test	Z: 2.58	Z: 1.96

Remember also that from the Z tables the Z statistic can be either positive or negative. This depends on the specific context of the problem. For example, in a one-tail test the critical tail might be on the left of the sampling distribution. Again, a sketch can be very useful.

TESTS ON MEANS

As well as a test on percentages we can conduct tests on means. The procedure is as before but with the standard error being $s/\sqrt{n}$ and the two hypotheses formulated in terms of μ. To illustrate and provide additional practice for this complex topic we shall consider the following problem.

A large store in London has recently changed suppliers for one of its products: 500 g packs of Scottish smoked salmon. Packs supplied are printed with 'average contents 500 g'. The manager of the food department is not convinced that the supplier is meeting this specification and has investigated the latest batch of salmon packs supplied. A sample of 100 packs was chosen at random from the last delivery and the sample mean weight calculated at 496 g, with a standard deviation of 4 g. Can we conclude by using a formal hypothesis test the manager's suspicion about the supplier?

We have:

$$H_0: \mu \geq 500$$
$$H_1: \mu < 500$$

The null hypothesis is that the packs are not underweight and are at least 500 g on average, with the alternative that they are underweight and weigh less than 500 g. We choose a significance level of 0.01 given the potentially serious consequences of the decision and this gives a test statistic of 2.33 since we have a one-tail test.

To locate the sample mean in this distribution we must calculate the appropriate statistic:

$$Z = \frac{\bar{X} - \mu}{\frac{s}{\sqrt{n}}}$$

giving:

$$Z_C = \frac{496 - 500}{4/\sqrt{100}} = \frac{-4}{0.4} = -10$$

with the appropriate sketch shown in Fig. 9.10.

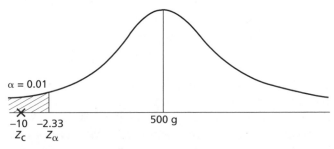

Fig. 9.10   One-tail test

Employers report jobs outlook still positive

By Andrew Bolger,
Employment Correspondent

The outlook for jobs remains positive for the fourth quarter of the year, according to a survey of employment prospects by Manpower, the independent employment agency.

However, Manpower says this is the first quarter for 2½ years in which the figures have shown a negative swing against a comparable period in the previous year. This negative swing continues the employment market's slowdown from its peak in the first quarter of 1994.

Ms Lilian Bennet, Manpower chairman, said: "There is no firm evidence yet as to whether the recovery is taking a breath or has turned downwards."

The survey, based on responses from more than 2,100 employers, shows 24 per cent are forecasting job increases in the three months to the end of December and 12 per cent are forecasting job losses, resulting in a positive balance of 12 per cent. Last year's survey showed a positive balance of 14 per cent.

All 12 regions surveyed forecast increased job levels. The East Midlands has become the most optimistic region, with a 24 per cent positive balance forecast, compared with 18 per cent for the same quarter last year.

The southern regions – London, home counties and South – have shown a fall in optimism against last year's and last quarter's figures.

The North-East of England has shown a strong increase in optimism with a positive balance of 16 per cent, compared with 5 per cent for last year's final quarter.

Manpower says the manufacturing sector continues to have a firm outlook with 24 per cent of employers forecasting an increase in job levels and 12 per cent a decrease.

Vehicle manufacturing continues its positive outlook with a balance of 22 per cent, the highest in the sector. Employers in private building, expect an increase in job levels by a margin of 8 per cent, but are less optimistic than last year when they registered a positive balance of 20 per cent.

The service sector has taken over from manufacturing as the most optimistic sector in the survey. This is helped

Employers forecasting job increases

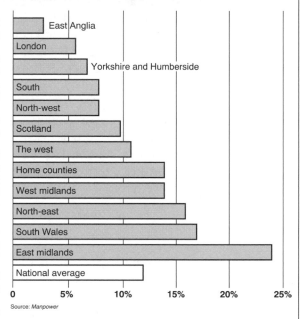

Source: *Manpower*

by an improvement in prospects for the energy and water industries. A positive outlook in the retail and hotel and catering industries also contributes to this sector's brighter outlook.

The public sector is underperforming the national average with a nil balance. The public building industry, like its private counterpart, has seen a decrease in optimism. Local government remains in the doldrums with healthcare the only industry in the sector that has improved. It shows a 13 per cent balance compared with 4 per cent last year.

Source: *Financial Times*, 25 September 1995

In other words, the sample mean is 10 SEs below the hypothesized population mean. This calculated value exceeds the critical value and we must reject the null hypothesis. At the 99% level we would conclude, based on the sample evidence, that the mean weight of packs of salmon was less than 500 g.

It is also worth practising how you might explain your result and your method to someone who is not familiar with statistical inference. Such an explanation might go something like the following. We think that we may be getting supplies which are underweight. We cannot check every single pack because this would be too costly and time-consuming so we take a random, representative sample of 100 of the supplies instead and find the mean weight of this sample. It would not be fair on the supplier to expect the mean weight of the sample to equal exactly 500 g since, after all, we have looked at only 100 packs. However, using some statistical theory we can predict the maximum difference we would expect between the sample mean weight and 500 g *if* packs actually have a mean weight of 500 g (this is the critical Z figure of 2.33 although we might not actually explain this to a manager). What we found was that the sample mean weight exceeded this maximum expected difference (even though the arithmetic difference might look small at only 4 g). So, we are 99% sure that the supplies we are getting have a mean weight which is less than the required 500 g, even though we only looked at 100 packs.

We have introduced in this section two common hypothesis tests: on a sample mean and on a sample percentage. You need to be aware that there are a considerable number of different tests available (one recent textbook summarizes details of the most common 100 tests!). Fortunately for all of us, whilst such tests are different in some ways, they are all based on the principles of statistical inference that we have introduced in this chapter. You will find as you progress through your studies that you come across some of these tests from time to time. If you properly understand statistical inference and the hypothesis test procedure that we have developed here then you will have no difficulty in learning how and when to use these tests properly.

SUMMARY

An understanding of probability and the normal distribution is essential for the area known as statistical inference: making an assessment of the likely characteristics of a population based only on sample data. Underpinning statistical inference is the concept of a sampling distribution which can be shown to be normal under certain conditions.

Given the amount of information that is produced today from some types of market research it is essential for a manager to be able to assess the value of such information and its limitations. This can only be achieved through the use of statistical inference either by constructing confidence intervals or by conducting a formal hypothesis test, both of which are two sides of the same coin. A confidence interval provides a range of values around some sample result whilst a hypothesis test allows us to compare a sample result against a specific numerical value. Whilst the principles of such a test are relatively straightforward it must be remembered that they are underpinned by some complex mathematics and statistics. We have provided an introduction to the principles of such tests. This is no substitute for obtaining expert advice when necessary to help you evaluate such information.

Now that you have completed this chapter you will appreciate that:

- It is usually necessary to base statistical analysis upon a sample taken from the population.

- Statistical inference is a use of statistics where we wish to infer the statistical characteristics of a population based on sample data.
- A confidence interval is a statistical attempt to establish limits for the estimation of a population value based on limited sample information.
- A hypothesis test is a procedure for assessing the likelihood of a population value against some sample information.
- The two basic types of test are a test on a sample mean and a test on a sample percentage.

EXAMPLE

We shall develop the following example to illustrate the use of statistical inference in a management context and also to illustrate typical computer output from a statistical software package.

A local hospital operates an outpatient clinic for patients who have been referred for medical tests by their GP (general practitioner, or family doctor). Such patients are sent a letter by the hospital telling them the date and time of the outpatient appointment. The hospital typically has three consultants working in the outpatient's clinic and patient appointments are scheduled for each consultant every 10 minutes. That is, a consultant would be scheduled to see a patient, say, at 9.00 a.m., the next at 9.10, the next and 9.20 and so on.

Naturally, life is not as obliging as this and inevitably it sometimes takes longer than 10 minutes to deal with a particular patient and this then means that patients with later appointments may have to wait beyond their appointment time. The hospital is keen to ensure that patients are not kept waiting for undue periods of time and the hospital manager has set a policy target that average (mean) waiting time of patients in the clinic must not exceed 15 minutes.

The problem is that no one currently has any idea as to whether the clinic is meeting this target or not. The hospital manager decides that patient waiting times must be recorded so that she can assess whether the clinic is meeting the target set. Patients have to come to the main reception desk when they arrive and it has been decided that the receptionist will record their arrival time on a special form. The nurses working with the consultants will also record the time when the patient finally gets to see the consultant. This data will then be used together with the appointment time of the patients to assess mean waiting time. Understandably, those involved are concerned that this data recording will interfere with their 'proper' work so it has been decided to take a sample of 200 patients.

Suppose that we have collected the following sample data:

Mean waiting time	12.2 minutes
Standard deviation	3.45 minutes
Sample size (n)	200

We can use the principles of hypothesis testing to assess, based on this information, whether the clinic is meeting the target.

Since we are dealing with means, we require a test on a mean and our two verbal hypotheses would be that the clinic is meeting the target, with the alternative that it is not meeting the target. The test would then be:

$$H_0: \mu \leq 10$$
$$H_1: \mu > 10$$
$$\alpha = 0.05$$
$$Z_\alpha = 1.64$$
$$Z = \frac{12.2 - 10}{3.45/\sqrt{200}} = \frac{2.2}{0.24} = 9.02$$

and since the calculated Z is greater than the critical we would reject the null hypothesis and be forced to accept that the mean waiting time in the clinic was currently greater than the 10 minute target.

Whilst the test itself is mechanically straightforward we must always recollect the underlying assumptions. Before using this result for management decision-making we would want to ensure that we had collected a properly representative sample for the population, with the result that we might also want to dig a little deeper into the data we have collected. Perhaps we might wish to use the statistical principles from earlier chapters to analyse the individual waiting times for the 200 patients. Although we have concluded through the test that average waiting time exceeds 10 minutes we do not know how many of the patients are affected. We might wish to calculate the median waiting time, for example, or construct a frequency table for waiting times to see how many are affected and by how much.

Such a test then for a manager is only part of the analysis that would need to be undertaken into the situation. If we have access to an appropriate computer package we might find that such tests can be undertaken as part of the routine analysis. Table 9.1 shows the output from such a program for the outpatient clinic data. From the raw data the mean and standard deviation are automatically calculated. The program allows the user to specify a numeric value for H_0 (here at 10) and also choose whether the test is one tail or two tail and if one tail the direction of the test. Here the null hypothesis is specified as less than or equal to 10 (LE) with the alternative of greater than 10 (GT). The user also controls the value of α used in the test, here at 0.05. The program then computes Z_C (at 9.02) and indicates a conclusion based on a comparison of Z_C with Z_α (see Fig. 9.11) – here the conclusion is to reject H_0.

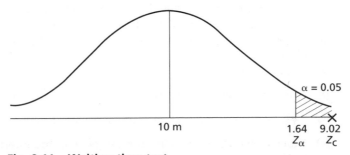

Fig. 9.11   Waiting time test

Table 9.1 One-sample analysis results

Sample Statistics:	Number of Obs.	200
	Mean	12.2
	Variance	11.0925
	Std. Deviation	3.45

Hypothesis Test for H0: Mean LE 10   Computed statistic = 9.02
                  vs Alt: GT
             at Alpha = 0.05   so reject H0.

SELF-REVIEW QUESTIONS

1 *What is the sampling distribution?*

2 *What is the standard error?*

3 *Why is the Central Limit Theorem important?*

4 *Why is a 95% confidence interval so called?*

5 *What is a hypothesis test?*

6 *What is H_0 in a hypothesis test?*

7 *What does the critical statistic in a hypothesis test show?*

STUDENT EXERCISES

1   In the chapter we used as an illustration a computer-based simulation for the Central Limit Theorem. The simulation program is available on the accompanying data disk and will run as a DOS program on an IBM-compatible PC.
    Switch to the DOS prompt on your PC. Switch to the floppy drive. Type:

    CLT and press Enter

and the program should load and run.
    Experiment with the program to assess the effect the sample size has on the sampling distribution.

2   A factory producing a product has recently introduced changes into the way that employees are regarded for their work and wishes to assess the effect on labour productivity. A representative sample of 100 employees have been monitored and the mean output per day calculated at 125 units with a standard deviation of 17.

(**a**) Calculate a 95% confidence interval for this problem.

(**b**) Calculate a 99% confidence interval for this problem.

(**c**) Explain why the interval in (**b**) is larger than the interval in (**a**).

3 A major oil company is considering the inclusion of a chemical additive to their unleaded petrol in order to increase the number of kilometres per litre obtained by a typical family car. An independent motoring organization has taken a number of cars – all of the same make and model – and driven the cars over the last few weeks with the additive in the petrol. A sample of 60 cars was tested and it was found that mean kilometres per litre obtained with the additive was 19.01, standard deviation 0.79. Performance of this type of car without the additive is 18 kilometres per litre.

Comment on whether the additive appears to improve performance in terms of kilometres per litre.

4 A large retail organization is thinking of introducing its own-brand lager into its stores nationwide. Before doing so, however, the organization commissioned some market research to assess the likely popularity of the product with customers. Across a sample of stores nationwide a cross-section of customers were asked to test the new product and indicate whether they would buy the product if available at a given price. Of the 2,400 customers surveyed 1,400 indicated that they would buy the product if available at the price indicated.

(a) Calculate a confidence interval around this sample result. Explain clearly how the confidence interval you have calculated can be interpreted and used.

(b) Draft a short management report explaining the background to the confidence interval you have calculated. You may assume that management reading the report have little knowledge of the relevant statistical theory.

5 A retail organization has recently been investigating its long-term strategy in terms of store location. As part of this it has analysed household income patterns for the UK as a whole and for one of its key regions – the South-East of England. The summary results are shown below (all figures are in £s and relate to household income):

	UK	South East
Mean income	337.19	401.34
Median	288.64	358.69
Standard deviation	234.39	255.80
Lower quartile	131.64	127.11
Upper quartile	368.60	536.54

Source: *Regional Trends 1993.*

(a) Using these statistics, and any others you can derive, compare and contrast household income in the South-East with that in the UK.

(b) A small market research exercise has recently been completed in part of the South-East where the organization is thinking of opening another retail outlet. In the exercise 400 representative households were asked to provide details of their income. A mean household income of £386.25 was obtained, standard deviation £256.24. Using an appropriate statistical test comment on whether the mean income in this part of the South-East is the same as that for the South-East as a whole.

6   A company provides a service to business customers in terms of providing an express delivery service for urgent correspondence and materials. One such service 'guarantees' to deliver such a package to any address in the UK by 9.00 a.m. the following morning if collected no later than 5.00 p.m. the previous day. The firm has a number of courier vans which deliver packages to given addresses with each van/driver allocated a specific geographical area. A sample of 150 days' deliveries found that the mean time taken for a van/driver to complete their deliveries each morning as 2 hours 18 minutes with a standard deviation of 35 minutes. By what time should the company ensure that these vans/drivers set off on their morning delivery round if they wish to meet their 'guaranteed' delivery time of 9.00 a.m.?

7   A chemicals factory is seeking to expand on its current site but has met resistance from local residents who are concerned about additional traffic and pollution. The company has decided to undertake a public relations campaign to reassure local residents and to persuade them of the benefits of the planned expansion, in terms of additional local jobs and income. A recent survey of 300 local residents has found that 59% were in favour of the planned expansion. A census carried out 12 months ago, before the PR campaign, revealed that 40% were in favour of the expansion

Draft a short report commenting on whether you think the PR campaign has been successful in terms of increasing the level of local support for the planned expansion.

8   In the current economic recession your company, a mail-order clothing firm, is becoming increasingly concerned about customers who do not pay for the items they have purchased through mail order (since items are sent on inspection with payment expected if the goods are kept by the customer). Last year the company found that 8% of customers had not paid for items they had kept. You have recently completed analysis of a sample of customer records for the current year and found that 35 out of 350 sampled have not paid for goods received. Would you conclude that non-payment has got worse since last year?

10 BUSINESS MATHEMATICS: LINEAR EQUATIONS AND GRAPHS

INTRODUCTION

In the preceding chapters we have seen the necessity for analysing and presenting information using a variety of *statistical* techniques. In the next few chapters we introduce some of the *mathematical* techniques that are frequently used by business. As with the statistical techniques we have introduced it is necessary to develop not only an ability to find the 'answer' to a mathematical problem but also to be able to understand the principles underlying the technique, the general areas of relevance for business applications and to interpret the 'answer' in a business context.

Mathematics offers a manager a convenient method of representing and analysing many business problems. Like the corresponding statistical techniques mathematics has its own terminology which will be introduced and explained where appropriate. Much of mathematical business analysis takes place through the use of linear equations. This chapter introduces such equations and their corresponding graphs and examines how sets of linear equations can be solved through the use of something known as simultaneous equations.

LEARNING OBJECTIVES

By the end of this chapter you should be able to:

- explain what is meant by a function;
- draw a graph of a linear equation;
- explain what is meant by the intercept and slope of a linear function;
- solve two linear equations using both graphs and simultaneous equations;
- use linear equations in a number of common business applications.

FUNCTIONS

In applying mathematics to business we are normally interested in trying to relate two or more variables to each other – such as sales and profit, price and sales, productivity and profit, costs and output and so on. This is initially achieved by expressing such a relationship in the form of what is known as a function.

Let us suppose that a company which manufactures a product has been collecting and analysing data on two variables of particular importance to management:

- the number of units of the product produced each week;
- the total cost of producing those units each week (measured in £000s).

If we show number of units produced as X and total costs as C then we can express the relationship between the two as a simple function:

$$C = f(X)$$

The term f( ) – 'a function of' – is the mathematical way of expressing a generalized relationship between two or more variables; here we are saying that C is a function of X. In business such a function between variables implies some sort of dependency or causal relationship. Here, in expressing the relationship in this way we are suggesting that the level of output in some way determines or 'causes' the level of total costs. In mathematical notation, C is referred to as the 'dependent' variable and X as the 'independent' or 'explanatory' variable. Whilst mathematically we could express the function the opposite way – output as a function of costs – it would make no sense to do so in a business context since it would imply that the level of output was determined by costs.

Student activity

Consider two variables: one is S, the amount of money you spend each week on food and drink. The other is Y, your weekly income. Write a function using the two variables. Numerically, what do you think will happen to S if Y increases? What will happen to S if Y decreases?

It seems sensible to have a function so that:

$$S = f(Y)$$

that is, spending on food and drink is a function of income. This implies that as Y changes then it will cause a change in S. This seems sensible since, other things being equal, the more money you have the more you might spend on food and drink (perhaps buying more expensive items that you couldn't afford before). Similarly, if you have less money then the chances are you will spend less on food (again perhaps substituting cheaper food and drink products for those you would normally buy).

LINEAR EQUATIONS

The expression of such a functional relationship between two variables is typically the first step in business mathematical analysis. However, for practical purposes we generally require more explicit information than that provided in a function. In our example, it is not sufficient to know that total costs are *in some way* dependent on output. We need to know exactly the numerical relationship between the two variables. Such a relationship may be expressed in the form of a linear equation such as:

$$C = 8.0 + 1.2X$$

As we shall see shortly, such an equation is referred to as 'linear' because when we show this type of equation on a graph we will get a straight line. The general form of a linear equation is given as:

$$Y = a + bX$$

where Y is the dependent variable, X is the independent variable and a and b are known as the *parameters* of the equation: they are the numbers that give the equation its specific form. Here a would be +8.0 and b +1.2. Be careful about the general use of X and Y and the variables you are using for a specific business problem. In the last Student activity we had a Y variable (income) but this was actually on the right-hand side of the function. The critical point is that the dependent variable appears on the left and the independent or explanatory appears on the right.

With such an equation we have a ready way of predicting values of C based on values of X. If we plan to produce 3(000) units of X then we can easily calculate C as:

$$
\begin{aligned}
C &= 8.0 + 1.2X \\
&= 8.0 + 1.2(3) \\
&= 8.0 + 3.6 \\
&= 11.6
\end{aligned}
$$

That is, with a level of production of 3(000) total costs will be 11.6 (£000).

GRAPHING A LINEAR EQUATION

Typically, we may wish to show the information in an equation visually in the form of a graph, just as we used diagrams to show data from tables. Graphs are often easier to use and understand than equations (although we need the equation first in order to draw the graph). There are a number of specific steps to follow in drawing the graph for a linear equation and we are assuming that you remember the key points about graphs from Chapter 5.

Step 1

Decide which variable is going on the vertical axis and which on the horizontal. In the case of equations this decision is taken for us: the dependent variable always goes on the vertical axis whilst the independent variable goes on the horizontal.

Step 2

Choose an appropriate numerical range for the X scale. Frequently it is apparent from the problem what the appropriate range of values for the X variable are. In other cases, we may simply have to make a reasonable assumption. Here, it is logical to set the lowest value of X to 0 (we cannot produce less than zero units after all). If we assume that the company can produce no more than 10(000) units of the product then the highest value for X can be assumed to be 10. (In a problem you are set you will usually be told the maximum value for the X variable.)

Step 3

Determine an appropriate range of values for the Y scale. This is easily done from Step 2. Using the equation we work out the Y value when X takes its lowest value. Here when $X = 0$ we can substitute the value for X into the equation and work out the corresponding value for Y:

$$C = 8.0 + 1.2X$$
$$= 8.0 + 1.2(0)$$
$$= 8.0$$

So, when $X = 0$ C equals 8.

Then we work out the corresponding Y value when X takes its upper value, here set at $X = 10$, by substituting again into the equation:

$$C = 8.0 + 1.2X$$
$$= 8.0 + 1.2(10)$$
$$= 8.0 + 12$$
$$= 20.0$$

So when $X = 10$ C must equal 20.

Step 4

Work out an appropriate scale for the Y variable (C in our equation). Here it would be sensible to set Y from 0 to 20 since this is the range of values that C must cover for the corresponding range of X values (0 to 10).

Step 5

Draw a suitable scale for the X and Y variables on the graph. Conventionally, the Y variable is shown on the vertical axis and the X variable on the horizontal. This then gives the graph we see in Fig. 10.1.

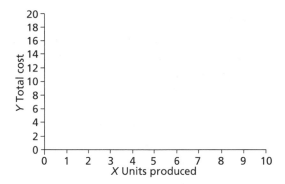

Fig. 10.1   Graph axes

Step 6

Taking the two pairs of X, Y values calculated in Step 2 plot each point on the graph – $(X = 0, Y = 8)$ and $(X = 10, Y = 20)$. These are shown in Fig. 10.2 as Point A and Point B.

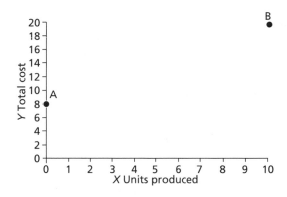

Fig. 10.2   Two points

Step 7

Join these two points carefully together with a straight line. This is the line for the given equation shown in Fig. 10.3.

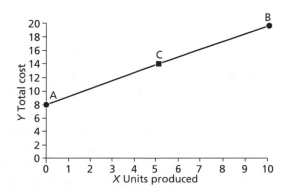

Fig. 10.3 $C = 8.0 + 1.2X$

Step 8

Until you have had adequate practice it is always worth checking you have drawn the line properly. Take another X value (typically somewhere in the middle of the X range) and calculate the corresponding Y value from the equation. Plot this point on the graph. If it falls on the line you have drawn then the line is correct.

Here, let us choose $X = 5$:

$$C = 8.0 + 1.2X$$
$$= 8.0 + 1.2(5)$$
$$= 8.0 + 6.0$$
$$= 14.0$$

which is plotted as Point C on Fig. 10.3. This falls on the line we have drawn confirming that the equation has been drawn correctly. If it had not fallen on the line then we would need to go back and check we had drawn the line properly on the graph.

Student activity

Suppose we had an equation linking your spending on food and drink to your income such that:

$S = 25 + 0.4Y$

If your weekly income is not expected to go above £100 draw a suitable graph for this equation.

We can use the steps we have identified:

Step 1. S goes on the vertical axis and Y on the horizontal.

Step 2. Income, Y, takes a value from 0 to 100.

Step 3. For $Y = 0$ we work out S as:

$$S = 25 + 0.4(0) = 25 + 0 = 25$$

and for $Y = 100$ we have:

$$S = 25 + 0.4(100) = 25 + 40 = 65$$

Step 4. A suitable scale for Y might be from 0 to 100 (it needs to be at least 65 and choosing a maximum of 100 makes some of the arithmetic for drawing the scale easier).

Steps 5–7. We can then do Steps 5–7 and draw the graph as shown in Fig. 10.4, with Point A showing $X = 0$, $Y = 25$ and Point B showing $X = 100$, $Y = 65$. Notice that, as with every diagram, we must ensure it is properly drawn, labelled and so on as we discussed in Chapter 5.

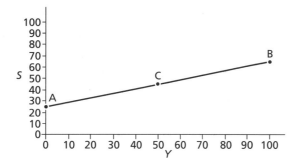

Fig. 10.4 $C = 25 + 0.4Y$

Step 8. We can check the line on the graph. If we set $X = 50$ (midway between 0 and 100) then we have:

$$S = 25 + 0.4(50) = 25 + 20 = 45$$

and we see that this point, $X = 50$, $Y = 45$, is at Point C which does indeed fall on the line we have drawn.

It is important to realize the relationship between the graph and the original equation. Both show *exactly* the same information. The graph shows the relationship between the two variables visually whilst the equation shows it mathematically. It is important to be able to use both methods and to be able to extract the same information from both. For example, if we wish to determine the value of S when $Y = 30$ then we can use the graph or the equation to obtain a value for S of 37, although it is evident that the graph may be less accurate depending on the scale shown.

PARAMETERS OF A LINEAR EQUATION

The two parameters of a linear equation – the a and b values – have particular importance both mathematically and in business. The a term is normally referred to as the intercept or constant whilst the b term is known as the slope or gradient.

The constant or intercept

The intercept is literally the point on the Y axis where the line of the equation crosses, or intercepts. In Fig. 10.3 – the cost example – the intercept is at $Y = 8.0$. It is evident that this intercept value is exactly the same as the numerical value of the a term in the equation. The a parameter actually determines the general position of the line, in terms of where it crosses the vertical axis. Should the a term change its value for any reason then the line will shift across the graph from one position to another as illustrated in Fig. 10.5:

- a positive value for *a* means the intercept will be above *Y* = 0;
- a negative value for *a* means the intercept will be below *Y* = 0;
- a value of *a* = 0 means the intercept will pass through the origin of the graph. When *a* = 0 the linear equation is often expressed solely in terms of *b* with *a* not appearing at all;

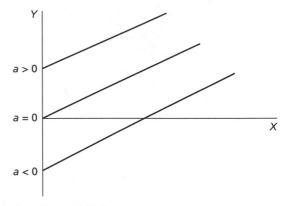

Fig. 10.5   Shift in *a*

- the larger the numerical value for *a* the further away from *Y* = 0 the intercept will be.

Apart from the mathematics, however, the *a* value frequently has a useful business interpretation. Naturally, this will vary depending on the problem. Here, *C* = 8.0 when *X* = 0. That is, when output is zero total costs are £8(000). It is evident that in this example, the intercept term represents the fixed cost element of production since fixed costs are defined as those costs which remain fixed no matter what the level of production.

Student activity

Return to the equation in the last activity:

S = 25 + 0.4*Y*

Explain what the a term measures in this example.

Suppose a friend came to stay with you for a few days. What would you expect to happen to the value of this 'a' term and what would happen to the line you have drawn on the graph?

For the spending equation *S* = 25 + 0.4*Y* the *a* term is 25. That is, when income, *Y*, is zero this is where the equation intercepts the vertical, *S*, axis and this is the value that *C* will take. In other words, with a zero income you will still spend £25 a week on food and drink. At first this might seem odd, since with no income where do you get the money to spend on food and drink? However, from another perspective the interpretation is fairly rational since, even with no income, you still have to eat and drink. You might perhaps be able to borrow money to buy food from friends or relatives or you might have some savings in a bank or building society which you can use. What is important is that for a business context equation we are able to interpret the *a* term in a contextual way.

As for the second part of the activity, with a friend visiting we would rationally expect a to increase since the amount of food and drink required, regardless of income, will increase. In other words even if your income does not change you will still have to increase your spending on S. This can only happen with an increase in a. On the graph the whole line would shift upwards as shown in Fig. 10.6.

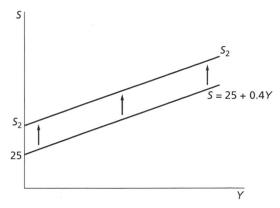

Fig. 10.6   New *a* term

Naturally we do not know by how much a increases but the whole line shifts upwards to line S_2 which is parallel to the original S equation. This is an important point because it implies that no matter what our level of income, Y, the change in S (i.e. the increase in a) will be the same no matter what our income. In other words the extra amount spent because of our friend's visit will be the same regardless of our income.

The slope or gradient

The second parameter of the linear function is the b term which is referred to as the slope or gradient of the function. The b parameter in a linear equation shows both the steepness of the line and the direction of its slope. Mathematically, the slope shows the change in Y that will occur for each unit change in X.

Let us return to the cost equation and assume that output is currently 4(000) units. From the equation we know that total costs will be:

$$C = 8.0 + 1.2X$$
$$= 8.0 + 1.2(4)$$
$$= 12.8$$

Let us now assume that output is set to rise to 5(000) units: a change of 1 in terms of units of X. The new C value will be given by:

$$C = 8.0 + 1.2X$$
$$= 8.0 + 1.2(5)$$
$$= 14.0$$

C has increased, therefore, by 1.2 as a result of X increasing by 1. This is obviously the value of the b parameter in the equation. Simply, the b parameter shows the change that will occur in Y for a given change in X. Similarly, if X were to change by 2, Y would change by 2.4 (i.e. 2×1.2). This is frequently expressed as:

$$\text{Slope} = \frac{\text{Change in } Y}{\text{Change in } X}$$

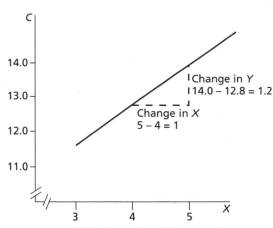

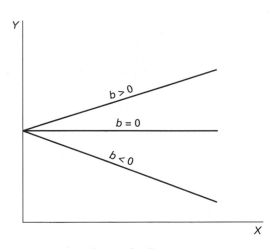

Fig. 10.7   Calculating slope from graph

Fig. 10.8   Slope of a line

The slope can also be identified from the graph of the equation as illustrated in Fig. 10.7 which shows the X and Y axes for part of their range. On the graph the numerical change in Y and change in X can be established and their ratio confirms the slope at 1.2. It is also evident from the graph of the linear equation that it will not matter where on the line we measure the slope, as we will always get the same numerical result. The slope of a linear function, in other words, is constant along its length.

As with the a parameter, the b term may take one of three general forms which are illustrated in Fig. 10.8:

- a line with a positive b value slopes upwards from left to right, implying that an increase in X will lead to an increase in Y;
- a line with a negative b value slopes downward from left to right, implying that an increase in X will lead to a decrease in Y;
- a line with a zero b value is parallel to the X axis, and implies that as X changes there will be no change in Y. X and Y, in other words, are independent of each other;
- the larger the b value the steeper the slope of the line.

As with the a term the slope usually has an important business interpretation. In this example, it shows how total costs change as output changes. Each unit extra of X leads to an increase in C of 1.2. Remembering the units of measurement this implies that an extra 1,000 units adds £1,200 to costs. It is evident that the b term shows variable costs in this example – that portion of costs which change with output.

Student activity

Return to the spending equation we have been using. How would you explain to someone who hadn't heard of slopes and gradients what the 'b' term at 0.4 actually showed? Suppose the 'b' term increased to 0.6: what would this mean? Could the 'b' term increase to a number greater than 1?

Our explanation might go something like this. We know there is a connection between our weekly income and the amount of that income we spend on food and drink. The equation is simply a way of calculating what we would spend on food and drink for any particular level of income. We also know that if our income changes then so does the amount we spend on food and drink. In this case, the equation tells us that if we get an extra £1 in income we would spend 40p of this (0.4) on food and drink (with the rest spent on other things). If the b term increased to 0.6 this implies that our propensity to spend income on food and drink has increased. In this case $b = 0.6$ implies we would spend 60p out of a £1 increase in income on food and drink. For the last part of the question we would not normally expect b to exceed 1 since $b = 1$ implies that of a £1 increase in income then £1 extra is spent on food and drink, which under normal circumstances is clearly the maximum that it would be possible to spend.

EQUATIONS FROM GRAPHS

Just as we have drawn a graph from an equation we were given, we can obtain a linear equation if we are given its graph. Consider Fig. 10.9 which shows the graph of some linear function. We see the graph is of a linear equation and we want to obtain the equation for this line. We know the equation is made up of two parts, a and b. a is the intercept indicating where on the Y axis the equation intercepts. From the graph we see that this line has an intercept of 1,000 so this must be the a value in the equation. How about the slope? We see that the slope of the line is negative so b must be negative also, since this shows the slope of the equation but how do we derive an appropriate number?

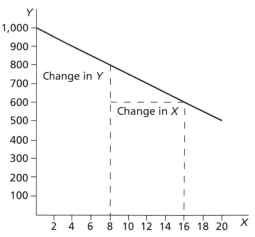

Fig. 10.9 $Y = a + bX$

Consider what we said earlier when we had:

$$\text{Slope} = \frac{\text{Change in } Y}{\text{Change in } X}$$

We can find the slope if we have a measure of a change in X and the corresponding change in Y. We can obtain these from the graph quite easily. Suppose we take $X = 8$ and let this change to $X = 16$ (we could take any of the X values – it wouldn't affect our answer). That is, the change in X is:

From 8 to 16 = +8

339

We see from the graph that when $X = 8$, $Y = 800$ and when $X = 16$, $Y = 600$. So, the corresponding change in Y is:

From 800 to 600 = –200

(we need to be careful to note that it is a negative change). This then gives:

$$\text{Slope} = \frac{\text{Change in } Y}{\text{Change in } X} = \frac{-200}{8} = -25$$

as the slope of this line. This then means that we have an equation:

$$Y = 1{,}000 - 25X$$

as the equation for the line we drew on the graph.

As ever we should check and we can do this quite easily. Suppose we let $X = 20$ then, from the equation, $Y = 500$ and we see from the graph that $Y = 500$ when $X = 20$ also confirming we have not made a mistake in obtaining the equation of this line.

Using this approach we can find the equation of a line graph although we must be careful about negative slopes and we must also be careful about the accuracy of our measures of change in X and Y given that it can be difficult to read precise values from a graph.

Student activity

From Fig. 10.10 obtain the equation of this line.

From the diagram we see that it has an intercept of –100 so this must be the *a* value of the equation. We see that the *b* value is positive since the line slopes upwards. You might have chosen a different set of X values to work out the slope. We chose $X = 75$ and $X = 100$. This gives:

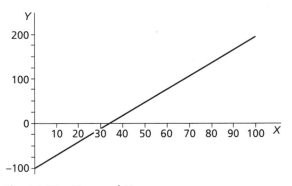

Fig. 10.10 $Y = a + bX$

Change in X = 75 to 100 = +25

From the graph we read the Y values as:

$X = 75$ $Y = 125$
$X = 100$ $Y = 200$

giving:

Change in Y = 125 to 200 = +75

and so the slope as:

$$\text{Slope} = \frac{\text{Change in } Y}{\text{Change in } X} = \frac{75}{25} = +3$$

and an equation of:

$$Y = -100 + 3X$$

We can check this is correct by taking another X value, say $X = 25$, and finding from the equation that $Y = -25$. We see from the graph that the line passes through the point (25,–25) indicating the equation is correct.

SETS OF LINEAR EQUATIONS

Typically, in a business context, we deal not with just one equation but with two or more. Such a situation is often referred to as a mathematical model and we need to see how to deal with such sets of equations. Let us assume that, in addition to the information on costs and output used earlier, we also have information on revenue and output: that is, on what we sell as well as what we produce. Assume that we have a linear revenue equation given by:

$$R = 2.8X$$

where X is output (again measured in 000s of units) and R is total revenue (measured in £000s). It is apparent that R is determined simply by the number of units sold multiplied by the price per unit. Using the concepts introduced earlier it is also clear that the R equation has an intercept of zero and a slope of 2.8. You should be aware that the intercept will logically be zero because if $X = 0$ (i.e. output is zero) the firm has no products to sell and therefore R will be zero also. The slope will be positive since the more we sell the more revenue we obtain and we can actually work out that the price per unit sold must be 2.8 also. The graph of this linear revenue equation will slope upwards as we look at it from left to right and will start from the origin.

So we have a situation with two linear equations:

$$C = 8.0 + 1.2X$$
$$R = 2.8X$$

Note that both equations have one variable in common: X, units of output. Typically in such a situation we wish to use both equations at the same time to analyse some problem, for example where we have been asked to determine the company's breakeven point, i.e. the level of output where costs are just balanced by revenue.

Since we have information in the form of an equation for both costs and revenue it seems logical that we should be able to use these equations to solve such a problem. In fact there are a number of methods we can adopt to find a solution. We shall introduce two: the graphical method and the method of simultaneous equations.

Graphical solution for a set of equations

The graphical solution method simply requires one graph showing both equations together. Figure 10.11 shows both the C and R functions. Note that we still have the common element, X, on the horizontal axis whilst the vertical axis now shows both dependent variables: C and R.

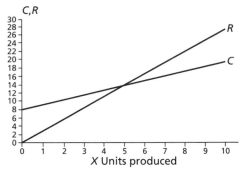

Fig. 10.11   C and R

Take a few minutes to study the diagram. We see that the lines for the two equations cross. It is also apparent that the point where the two lines cross will be the point where C and R are equal for a given value of X. This point will then be the solution to the problem: the breakeven point where total cost equals total revenue. From the graph it can be seen that this point will occur when $X = 5$. At this point from the graph both C and R take a value 14.

Because graphs are not always precise given the scales used it is advisable to confirm the graphical solution from the original equations. We can check from the C and R equations that when $X = 5$ both C and R do actually equal 14. Let $X = 5$ then:

$$C = 8.0 + 1.2(5) = 14.0$$
$$R = 2.8(5) = 14.0$$

That is, we confirm that when output is 5(000) units the company breaks even.

Student activity

A company is thinking of getting a photocopier for use in its office. It has the choice of leasing a copier from the copier company or buying a copier outright. If it leases the copier then it will have to pay an annual leasing charge of £3,000 plus 10p per copy to the rental company who will be responsible for all other costs (such as paper, toner, repairs etc.). If it decides to buy the copier then it will pay £5,000 to buy the machine outright and will have to pay for paper etc. itself at an estimated cost of 2p per copy. The firm is not sure what to do although it does know that its copying each year runs to less than 50,000.

Derive two equations for the lease option and the buy option. Draw both equations on the same graph and use the graph to advise the firm what to do.

This is the first time we've actually had to derive equations from information but it's actually quite straightforward as long as we remember the principles of linear equations. Let's start by defining our variables. Suppose we use the following:

C_l as the cost of leasing a copier
C_b as the cost of buying the photocopier
X as the number of copies made

and we assume two functions so that:

$C_l = f(X)$
$C_b = f(X)$

For C_l we know that the two costs are the leasing cost per year of £3,000 and the cost of 10p per copy made. The leasing cost will have to be paid regardless of the number of copies made. That is, even if the firm makes no copies at all it will still have to pay the annual leasing cost of £3,000. In a mathematical context this fixed element would then be the a term in a linear equation. The company also knows that each extra copy made will increase costs, C_l, by 10p or £0.1. The b term in this equation then will be 0.1. We then have:

$C_l = 3,000 + 0.1X$

where $a = 3,000$ and $b = 0.1$.

If we apply the same sort of logic to C_b we see that the cost per copy is 2p, or £0.02 whilst the firm must pay £5,000 regardless of how many copies it makes, so this must be a, giving:

$C_b = 5,000 + 0.02X$

as the cost equation for buying the copier.

Notice that we must be very careful about units of measurement when deriving an equation from information we have been given. Some of the information was in £s whilst some was in pence. It does not matter whether we use £s or pence but we *must* use the same units for each and every part of an equation. Suppose for the C_b equation we had not noticed this and written:

$C_b = 5,000 + 2X$

Can you see why this would be wrong? We have mixed the a term in £s with the b term in pence. When we came to work out C_b, the cost to the company of buying and using a copier, would this cost have been in £s or pence? (The answer would actually be neither or both!) So we must be careful about ensuring consistent units of measurement.

We could have written the two equations in pence form if we'd wanted as:

$C_l = 300,000 + 10X$
$C_b = 500,000 + 2X$

Notice that the b terms are now in pence but so is the £3,000 leasing cost and the £5,000 purchase cost. It doesn't really matter which set of equations we use – those in pence or those in pounds.

If we use our two cost equations in £s we can proceed to plot them together on a graph. We are told that the company will have no more than 50,000 copies per year so our X scale runs from 0 to 50,000. We can then work out a suitable Y scale for the two equations by substituting $X = 0$ and $X = 50,000$. We then have:

When $X = 0$:

$C_1 = 3,000 + 0.1X = 3,000 + 0.1(0) = 3,000$
$C_b = 5,000 + 0.02X = 5,000 + 0.02(0) = 5,000$

When $X = 50,000$:

$C_1 = 3,000 + 0.1X = 3,000 + 0.1(50,000) = 8,000$
$C_b = 5,000 + 0.02X = 5,000 + 0.02(50,000) = 6,000$

So, we need a Y scale that covers at least a range from 3,000 to 8,000, and since we are not starting the Y axis at zero we shall need to be careful to show this on the completed graph.

We then need to plot two points for each equation and draw the line joining them together. For the first equation, C_1, we have $X = 0$, $Y = 3,000$ and $X = 50,000$, $Y = 8,000$. For the second equation, C_b, we have $X = 0$, $Y = 5,000$ and $X = 50,000$, $Y = 6,000$. Plotting these two sets of points then gives the graph as in Fig. 10.12. We see the C_1 starting from 3,000 on the Y axis and C_b starting at 5,000. We also see quite easily that C_1 has a steeper slope or gradient which is consistent with the numerical value of b in the two equations (that for C_1 is 0.1 and higher than that for C_b at 0.02).

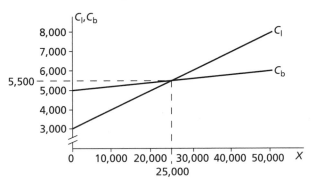

Fig. 10.12   Photocopy costs

The two lines (and their equations) can be used to calculate photocopier costs at any level of use between 0 and 50,000 copies. However, we can also use the graph to help in management decision-making. The company were not sure whether to lease or buy the copier. The graph will now help them make a decision. We see that for a level of use of up to 25,000 copies then the C_1 line is always below that for C_b. Think carefully about what this means in the context of the question. This means that up to this level of use the numerical values for C_b will be greater than those for C_1 or, in other words, it will be more costly to buy the copier than to lease it. On the other hand, we also see that if the number of copies exceeds 25,000 then the C_1 line is always above the C_b line implying that leasing costs are above the cost of buying the machine. We can refer to the level of use of 25,000 as the critical value for X. If the company thinks it will use less than 25,000 copies a year then it should lease the copier. If it thinks it will use more than 25,000 copies it should buy the copier. (And any smart-alec who asks what should we do if we think we will use *exactly* 25,000 copies should be told that it doesn't matter whether you lease or buy since the two costs will be exactly equal at this level of use.)

Using simultaneous equations to find a solution

Whilst such a graphical method of solution is straightforward it is not always practical: it may be difficult to read precise values from the graph and a complex problem we face may not be capable of being easily graphed. A more general method of algebraic solution is necessary. This method is known as the *method of simultaneous equations*.

Let us return to the cost/revenue example. Recollect that we had the general form of a linear equation as $Y = a + bX$, with Y as the dependent variable and X as the independent. In this example Y is both C and R. The method takes its name from the fact that we are looking for a combination of X and Y values that will satisfy *both* equations simultaneously. Clearly this will give us the same intersection point that we derived from the graph. However, there are frequently occasions when we wish to find such a point without having to draw a graph of the problem.

In order to be able to develop a general method of solution it is necessary to understand the general principles of the algebraic manipulations we shall be performing. It is important to remember that an equation is simply a precise statement of some relationship between variables. Suppose we have an equation such that:

$$5X = 50$$

Obviously, here $X = 10$. However, suppose we have an equation instead such that:

$$10X = 100$$

X clearly still equals 10. Although the two equations look different they are in fact expressing the same relationship.

We can generalize this to say that we can change an equation into a different form as long as we change both sides of the equation in the same way. It is apparent in the simple example above that this is what we have done. The original equation was:

$$5X = 50$$

Suppose we multiply the left-hand side (LHS) by 2. The relationship expressed in this equation will remain unchanged as long as we also change the right-hand side (RHS) in the same way:

$$5X \times 2 = 50 \times 2$$

giving:

$$10X = 100$$

So, we can make any arithmetic change to the LHS of an equation as long as exactly the same change is undertaken on the RHS (and it doesn't matter if the arithmetic is multiplication, addition, subtraction, division).

How does this help? Let us return to the R and C equations. We have:

$$C = 8.0 + 1.2X$$
$$R = \qquad 2.8X$$

We are looking for a point where $C = R$ (that is a value for X which gives an identical numerical value for C and for R). We now know of course that where $C = R$ is where the two lines cross on the graph but we are looking for a strictly numerical solution. So we have:

$$C = R$$

But we have another expression for C and for R. We know that $C = 8.0 + 1.2X$ and that $R = 2.8X$. If we substitute these for C and R we then have:

$$8.0 + 1.2X = 2.8X$$

as an identical expression for $C = R$. What this means is that if we can find a value for X which makes both sides of this equation the same then we have also found a value for X which will make $C = R$.

What we need to do now is to manipulate this equation so that we get all the terms involving X on the same side. Suppose we subtract $1.2X$ from each side (remembering that as long as we carry out the same arithmetic on both sides of an equation we are not really altering it – it just looks different). We then have:

$$8.0 + 1.2X - 1.2X = 2.8X - 1.2X$$

On the left-hand side the two terms involving X cancel each other and on the right-hand side we can subtract 1.2 from 2.8 to give 1.6. This gives an equation:

$$8.0 = 1.6X$$

We can now find the value of X which 'solves' this equation by dividing both sides through by 1.6. This gives:

$$\frac{8.0}{1.6} = \frac{1.6X}{1.6}$$

8.0/1.6 is equal to 5 whilst 1.6/1.6 is the same as 1 so we have:

$$5 = 1X \qquad \text{or} \qquad 5 = X$$

That is when X is 5 we have 'solved' the equation.

But remember what we were doing. We were trying to find a value for X which would make C and R equal to each other. So, we now know that when $X = 5$, $C = R$. We could of course check by substituting $X = 5$ into each of the C and R equations in turn and we should get the same result (of 14).

To summarize what we have done:

- We set the two equations equal to one another.
- We performed arithmetic on the equation to collect all the terms involving X on one side.
- We performed arithmetic on the equation to collect all the terms involving just numbers on the other side.
- We can then solve for X.

Student activity

Return to the two equations derived in the last activity on photocopying costs. Use simultaneous equations to confirm the solution.

Using the two equations we derived earlier we have:

$$C_l = C_b$$
$$3{,}000 + 0.1X = 5{,}000 + 0.02X$$

(**a**) Subtract $0.02X$ from both sides:

$$3{,}000 + 0.1X - 0.02X = 5{,}000 + 0.02X - 0.02X$$
$$3{,}000 + 0.08X = 5{,}000$$

(**b**) Subtract 3,000 from both sides:

$$3{,}000 + 0.08X - 3{,}000 = 5{,}000 - 3{,}000$$
$$0.08X = 2{,}000$$

(Be careful with the decimal places when subtracting.)

(**c**) Divide both sides by 0.08:

$$\frac{0.08X}{0.08} = \frac{2{,}000}{0.08}$$
$$1X = 25{,}000$$

confirming our solution (again be careful when dividing by the decimal to check your answer).

We also begin to see the usefulness of the mathematical approach if we wish to consider how the situation might change. Suppose the photocopier leasing company now decides to increase the purchase price of the copier from £5,000 to £6,000. How will this affect our decision as to whether to lease or buy?

First of all we can examine the graph to assess the general impact such a change will have. From what we know of linear equations if the a term in C_b increases from 5,000 to 6,000 then the intercept of this line increases and it will shift upwards, starting at 6,000 now but still parallel to the original C_b line. This will have the effect of changing the point where C_b and C_l intersect. As the C_b line shifts upwards then the intersection point will be to the right and above where it currently is. This means that the critical value of X, in terms of number of copies, will increase. In other words we will need to use even more than 25,000 copies a year before it is more effective to buy the machine rather than lease it.

Whilst we could draw the new line on the graph and find the new X value it is quicker, easier and more accurate to use simultaneous equations. We now have:

$$C_l = C_b$$

where:

$$3,000 + 0.1X = 6,000 + 0.02X$$

(**a**) Subtract $0.02X$ from both sides:

$$3,000 + 0.1X - 0.02X = 6,000 + 0.02X - 0.02X$$
$$3,000 + 0.08X = 6,000$$

(**b**) Subtract 3,000 from both sides:

$$3,000 + 0.08X - 3,000 = 6,000 - 3,000$$
$$0.08X = 3,000$$

(**c**) Divide both sides by 0.08:

$$\frac{0.08X}{0.08} = \frac{3,000}{0.08}$$
$$1X = 37,500$$

That is, the critical number of copies per year is now 37,500.

We should also note that some sets of linear equations may not have a solution. Consider two equations where the lines were parallel to each other (which, of course, means they have the same slope). These two lines would never cross and hence would not have a solution as such – that is there would never be an X value which would give the same Y value in both equations. This would be apparent from the graph and from the simultaneous equations approach since we would not be able to find a unique solution that satisfied both equations simultaneously. Of course, if you are using the simultaneous equations method and cannot find a solution you must check that you have not made an arithmetic mistake somewhere before deciding the equations do not have a solution.

SUMMARY

Linear functions are – with relatively little practice – easy to use in business and easy to interpret. They can be used to develop simple models of business situations. By understanding and interpreting the parameters of such equations – the intercept and slope – we can produce useful management information and by solving sets of equations – either graphically or using algebra – we can identify solutions to business problems. However, linear equations cannot always be reliably applied to all business problems. In particular, there are two aspects of linear functions which are inadequate in a business context.

The first is that the linear function we have introduced only allows for one independent (X) variable. Frequently in business analysis this may be a reasonable simplifying assumption. There will be other times when it is not. In our example, we have assumed that output is the only factor affecting costs. Whilst output may be the major factor there are likely to be other variables that will affect costs in some way.

The second is that not all relationships are linear: many business applications require the use of non-linear functions which are developed later in the text.

Now that you have completed this chapter you will appreciate that:

● A functional relationship expresses two, or more, variables in terms of their cause and effect pattern.

● A linear equation is represented as a straight line on a graph, and consists of two parameters – a and b.

● The constant or intercept value (the a term) indicates where on the vertical axis the line will cross.

● The slope or gradient value indicates the steepness of the line and is represented by the b term. The slope measures the change in the Y value that will occur for a unit change in the X value.

● Simultaneous equations are a general method of finding X and Y values that satisfy two or more equations. Such a solution is shown graphically where the lines representing the equations intersect.

EXAMPLE

Suppose we are told that a small firm manufactures some product. On a weekly basis the firm's accountant has indicated that overheads are £15,000. The product costs £20 per item on average to produce and the firm has a long-term contract with a major customer who has agreed to buy all the firm's output at a price of £22.50 per unit. The firm wants to know how many units it needs to produce to break even on a weekly basis.

In this case we are not given the equations as such but we have to derive them from the information supplied. Let us denote the weekly output as X. Total costs will then comprise: fixed costs and variable costs. Fixed costs are the same as overheads at £15,000. Variable costs are £20 per unit of X so the total cost equation is:

$$C = 15,000 + 20X$$

Total revenue represents the income the firm gets from selling its product. Clearly if it sells nothing ($X = 0$) the total revenue will be zero. In other words the intercept of the R equation will be zero. Each unit can be sold for £22.50 so we have a total revenue equation:

$$R = 22.5X$$

To determine the breakeven level of output (where $C = R$) we could draw a graph but we shall instead use simultaneous equations. Using the method introduced we have:

$$C = R$$
$$15{,}000 + 20X = 22.5X$$
$$15{,}000 + 20X - 20X = 22.5X - 20X$$
$$15{,}000 = 2.5X$$
$$\frac{15{,}000}{2.5} = X$$
$$X = 6{,}000$$

and derive $X = 6{,}000$ as the breakeven level of output.

Substituting $X = 6{,}000$ into the C equation we get $C = 135{,}000$ and into the R equation we get $R = 135{,}000$. Since the two are the same ($C = R$) this implies that we have not made an arithmetic mistake in the calculation and therefore this value for X represents the breakeven level of output.

To see how this can be further used to help management, consider the following scenario. The major customer is now wanting to renegotiate the contract under which all production is sold at £22.50. The company wants to buy the production at £22 per unit. How will this affect the breakeven level of output?

Fortunately we do not need to go through all the calculations again. Previously we required:

$$2.5X = 15{,}000$$

as the solution for X. All that has altered in the problem is the b term for the R equation. This will alter the expression required to:

$$2X = 15{,}000$$

and the new solution will require 7,500 units of X for the breakeven position.

You should be able to see why the breakeven level of output rises. The selling price has fallen so, to cover costs, we need to sell more of the product. It is also worth noting that if we had used the graphical method for solution originally we would have had to draw a completely new line for the R function to find the solution.

SELF-REVIEW QUESTIONS

1 *What is the difference between the dependent and independent variable in a function?*

2 *How would you calculate the slope of a linear function from the graph?*

3 *You are told that a linear function has a negative intercept. What does this mean?*

4 *What is meant by a functional relationship?*

5 *What are the two parameters of a linear function?*

6 *What are the two methods of finding the solution to a set of linear equations?*

7 *If you are told one linear equation has a slope of +1 and another of –1 what is the key difference between them?*

8 *What is the difference between a linear equation with a positive intercept and one with a negative?*

9 *What would a linear function look like if it had a zero slope?*

10 *What is the advantage of solving a set of linear equations using simultaneous equations rather than a graph?*

STUDENT EXERCISES

1 For each pair of equations shown below:

- draw a graph for the two equations;
- find the graphical solution to the two equations;
- confirm the graphical solution using simultaneous equations.

(a) $Y_1 = 10 + 3X$
$Y_2 = -10 + 5X$

(b) $Y_1 = 120 - 2X$
$Y_2 = 140 - 3X$

(c) $Y_1 = 10 + 5X$
$Y_2 = -30 + 5X$

2 Return to the total costs and total revenue equations used in the chapter where:

$C = 8 + 1.2X$
$R = 2.8X$

(a) You are told that the company's overheads increase by £2,000. Determine the new C and R equations.

(b) Graph these on the same diagram.

(c) Find the new breakeven point graphically.

(d) Confirm your answer to **(c)** by using simultaneous equations.

(e) You are now told that, in addition to the change in overheads, the R equation has changed to:

$R = 3X$

Find the new breakeven point.

3 In a particular company store some data have been collected on the sales of one product and two equations derived:

$Q_d = 100 - 10P$ (known as the demand function)

and:

$Q_s = -25 + 5P$ (known as the supply function)

where: Q_d is the quantity demanded of the product (000s units);
$\quad\quad\quad$ Q_s is the quantity supplied (i.e. offered for sale) (000s units);
$\quad\quad\quad$ P is the price charged per unit.

(a) Why in both cases is Q expressed as a function of P?

(b) Draw both equations on the same graph.

(c) Why is it logical for the demand function to have a negative slope?

(d) Why is it logical for the supply function to have a positive slope?

(e) Why is it logical for the supply function to have a negative intercept?

(f) At what price will Q_d and Q_s be the same?

(g) What will happen if the store charges a higher or lower price than this?

4 The store now realizes that the demand function has altered. The store manager has noted that when a price of £5 was charged customers bought 50(000) units whilst when a price of £3 was charged customers bought 90(000) units.

(a) From this data determine the new demand function.

(b) Find the new point where $Q_d = Q_s$, assuming the supply function remains unchanged.

(c) Compare the new demand function with the previous one. What factors can you suggest that might have brought about such a change?

5 The sales director has recently crashed his company car and later this week must travel to one of the stores for a meeting with the manager. He has asked you to arrange for a car to be hired for the day. You have contacted two car hire firms. Firm A will rent a car for £60 per day. Firm B will rent a car for £10 per day plus £0.10 per mile travelled.

(a) Determine an equation representing the cost of hiring the car from each of the two firms.

(b) Draw a graph of these two equations.

(c) Which firm would you recommend the car is hired from?

BUSINESS MATHEMATICS: NON-LINEAR FUNCTIONS AND CALCULUS

INTRODUCTION

The type of mathematics that we introduced in the previous chapter – that covering linear relationships – will not be helpful in every area of business analysis. There are some business relationships where it is unrealistic to assume that the connection between two variables is linear – a straight line. Many business relationships are non-linear and this chapter looks at non-linear equations in general and one particularly common non-linear function – the quadratic. We shall also be looking at a general method for handling non-linear equations: that of differential calculus.

LEARNING OBJECTIVES

By the end of this chapter you should be able to:

- draw a graph of common non-linear equations;
- recognize a quadratic equation;
- find the roots to a quadratic equation;
- solve sets of quadratic equations;
- apply the simple differentiation rule;
- use calculus to determine the slope and optimal point of a non-linear equation.

QUADRATIC FUNCTIONS

Just as we had the general form of a linear equation as:

$$Y = a + bX$$

so the general form of the type of equation known as a quadratic is given as:

$$Y = a + bX + cX^2$$

where X and Y are the two variables and a, b and c are appropriate numbers or parameters. Effectively, as we can see, the quadratic has an extra term involving X^2. That is, it has a term which involves the square of the X variable. Such an equation will take one of two general shapes when drawn on a graph as illustrated in Fig. 11.1. A quadratic function will have what is known as a parabolic shape: it will either follow a U-shape as in part (a) of the diagram or the function may follow what is known as an inverted U-shape as in part (b).

Let us consider the implications of each type of quadratic in terms of the link between X and Y. In part (a) we see that as X gradually increases in value then to begin with Y has a fairly high value. However, as X increases the value of Y slowly decreases. Eventually Y reaches a minimum position and then, as X continues to increase further, the Y value gradually climbs back up again. In part (b) of the diagram we have a different type of relationship. There, Y starts off with a fairly low value. As X increases Y gradually increases also until it reaches a maximum value. As X increases further the Y value gradually begins to fall.

This behaviour is quite typical of quadratic equations and, as you may be able to imagine, is very useful for business modelling. The potential usefulness of quadratics arises because such a function moves towards some *optimum* position: a maximum or minimum value for the Y variable. If an organization can model part of its situation using quadratics this allows it to consider finding some optimum position in the context of whatever variable it is examining. So, a firm may be able to find the level of output which maximizes profit, or a sales level which maximizes revenue, or a production process which minimizes costs and so on.

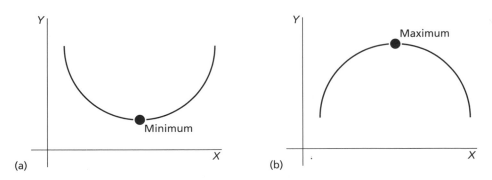

Fig. 11.1   General forms of a quadratic equation

The concept of maximum and minimum is particularly relevant and important for non-linear functions – which of course is why we introduce them into our studies. As we shall see soon, you can actually tell which of these two general types of situation we would get just by looking at a quadratic equation (assuming of course that you know what to look for). Just like a linear equation the quadratic function may of course intercept either or both of the two axes, depending on the specific numerical value of the parameters in the equation.

GRAPHING A QUADRATIC EQUATION

Drawing a graph of a quadratic equation is almost as straightforward as that for a linear equation. We shall illustrate by reference to the quadratic equation below:

$$P = -100 + 100X - 5X^2$$

We assume that this represents a profit equation for some company. X relates to number of units of some product produced (in 000s) and P is profit measured in £000s. Just like any equation, this one allows us to work out what profit would be for any level of production. If $X = 10$, for example, we substitute this value of X into the equation and work out P:

$$P = -100 + 100X - 5X^2$$
$$= -100 + 100(10) - 5(10)^2$$
$$= -100 + 1,000 - 5(100) = -100 + 1,000 - 500$$

giving:

$$P = 400$$

You will remember that with a linear equation it was necessary only to determine two pairs of points (coordinates) in order to be able to draw a graph of the straight line representing the equation. With quadratic equations – and other non-linear equations – it is necessary to obtain more pairs of points than this in order to accurately draw the parabola.

Before starting to draw a graph, however, it will be useful to know the general shape that the equation will take (since this will give us a hint as to what our graph should look like). We know that it will take one of the two general patterns illustrated in Fig. 11.1. In fact it is the c term in the quadratic expression which determines which of the two forms the quadratic function follows. If the c term is a positive number ($c > 0$) the function will take the standard U-shape, whilst if the c term is a negative number ($c < 0$) the function will follow the inverted U-shape pattern.

Student activity

What do you think the graph would look like if the 'c' term was not positive or negative but actually zero?

355

It may be evident that if c is neither positive nor negative but zero then the equation is not really a quadratic at all! In fact, without this c term the equation would actually be linear:

$$P = -100 + 100X$$

It is the presence of the X^2 term which makes an equation quadratic. We could remove either or both of the other two terms and the equation would still be quadratic. That is:

$$P = -100 - 5X^2$$
$$P = 100X - 5X^2$$
$$P = -5X^2$$

are all quadratic equations (although they are different and will give different graphs).

However, just because an equation contains the term X^2 doesn't necessarily mean it is a quadratic. If the equation contains any other X terms involving powers then it is not quadratic but some other non-linear equation. For example, the equation:

$$Y = 3X^2 - 0.3X^3$$

is not quadratic since it has another X term, X^3, involving powers.

But to return to our quadratic profit equation. In this example the c term is -5 so we know that the function will follow the inverted U-shape climbing up to some maximum Y value and then dropping away again. We can also see that once we have the graph we will be able to see what level of X will lead to this maximum Y (profit) value: that is, what output level will maximize the firm's profit.

Knowing the general shape the graph will take we can now follow the same steps as with a linear function to draw a graph.

Step 1

Choose an appropriate range for the X scale. Here suppose we decide that X will range from 0 to 20 units. If you are set a problem involving a quadratic equation you will often be told over what range for X to draw the function.

Step 2

Work out an appropriate range of values for the Y scale. We must use the equation to determine the Y values corresponding to specified X values. As a rule of thumb, approximately ten pairs of X, Y values should be sufficient, spaced equally over the X range, to draw a non-linear graph accurately. Since X ranges from 0 to 20 and since we want about ten X, Y sets of values it seems sensible to take $X = 0$ and then increase X by 2 each time. For each of the X values we can then substitute this into the quadratic equation to work out profit, P. These calculations are:

X value	Y value	Equation
0	−100	$Y = -100 + 100(0) - 5(0)^2$
2	80	$Y = -100 + 100(2) - 5(2)^2$
4	220	$Y = -100 + 100(4) - 5(4)^2$
6	320	$Y = -100 + 100(6) - 5(6)^2$
8	380	$Y = -100 + 100(8) - 5(8)^2$
10	400	$Y = -100 + 100(10) - 5(10)^2$
12	380	$Y = -100 + 100(12) - 5(12)^2$
14	320	$Y = -100 + 100(14) - 5(14)^2$
16	220	$Y = -100 + 100(16) - 5(16)^2$
18	80	$Y = -100 + 100(18) - 5(18)^2$
20	−100	$Y = -100 + 100(20) - 5(20)^2$

So, we now have 11 sets of X, Y values for the equation.

Step 3

Work out an appropriate scale for the Y variable. Here, Y (profit) ranges from −100 to 400 so we decide to set the Y scale from −100 to 500 to make it easier to draw.

Step 4

Draw a suitable scale for the X and Y variables on the graph, ready to plot the X, Y coordinates. This is shown in Fig. 11.2.

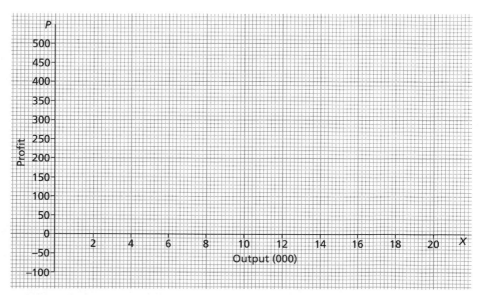

Fig. 11.2 X and Y scales

Step 5

Taking each pair of X, Y values calculated in Step 2 in turn, plot the corresponding point on the graph. This is shown in Fig. 11.3. Until you have prac-

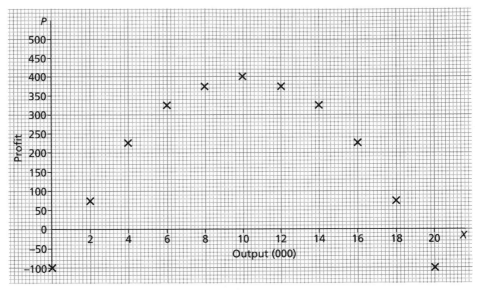

Fig. 11.3   Plot of points

tised you need to be careful about plotting points for a non-linear equation
and should check these carefully.

Step 6

Now we join these points together as smoothly as we can with a curved line.
This is the line for the given equation. The corresponding graph is shown in
Fig. 11.4. Notice that we should not join the points together with a straight
line (perhaps using a ruler) but try to get a curve between the points.

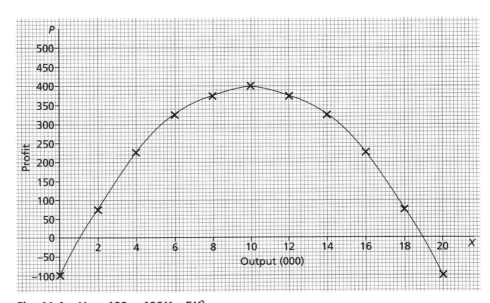

Fig. 11.4 $Y = -100 + 100X - 5X^2$

Obtaining information from the graph

Just as with a linear equation you should ensure that you can obtain information either by calculating from the equation or from the corresponding graph by reading values from the graph. We can now see from Fig. 11.4 that an output level of 10,000 ($X = 10$) will put us at the highest point on this curve and will lead to maximum profit (at £400,000).

Student activity

The same firm has worked out its cost equation and found that this is given by:

$C = 100 + 2X^2$

where C is total costs and X is output.

(a) What general type of quadratic will this be?

(b) Draw a graph of this equation for X = 0 to 20.

We have another quadratic equation, this time linking the firm's costs to its production level. From Fig. 11.1 we recognize this quadratic as taking the U-shape since the c term is positive, at $+2$. To draw the graph it makes sense to use the same X values to work out C as we did for the profit equation earlier. The calculations are shown below:

X	$C = 100 + 2X^2$
0	100
2	108
4	132
6	172
8	228
10	300
12	388
14	492
16	612
18	748
20	900

The corresponding graph is shown in Fig. 11.5. Notice that we have only drawn the graph up to $X = 14$ so as to use the same Y scale as we did for profit. Notice also that as we look at the graph we do not necessarily recognize the curve as a quadratic. The reason for this, if you remember Chapter 5, is that the rest of the quadratic appears in the adjacent quadrant which we have not drawn (since it makes no sense to draw the rest of the graph for negative output levels). Again, this is quite common when using quadratic and other non-linear equations.

As with every equation in business, we should make sure we realize the business implications behind the mathematics. From the graph we see that as X increases so does C, that is as the firm produces more output its total

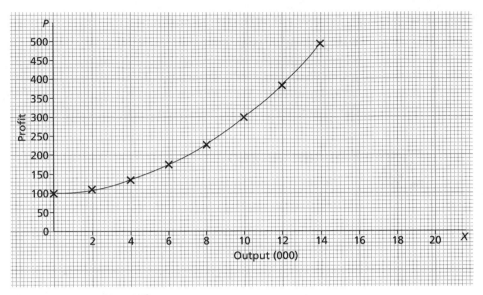

Fig. 11.5   C = 100 + 2X²

costs increase. This is quite logical and sensible since to produce more the firm will need more raw materials, more staff, more equipment, more energy and so on. But notice that the relationship is not linear. That is, the extra cost as we produce extra output does not remain constant (remember that a linear equation has a constant slope). For this function we see that the curve starts to slope upwards. At low levels of output, say $X = 4$, increased production increases costs but by a relatively small amount. At higher levels of out, say $X = 12$, increased production increases costs by much more.

With some thought we can see the logic behind this. When X is, say, 4 then we may be able to get an increase in production by increasing the productivity of our workforce (i.e. without paying them any extra) so the extra costs will relate to the raw material costs and so on, not to any extra labour costs. When X is 12, though, our workforce may already be working at their maximum productivity. To increase production further at this point we might have to take on additional staff (which is expensive) or perhaps pay our existing workforce overtime or bonuses for increasing production further (which is also expensive). This feature of quadratics of not having a constant slope is a useful one for business modelling as we shall see.

PARAMETERS OF A QUADRATIC EQUATION

With a linear equation we saw that there were two important parameters: the intercept and the slope. The same is true of a quadratic function. Let us illustrate with the profit function we have been using. The intercept – as with the linear function – is given by the a term in the equation, here at -100. This is the point where the quadratic equation crosses the Y axis as we see from

Fig. 11.4. Note also that – as with a linear equation – the intercept frequently has a business meaning in the context of the problem. Here, as with a linear equation for profit, this is the level of profit when output is zero. The equation (and graph) indicates that profit will be –£100(000) at zero level of output. This actually means the firm is making a loss of £100(000).

On reflection you will see the logic of this. If the firm is producing zero output its revenue will also be zero. However, it is still likely to incur overheads and fixed costs. Given that profit is simply the difference between revenue and costs, the company will be operating at a loss of £100(000) at such a level of output.

Student activity

Return to the cost function used in the last activity. How would you interpret the intercept of this equation?

For the cost function, with an intercept of 100 we would simply consider that this represented the fixed cost element out of total costs. That is, the firm has fixed costs to pay of £100(000) even if it produces nothing. Notice that this equates directly with the intercept of –100 for the profit function. This is because we have profit as the difference between the firm's revenue (its income from selling its output) and its costs. When $X = 0$ revenue will be zero (since if the firm produces nothing it has nothing to sell). But at zero output fixed costs still have to be paid hence the negative profit arises from the fixed costs.

The slope of an equation also has an important meaning. We saw with a linear function that the slope was constant (the same no matter what the value for X) and was given by the b term in the linear equation. However, the slope of a quadratic equation is not constant but changes depending where we are on the X axis. You will see from Fig. 11.4 for the Profit function that to begin with, for low values of X, the slope is positive (it moves upwards from left to right). The steepness of the slope gradually gets less and less until – in this example when $X = 10$ – the direction of the curve changes and the slope becomes negative (downwards from left to right). The calculation of the slope is not as straightforward as for a linear equation and we must wait for the techniques introduced later in this chapter before we can quantify the slope of a quadratic function. The meaning of the slope, however, remains the same. In the case of our equation it refers to the change in profit as output changes. That is, the extra profit achieved as we increase output. This is of obvious importance to any organization.

THE TURNING POINT OF A QUADRATIC FUNCTION

One specific feature of a quadratic equation that is usually of considerable importance to business is the point where the slope changes sign (from positive to negative or from negative to positive). In this example, we can observe from the graph that this will occur when $X = 10$. Such a point is referred to as the *turning point*. If we refer back to the profit equation in Fig. 11.4 it is clear that the turning point occurs at the maximum position of the function – that is where profit is at its highest value. Similarly, if we had been dealing with a quadratic equation which took the opposite shape, the U-shape, then the turning point would represent a minimum Y value.

You may well be aware that such concepts – maximization and minimization – are especially important in the study of business and economics. Apart from profit maximization, such situations as maximizing production, minimizing costs, minimizing the use of resources and so on are all common. At this stage, we can find the turning point of a quadratic equation in two ways:

- directly from the graph;
- using algebra to determine what are known as the roots of the equation.

THE ROOTS OF A QUADRATIC FUNCTION

Whilst the graph can be useful for helping us determine the approximate value of the turning point it is not always as accurate as we might like so we need a mathematical way of finding this point also. As we have noted before extracting precise information from a graph is an inaccurate method and we shall concentrate on the algebraic method here.

In mathematical terms the *roots* of a quadratic equation are simply the X values which generate a value for Y equal to zero. In other words, the roots represent the X values where the equation line intercepts the X axis (for here $Y = 0$). Typically in most (but not all) quadratic equations there will be two such roots. In other cases there may be one or none. In our profit example, it can be seen that the equation crosses the X axis at two points: these are the two roots of the equation and we require a general algebraic method of finding them.

The equation below is generally used to determine the roots:

$$\text{Roots } X_1, X_2 = \frac{-b \pm \sqrt{b^2 - 4ac}}{2c}$$

where a, b, c are the appropriate parameters from the quadratic function. In our example they would take the values:

$$a = -100 \quad b = 100 \quad c = -5$$

and substituting into the formula we would then have:

$$\frac{-b \pm \sqrt{b^2 - 4ac}}{2c}$$

$$= \frac{-100 \pm \sqrt{100^2 - (4)\,(-100)\,(-5)}}{2(-5)}$$

$$= \frac{-100 \pm \sqrt{10,000 - 2,000}}{-10}$$

$$= \frac{-100 \pm 89.44}{-10}$$

To find the two X values we work out this expression by using the '+' and '−' signs in turn (it doesn't matter in what order). This gives:

$$\text{Using } + \quad X_1 = \frac{-100 + 89.44}{-10} = \frac{-10.56}{-10} = 1.056$$

$$\text{Using } - \quad X_2 = \frac{-100 - 89.44}{-10} = \frac{-189.44}{-10} = 18.944$$

That is, the two roots of this equation are 1.056 and 18.944. This means that the quadratic function crosses the X axis when $X = 1.056$ and again when $X = 18.944$.

These two points can be confirmed from Fig. 11.4 and from substitution into the original profit equation – that is, if we substitute each of these root values in turn back into the profit equation we should get a profit value of zero (since this is what a root shows). This is a useful way of checking your answers.

The roots of a quadratic equation often have a specific meaning in the context of the business problem we are examining and we must always take care to understand this meaning. From a business context the roots of this equation represent the two breakeven points, i.e. where profit = 0.

It is also important to understand what we have done with this calculation. In general by finding the roots of a quadratic function we find the two X values which will give $Y = 0$. Graphically we have found the points on the X axis where the line of this function would cross. We must also make sure that we take care when using the formula to ensure that the correct values for a, b, c and the correct arithmetic signs are used. A frequent (and careless) mistake seen on many exam answers is for a student to confuse the negative signs shown in the calculation. One way of noticing whether you have done this is to check the final number for which you are trying to find a square root (here we wanted $\sqrt{8,000}$). If you get the signs of the numerical values wrong you can often end up with trying to find the square root of a negative number. This is a sure sign you have made a mistake since, as far as our mathematics is concerned, there is no such thing as the square root of a negative number.

FINDING THE TURNING POINT

Whilst we are frequently interested in the values of the roots of a quadratic function in their own right we are also interested in the turning point of the quadratic equation: that is, the X value which generates either the maximum or minimum Y value (depending on the type of quadratic function). We can readily use the two roots to determine such a turning point. Without proof, we simply state that:

The turning point of a quadratic function will be found midway between the two roots.

In this example the two roots, the X values, are 1.056 and 18.944. The point midway between them is found by:

$$\text{Lowest root} + \frac{(\text{Highest root} - \text{Lowest root})}{2}$$

In this example:

$$1.056 + \frac{(18.944 - 1.056)}{2} = 1.056 + 8.944 = 10$$

When $X = 10$ the equation is at its maximum point, confirming what we saw on the graph.

In a business context the group will achieve maximum profit for this product when output is 10(000) units. To determine profit at this level of output we return to the profit equation:

$$
\begin{aligned}
\text{Profit} &= -100 + 100X - 5X^2 \\
&= -100 + 100(10) - 5(10^2) \\
&= -100 + 1,000 - 500 \\
&= 400
\end{aligned}
$$

So, profit is £400(000) at its highest point.

As with most mathematical calculations it is always worthwhile checking your answer wherever possible. We can make use of our knowledge of quadratic equations to confirm the result since, even with practice, it is quite easy to make small mistakes in the calculations. If profit is maximized when $X = 10$ then we know – from the general shape of the function – that when X is slightly less than 10 and when X is slightly more than 10 profit

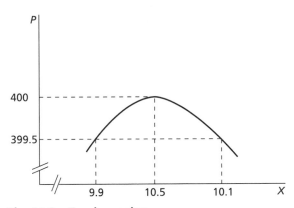

Fig. 11.6   Turning point

should be less than the maximum of 400. Let us set $X = 9.9$ and $X = 10.1$ and find the corresponding values for Y. Using the profit equation you should confirm that this will give profit at:

$$X = \ \ 9.9 \quad \text{Profit} = 399.95$$
$$X = 10.1 \quad \text{Profit} = 399.95$$

Both of these are slightly less than the maximum at 400. From Fig. 11.6 you can see that such a combination of profit and X values can only occur at one point – at the top of the function – thus confirming that when $X = 10$ profit is at the maximum point.

Student activity

The firm has also found its revenue function, showing the total revenue (or income) it will get from selling its production. This is:

$R = 100X - 3X^2$

Using algebra find the turning point of this equation. Does this represent a maximum or a minimum?

For the equation:

$$R = 100X - 3X^2$$

we have:

$a = 0$
$b = 100$
$c = -3$

and substituting these into our roots equation we have:

$$\frac{-b \pm \sqrt{b^2 - 4ac}}{2c}$$

$$= \frac{-100 \pm \sqrt{100^2 - (4)\,(0)\,(-3)}}{2(-3)}$$

$$= \frac{-100 \pm \sqrt{10{,}000 - 0}}{-6}$$

$$= \frac{-100 \pm 100}{-6}$$

To find the two X values we work out this expression by using the '+' and '−' signs in turn. This gives:

$$\text{Using } + \quad X_1 \quad = \frac{-100 + 100}{-6} = \frac{0}{-6} = 0$$

$$\text{Using } - \quad X_2 \quad = \frac{-100 - 100}{-6} = \frac{-200}{-6} = 33.33$$

That is, the two roots for the R equation are $X = 0$ and $X = 33.33$.

The root of zero might seem odd but all that this means is that the equation takes a zero value (i.e. $Y = 0$) when $X = 0$ – that is the curve passes through the origin. This is quite sensible in the business context of the equation which, after all, represents revenue earned from selling products. If the firm produces nothing ($X = 0$) then by default its revenue will be zero also. Using the two roots we can find the turning point:

$$\text{Lowest root} + \frac{(\text{Highest root} - \text{Lowest root})}{2}$$

$$0 + \frac{(33.33 - 0)}{2} = 16.67$$

That is, the turning point for the revenue function occurs when $X = 16.67$. In the context of the problem the firm will achieve maximum revenue by producing $16.67(000)$ units of output (and we know the turning point will be a maximum because the c term in this quadratic is negative indicating the function follows the inverted U-shape with a maximum point).

SETS OF QUADRATIC EQUATIONS

Just as with linear equations there are times when we may have two or more quadratic equations and we wish to determine the point or points where the equations intersect. To find such points we can again use the concept of roots of quadratic equations. In this case, however, we are using the concept in a slightly different way.

Let us return to the firm's profit and cost function that we have been analysing. We had:

$$P = -100 + 100X - 5X^2$$

and:

$$C = 100 + 2X^2$$

However, using some simple logic it is evident that:

Profit = Revenue − Cost

or:

$$P = R - C$$

That is, profit is simply the difference between the total revenue, R, the firm earns from selling its product and its total cost C. But we already have an equation for profit and C so we should be able to derive one also for R, the revenue function. We can rearrange the expression:

$$P = R - C$$

if we add C to both sides to produce:

$$P + C = R - C + C = R$$

(since the two C terms cancel). If we now substitute the two quadratic equations for P and C we have:

$$(-100 + 100X - 5X^2) + (100 + 2X^2) = R$$

and we can simplify the left-hand side of the equation. First let us remove the brackets:

$$-100 + 100X - 5X^2 + 100 + 2X^2 = R$$

We see that we have two terms that cancel (-100 and $+100$) giving:

$$100X - 5X^2 + 2X^2 = R$$

and we have two terms which are both expressed as X^2 so if we add these together we get:

$$100X \, (- 5X^2 + 2X^2) = R$$
$$100X - 3X^2 \qquad\quad = R$$

as the revenue function (and you will recognize this from the last activity).

So we now have a set of equations such that:

$$P = -100 + 100X - 5X^2$$
$$C = 100 + 2X^2$$
$$R = 100X - 3X^2$$

What we will now do is to look at these equations as a set and look for a solution to this set. We know that we have already done this and we know the solution that will maximize profit. However, we want to find the solution using a different approach and it will be helpful if we already know the solution so that we can see what is happening. Once we have developed a solution method we will then look at a different problem in a Student activity.

Suppose the firm wanted to know over what range of output it would make a loss (because costs were higher than revenue) and over what range of output it would make a profit (since revenue was greater than costs). Whilst we could derive this from the profit equation, let us suppose for the moment that we didn't have the profit function but only the C and R equations. In fact we are interested not in these two equations as such but in the difference between them (since the difference will show whether the firm is making a profit or loss).

Let us define the difference between them as:

$$Y = R - C$$

that is, the difference, Y, is simply R minus C. Both R and C are expressed as a function of X (output) so Y will be a function of X also. We are interested in finding the levels of X which generate a loss and those which generate a profit. The easiest way to do this is to try to find the breakeven levels of output – those levels where R and C will be exactly equal. If we find the breakeven levels of output then we know for all other levels of output R and C will *not* be equal. The breakeven levels of output will occur when:

$$Y = R - C = 0$$

So, we want to find the levels of output, X, which will cause Y to take a zero value.

However, let us go back to the 'definition' of the roots of a quadratic equation. We said earlier that the roots of a quadratic showed the X values which gave $Y = 0$. So, to find the breakeven points we need to find the roots of the quadratic equation, Y. By using the equations for R and C we can derive an equation for Y and then find the roots of this equation:

$$Y = R - C$$
$$= (100X - 3X^2) - (100 + 2X^2)$$

If we multiply out the brackets (taking care with the minus sign) we get:

$$Y = 100X - 3X^2 - 100 - 2X^2$$

and rearranging and collecting terms together gives:

$$Y = -100 + 100X - 5X^2$$

which, on inspection is the profit equation we started off with. We would now find the roots of this equation but in fact have already done so at 1.056 and 18.944. These we now know represent the break even levels of output: that when $X = 1.056(000)$ units the firm breaks even as it does when $X = 18.944(000)$ units.

But over what range of output does it make a loss and when does it make a profit? We could resort to a graph but in fact can use what we know about quadratics. We see from the Y equation we have derived that the c term is negative so we must have a quadratic taking the inverted U-shape. Applying a bit of logic we know that one of the roots is when $X = 1.056$. This means that Y (profit) takes a zero value at this point.

But what would happen to Y if X were less than 1.056? From what we know of the shape of this quadratic (an inverted U) then if X is less than 1.056 Y *must* take a negative value (you can check this from Fig. 11.4 if you need to). So, if the company produces less than 1.056(000) units profit will be negative: the company will make a loss.

Let's look at the other root: what value will Y take if X is greater than 18.944? Again, we know that $Y = 0$ at this point and from the inverted U-shape we also know that Y will take a negative value if X takes a value higher than this. Again, if the firm produces more than 18.944(000) units it will make a loss.

But what of output levels *between* the two roots? Well, between these two output levels the firm must have a positive profit. So we can summarize as:

Output (000)	*Financial Position*
< 1.056	Loss
1.056	Breakeven
> 1.056 but < 18.944	Profit
18.944	Breakeven
> 18.944	Loss

What is important to realize is that although we had already looked at this problem earlier in the chapter we could have reached this conclusion simply by the mathematical analysis of the C and R equations (no graph would have been necessary). Adopting this approach for other business problems can be quite useful. If we are looking for a point where two quadratic equations intercept each other (that is where they are equal) we can find these points by subtracting one equation from the other and finding the roots of the equation which forms the difference between them. In this example these two points represent breakeven, in other problems the points are likely to represent something else and we will need to interpret them in the context of the problem set.

Finally, it may help to show all three equations together on the same diagram as in Fig. 11.7. All three equations are shown and the relationship between the various X values we have found and the three functions is evident. X_1 is the first breakeven point (root) and we see that this occurs where C and R intersect (which also coincides with the point where P crosses the X axis, i.e. $P = 0$). X_2 shows the second breakeven position (root), again where R and C intersect and again coinciding with where the P equation crosses the X axis.

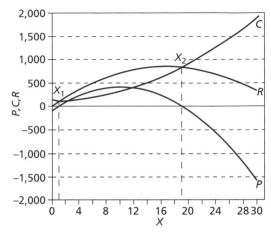

Fig. 11.7 P, C, R

Student activity

The following activity is more complex than normal so may take you some time. However, it brings together all the key points we have covered so far and you will find it useful to complete at this stage.

A firm selling a product has determined what is known as its demand function: the quantity of its product that will be demanded by its customers at any given price. This is:

$Q_d = 100 - 10P$

where Q_d is the quantity of the firm's product demanded (000s) and P is the price charged per unit (£s). The firm has also determined what is known as its supply function: the quantity of the product it is willing to sell at any given price. This is:

$Q_s = -25 + 3P^2$

where Q_s is the quantity supplied by the firm (000s units).

(a) *For a price range from −£10 to +£10 plot these two functions on one graph. (You will see soon why we asked you to use negative P values.)*

(b) *Since the graph you have drawn covers two quadrants which of the two would we normally use?*

(c) *Comment on the nature of the Q_d equation. Does it make sense for it to have a negative slope?*

(d) *How would you interpret the negative intercept for Q_s in a business context?*

(e) *Using algebra find the points where $Q_d = Q_s$. Which of these represents a meaningful business position?*

369

As we said this is quite a complex activity but will be very useful at showing how the various aspects of mathematics we have looked at so far can be brought together. First, we should note that the Q_d equation is linear and that for Q_s is quadratic. Mixing different types of equations in business modelling is not uncommon. The two equations are plotted together on Fig. 11.8, for P = −10 to +10. Normally, we

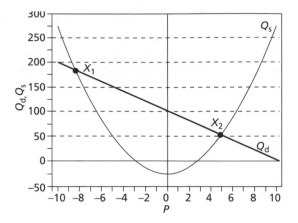

Fig. 11.8 Q_d, Q_s

would use only the right of these two quadrants (the one with values for P and Q_d, Q_s that are not negative since it makes no sense to talk of negative prices. However, we will see later why it is helpful to have both quadrants on the graph.

For Q_d we see that it has a positive intercept (at 100) and a negative slope (at −10). The negative slope implies that as P increases, Q_d increases. From a business context this is quite sensible, since if a firm puts its prices up, other things being equal, then it will probably sell less since customers will typically respond to a higher price by buying less of that product.

For Q_s (restricting our comments only to non-negative values for P) we see that this has a negative intercept (at −25) and a positive (but changing) slope. The slope implies that as the price increases, other things being equal, the firm will be willing to produce and sell more of the product (since higher prices usually mean higher profits for the firm).

The negative intercept may have had you puzzled. This implies that at a zero price the firm is willing to supply −25 units! However, if we look at the curve for this equation for positive P values we see that the curve crosses the P axis at $P = 3$. At this point Q_s will be 0 and after this, for higher values of P, Q_s will be positive. What this actually means is that for prices below £3 the firm will be unwilling to sell anything (presumably because a price of £3 or less means the firm will be making a loss). Only for prices higher than £3 will the firm be willing to sell its product. What we have done is to use the features of a quadratic equation to represent rational business behaviour although it may take us a little while to figure this out.

Now that we understand the two equations and their business implications we can proceed to find the two points where the equations intersect. We can adopt the usual approach of saying we will create a new equation, Y, which is the difference between Q_d and Q_s and then find the roots of this equation (which will be quadratic). This will represent the two points marked on the graph as X_1 and X_2. We have:

$$Y = Q_d - Q_s$$

(Note we could have written it the other way, $Y = Q_s - Q_d$, but we would still get the same solution since we are finding the values that equate to $Y = 0$). Substituting for Q_d and Q_s we then have:

$$Y = (100 - 10P) - (-25 + 3P^2)$$

Removing brackets and then rearranging (taking care over double negatives) we have:

$$Y = 100 - 10P + 25 - 3P^2$$
$$= 125 - 10P - 3P^2$$

We now want the roots of this equation (which will show where Y, the difference between Q_d and Q_s, is zero). Using the roots formula we have:

$$a = 125$$
$$b = -10$$
$$c = -3$$

and:

$$\frac{-b \pm \sqrt{b^2 - 4ac}}{2c}$$

$$= \frac{(-10) \pm \sqrt{(-10)^2 - (4)(125)(-3)}}{2(-3)}$$

$$= \frac{10 \pm \sqrt{100 - 1,500}}{-6}$$

$$= \frac{10 \pm 40}{-6}$$

To find the two X values we work out this expression by using the '+' and '−' signs in turn. This gives:

Using + $X_1 = \dfrac{10 + 40}{-6} = \dfrac{50}{-6} = -8.33$

Using − $X_2 = \dfrac{10 - 40}{-6} = \dfrac{-30}{-6} = 5$

That is, the two roots of the Y equation occur when $P = -8.33$ and when $P = 5$. Since the two roots of the Y equation represent where Q_d and Q_s are equal this means we have found the two points where the supply and demand equations intersect (X_1 and X_2).

You might now see why we asked you to draw the graph for negative P values. One of our solution points, whilst mathematically correct at $P = -8.33$, makes no sense in the context of the business problem. Going up to the managing director of this firm and announcing that you have calculated the firm will balance supply and demand when it sets a price of −£8.33 is unlikely to get you promoted! Clearly, in the context of the problem, only the solution of $P = 5$ makes any sense. However, we asked you to draw the graph for negative P values so that you could see what it was you were actually finding by calculating the two roots. If you had simply used the roots formula and found two answers but then only saw one intersection on the graph (in the positive quadrant) you might have been somewhat puzzled as to what the other solution was for. In practice, and in an exam, you would only have to draw the graph for $P = 0$ to 10. So when $P = 5$, supply and demand are equal and we can confirm from the two equations that $Q_d = Q_s = 50$ at this point.

Although this has been a complex activity it has illustrated the use of equations in business and reinforced the point that you cannot simply look at the maths by itself: you have to be able to interpret the mathematical results in the context of the business problem.

OTHER TYPES OF NON-LINEAR EQUATIONS

Occasionally, business problems may be represented by other types of non-linear equations rather than the quadratic. The solution of such equations is rarely required and, indeed, there is no common method of solution: the method employed depends entirely on the type of function used. A graph of the function is usually helpful, however, and you should be able to produce such graphs. The method is the same as that for graphing a quadratic function. It is necessary to determine a number of (X, Y) values in order to plot the function accurately.

For example, suppose we have:

$$Q = 12L^2 - 0.75L^3$$

where Q represents the number of units of output produced by a company (000s) and L is the number of people employed on the production line. Clearly, we have a non-linear function linking production to employee levels and the function is not quadratic (since it involves a term involving powers other than squares). Suppose that we wish to plot this function from $L = 0$ to $L = 15$. Following the standard steps for a non-linear graph we need to determine the corresponding Y values over this range by taking X values, substituting these into the equation and finding the corresponding Y value (or Q here). In this case since L ranges only from 0 to 15 we decide to use L in steps of 1 and the calculations are then:

L	Q	L	Q	L	Q	L	Q
0	0.00	4	144.00	8	384.00	12	432.00
1	11.25	5	206.25	9	425.25	13	380.25
2	42.00	6	270.00	10	450.00	14	294.00
3	87.75	7	330.75	11	453.75	15	168.75

Once again you should confirm the values for Q for yourself from the equation. Note that if you are unsure of the general shape of the function you are plotting you should calculate the Y value for as many X values as is practical. Of course if you are using a computer package for graphics then it isn't really a problem. It would be sensible to use a Y scale from 0 to 500 here, and Fig. 11.9 shows the function plotted. Virtually any non-linear function can be graphed in this way.

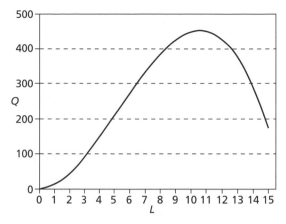

Fig. 11.9 $Q = 12L^2 - 0.75L^3$

Student activity

How would you explain why the Q equation takes the shape it does, in a business context?

Again, we might need to think about this but it is important that we can comment on any mathematical relationship from a business perspective. Typically, there are two key aspects of any such relationship we need to try to explain: the intercept and the slope. Here, we have a relationship between the level of production, Q, and the number of production staff employed, L. We see first of all that the function has a zero intercept: this is sensible since without production staff it seems unlikely we would be able to produce anything. As we increase the number of production staff then Q begins to rise (that is, it has a positive slope). This again is sensible since we would expect an increase in production as we increased staff numbers. However, the curve then reaches a maximum and begins to decline. This implies that there will be an optimum number of staff to employ (here at about 11) which will give maximum production. If we continue to employ additional staff after this level we see that Q actually begins to decline (the curve has a negative slope). This implies that after some point we actually have too many staff: on a production line, for example, where the amount of machinery and equipment is fixed we may well have more staff than we need and productivity suffers as a result. This is what the curve is showing.

DIFFERENTIAL CALCULUS

The importance of the slope of a function was stressed earlier. The slope provides a method of determining the change in the Y value that is associated with a given change in the X value. In a business context, the slope is of fundamental importance. Businesses wish to know how profit will change with output, how costs and revenue will change with output, how sales will change with the level of advertising, how productivity will change with the size of the labour force, how sales will change with price and so on.

When we were looking at linear functions we saw that the slope was readily identifiable from the equation – with the b term indicating the value of the slope directly. With quadratics – and indeed with any type of non-linear function – the slope is not immediately obvious. In fact, as we saw with quadratics, the slope of a non-linear equation changes depending where on the function we are and does not remain constant.

It is evident that we require some general method of determining the slope of any type of function. Such a method is provided through the use of what is known as *differential calculus*. This is a method whereby we can determine the slope of a function relatively easily, no matter what type of function we are dealing with. Let us return to the profit equation used earlier:

$$P = -100 + 100X - 5X^2$$

where X is output. We saw from the corresponding graph of this equation, Fig. 11.4, that the slope of the function changed with X. The slope started off as very steep and positive, gradually became less steep and then reversed direction and became negative. In a business context the slope of the profit function shows how profit will change as output changes: this is frequently referred to as a *marginal* concept – the extra (or marginal) profit achieved as an extra unit of output is produced. From the corresponding graph we can see that at low levels of output considerable extra profit can be achieved by increasing output. This extra profit gradually gets less and less as output increases and there finally comes a point where extra output has a negative effect on profit.

The derivative

In order to find the slope of such a function we must introduce the idea of a derivative. When we have a function which takes the general form:

$$Y = kX^n$$

then the derivative of that function can be expressed as:

$$\frac{dY}{dX} = nkX^{n-1}$$

where dY/dX (pronounced 'dee Y by dee X') is the general symbol for the derivative.

The derivative, as we shall see, is simply an expression which shows the slope of any function at any point on that function. Like some of the other formulae we have introduced in this text, we cannot show how the derivative has been obtained since it requires some fairly complex mathematics. However, as we begin to apply it you will see that it does work: it allows us to calculate the slope for any function we are likely to encounter. We shall illustrate with a simple example. Suppose we have a linear function such that:

$$Y = 100X$$

Because it is a linear function we already know that its slope will be 100 (that is, identical to the *b* term). But we shall also use the derivative method. The linear function corresponds to the function form:

$$Y = kX^n = 100X^1$$

where $k = 100$ and $n = 1$. Using the derivative rule we have:

$$\frac{dy}{dx} = nkX^{n-1} = 1(100)X^{1-1} = 100X^0 = 100$$

You will remember that any variable raised to the power zero equals 1 so $X^0 = 1$. The derivative expression shows the slope of the original (linear) function. That is, the derivative indicates that the slope of $Y = 100X$ is 100, confirming what we already knew from the value of *b*.

Obviously for a linear function there is no advantage in using the derivative approach to obtain the slope since we can do this by inspection of the equation parameters. For non-linear functions, however, we cannot obtain the slope simply by inspection but we can by applying the derivative rule. If we have a quadratic function rather than a linear one the derivative rule is just as straightforward. Suppose we have:

$$Y = -5X^2$$

Here, $k = -5$ and $n = 2$ so the derivative would be:

$$\frac{dy}{dx} = 2(-5)X^{(2-1)} = -10X^1 = -10X$$

What does this mean? Since the original expression ($Y = -5X^2$) was quadratic we know that its slope is not constant. The derivative is an equation which shows the slope of the original equation anywhere along its length: for any value of X. So if we wish to know the slope of $Y = -5X^2$ at the point when $X = 10$ we would substitute $X = 10$ into the derivative expression:

$$\frac{dy}{dx} = -10X = 10(-10) = -100$$

When $X = 10$ the slope of the original equation is -100. That is, at this point if X were to change by some (small) amount Y would change by -100 times that amount. If we now wanted the slope when $X = 4$ we would again use the derivative expression and find the slope to be -40. That is, at this point on the original function there is a change in Y of -40 times the change in X. The derivative, therefore, provides a simple method of calculating the slope for any value of X for any function.

Let us now return to the profit function:

$$P = -100 + 100X - 5X^2$$

To find the derivative of this function we can represent each part of the function in turn in the standard format and find the derivative of each part. Then, reassembling the derivative components will give the derivative for the whole function.

This sounds more complicated than it is. We have:

$$P = -100 + 100X - 5X^2$$

and we can break this into three parts:

(**a**) −100

(**b**) + 100X

(**c**) −5X²

So for part (**a**):

−100 becomes $-100X^0$

and its derivative = $0(100)X^{(0-1)} = 0$

In other words, as $Y = -100$ represents a line parallel to the X axis the derivative confirms that such a function has a zero slope: Y does not change as X changes. Similarly for part (**b**):

+100X has a derivative:

$+1(100)X^{(1-1)} = +100X^0 = +100$

and finally part (**c**):

−5X² has a derivative:

$2(-5)X^{(2-1)} = -10X^1 = -10X$

Reassembling the derivatives of (**a**), (**b**) and (**c**) gives:

$$\frac{dP}{dX} = 0 + 100 - 10X = 100 - 10X$$

This derivative (itself a linear function) allows us to calculate the slope of the profit function at any level of output. Suppose we wanted to find the slope of this function when $X = 5$. We simply substitute $X = 5$ into the derivative equation and solve:

$$\frac{dP}{dX} = 100 - 10X = 100 - 10(5) = 50$$

That is, at a level of output of 5 a marginal (small) change in this output will lead to a corresponding change in total profit of +50 times the change in output.

Student activity

Using the original profit equation, calculate profit when X = 5. Calculate profit again when X = 5.01. Determine the change in profit. How does this relate to the slope that we found of 50?

Using the derivative calculate the slope when X = 2,8,10,14,18. Compare these slope values with Fig. 11.4. Are they what you would expect?

Using the original profit function we have:

When $X = 5$:

$$P = -100 + 100(5) - 5(5)^2 = 275$$

When $X = 5.01$:

$$P = -100 + 100(5.01) - 5(5.01)^2 = 275.4995$$

Remember that the slope is simply:

$$\frac{\text{Change in } Y}{\text{Change in } X} = \frac{275.4995 - 275}{5.01 - 5} = \frac{0.4995}{0.01} = 49.95$$

That is, a small change in X (of 0.01 units) has brought about a change in Y of (almost) 50 times the change in X. This is not to say that profit has increased 50 times, but that the increase in profit is 50 times the increase in X.

Notice that there is a small difference between calculating the slope using the original function (49.95) and using the derivative (50). The reason for this is that we can only approximate the slope using the original function: the derivative approach is more accurate. Note also, that the slope for any value of X is accurate only for small (marginal) changes in X. We could not say that if X increased from 5 to 8 then the change in profit would be (50×3). The slope for a non-linear function is correct only for very small changes in X (since, of course, the slope is constantly changing). It is important to realize – from the mathematical theory supporting the derivative – that these derivative values are applicable only for marginal changes in output: that is for particularly small changes in X. We can use the derivative to answer the rest of the activity quite simply:

$$dY/dX = 100 - 10X$$

$X = 2$	$dY/dX = 80$
$X = 8$	$dY/dX = 20$
$X = 10$	$dY/dX = 0$
$X = 14$	$dY/dX = -40$
$X = 18$	$dY/dX = -80$

By using Fig. 11.4 we can see how these figures fit in with the curve we have drawn. We see from the graph that when $X = 2$ the slope on the graph is positive (and quite steep – i.e. a high positive number). Compared with this, when $X = 8$ the slope is still positive but less so (i.e. a smaller positive number). We already know when $X = 10$ we have reached the turning point of this quadratic. We see from the derivative that at this value for X the slope is actually zero – neither positive or negative (which of course is why we call it the turning point since it is about to turn from a positive slope to a negative). For values of X greater than 10 we know the slope is negative and this is confirmed from the derivatives. When $X = 14$ the slope is negative, as it is when $X = 18$ with the negative slope increasing (i.e. taking larger negative values as X increases).

The relationship between the original profit function and its derivative is shown in Fig. 11.10 (and of course the derivative is easy to graph since it is a linear function). Up to an output level of 10 units the slope is positive (above the origin), but decreasing as X increases. After an output of 10 units the slope is negative and becomes more and more so. At a level of output of 10 units it is apparent that the slope is zero. The derivative can, in fact, be applied to any type of mathematical function that is typically used in business and not simply to quadratics.

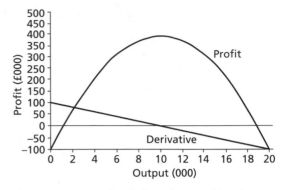

Fig. 11.10   Quadratic function and its slope

Student activity

Return to the C and R functions that we were using earlier. Obtain the derivative for each equation.

(a) *Give an explanation of the meaning of each derivative in a business context.*

(b) *Calculate each derivative when X = 10.*

Earlier we had the two functions as:

$$C = 100 + 2X^2$$
$$R = 100X - 3X^2$$

Let us take the C function first. We can differentiate each part of the equation. We can write 100 in our standard notation as $100X^0$. Then $k = 100$ and $n = 0$ giving its derivative as:

$$(0)100X^{(0-1)} = 0$$

and for $2X^2$ $k = 2$ and $n = 2$ giving:

$$(2)2X^{(2-1)} = 4X^1 = 4X$$

Re-assembling gives a derivative:

$$\frac{dC}{dX} = 4X$$

For the R equation we have $100X$, where $k = 100$ and $n = 1$ giving:

$$(1)100X^{(1-1)} = 100X^0 = 100 \text{ (since anything to the power 0 equals 1)}$$

and also $-3X^2$ (remembering the negative sign is important) where $k = -3$ and $n = 2$ to give:

$$-(2)3X^{2-1} = -6X^1 = -6X$$

Re-assembling gives:

$$\frac{dR}{dX} = 100 - 6X$$

So our two derivatives are:

$$\frac{dC}{dX} = 4X$$

$$\frac{dR}{dX} = 100 - 6X$$

We know that the derivatives are simply a mathematical expression allowing us to calculate the slope of the original function. In a business context though, they show the change in the original function from some small change in X (output). The derivative of the cost function will show the change in C as we change X by some small amount. We see that this derivative, often referred to as the marginal cost equation, has a positive slope (of 4, since it is linear) implying that as we increase output costs will always increase and we could use the derivative to calculate the change in costs for any marginal change in X. Similarly, for the derivative of the revenue function, often known as the marginal revenue equation. This shows the change in revenue as X changes.

We are also asked to find the value of each derivative when $X = 10$. We have:

$$\frac{dC}{dX} = 4X = 4(10) = 40$$

$$\frac{dR}{dX} = 100 - 6X = 100 - 6(10) = 40$$

That is, when $X = 10$ the two derivatives are equal and this means that the slopes of C and R are equal at this level of output. On reflection this makes sense since as we know the slope of the profit function is zero at this point and the profit function is only the difference between C and R functions, so the difference between their two slopes must be zero also.

You may have begun to realize that for the types of functions we have been dealing with certain basic 'rules' when differentiating begin to emerge:

Term involving	Derivative
Constant	0
X	1
X^2	$2X$
X^3	$3X^2$
X^4	$4X^3$

If we are differentiating a constant term this will have a derivative of zero; a term involving X will itself become a constant (with X disappearing); an X^2 term will become a term involving X and so on. It is worth remembering this when differentiating more complex equations just to check you haven't made any obvious mistakes. It is also important to constantly remind yourself of what the derivative is actually measuring and the relationship between the derivative and the original function.

FINDING THE TURNING POINT USING DIFFERENTIAL CALCULUS

Figure 11.10 leads us to one of the particularly important uses of the derivative. We saw earlier in the chapter that it is frequently important to find the turning point of a quadratic equation: the X value which gives the maximum or minimum Y value for the function. Up to now, we have used the two roots of the quadratic to determine the turning point. We can now find this point in a much easier way using the derivative.

We saw earlier in the chapter that the turning point for any quadratic will occur when the slope is zero. Given that the derivative is an expression for calculating the slope at any point on the original function then we can use the derivative to find the turning point directly. In this example we wish to find the level of output when the slope of the profit function (that is the value of the derivative) is zero. Setting the derivative to zero and solving gives:

$$\frac{dP}{dX} = 100 - 10X = 0$$

We require a value for X which will cause dY/dX to take a zero value:

$$100 - 10X = 0$$

adding $10X$ to both sides:

$$100 - 10X + 10X = 10X$$
$$100 = 10X$$

and dividing through by 10 gives $X = 10$. When X is 10 units, therefore, we have reached a point on the profit function with a zero slope and this must represent the turning point for this quadratic function where profit is maximized.

In general such a turning point can be found for any quadratic by:

- finding the derivative expression;
- setting the derivative to zero;
- solving for the X value in the derivative.

Student activity

For the equation:

$$Y = 100 - 30X + 5X^2$$

find the turning point and determine whether the turning point represents a maximum or a minimum.

We can easily find the derivative as:

$$\frac{dY}{dX} = -30 + 10X$$

(the constant disappears, $-30X$ becomes -30 and $5X^2$ is $(2)5X^{2-1}$).

To find the turning point we set the derivative to zero and solve for X:

$$-30 + 10X = 0$$
$$-30 = -10X$$
$$X = \frac{-30}{-10} = 3$$

So, the turning point of the original Y function occurs when $X = 3$. We see from the original function that it is quadratic with the c term positive so the curve follows the U-shape implying that the turning point at $X = 3$ represents a minimum value for the Y function.

The second derivative

In the activity above we recognized that the turning point derived using calculus represented a minimum turning point. In other situations, however, particularly if we develop business models using higher power expressions, it is necessary to be able to check whether the turning point represents a maximum or a minimum position without resorting to a graph. This is achieved through the use of what is known as the *second derivative*.

A simple rule applies in determining whether the turning point we have found represents a maximum or minimum. Having determined the first derivative and used this to obtain the X value at the turning point we can decide whether this turning point represents a maximum or minimum value by taking the derivative of the first derivative function. If this second derivative is negative the zero-slope point found is a maximum. If the second derivative is positive we have a minimum point.

This sounds complicated but is easier to do than to explain. Let us return to the profit function we have been using. We had:

$$P = -100 + 100X - 5X^2$$

In this example, the (first) derivative was:

$$\frac{dP}{dX} = 100 - 10X$$

and we used this to derive a turning point of $X = 10$. However, this derivative is itself a function and we can apply the derivative rule to it – that is, we can differentiate this equation in turn.

Applying the same rule of differentiation we can find the (second) derivative of this expression:

$$\frac{d^2P}{dX^2} = -10$$

The term 2 (i.e. d^2 and X^2) is used to indicate this is a second derivative so that we can distinguish it from the first derivative and the expression would be pronounced as 'dee two P by dee X squared'. Here, the second derivative is a constant and takes a negative value, indicating that the turning point found using the first derivative related to a maximum point on the curve. If the second derivative had been positive then it would indicate that the turning point we had found was a minimum.

To summarize the method of finding the turning point using calculus and determining whether the turning point represents a maximum or minimum we need to:

1 Find the first derivative expression of the original function.
2 Set the first derivative to zero.
3 Solve for the X value in the first derivative.
4 Find the second derivative by differentiating the first derivative:
   - if the second derivative is positive then the turning point found in 3 is a minimum;
   - if the second derivative is negative then the turning point found in 3 is a maximum.

We should note that some higher power functions may have more than one turning point. This will result in more than one value of X at step 3. To find which is a maximum and which is a minimum then we substitute each value of X found at step 3 into the second derivative and solve for the second derivative value. The negative/positive rule will then tell us which is a maximum turning point and which is a minimum.

To illustrate this we shall use the equation:

$$Y = 500 + 10X - 25X^2 + 7.5X^3$$

This is a more complex function than those we have met so far but its derivative is easily found using the basic rule and differentiating by parts:

$$\frac{dY}{dX} = 10 - 50X + 22.5X^2$$

To find the turning point we set this derivative to zero and solve for X. Setting to zero we have:

$$10 - 50X + 22.5X^2 = 0$$

But it is now apparent that there is no easy way to find the X values that make this equation equal zero. However, we should recognize the derivative equation as a quadratic and what we actually require is to find the X values for this quadratic when it takes a zero value.

This is actually the same as saying we want the roots of the quadratic (since the roots show the X values that make the quadratic take a zero value). And, of course, we know how to find the roots of a quadratic equation – we use the roots formula we introduced earlier in the chapter. Using this (and we won't bother showing the full calculations) we get:

$$X_1 = 0.22$$
$$X_2 = 2$$

as the two roots of the quadratic.

It is important to remind yourself what these values represent. They do represent the roots of this quadratic but since the quadratic is actually the derivative of our original Y function, what we have found with the two roots are the values of X when the original function, Y, has a zero slope. In other words when $X = 0.22$ and when $X = 2$ the Y function has a turning point – in fact this function has two turning points. But how do we decide whether these turning points represent a maximum or minimum value for Y?

The answer, of course, is that we use the second derivative. The second derivative (the derivative of the first derivative) is:

$$\frac{d^2Y}{dX^2} = -50 + 45X$$

But is this second derivative positive or negative (which we need to know to figure out whether we have a maximum or minimum turning point)? The answer is: it depends on the specific numerical value of X.

Let us take the first turning point when $X = 0.22$. If we substitute into the second derivative we have:

$$\frac{d^2Y}{dX^2} = -50 + 45X = -50 + 45(0.22) = -40.1$$

that is, when $X = 0.22$ (which is one of our turning points) the second derivative takes a negative value indicating that this turning point is actually a maximum (Y, in the original function, reaches a maximum value when $X = 0.22$).

If we repeat this for the second turning point, $X = 2$ we have:

$$\frac{d^2Y}{dX^2} = -50 + 45X = -50 + 45(2) = +40$$

that is, when $X = 2$ the second derivative takes a positive value and hence must represent a minimum turning point on the original function.

Although it sounds a little complicated to begin with – with different functions floating about – this method is actually quite logical and straightforward if we are asked to determine turning points for a function. We should always use the second derivative to confirm whether a turning point is a maximum or minimum as we did here. Fig. 11.11 (overleaf) shows a graph of both the original function and the first derivative just so you can visually confirm the result.

SUMMARY

In this chapter we have introduced mathematics which allow us to extend business analysis to include non-linear equations. One common type of non-linear equation, the quadratic, is a useful function for describing many business situations. We have introduced a method for finding the roots of a quadratic equation as these points frequently have an important business meaning. We also introduced calculus as a general method for finding the slope of a non-linear function, for determining the turning point of a non-linear function

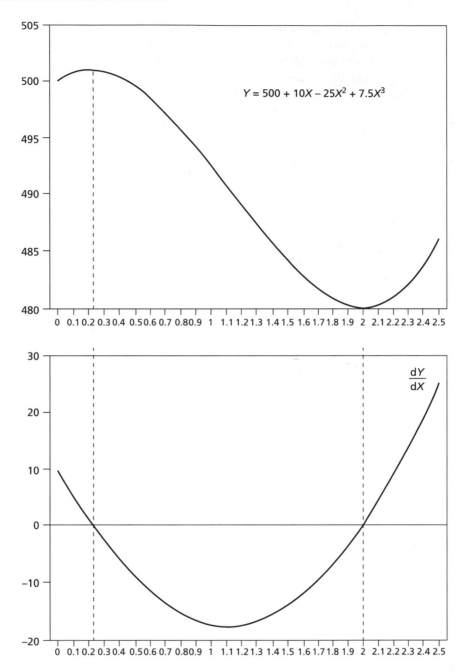

$$Y = 500 + 10X - 25X^2 + 7.5X^3$$

$$\frac{dY}{dX}$$

Fig. 11.11   Function and derivative

and for determining whether the turning point represented a maximum or a minimum value for the original function. The use of differential calculus is extremely common in business mathematics. The derivative in particular is used extensively in marginal analysis and typical business applications include marginal revenue, marginal cost, profit maximization, cost minimization, and applications to demand and supply problems.

Now that you have completed this chapter you will appreciate that:

- Non-linear functions are common in business mathematics and can take almost any form.

- A quadratic function is a particular type of non-linear function commonly used in business modelling. It is given in the general form: $Y = a + bX + cX^2$.

- In a quadratic function the points where the function crosses the X axis are known as the 'roots' and show the X values where $Y = 0$. There may be two, one or no roots depending on the parameters of the quadratic.

- Graphing a non-linear equation follows the same steps as for a linear function, with the exception that a reasonably large number of points need to be plotted to identify the specific shape of the function.

- The derivative is simply an expression which shows the slope of the original function at any point along its length.

- The derivative is frequently used to find the turning point of a function: when the slope = 0.

- The second derivative results from differentiating the derivative of a function and is used to confirm whether the turning point identified is a maximum or minimum value.

EXAMPLE

Finally, let us work through an example problem to see how we can use the concepts we have introduced in this, and the previous, chapter. Let us suppose that a firm has been able to quantify its total costs of production, C, as:

$$C = 400 + 0.005X^3 - 0.75X^2 + 37.5X$$

where X is output produced. The firm is able to sell all its output at a price of £25 per unit and the firm has asked us to advise how much output it should produce in order to maximize profit. The firm also wants to know its average cost of production per unit at this output level.

In order to tackle this problem we need the firm's profit equation. This will be given by:

$$P = R - C$$

where P is profit, R is revenue and C is cost. C we already have and R will be:

$$R = 25X$$

since the firm can sell output at a price of £25. This then gives:

$$
\begin{aligned}
P &= R - C \\
&= 25X - (400 + 0.005X^3 - 0.75X^2 + 37.5X) \\
&= 25X - 400 - 0.005X^3 + 0.75X^2 - 37.5X \\
&= -400 - 0.005X^3 + 0.75X^2 - 12.5X
\end{aligned}
$$

To find the profit maximizing level of output we require the turning point of this equation (where the slope is zero). This requires the first derivative:

$$\frac{dP}{dX} = -0.015X^2 + 1.5X - 12.5$$

Setting this to zero we require the values for X such that $dP/dX = 0$. The derivative is clearly a quadratic so for dP/dX we need the two roots. Using the roots formula (and without showing the full calculations) we find the two roots to be:

$X_1 = 9.167$
$X_2 = 90.83$

We then require the second derivative to determine which of these roots represents a maximum turning point. We have:

$$\frac{d^2P}{dX^2} = -0.03X + 1.5$$

When $X = 9.167$ the second derivative is positive and when $X = 90.83$ the second derivative is negative. This implies that profit will be maximized when $X = 90.83$.

To determine the average cost per unit produced at this output level we require an average cost equation. This would be:

$$AC = \frac{C}{X}$$

that is, average cost is simply the total cost divided by the number of units produced. From the C equation this is then:

$$AC = \frac{C}{X} = \frac{400 + 0.005X^3 - 0.75X^2 + 37.5X}{X}$$

giving (by dividing each term through by X):

$$AC = 400/X + 0.005X^2 - 0.75X + 37.5$$

When $X = 90.83$ (the profit maximizing level of output) then AC will be £15.03 implying that, since the firm sells its output at £25, it is making a profit per unit sold of almost £10.

SELF-REVIEW QUESTIONS

1 *Which part of the quadratic equation shows the intercept?*

2 *What does the 'c' term in the quadratic tell us?*

3 *What are the 'roots' of a quadratic?*

4 *What is the 'turning point' and how is it found?*

5 *What is the derivative rule?*

6 *What does a derivative measure?*

7 *What is the derivative of a constant?*

8 *How is the derivative used to find the turning point?*

9 *What is the second derivative?*

10 *Why is the second derivative calculated?*

STUDENT EXERCISES

1 Plot the following quadratic equations and determine the roots and turning point:

(a) $Y = 50 - 5X + 2.5X^2$ (for $X = 0$ to 20)

(b) $Y = 45 + 5X - 3X^2$ (for $X = -5$ to $+5$)

(c) $Y = -100 + 50X - 5X^2$ (for $X = 0$ to 10)

(d) $Y = -500 + 50X - 5X^2$ (for $X = 0$ to 10)

(e) $Y = 100 + 50X - 5X^2$ (for $X = 0$ to 10)

Why is it impossible to find roots for certain of these functions?

2 In the chapter we had a function such that:

$$Q = 12L^2 - 0.75L^3$$

where Q was production and L the number of people employed. Determine the optimum number of people the firm should employ.

3 Return to the worked example at the end of the chapter. Plot on one graph:

(a) the equations for P, dP/dX and d^2P/dX^2;

(b) the equations for P, C, AC.

4 A firm producing floppy disks has found that the total production on its production line depends on the number of production staff employed and the relationship between output and employment has been found to be:

$$Q = 30L + 3L^2 - \frac{L^3}{3}$$

where Q is the number of floppy disks produced and L the number of production staff employed.

(a) Draw a graph of the firm's production function.

(b) Obtain an equation for the firm's marginal product (the derivative of Q).

(c) Over what range of employment does marginal product increase and over what range does it decrease?

(d) How many people should the firm employ?

5   A firm has found that its cost function is given as:

$$C = 1{,}000 + 20Q + 0.5Q^2$$

where C is cost and Q is production. The firm has also found that its demand function is:

$$Q = 80 - \frac{2P^2}{3}$$

where P is the price at which the product is sold.

(a) Find an equation for the firm's total revenue, R, as a function of Q.

(b) Find an equation for profit.

(c) Find the firm's profit maximizing level of production.

(d) Find the price the firm should charge at this profit maximizing level of production.

(e) Find the output level over which the firm will at least break even.

(f) Find the two price levels corresponding to the output levels in (e).

6   Over the last few years a firm has collected information on the price it has charged for its product and the amount of the product it has sold:

Price charged	£20	£14	£23
Units sold	4,000	8,000	2,000

The firm's accountant has indicated that fixed costs are £20,000 whilst variable costs per unit produced are:

$$V = 8Q + 0.25Q^2$$

where V is variable cost and Q is output.

(a) Obtain a linear demand equation where:

$$P = f(Q)$$

where P is price.

(b) Why does V have a zero intercept?

(c) Find an equation for profit.

(d) Determine the profit maximizing level of output for this firm.

(e) Determine the cost minimizing level of output.

(f) Determine the revenue maximizing level of output.

12 BUSINESS FORECASTING: SIMPLE LINEAR REGRESSION

INTRODUCTION

In Chapter 10 linear equations were introduced and discussed and their potential usefulness in a variety of business applications illustrated. Up to now we have simply assumed that such equations have been provided without any concern for their source or derivation. This chapter is concerned with how such linear relationships can be quantified from the raw data using the technique of simple linear regression and with how regression provides a powerful forecasting tool for business.

LEARNING OBJECTIVES

By the end of this chapter you should be able to:

- explain the principles of simple linear regression;
- calculate a regression equation;
- interpret the results of a regression equation;
- evaluate the potential usefulness of a regression equation in a business context.

FORECASTING IN BUSINESS

Mercedes-Benz forecasts higher earnings in year

It will be clear by now at this stage in the text that any organization will need to try to forecast key variables. A production company will need to try to forecast future sales, cash flow, profitability, raw material requirements, employment levels and so on. A hospital will need to try to forecast the number of patients needing treatment, the type of treatment needed, future requirements in terms of drugs, medicines, blood supply. A school will need to try to predict enrolment of new pupils, which academic subjects to offer, costs of teaching and learning materials and so on. Any organization will wish to try to develop some view as to the likely values of some important variable. In this chapter and the next we shall introduce two important techniques which are specifically concerned with helping a manager try and predict the future value of some variable. In this chapter we introduce the technique of simple linear regression and in the next chapter that of time series analysis.

Shares hit as broker downgrades forecast

Forecast global value of the datacoms market, 1995–2000

1993 ($m)	Market value	% growth
1995	18,510	17.9
1996	20,873	12.8
1997	23,072	10.5
1998	24,828	7.6
1999	26,331	6.1
2000	27,773	5.3

Source: MarketLine

Source: *Financial Times*, 3 October 1995

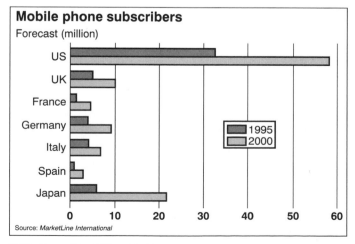

Mobile phone subscribers
Forecast (million)

Source: MarketLine International

Source: *Financial Times*, 3 October 1995

SIMPLE LINEAR REGRESSION

We shall illustrate the principles of the technique with a simple numerical example, which will allow us to focus on the key principles and concepts. At the end of the chapter we shall examine an application using real data.

Let us return to the linear equation introduced in Chapter 10 relating total costs to output:

$$C = 8 + 1.25X$$

where C was total costs measured in £000 and X was output measured in 000 units. We saw in Chapter 10 how we could use such a linear equation. But a critical question arises: how would such an equation be derived in practice?

Let us assume that over the past 12 months the company has collected monthly data on the two variables. The production department anticipates that next month's production will be 7.5(000) units and wishes to estimate likely costs. The data collected are shown in Table 12.1.

Table 12.1
Monthly costs and output levels for 1995

Total costs (£000)	Monthly output (000 units)
10.3	2.4
12.0	3.9
12.0	3.1
13.5	4.5
12.2	4.1
14.2	5.4
10.8	1.1
18.2	7.8
16.2	7.2
19.5	9.5
17.1	6.4
19.2	8.3

Source: Production department.

We shall assume that the data shown in Table 12.1 is typical and representative of the company's situation. Clearly the company is assuming that costs, C, are affected by output X. In our jargon that:

$$C = f(Y)$$

One useful first step is to use a scatter diagram (that we introduced in Chapter 5) to check visually whether there is any obvious pattern or relationship between the two variables – as there ought to be if there is a functional relationship between the two. Figure 12.1 shows the two variables plotted on such a scatter graph. On the vertical axis we have total costs, C (since this is the dependent variable) and on the horizontal axis the output level, X (since this is the independent or explanatory variable).

It should be apparent why C has been placed on the vertical axis. In terms of convention the dependent variable is put on this axis and it is logical to suggest that C is dependent on X. Thus, C is denoted as the Y variable and output as the X variable. The diagram is known as a scatter diagram because it shows the scatter of points of the two variables and is an essential first step in regression analysis. It allows us to see whether there is any evidence of a linear relationship between the two variables in question.

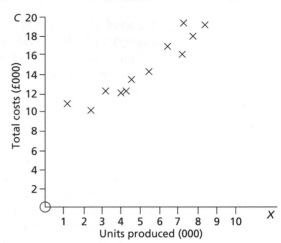

Fig. 12.1   Scatter diagram

Student activity

What observations can you make about the assumed relationship between costs and output based on the scatter diagram?

There are a number of things you could say about the apparent relationship between the two variables:

- In general, the higher the level of production the higher are costs.
- The scatter of points represents a reasonably close pattern running from bottom left to top right.
- Whilst the pattern of points is reasonably close together it is not perfectly so.

We shall examine these points in more detail shortly.

We confirm then from the diagram that there is indeed some connection between the two variables, with C rising as X rises, although it is also evident that the relationship between the two variables is not perfectly constant as the points do not all fit on a single straight line. There is some variability in the apparent linear relationship. It is important to realize the relationship we are trying to establish between the two variables in our investigation. In general we are assuming that:

Cost = f(Output)

that is, that costs are a function of output. In general we would have:

Y = f(X)

where X is the independent, or explanatory, variable and Y is the dependent variable.

The linkage between the two variables – which is dependent and which is independent – must be our choice and must be based on what we assume to be the appropriate relationship between the two variables. It would not make sense, in this example, to assume that:

Output = f(Costs)

i.e. that output is dependent on costs. However, in other situations the choice of dependent variable may be more difficult. Consider the two variables:

S = sales of a product per month
P = price charged per item

Student activity

Which variable do you think should be the dependent and which the independent?

You probably said that sales should be dependent and price independent – that is:

Sales = f(Price)

This may be very logical but we might also argue that in some cases the price we charge for the item will, in part, depend upon the sales levels we can achieve. If we are able to achieve very high sales levels we may be able to offer the item for sale at a lower price (perhaps because of economies of scale in the production process). We are then saying that:

P = f(Sales)

It is particularly important, therefore, to be able to justify your choice of X and Y variables in the problem you are investigating.

A second important point relates to the scatter of points we have on the diagram. Whilst there is obviously a strong relationship between the two variables – in this case as output increases costs increase – it is clear that this relationship is not a perfectly constant one. There is some variability in the relationship. For example, the second and third sets of data in Table 12.1 both show costs at 12 and yet output levels were different – at 3.9 and 3.1 respectively. There may be many reasons why the relationship between two variables is not perfectly constant. One of these reasons relates to the fact that we are limiting the relationship to only two variables – costs and output – and implicitly we are assuming in the functional expression that output is the only variable 'explaining' the level of costs. Clearly this assumption will not always be valid.

Student activity

What other variables do you think might influence costs apart from output?

Other variables might include the number of people employed in this production process, the stock policy of the company, production of other products, the level of inflation, the exchange rate if the firm uses imported materials in the production process. In our function we are assuming (rightly or wrongly) that output is the most important variable affecting costs. We shall see in a later section how we may be able to assess the strength of this assumed relationship.

Student activity

A firm has collected data on the price at which its product has been sold over the last few months, P, and the amount of the product bought by customers, Q. Q is measured in 000s of units whilst P is measured in pence.

Q	P		Q	P
40	80		40	72
52	60		48	65
37	85		37	83
44	70		44	75
45	68		45	68

Draw a scatter diagram for the data and comment on the results.

In this case it makes sense to say that:

$$Q = f(P)$$

that is, the amount sold depends on the price charged. In a linear format we would have:

$$Q = a + bP$$

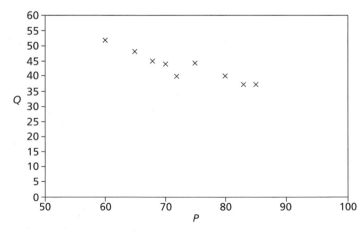

Fig. 12.2 *Q = f(P)*

where Q is Y and P is X. The scatter diagram is shown in Fig. 12.2. We see a negative relationship between Q and P, implying that as P increases as Q decreases (which is a reasonable thing to happen since as prices rise customers will probably buy less of the product). Whilst we are expecting a negative slope we cannot from the diagram see the likely value for a since we have a P scale from 50 to 100 – we would need to draw the diagram with a P scale including 0 in order to estimate the intercept from the graph.

LINE OF BEST FIT

Returning to our data and the scatter diagram, we are trying to obtain a linear equation that best represents the scatter of data that we have in the diagram, in the terminology of regression we are looking for the *line of best fit*. That is, the one line which best fits the scatter of points on the diagram and which best represents the numerical relationship between our two variables. From such a line we could obviously derive a linear equation. Such an equation will be the one that comes closest to the data set.

We could draw such a line ourselves, superimposing the straight line onto the scatter diagram. In doing this we would probably try to draw the line so that it came as close as possible to as many as possible of the various points on the graph. Once we had drawn this line of best fit we could then obtain its equation from the graph by determining the intercept and the slope of the line as we did in Chapter 10.

Such a method, however, is entirely subjective and unlikely to be perfectly accurate. Different people will draw slightly different lines (and thereby get slightly different equations). Clearly, we need a mathematical method of finding the equation. This method is known as finding the line of best fit (sometimes also referred to as the *method of least squares*).

Whilst we need not concern ourselves with the exact mathematical underpinning of the method the general approach will be worth considering. We require the line that comes closest to the points in the scatter diagram. This does not necessarily mean that the line will go through all – or indeed any – of the points. One approach would be to produce a line so that the distance between the line itself and all the points in the data set was the minimum possible. However, since some points would be below the line and some above then minimizing the total deviations of points from the line clearly would not be appropriate (as positive deviations would cancel negative ones).

Adopting a similar approach to that of the standard deviation calculation in Chapter 7 we could then consider squaring the individual deviations from the line and finding the line that minimized this total deviation value. This is precisely what the line of best fit does. It minimizes the sum of the squared deviations (hence the alternative name as the *method of least squares*). The line that we then derive will literally be the line that comes closest to the individual points in the data set we are examining.

CALCULATING THE LINE OF BEST FIT

You will remember that the general form of a linear equation is given as:

$$Y = a + bX$$

where a and b are the appropriate parameters for the equation. The equation representing the line is actually obtained through two formulae used for estimating the b and a parameters of a linear equation:

$$b = \frac{n\Sigma XY - \Sigma X \Sigma Y}{n\Sigma X^2 - (\Sigma X)^2}$$

$$a = \frac{\Sigma Y}{n} - \frac{b(\Sigma X)}{n}$$

where

X represents the independent variable;

Y represents the dependent variable;

n is the number of pairs of observations in the data sat.

The method of applying these formulae to the data is often referred to as estimating the equation using simple linear regression. Regression is the technique for deriving such an equation. In this context we are obviously concerned with obtaining a *linear* equation and it is known as *simple* linear regression – not because the calculation is an easy one but because we have only one explanatory variable in the equation (and hence have the simplest type of function). Although the formulae look complicated the arithmetic is relatively straightforward and best approached using a tabular format as illustrated below. We have five columns of calculations and it is the totals for these columns that we are interested in. The first two columns are simply the Y and X data for our problem. The remaining columns show:

- the X and Y values multiplied together, so the first pair of X,Y values give $10.3 \times 2.4 = 24.72$;
- X^2, which for the first value gives $2.4^2 = 5.76$;
- Y^2, which for the first value gives $10.3^2 = 106.9$.

Such calculations are, of course, ideally suited for a spreadsheet but if you are doing them manually make sure you are multiplying and squaring the right values in each column. We then total each column to give the totals as shown in Table 12.2.

Table 12.2
Calculations for linear regression

Y	X	XY	X^2	Y^2	
10.3	2.4	24.72	5.76	106.09	
12.0	3.9	46.80	15.21	144.0	
12.0	3.1	37.20	9.61	144.0	
13.5	4.5	60.75	20.25	182.25	
12.2	4.1	50.02	16.81	148.84	
14.2	5.4	76.68	29.16	201.64	
10.8	1.1	11.88	1.21	116.64	
18.2	7.8	141.96	60.84	331.24	
16.2	7.2	116.64	51.84	262.44	
19.5	9.5	185.25	90.25	380.25	
17.1	6.4	109.44	40.96	292.41	
19.2	8.3	159.36	68.89	368.64	
175.2	63.7	1,020.7	410.79	2,678.44	Totals

So we have:

$$\Sigma Y = 175.2$$
$$\Sigma X = 63.7$$
$$\Sigma XY = 1,020.7$$
$$\Sigma X^2 = 410.79$$
$$\Sigma Y^2 = 2,678.44$$
$$n = 12$$

We can now substitute these values into the equations for a and b, again taking care that we are using the right totals in the formula. We must work out b first:

$$b = \frac{n\Sigma XY - \Sigma X \Sigma Y}{n\Sigma X^2 - (\Sigma X)^2}$$

and substituting for the totals we have (using brackets to help the calculations):

$$b = \frac{12(1,020.7) - 63.7(175.2)}{12(410.79) - (63.7)^2}$$

Notice that the second term on top is $\Sigma X \Sigma Y$ and *not* ΣXY, and that the second term on the bottom is $(\Sigma X)^2$ and *not* ΣX^2.

We then simplify:

$$b = \frac{12,248.4 - 11,160.24}{4,929.48 - 4,057.69} = \frac{1,088.16}{871.79} = 1.248$$

So, the slope of the regression line (the line of best fit) is +1.248.

We can now calculate the a term for the regression equation:

$$a = \frac{\Sigma Y}{n} - b\frac{(\Sigma X)}{n}$$

$$= \frac{175.2}{12} - \frac{1.248(63.7)}{12}$$

$$= 14.6 - 6.6248$$

$$= 7.9752$$

Thus, the equation representing the line of best fit is:

$$Y = 7.9752 + 1.248X$$

where Y is the total costs and X is the output. For practical use we may wish to round this to:

$$Y = 8 + 1.25X$$

Interpretation of the line of best fit is the same as for any linear equation. The a term – at 8 – denotes the intercept and the b term – at 1.25 – denotes the slope of the line. The formulae for calculating a and b are quite complex and you should double check any calculations. One quick check you can make is to look back at the scatter diagram, and use our knowledge of linear equations. We see from the scatter diagram that the scatter of points has a positive slope and an intercept of about 8. If we had calculated, for example, b as a negative slope using the formula or a as a number considerably different from 8 then this ought to indicate to us that we have probably made a mistake somewhere and ought to go back and check the calculations.

The line of best fit we have obtained has been superimposed on the scatter diagram in Fig. 12.3. The line, as the name suggests, is that which comes closest to the set of data points that we have. As we can see from the figure, however, there are some differences between the observed points and the best fit line. That is, the line we have calculated is not a perfect fit to the scatter of data. Any line is likely to deviate – to a large or small extent – from the observed data. The regression equations used above find the line where this deviation is at a minimum.

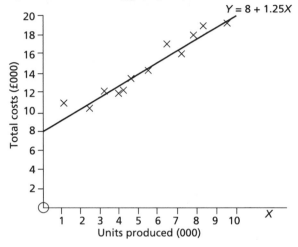

Fig. 12.3   Line of best fit

Student activity

Obtain the regression line for P/Q data used in the previous activity.

The relevant calculations are shown in Table 12.3.

Table 12.3
Calculations for linear regression

Y	X	XY	X^2	Y^2
40	80	3,200	6,400	1,600
52	60	3,120	3,600	2,704
37	85	3,145	7,225	1,369
44	70	3,080	4,900	1,936
45	68	3,060	4,624	2,025
40	72	2,880	5,184	1,600
48	65	3,120	4,225	2,304
37	83	3,071	6,889	1,369
44	75	3,300	5,625	1,936
45	68	3,060	4,624	2,025
432	726	31,036	53,296	18,868	Totals

For *b* we then have:

$$b = \frac{n\Sigma XY - \Sigma X\Sigma Y}{n\Sigma X^2 - (\Sigma X)^2} = \frac{10(31,036) - 726(432)}{10(53,296) - (726)^2} = \frac{-3,272}{5,884} = -0.556$$

confirming that we have a negative slope. For *a* we have:

$$a = \frac{\Sigma Y}{n} - \frac{b(\Sigma X)}{n} = \frac{432}{10} - \frac{(-0.556)(726)}{10} = 83.57$$

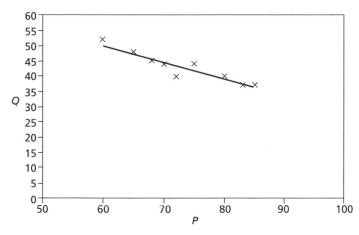

(taking care over the double negative with *b*) giving an intercept of 83.57. We then have a regression equation such that:

$$Q = 83.57 - 0.556P$$

The regression line is superimposed on our earlier scatter diagram in Fig. 12.4 and we see that the line comes reasonably close to all the points.

Fig. 12.4   Q = f(P) line of best fit

FORECASTING WITH THE REGRESSION LINE

Now we have established the parameters of the regression line we can use it for forecasting purposes. Returning to our cost equation we had:

$$C = 8 + 1.25X$$

and you may remember at the start of this chapter we said that the production department thought next month's production was likely to be 7.5(000) units. Clearly we can now use the equation to forecast likely costs associated with this level of output. We know that output next month is planned to be 7.5. We wish to establish – perhaps for cash flow purposes – the likely costs associated with this output. Substituting $X = 7.5$ into the regression equation we have:

$$C = 8 + 1.25(7.5) = 17.375 \ (\pounds000)$$

This is the predicted level of costs, £17.375 (000) based on a level of output of 7.5(000).

Given that we have a line of best fit which visually on the scatter diagram comes close to most of the points we would tend to regard such a forecast as being reasonably accurate and it could be used with a high degree of confidence in its reliability, although we would expect some slight discrepancy between the forecast costs and the outturn costs. However, it is also important to distinguish between two general situations when using regression for forecasting purposes.

Interpolation and extrapolation

From Table 12.1 and the associated scatter diagram it is apparent that over the last 12 months output has varied between 1.1 and 9.5(000) units. Strictly speaking the line of best fit we have established is appropriate only within this range of output. We actually have no information on what happens to total costs if output were to go outside this range. In the example of forecasting above (with $X = 7.5$) we would be reasonably confident about the validity of the forecast produced because the X value lies within the range used to determine the line of best fit. Such a forecast is based on *interpolation* – where we are basing the forecast on an X value within the observed range.

Suppose, however, we were required to forecast C when $X = 12.1$. Although we can use the same regression equation to produce a forecast value for C of 23.125 we should regard the forecast with much greater suspicion. This is because we are now *extrapolating* – basing the forecast on a value for X outside the observed range. In effect we would have to say that we do not actually know what the relationship between X and C is at such output levels. All we can do is assume it remains unchanged from that specified in the regression equation. Our forecast, therefore, is based on the assumption that the relationship between X and Y we have obtained will remain exactly the same at higher output levels. This may or may not be the case for a variety of reasons. Factors such as economies of scale may come into effect, there may be capacity limits on production, there may be limits on normal working hours. We need to be more cautious about the reliability of an extrapolated forecast.

Student activity

Return to the Q/P equation estimated in the previous activity. Forecast Q when P = 73 and when P = 90. What reasons can you suggest as to why the extrapolated forecast may be less accurate?

Simply substituting each of the P values into the equation gives:

$Q = 83.57 - 0.556P$

$P = 73$: $Q = 42.982$ or 43 rounded
$P = 90$: $Q = 29.955$ or 30 rounded

The extrapolated forecast of $Q = 30$ has a higher degree of uncertainty attached to it simply because we do not know, based on the data supplied, how customers will react to prices over 83p (which is the highest observed price). It may be that their buying behaviour changes quite radically – there may, for example, be a psychological barrier attached to a particular price and if that barrier has been reached at a price of 90 then they may stop buying this product entirely (think about how many products are sold with a 99p tag on the price – £9.99, £19.99, £29.99, etc.).

THE CORRELATION COEFFICIENT

Whilst we can use the regression equation for forecasting, one aspect of our forecast that we have not yet considered is how good, or accurate, a forecast it is likely to be. Since the forecast is based on the equation which quantifies the relationship between the X and Y variables this is effectively the same as asking how strong a relationship there is between X and Y.

This is an important point in regression analysis which managers and students frequently fail to appreciate. Using the equations introduced in the last section we *always* obtain the line of best fit for some set of data. The regression equation will always be the one that comes closest to the scatter of observed points. However, this does not really tell us how close the line comes to the data points and whether the line is a good one in relation to the scatter of points. Just because we derive the line of *best* fit doesn't necessarily mean it's a *good* fit. Think about going into a clothing shop and trying on several pairs of jeans. One pair fits better than all the others but they're still the wrong waist size and the legs are too long. Even though they're the best fitting pair available you still wouldn't buy them as they didn't fit well enough.

Look at Fig. 12.5 which shows a scatter diagram for two sets of data: in the first set the line of best fit comes very close to most of the points. In the second case, although we still have the line of best fit, it doesn't fit the data particularly well (even though it is the best line we can get from the technique). Clearly we would have far more confidence in the regression equation for the first set of data than for the second – and in any forecasts produced.

Given that we are using regression to measure relationships between variables and that we wish to use such equations for forecasting it is essential that we have some measure of how accurate and reliable the equation we

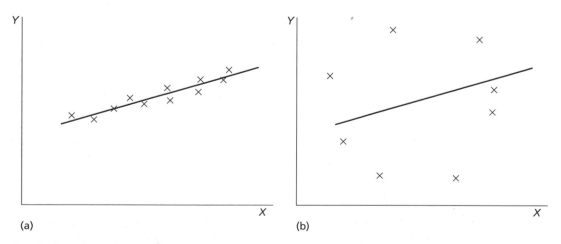

(a) (b)

Fig. 12.5 Lines of best fit

have obtained is. Obviously, we can obtain a visual assessment by superimposing the line of best fit onto the scatter diagram as we did in Fig. 12.2. Visually, it appears that the regression line for costs and output is reasonably close to the observed data and hence we would view predictions obtained from the equation with reasonable confidence.

Such a visual impression, however, is insufficient. We also require some statistical measure of accuracy. One such measure is to calculate a statistic known as the correlation coefficient or, more precisely, as Pearson's product moment correlation coefficient denoted as r. The formula is:

$$\text{Correlation coefficient} = r = \frac{n\Sigma XY - \Sigma X\Sigma Y}{\sqrt{[(n\Sigma X^2 - (\Sigma X)^2)\,(n\Sigma Y^2 - (\Sigma Y)^2)]}}$$

Whilst the formula looks horrendous, the calculations are actually quite straightforward and the appropriate totals can again be found from Table 12.2. We need the following values:

$$\Sigma Y = 175.2$$
$$\Sigma X = 63.7$$
$$\Sigma XY = 1{,}020.7$$
$$\Sigma X^2 = 410.79$$
$$\Sigma Y^2 = 2{,}678.44$$
$$n = 12$$

and we substitute these – with considerable care and double-checking – into the correlation coefficient equation:

$$
\begin{aligned}
r &= \frac{n\Sigma XY - \Sigma X\Sigma Y}{\sqrt{[(n\Sigma X^2 - (\Sigma X)^2)\,(n\Sigma Y^2 - (\Sigma Y)^2)]}} \\[2mm]
&= \frac{12(1{,}020.7) - (63.7)(175.2)}{\sqrt{(12(410.79) - 63.7^2)(12(2{,}678.44) - 175.2^2)}} \\[2mm]
&= \frac{12{,}248.4 - 11{,}160.24}{\sqrt{(4{,}929.48 - 4{,}057.69)(32{,}141.28 - 30{,}695.04)}} \\[2mm]
&= \frac{1{,}088.16}{\sqrt{(871.79)(1{,}446.24)}} = \frac{1{,}088.16}{\sqrt{1{,}260{,}817.5}} = \frac{1{,}088.16}{1{,}122.861} = 0.969
\end{aligned}
$$

So we have a correlation coefficient of 0.969. But what does this mean and how can we use this statistic?

The correlation coefficient measures the strength of the relationship between the X and Y variables. Mathematically the coefficient can take a value anywhere between -1 and $+1$ (which means that if you work out a correlation coefficient of 5.2 you've done something wrong!). The sign of the coefficient (i.e. + or −) indicates the direction of the relationship between the two variables. A positive sign (as in this case) implies that the two variables move together in the same direction. That is if one variable increases the other increases whilst if one decreases the other decreases also. A negative sign would have indicated that as one variable increased the other decreased – that is the two variables would move in opposite directions. In absolute terms the coefficient can take a value between 0 and 1. A value of zero implies that, literally, there is no correlation between the two variables – the two variables are statistically independent. A value of 1 (either positive or negative) implies the two variables are perfectly correlated.

Student activity

Return to the two scatter diagrams we had in Fig. 12.5. For each diagram decide whether the correlation coefficient would be positive or negative. Considering the two diagrams which do you think will have a correlation coefficient closer to 0 and which closer to 1?

Both sets of data will have a positive correlation since it is evident that in both cases the two variables move together in the same direction. The first diagram will have a correlation coefficient closer to 1 than the second as it is apparent that the scatter points are generally closer to the line (which represents the estimated relationship). Suppose all the scatter points had fallen on the line of best fit. What do you think the correlation coefficient would be in such a case? The correlation coefficient in this case would be 1 – indicating a perfect relationship between the two variables. As a rule of thumb we would be seeking a correlation coefficient of at least 0.7 for a set of data before we had any real confidence in the reliability of our results.

Returning to our cost example the correlation coefficient is +0.969. The correlation coefficient is positive and takes a value very close to 1. Although there is not a perfect correlation between the two variables it is nearly so. The company would be reasonably confident about any forecasts produced using such a regression line (at least for interpolation). If the correlation coefficient had been lower – say 0.6 – the company would have been less confident about the reliability of forecasts produced using the regression equation.

There are three further points to be made about using the regression technique.

- The first is that the correlation coefficient we have calculated is strictly known as *Pearson's product moment* correlation coefficient.

- The second point is that the correlation coefficient simply indicates whether two variables are connected. It does not 'prove' that one variable causes the other. If you look carefully at the correlation coefficient formula you will notice that if we were to change round the X and Y variables the formula would effectively be the same. It does not in fact matter – for the calculation of correlation – which variable is dependent and which independent.

- The third point is that the correlation coefficient actually only measures the strength of a *linear* relationship between two variables. A low value for the correlation coefficient indicates that there is little linear connection between the two not necessarily that there is no connection of any kind. Consider Fig. 12.6. This shows a scatter of points between two variables. It is evident that there is a strong relationship between the two variables but that this relationship is non-linear (in fact it is quadratic). If you were to calculate the correlation coefficient for this data you would actually get a correlation coefficient of 0 (or close to it). But all this strictly indicates is that there is no *linear* relationship between the two variables.

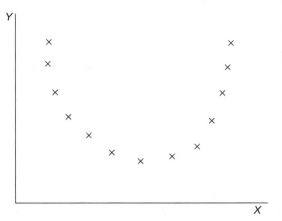

Fig. 12.6   Non-linear correlation

Student activity

Return to the Q/P equation derived in an earlier activity. Calculate the correlation coefficient for this data and comment on its value.

Returning to the P/Q problem we had the following totals:

n = 10
ΣY = 432
ΣX = 726
ΣXY = 31,036
ΣX^2 = 53,296
ΣY^2 = 18,868

Using the correlation coefficient formula we have:

$$r = \frac{n\Sigma XY - \Sigma X \Sigma Y}{\sqrt{[(n\Sigma X^2 - (\Sigma X)^2)\,(n\Sigma Y^2 - (\Sigma Y)^2)]}}$$

$$= \frac{10(31{,}036) - (726)(432)}{\sqrt{(10(53{,}296) - 726^2)(10(18{,}868) - 432^2)}}$$

$$= \frac{310{,}360 - 313{,}632}{\sqrt{(532{,}960 - 527{,}076)(188{,}680 - 186{,}624)}}$$

$$= \frac{-3{,}272}{\sqrt{(5{,}884)(2{,}056)}} = \frac{-3{,}272}{\sqrt{12{,}097{,}504}} = \frac{-3{,}272}{3{,}478.146} = -0.941$$

giving a correlation coefficient of –0.941, again a relatively high linear correlation between the two variables.

SUMMARY OF SIMPLE LINEAR REGRESSION

Finally, let us summarize the method we have developed.

Step 1

Obtain data for the two variables being analysed. There are two particular points to note here. The first is that if we are using non-annual data (i.e. data which is daily, monthly, quarterly) then we should ensure the data used is seasonally adjusted. This is described in detail in the next chapter but effectively means that we must have removed the effects from the data of the time of the year.

The second point is that if we are using financial data over a period of time then we must ensure the data is expressed in real terms and not money terms. In both cases regression analysis on data which is not seasonally adjusted or which is expressed in money terms is highly suspect.

Step 2

Decide which variable is X and which is Y (which requires you to specify the functional form of the relationship).

Step 3

Draw a scatter diagram of the data.

Step 4

From the scatter diagram assess:

- whether the scatter looks linear (if it doesn't there's no point calculating a linear regression equation);
- the slope (positive or negative);
- the intercept (as an estimate).

Step 5

Calculate the line of best fit using the a and b equations, calculating b first and then a.

Step 6

Check the slope and intercept from the equation against those you'd identified from the scatter diagram in Step 4.

Step 7

Calculate the correlation coefficient.

Step 8

If you're reasonably confident about the analysis you can use the equation for forecasting (but bear in mind the interpolation/extrapolation discussion we had earlier).

We should also note that we have really only touched on the very basics of regression here. The technique is a large and complex topic and can be extended to include:

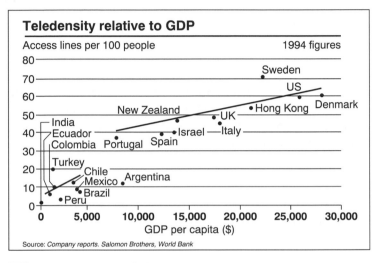

Teledensity relative to GDP

Access lines per 100 people   1994 figures

Source: *Company reports. Salomon Brothers, World Bank*

FT Source: *Financial Times*, 3 October 1995

- a statistical assessment of the reliability of the equation parameters using the principles of hypothesis testing;

- multiple regression where we have several X variables and not just one as in our case;

- non-linear regression where we estimate non-linear lines of best fit.

Finally, you should note that no one in their right mind actually calculates a regression equation using the formula we introduced. Instead we use a statistical package or a spreadsheet which will have regression calculation facilities built into it. You should familiarize yourself with the type of regression output that your own software uses when calculating regression.

SUMMARY

In this chapter we have introduced the principles of simple linear regression as a means of estimating the equation of the best fit line for a set of data which we can then use for forecasting. Regression is a particularly useful technique for organizations concerned with trying to predict the future value of some variable based on past relationships. The principles of the technique are relatively straightforward but caution is required in applying the technique properly.

Now you have completed this chapter you will appreciate that:

- Simple linear regression is a method used to obtain the equation of the line of best fit.

- The line of best fit is the line that comes closest to a set of data points by minimizing the squared deviations from the line.

- The scatter diagram is a visual method for assessing whether there is any apparent link between two variables and whether the relationship is linear.

- A correlation coefficient measures the strength of a linear relationship between two variables.

- Regression is particularly useful for forecasting a variable. A distinction must be made between forecasts based on interpolation and those on extrapolation.

EXAMPLE

Finally, let us see how regression can be used on a set of real data. You may remember that in Chapter 5 (Table 5.1) we looked at some data taken from the *Economic Trends Annual Supplement* on per capita disposable income and consumers' expenditure on certain types of products. The relevant data are reproduced below:

	PDI[1]	Durables[2]	Food[3]	Drink[4]
1970	3,912	11,865	36,280	26,349
1971	3,940	14,065	36,312	26,975
1972	4,256	17,096	36,248	28,882
1973	4,523	18,029	37,120	31,875
1974	4,487	15,790	36,470	32,189
1975	4,514	16,059	36,480	31,576
1976	4,501	16,850	36,866	31,490
1977	4,409	15,671	36,547	31,119
1978	4,734	17,926	37,217	32,000
1979	4,998	20,221	38,046	32,922
1980	5,067	19,276	38,095	31,706
1981	5,025	19,634	37,849	30,222
1982	5,004	20,652	37,942	28,963
1983	5,133	24,234	38,582	29,632
1984	5,309	24,059	37,925	29,695
1985	5,472	25,192	38,402	29,819
1986	5,703	27,912	39,610	29,630
1987	5,882	30,317	40,621	29,976
1988	6,221	34,950	41,541	30,478
1989	6,506	36,815	42,281	30,433
1990	6,621	34,745	41,816	30,272
1991	6,561	30,472	41,870	29,437
1992	6,717	30,752	42,380	28,667

[1]PDI: Per capita disposable income, £s at 1990 prices.
[2]Durables: Consumers' expenditure on durable goods, £ million at 1990 prices.
[3]Food: Consumers' expenditure on food, £ million at 1990 prices.
[4]Drink: Consumers' expenditure on alcoholic drink and tobacco, £ million at 1990 prices.

We thus have data on four variables as shown. Note that all the data is shown in real terms (at 1990 prices) so that the effects of inflation over this period will not affect the analysis.

Consider a retail organization which is strategically reviewing its areas of activity in terms of the type of products it offers for sale in its stores. We see that over this 20-year period per capita PDI has fairly steadily increased. Rationally, as people get more money – as their real per capita income increases – then it is reasonable to assume that they will use at least some of this extra income to increase their purchases of different types of goods and services. However, as we all know, if your income increases, say by 10%, this does not necessarily mean that you will increase your purchases of all the things you buy by 10%. For some items you may not actually increase purchases at all (basic foodstuffs for example) whilst for other products you may now decide that, whereas before you could not afford them at all, now you can – a home computer for example, or a car CD player.

Clearly for a retail organization it is important to have an understanding of which types of goods and services people will want more of if their income increases and which types are likely to experience little or no increase in purchasing. In our data set we have three broad areas of expenditure: durable goods, food, and alcoholic drink and tobacco. We can use the principles of regression to examine the relationship between income levels and spending on these product groups.

What we are saying is that we assume:

Durables = f(PDI)
Food   = f(PDI)
Drink   = f(PDI)

that is that spending on each product group is assumed to be a function of per capita income and that we assume a linear relationship for each. This does not mean of course that the regression equation for each product group will be the same (in terms of the *a* and *b* parameters). Given the preceding discussion we would expect different equations from our analysis and a comparison of these different equations will help us assess the differing effects of a change in PDI.

Having collected data our next step is to produce scatter diagrams for the three relationships. These are shown in Figs 12.7–12.9. Note that all the graphs have the same X scale but different Y scales and that none of the X scales include zero. From Fig. 12.7 for durables we see evidence of a strong positive relationship between the two variables with the relationship looking reasonably linear, although at the top of the X scale there are some data points which appear to be 'drifting' away from the linear pattern. Figure 12.8 shows food and again we have evidence of a strong positive linear relationship.

Figure 12.9 on the other hand which shows alcoholic drink and tobacco has a scatter of points which are all over the place. It is evident from this diagram that there is little evidence of any sort of relationship between the

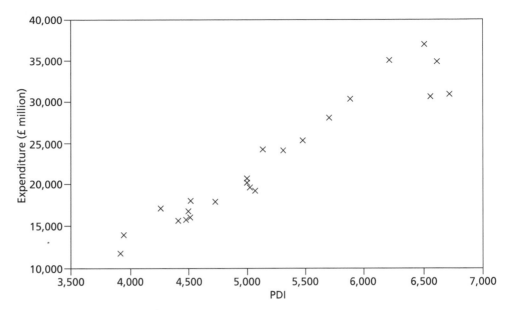

Fig. 12.7   Durable goods

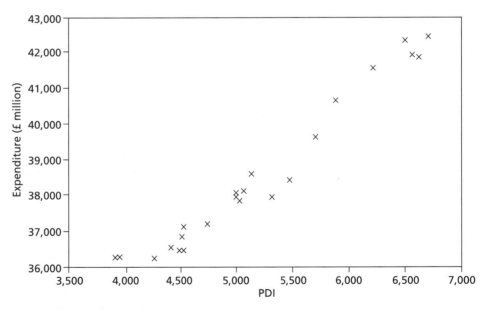

Fig. 12.8   Food

two variables. This is a little surprising and we might want to investigate this in more detail. It might be, for example, that by aggregating expenditure on alcoholic drink with that on tobacco we have two conflicting patterns. It may be that spending on drink is increasing whilst that on tobacco is decreasing but by merging the two together perhaps the two patterns are cancelling each

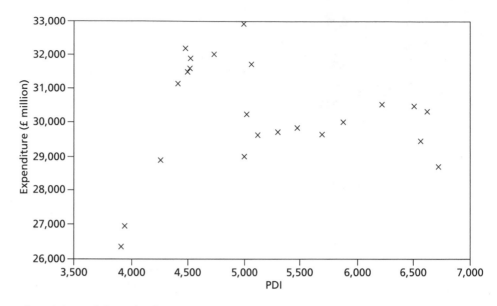

Fig. 12.9   Drink and tobacco

other out. Clearly, there would be little point in practice in calculating a regression equation for drink (although we shall do this anyway to show the results from this type of situation).

Table 12.4 shows the output from a statistical package that computes regression equations.

Table 12.4
Regression analysis – linear model: $Y = a + bX$

Dependent variable: Durables
Independent variable: PDI

Parameter	Estimate	Standard Error	T Value	Prob. Level
Intercept	−19408.8	2630.39	−7.37869	.00000
Slope	8.109	0.499589	16.2313	.00000

Analysis of Variance

Source	Sum of Squares	Df	Mean Square	F-Ratio	Prob. Level
Model	1.1023E0009	1	1.1023E0009	2.635E0002	.00000
Residual	87860459	21	4183831		

Total (Corr.)   1.1901E0009   22
Correlation Coefficient = 0.96238   R-squared = 92.62 percent
Stnd. Error of Est. = 2045.44

The first set of output relates to a regression for PDI and durables. Notice that the output is quite complex and involves a number of statistics that we have not covered reinforcing the point that there is much more to regression than we have looked at in this chapter – although you may recognize some of the terminology such as standard error and probability. However, from the first part of the output we can extract the regression equation and from the bottom of the output the *r* value:

$$\text{Durables} = -19{,}408.8 + 8.109\text{PDI}$$
$$r = 0.96238.$$

The equation has a positive slope of just over 8 and a high correlation coefficient. The slope value implies that for a unit increase in PDI there will be an 8 unit increase in spending on durables (although we need to be careful since the two variables have different units of measurement). The equation has a high degree of fit, as shown by the correlation coefficient and this is confirmed by superimposing the line of best fit equation on the scatter diagram

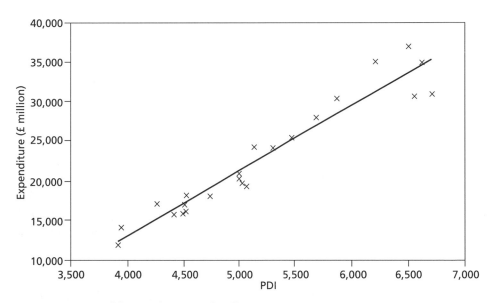

Fig. 12.10   Durable goods regression line

as shown in Fig. 12.10. However, we also notice from the diagram that for the five or six data points on the right of the *X* scale (which relate to the last five years' data in the data set) the points are further away from the line than the points for earlier years. Although we appear to have a good statistical fit for the data we might be a little cautious about our use of the results since it may be that the relationship between PDI and spending on durables is changing over time.

The output for the food regression is shown in Table 12.5.

Table 12.5
Regression analysis – linear model: $Y = a + bX$

| Dependent variable: Food | | | | |
| Independent variable: PDI | | | | |

Parameter	Estimate	Standard Error	T Value	Prob. Level
Intercept	26051.4	575.261	45.2863	.00000
Slope	2.40443	0.109259	22.0067	.00000

Analysis of Variance					
Source	Sum of Squares	Df	Mean Square	F-Ratio	Prob. Level
Model	96911265	1	96911265	4.843E0002	.00000
Residual	4202256.7	21	200107.5		

Total (Corr.)   1.0111E0008   22
Correlation Coefficient = 0.979   R-squared = 95.84 percent
Stnd. Error of Est. = 447.334

In this case we obtain the equation:

$$Food = 26{,}051.4 + 2.40443 PDI$$
$$r = 0.979$$

Again we have a positive slope with a high r value at 0.979.

It is worthwhile comparing this equation with that for durables. For durables we had a negative intercept whilst for food we have a positive. A positive intercept implies that when PDI is zero food spending will be greater than zero (it will be 26,051.4 to be exact). This appears reasonable since people still have to eat no matter what their current income. The negative intercept for durables, however, implies that spending on durables will not commence until income has reached a critical level. Again this appears sensible since most durable goods can be classed as 'luxury' or non-essential items and will not be bought if income levels are low. Both slopes are positive implying that an increase in PDI will increase spending on durables and spending on food. However, the two slope coefficients are different with that for durables over three times higher than that for food (8.108 compared to 2.40443). This implies that people will respond to an increase in income more positively for durables spending than for food: that is, an increase in PDI will lead to a larger increase in spending on durables than it will on spending on food. Again, this appears sensible in the context of the problem. Once people's basic food needs have been met they are likely to spend extra income on TVs, videos, CD players and so on to improve their living standards. For a retail organization the implications are that, if it believes that PDI will increase over the next few years, then it can anticipate more growth in income from durables than for food. Figure 12.11 shows the scatter diagram for food with the regression line superimposed and we see that over this period the scatter of points is consistently close to the regression line.

Finally we show the output for drink in Table 12.6.

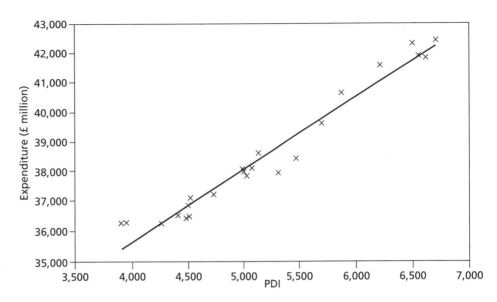

Fig. 12.11   Food regression line

Table 12.6
Regression analysis – linear model: $Y = a + bX$

Dependent variable: Drink				
Independent variable: PDI				
Parameter	Estimate	Standard Error	T Value	Prob. Level
Intercept	30014.4	2113.53	14.2011	.00000
Slope	0.0332723	0.401422	0.0828863	.93473
Analysis of Variance				
Source	Sum of Squares	Df	Mean Square	F-Ratio	Prob. Level
Model	18557.331	1	18557.331	.01	.93473
Residual	56724317	21	2701158		
Total (Corr.)	56742874	22			
Correlation Coefficient = 0.0180843			R-squared = .03 percent	
Stnd. Error of Est. = 1643.52				

The line of best fit gives an equation of:

Drink = 30,014.4 + 0.0332723PDI
$r = 0.018$

We see from the correlation coefficient that we have a very poor fit for the data and this is confirmed from the b coefficient in the equation which is very close to zero. Consider the implications of this. The b coefficient indicates the relationship between drink and PDI. If this parameter is effectively zero it implies that the relationship between the two variables is effectively zero also – changes in PDI do not appear to bring about any predictable changes in drink. Naturally, this simply confirms what we had already seen on the scatter diagram.

SELF-REVIEW QUESTIONS

1 *What is meant by 'the line of best fit'?*

2 *Why is a scatter diagram essential in regression?*

3 *What does the Pearson correlation coefficient show?*

4 *Why cannot the correlation coefficient be used to show cause and effect?*

5 *What does a correlation of 0 mean in regression?*

6 *What is the difference between interpolation and extrapolation?*

7 *What is the difference between a negative and a positive correlation?*

STUDENT EXERCISES

1 A company has a variety of microcomputers in use by management. For seven of the machines information has been collected on their age and the annual maintenance cost last year.

Machine	Maintenance costs (£ per year)	Age of machine (years)
A	1,220	6
B	500	2
C	1,800	7
D	600	4
E	1,100	4
F	200	1
G	600	3

(**a**) Forecast annual maintenance costs for a computer that is five years old.

(**b**) Forecast annual maintenance costs for a computer that is eight years old.

(**c**) Which forecast do you think will be more reliable and why?

2 A company has recently carried out some market research into the background of their customers and the proportion of customers who have purchased a video camcorder.

Year	Average weekly income £ (1990 prices)	Proportion of customers with a camcorder
1984	123.7	32
1985	134.5	37
1986	143.9	39
1987	142.7	43
1988	142.6	47
1989	141.6	51
1990	139.3	54
1991	149.6	59
1992	158.3	63
1993	160.6	65
1994	166.6	68
1995	170.5	72

(a) Determine an appropriate equation for forecasting the proportion of customers with camcorders.

(b) Assess the potential accuracy of your equation.

(c) How could the equation provide information useful to management?

3 Data has been collected on two variables as shown below:

    Y: 108   116   105   130   128   107   116
    X: 2   3.5   1.4   5.2   5.1   1.8   3.4

Calculate the correlation coefficient and comment on the relationship.

4 Return to the data shown in Chapter 5, Table 5.1. Calculate a regression equation for PDI and the number of new car registrations. Obtain a value for PDI for 1995 and forecast new car registrations for 1995 and comment on the accuracy of your result.

5 A large retail organization has been analysing the profitability of a sample of its outlets in a particular geographical region. Data has been collected for 20 outlets for the last financial year on two variables:

   Profit: the pre-tax profit of the outlet (measured in £000)
   Sales: the annual sales of the outlet (measured in £000)

The data has been analysed through the technique of simple linear regression and the following results obtained:

   $Y = -2.418386 + 0.061373X$
   $r = 0.9647$

You have been asked to comment on the results of the model in terms of its suitability for forecasting future profit levels of these outlets.

(a) Explain the principles of simple linear regression in the context of this problem.

(b) Explain the results of this regression analysis in both a statistical and business context.

6 A company has a number of home furnishing outlets in a particular region – selling products such as carpets, curtains, domestic furniture and fittings. The organization has been affected badly by the downturn in domestic property sales in the region over the last few years as it has found that much of its business comes from customers redecorating or refurnishing a home they have just purchased. The company has collected and analysed data over the past two years to try to assess the impact that regional property sales have on its business. Two variables in particular have been specified:

● the number of house sales in the region on a monthly basis (000);
● gross monthly sales in the organization's outlets in the region (£000,000).

Data has been obtained for the last 24 months on these two variables and the data analysed through a spreadsheet package using simple linear regression with the number of house sales as the X variable:

$$Y = -0.532 + 0.476X$$
$$r = 0.914$$

(a) Explain the results of this regression analysis in both a statistical and business context.

(b) Assess and comment on the reliability of this analysis for forecasting purposes.

13 BUSINESS FORECASTING: TIME SERIES ANALYSIS

INTRODUCTION

Much of business analysis is concerned with investigating the movement of a variable over a period of time and trying to predict the future movement of that variable. We may be looking at sales, profits, costs, share prices or whatever, and our interest initially is to try to quantify the general movement in the variable over time. In this chapter we shall be seeing how some simple mathematics can be applied to help us try to analyse and predict the future values of some business variable over some period of time. This chapter is largely concerned with a technique that is specifically employed in quantifying the movement in a variable over time and which is generally referred to as *time series analysis*.

LEARNING OBJECTIVES

By the end of this chapter you should be able to:

■ state the principles of seasonality and trend;

■ calculate and graph a trend using moving averages;

■ calculate seasonal components;

■ interpret the seasonal components in a business context;

■ calculate and graph seasonally adjusted data.

SEASONAL VARIATION

HOT WEATHER HITS AUGUST CLOTHING SALES

By Robert Chote, Economics Editor

Sales of clothing dropped sharply in British shops last month, as the hot weather meant consumers were not yet in the mood to restock their winter wardrobes from newly arrived autumn ranges.

The Central Statistical Office said yesterday that the volume of goods sold in textile, clothing and footwear stores had dropped by 3.5 per cent last month, after adjusting for normal seasonal patterns. This followed a 1.4 per cent rise in July, when shoppers were snapping up summer outfits.

FT Source: *Financial Times*, 15 September 1995

Many business variables follow a regular – and hence potentially predictable – pattern over a given 12-month period. Such a pattern is referred to as the *seasonal variation* in that variable – the regular movement in the variable over a period of a year. We shall illustrate the principles involved with a simple numerical example and at the end of the chapter look at some real data to which we can apply the technique.

Look at the data in Table 13.1 which shows sales of computers by a high street store for each quarter in a year (where a quarter relates to three months) for the period 1992 to 1996. The computers are sold mainly for personal use and are often bought by individuals for home use.

Table 13.1
Sales of computers in a store
(000 units per three-month period)

Time		Sales
1992	I	86.7
1992	II	94.9
1992	III	94.2
1992	IV	106.5
1993	I	105.9
1993	II	102.4
1993	III	103.1
1993	IV	115.2
1994	I	113.7
1994	II	108.0
1994	III	113.5
1994	IV	132.9
1995	I	126.3
1995	II	119.4
1995	III	128.9
1995	IV	142.3
1996	I	136.4
1996	II	124.6
1996	III	127.9

Source: Sales department.

As usual such data is far better understood shown on a diagram and Fig. 13.1 shows the corresponding time series graph. We can see from the diagram that there appear to be two forces at work on this variable. One is a long-term movement in the variable. Over this five-year period sales are seen to be generally increasing. Such a long-term movement is referred to as the *trend*. The second force at work is a pattern which appears to repeat itself at the same time each year and is more of a short-term influence. It can be seen that each year sales tend to rise dramatically in Quarter IV and fall in Quarter II. Such a pattern within a year is known as the *seasonal variation* or *seasonal pattern* because it repeats itself at the same season each year. In general we need to be able to distinguish between these two effects as they have important – but different – implications for management and we need to be able to quantify the differing influences of these two effects.

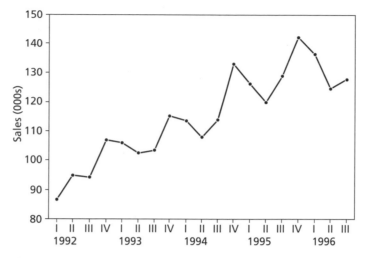

Fig. 13.1   Sales

Student activity

Why do you think management will want to distinguish between these two types of effect?

It is important for management to be able to distinguish between these two factors so they can assess the implications for the company and reach appropriate decisions about changes in the variable (sales) that they see occurring. We see from the diagram that sales have fallen since 1995 IV. We need to know whether this is a temporary seasonal phenomenon which will correct itself without any intervention from us at a later time in the year, or whether it represents a fundamental downturn in sales. In time series jargon, is the downturn in sales due to the seasonal factor or is it more related to a downturn in the trend? If it is the first then management do not really need to take any action as they know that sales in future quarters will pick up again by themselves. If it is the second, however, they may need to consider action to prevent sales falling further – such as cutting prices, advertising, having special promotions and so on.

Student activity

In the case of this company why do you think that sales in quarter IV each year increase only to fall again in quarters I and II? What other examples of business variables can you give which will follow some sort of strong seasonal pattern through a year?

In the case of this firm and this product then we would probably expect sales of computers from a high street store to increase markedly in the last quarter of the year since this will include Christmas buying on the part of consumers

419

when many of these products are likely to be bought. Similarly, in other parts of the year, notably quarters I and II, sales tend to fall since this is not a time when many consumers would think of purchasing this type of item. In fact, many variables will have their own seasonal pattern. Think of Christmas cards, for example, sun-tan lotion, swimming costumes, ice-cream. The list goes on and on.

In fact it is quite difficult to think of variables which are unlikely to have a strong seasonal pattern. Whilst you might agree that Christmas card sales will be highly seasonal you might argue that birthday card sales, for example, will not be. However, if you look at some supplementary statistics on the seasonal pattern of births in the UK you might change your mind since there are some months of the year which consistently have a higher number of births occurring in them than others (use your imagination as to why!) and this obviously will affect the number of birthdays and hence birthday card sales in each month.

However, what is important for management is to be able to measure both this seasonal effect and any trend which may be evident. It's all very well going back to the store and informing the manager that the store will sell more computers in the last quarter of the year. The manager will want to know how many more – so that orders can be placed and related decisions taken on staff levels and training well before this last quarter happens. Similarly, if any long-term trend in sales is emerging a manager will want to be able to measure this and potentially to project it into the future to pose 'what-if' questions about future decisions.

TIME SERIES MODELS

In general a time series such as that shown above can be broken into three major components (hence the alternative name for the technique of *time series decomposition*) where:

$$D = T + S + R$$

and where:

- D is the original data series;
- T the trend;
- S the seasonal variation;
- R the residual.

So sales in a particular quarter, D, will comprise both a trend element, T, and an element of seasonal variation, S (which of course will depend on the time of the year). In addition, there may be random events, R, which affect sales in a particular quarter but which are unlikely to be repeated in future quarters. These events would include periods of extreme weather, labour disputes, changes in government tax policy, a special one-off sales promotion, a competitor opening a new store nearby, for example. These residual elements are unpredictable factors affecting sales in a particular period which have nothing to do with either seasonal variations or the underlying trend in sales.

Time series analysis is concerned with quantifying the effects of these different elements. The calculations appropriate for the analysis take place in a number of stages:

- Calculate the trend for the series.
- Calculate the deviation of actual sales from the trend.
- Calculate an average deviation.
- Calculate the seasonal variation.
- Calculate the seasonally adjusted series.

We shall examine each of these in turn.

CALCULATION OF THE TREND

By definition, the trend is the underlying, long-term movement in the variable whilst the seasonal variation is the temporary (and repetitive) variation that occurs over a 12-month period. Over any 12-month period, therefore, the seasonal fluctuations in a series should cancel out, given that in any one quarter or month such variation is, by definition, temporary. That is, over the year the seasonal fluctuations will cancel each other out since, logically, higher than average sales in one quarter will be counterbalanced by lower than average sales in another.

Returning to the trend, therefore, it seems that if we were to take a set of four quarterly figures (which cover a full 12-month period) and average them then this average should not contain any seasonal effect but could rather be regarded as a long-term average (i.e. the trend). Referring to Table 13.1 for the first four quarters, if we total the actual sales (86.7 + 94.9 + 94.2 + 106.5) to get 382.3 – a total for the 12 months between the first quarter 1992 and the last quarter. Given that this figure covers a full 12-month period the seasonal variation between quarters should have cancelled out. Similarly we can take the next 12 month period – from the second quarter 1992 to the first quarter 1993. This also covers a full 12 month period and again will have the seasonal effects removed. These totals are known as the four-period totals.

Student activity

Calculate the rest of the four-period totals for Table 13.1.

The rest of the totals will appear as in Table 13.2.

We might think that these figures, the four-period totals, could now be averaged (by dividing each by 4 since we have totalled sets of 4 sales values) and that this would give the trend for each quarter. The problem is, as you might have noticed, that these four-period totals do not actually line up with specific quarters. The first figure of 382.3, for example, is actually for the middle of the 12-month period covered (between quarters II and III) rather than for a specific quarter. When we wish to compare actual sales against trend (as we shall do shortly) this will cause difficulties in actually lining up each quarter with each average.

Accordingly we must undertake an adjustment known as *centring the trend* – effectively to make it line up with a specific quarter. The process of centring is quite straightforward but as is often the case sounds more complicated than it is. We take the first four-period total (of 382.3) and add it to the second four-period total (of 401.5). This then gives a total of 783.8. If we then average this (dividing by 8 since it now covers eight quarters) we get 98.0 which is now centred (i.e. corresponds to 1992 III) and an average for the third quarter of 1992 and represents trend sales in this quarter. We can see the logic of this process in Table 13.3.

The first four-period total of 383.2 represents a 12-month value for the period in between quarters II and III. Similarly, the second four-period total of 401.5 represents the next 12-month total for the period in between quarters III and IV. By taking these two totals, adding them and then averaging, the result corresponds to quarter III. The next calculation would be $(401.5 + 409.0)/8 = 101.3$ representing trend sales for the fourth quarter of 1992. In such a way we can calculate the centred trend for each of the other quarters.

Table 13.2
Calculation of a moving average trend

Time		Sales	Four-period total
1992	I	86.7	
1992	II	94.9	
			382.3
1992	III	94.2	
			401.5
1992	IV	106.5	
			409.0
1993	I	105.9	
			417.9
1993	II	102.4	
			426.6
1993	III	103.1	
			434.4
1993	IV	115.2	
			440.4
1994	I	113.7	
			450.4
1994	II	108.0	
			468.1
1994	III	113.5	
			480.7
1994	IV	132.9	
			492.1
1995	I	126.3	
			507.5
1995	II	119.4	
			516.9
1995	III	128.9	
			527.0
1995	IV	142.3	
			532.2
1996	I	136.4	
			531.2
1996	II	124.6	
1996	III	127.9	

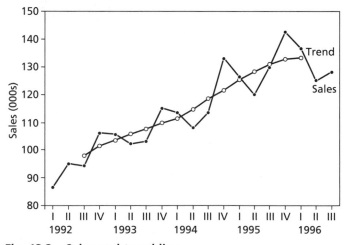

Fig. 13.2   Sales and trend line

Table 13.3
Calculation of a moving average trend

Time		Sales	Four-period total	Eight-period total	Trend
1992	I	86.7			
1992	II	94.9			
			382.3		
1992	III	94.2		783.8	98.0
			401.5		
1992	IV	106.5		810.5	101.3
			409.0		
1993	I	105.9		826.9	103.4
			417.9		
1993	II	102.4		844.5	105.6
			426.6		
1993	III	103.1		861.0	107.6
			434.4		
1993	IV	115.2		874.4	109.3
			440.4		
1994	I	113.7		890.4	111.3
			450.4		
1994	II	108.0		918.5	114.8
			468.1		
1994	III	113.5		948.8	118.6
			480.7		
1994	IV	132.9		972.8	121.6
			492.1		
1995	I	126.3		999.6	125.0
			507.5		
1995	II	119.4		1,024.4	128.1
			516.9		
1995	III	128.9		1,043.9	130.5
			527.0		
1995	IV	142.3		1,059.2	132.4
			532.2		
1996	I	136.4		1,063.4	132.9
			531.2		
1996	II	124.6			
1996	III	127.9			

The appropriate calculations are shown in Table 13.3 and you might want to work through them yourself to confirm exactly what we are doing.

The trend values calculated show the underlying – or long-term – movement in the series as it is averaged over time. These trend values are shown together with actual sales in Fig. 13.2 and the underlying trend in sales is readily visible. The patterns we had earlier in Fig. 13.1 have now been smoothed out to give the trend sales – the long-term average per quarter. We see that the trend is relatively smooth and shows a long-term positive growth (it has a positive slope in the jargon of Chapters 10 and 11) implying that sales are steadily increasing over this period.

The method we have used is actually referred to as finding the trend by centred moving averages. Note that the method cannot give us the trend for the first two and last two quarters in the series because of the averaging process.

Whilst the trend is obviously useful we need to go further in our analysis. It is clear that sales in each quarter vary from this trend (which is after all only an average). We now wish to quantify this variation.

Note that by superimposing your trend line on the graph of actual sales you can check that you have not made any obvious mistakes in calculating the trend. It should pass through the middle of the actual data series. If it doesn't then you've probably made a mistake somewhere in the trend calculations.

CALCULATION OF THE SEASONAL VARIATIONS

The trend values can now be used to determine the quarterly seasonal variations. If we ignore the residual terms which are random and unpredictable by definition then we have:

$$D - T = S$$

That is, we can estimate the seasonal variation in each quarter of the year by removing the trend from the original series. The next step then is simply to calculate a difference – known technically as a deviation – between the actual value and the trend for each quarter. The relevant data is shown in Table 13.4.

Table 13.4
Calculation of the seasonal deviations

Time		Sales	Trend	Deviation from trend
1992	I	86.7		
1992	II	94.9		
1992	III	94.2	98.0	−3.8
1992	IV	106.5	101.3	5.2
1993	I	105.9	103.4	2.5
1993	II	102.4	105.6	−3.2
1993	III	103.1	107.6	−4.5
1993	IV	115.2	109.3	5.9
1994	I	113.7	111.3	2.4
1994	II	108.0	114.8	−6.8
1994	III	113.5	118.6	−5.1
1994	IV	132.9	121.6	11.3
1995	I	126.3	125.0	1.3
1995	II	119.4	128.1	−8.7
1995	III	128.9	130.5	−1.6
1995	IV	142.3	132.4	9.9
1996	I	136.4	132.9	3.5
1996	II	124.6		
1996	III	127.9		

You will see that for each quarter we have calculated the difference (deviation) of the actual sales figure from the trend. A positive deviation implies that actual sales were above the trend (i.e. above the long-run average) whilst a negative deviation implies that actual sales were below the trend. Similarly, the larger the deviation the further away from the trend actual sales were. So, for example, in quarter III of 1992 sales were 3.8 below the trend whilst in quarter IV of 1992 sales were 5.2 above the trend. If we examine these deviations for the fourth quarter of each year, for example, we can also see that there is a repetitive pattern each year in that in each quarter at this time of year there is a large positive deviation. That is, at this time of year sales are always above the trend.

Student activity

Why do you think that the deviations for a given quarter vary from year to year?

We can see from Table 13.4 that these deviations in a particular quarter are not perfectly constant from year to year. The reason for this lies with the R term, the residual element of the series. The deviations include not only the seasonal variation but also any residual or random variation which will vary from year to year. So, for example, although we see that quarter IV sales in each year are always above the trend the amount above the trend differs from one year to the next. Perhaps, for example, in 1994 we had some special promotion or marketing campaign in the run-up to Christmas sales which boosted this quarter's sales even more than usual at this time of the year for a positive deviation of 11.3.

So, given that we are trying to work out an average (or typical) deviation of sales in each quarter, what do we do about this random variation? It seems reasonable to assume that over a number of years such residuals will tend to cancel each other. If, then, we were to take the individual deviations for a particular quarter and average them we can expect this to provide a reasonable estimate of the seasonal variation in this quarter. We can collect the deviations together as in Table 13.5 and calculate the average seasonal deviation.

Table 13.5
Calculation of average seasonal deviation

	1	*2*	*3*	*4*
1992			−3.8	5.2
1993	2.5	−3.2	−4.5	5.9
1994	2.4	−6.8	−5.1	11.3
1995	1.3	−8.7	−1.6	9.9
1996	3.5			
Total	9.7	−18.7	−15.0	32.3
Average deviation	2.425	−6.233	−3.750	8.075

The average (the mean) is calculated by adding together the individual deviations for a specific quarter of the year and dividing by the number of deviations that make up the total. So, for quarter I we add together the deviations in this quarter for 1993, 1994, 1995 and 1996 to give 9.7 and divide by 4 to give an average deviation of 2.425.

Student activity

If you were to add the four average deviations together what total should they give?

In principle they should total to zero. This is because we said that over a 12-month period the seasonal variations should cancel out. In our case they total to 0.517. This does not necessarily mean we have made a mistake but rather is associated with this type of calculation. As you will appreciate for convenience we are dealing with rounded numbers. Because of this and because of the random events that are not included in our calculations it is not unusual for such a non-zero figure to occur. If the deviations do not total to zero we need to make an adjustment to them.

Strictly speaking we now need to force these average deviations to total to zero before we can call them the seasonal variations. We do this quite simply. The sum of the average deviations is 0.517 too high so we need to reduce these deviations by this much so that they total to zero. We do this simply by reducing each average deviation by 1/4 of 0.517. You should be able to see that this will then make sure the four average deviations total to zero.

Quarter	1	2	3	4
Average deviation	2.425	−6.233	−3.750	8.075
Adjustment	−0.129	−0.129	−0.129	−0.129
Seasonal variation	2.296	−6.362	−3.879	7.946

We also see that the adjusted deviations now total to −0.001 which is as close to zero as we need to be.

The interpretation of these values – labelled seasonal variation – is straightforward. Looking at quarter III, for example, we see that, on average, sales fall by 3.879(000) at this time of year only to rise on average by 7.946(000) in the following quarter. These seasonal variations are an indication to management of the typical change in the variable (sales) that occurs at a given time of the year.

The implications of these deviations are important. It implies that there is nothing for management necessarily to worry about if sales in the second quarter of a year, for example, have fallen. We would expect this at this time of the year. Of course, if sales in the second quarter had fallen by more than the seasonal variation management would need to investigate as sales would have fallen by more than usual for the time of year.

SUMMARY OF METHOD

It will be worthwhile summarizing the method we have used so far to produce these calculations. We will need to amend them slightly for other situations as we shall see later but the summary will still be useful here.

Step 1

Graph the time series so you have a visual check on the apparent trend and any apparent seasonal variation. This can be important as it can be easy to make arithmetic errors later in the calculations. It is not unusual for students, for example, to produce a downward sloping trend in their calculations even though it is evident from the graph that the trend should be upward sloping.

Step 2

Calculate a four-period total through the series.

Step 3

Calculate an eight-period total and then a trend by dividing through by 8. Draw a graph showing both the actual variable and its trend (the trend line should more or less go through the middle of the variable over the period).

Step 4

Subtract the trend in each quarter from the actual figure to produce a quarterly deviation.

Step 5

Produce a table of the deviations where the columns are the four quarters. Calculate an average (mean) deviation for each quarter.

Step 6

Total the average deviations. If they do not add to zero you will need to adjust them. Take the total you have calculated, divide by 4 and subtract this from each of the deviations. These are then the seasonal variations in each quarter.

Step 7

Look back at your graphs and your statistics and see if they are consistent and are more or less what you think they should be.

SEASONALLY ADJUSTED SERIES

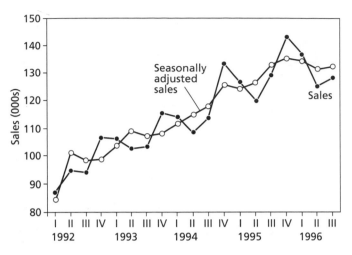

Fig. 13.3   Sales and seasonally adjusted sales

Sometimes, rather than use the seasonal variation statistics we have calculated, management might wish to adjust the original time series to take these seasonal variations into account. This adjusted series is usually referred to as the seasonally adjusted series. This is shown in Table 13.6 and in Fig. 13.3. The original series simply has the appropriate quarter's seasonal variation subtracted from it (remember that if the seasonal variation is negative this will have the effect of making the adjusted series larger than the original).

Table 13.6
Calculation of the seasonally adjusted series

Time		Sales	Seasonal factor	Seasonally adjusted sales (rounded to 1DP)
1992	I	86.7	−2.296	84.4
1992	II	94.9	−(−6.362)	101.3
1992	III	94.2	−(−3.879)	98.1
1992	IV	106.5	−7.946	98.6
1993	I	105.9	−2.296	103.6
1993	II	102.4	−(−6.362)	108.8
1993	III	103.1	−(−3.879)	107.0
1993	IV	115.2	−7.946	107.3
1994	I	113.7	−2.296	111.4
1994	II	108.0	−(−6.632)	114.6
1994	III	113.5	−(−3.879)	117.4
1994	IV	132.9	−7.946	125.0
1995	I	126.3	−2.296	124.0
1995	II	119.4	−(−6.632)	126.0
1995	III	128.9	−(−3.879)	132.8
1995	IV	142.3	−7.946	134.4
1996	I	136.4	−2.296	134.1
1996	II	124.6	−(−6.632)	131.2
1996	III	127.9	−(−3.879)	131.8

All that we have actually done is to adjust (remove) the effects of the seasonal variation from each quarter's sales figure. Effectively we have said that we now know what the effect on sales of each quarter will be (that is after all what the seasonal factor shows). So, if we remove this from the actual sales data we will get a better picture of underlying sales without the distorting effects of the seasonal factors.

In general, for analysis and decision purposes, it is this seasonally adjusted series that we should focus upon for it allows us to examine the longer-term movement in the data without being distracted by temporary seasonal fluctuations. The seasonally adjusted data is more useful as a series than the original figures. These, after all, contain the seasonal fluctuations and make it difficult to decide on the causes of change from one quarter to another. Many government, or official, statistics will be presented both in the original, unadjusted form and in seasonally adjusted form.

In the case of sales of microcomputers we can see a strong upward pattern in sales since 1992. The last three quarters sales however, since 1995 IV are beginning to show cause for concern. Seasonally adjusted sales (that is sales adjusted for the normal seasonal variation) have slowly been decreasing. Management should be made aware of this movement and we would want to investigate further the recent sales of this product to identify the possible causes of such a movement.

USING MONTHLY DATA

Many series are available not only in quarterly but also in monthly form. Calculating the trend and the seasonal factors for a monthly series follows exactly the same process except for the calculation of the trend. In this case we would first work out a moving 12-month total (instead of a four-quarter total) and then add successive pairs of 12-month totals together to calculate a 24-month total which can then be divided by 24 (rather than 8) to provide the trend.

The remaining calculations remain unchanged – we would then subtract the trend from each month's actual figure; we would average these deviations for the same month in each of the years; we would adjust these average monthly deviations if necessary to give seasonal variations for each month; we would then subtract these monthly seasonal variations from each month's actual to give the seasonally adjusted series.

Such calculations, however, are recommended only with a spreadsheet as they are extremely lengthy and tedious. You should also note that whereas we 'lost' two periods of trend values at either end of the series for a quarterly moving average we will 'lose' six periods of trend values at either end of a monthly series.

ADDITIVE AND MULTIPLICATIVE MODELS

The method we have used thus far is referred to as the *additive* model since that the components of the series are literally added together:

$$D = T + S + R$$

There is an alternative model available where the component terms are expressed in multiplication terms (and known logically as the *multiplicative* model):

$$D = T \times S (+ R)$$

In such a case the seasonal factors would now be calculated as:

$$\frac{D}{T} = S$$

The seasonal factors for the multiplicative model will be ratios rather than differences. As ratios they will vary about the value 1.0 and will show the relative seasonal fluctuation. Thus a seasonal factor of, say, 1.08 for a data series using this type of model indicates that the data is 8% above the trend in this period. The sum of such ratios should be 4 for quarterly data and 12 for monthly data, and an adjustment to the ratios so that they total to this value should be made accordingly.

The additive model implies that the seasonal variation around the trend maintains a constant difference. Thus, in our example no matter what the trend we are always adjusting the first quarter of the series by the same amount of seasonal variation. The multiplicative model assumes instead that the seasonal variation is a constant proportion around the trend rather than a constant amount. Accordingly, this model is often more useful in situations where the trend is undergoing considerable change. It may have been more appropriate in the example used in this chapter to use the multiplicative rather than additive model, although for short periods of time there will be little apparent difference in the results. If we had applied the multiplicative model to our data we would have obtained the results shown in Table 13.7.

Table 13.7 shows the calculated deviations from the trend (note that the trend values are exactly the same as before: we still use a moving average value). These are now expressed as ratios around 1 (calculated as D/T) with a ratio less than 1 implying an actual sales figure below the trend and a ratio above 1 implying an actual sales figure above the trend. The deviation for 1992 III, for example, indicates that actual sales are 0.96122 of the trend value.

As before we can collect these deviations for the same quarters in different years together. This is shown in Table 13.8.

If we aggregate the deviations for a given quarter we get the total figure shown. Dividing through by the number of deviations in each column gives the average deviation (shown as 1.020619 for I for example). As usual in the

Table 13.7
Deviations from trend: multiplicative model

Time		Sales	Trend	Deviation
1992	I	86.7		
	II	94.9		
	III	94.2	98.0	0.96122
	IV	106.5	101.3	1.05133
1993	I	105.9	103.4	1.02418
	II	102.4	105.6	0.96970
	III	103.1	107.6	0.95818
	IV	115.2	109.3	1.05398
1994	I	113.7	111.3	1.02156
	II	108.0	114.8	0.94077
	III	113.5	118.6	0.95700
	IV	132.9	121.6	1.09293
1995	I	126.3	125.0	1.01040
	II	119.4	128.1	0.93208
	III	128.9	130.5	0.98774
	IV	142.3	132.4	1.07477
1996	I	136.4	132.9	1.02634
	II	124.6		
	III	127.9		

Table 13.8
Deviations and seasonal variations

Year	I	II	III	IV
1992			0.96122	1.05133
1993	1.02418	0.96970	0.95818	1.05398
1994	1.02156	0.94077	0.95700	1.09293
1995	1.01040	0.93208	0.98774	1.07477
1996	1.02634			
Total	4.082476	2.842547	3.864140	4.273013
Average	1.020619	0.947515	0.966035	1.068253
Adjustment	0.999394	0.999394	0.999394	0.999394
Seasonal variation	1.020001	0.946942	0.965450	1.067606

multiplicative model these average deviations should total to 4.0. In fact they total to 4.002423, 0.002423 too high. So we need to adjust the average deviations. We do this by calculating a ratio of 4/4.002423 and multiplying each average deviation by this adjustment. The adjustment works out at 0.999394 and using this to adjust the average deviation produces the figures shown as seasonal variation. For quarter I, for example, at 1.020001 we see that sales in this quarter are typically 2% higher than the trend whilst in quarter II they are 5.3% below the trend on average.

SUMMARY OF METHOD

Finally, let us review the method for time series analysis taking into account that the periods within the year could be quarterly or monthly and that we might have either the additive or the multiplicative model.

Step 1

Draw a graph of the data over the period to be analysed.

Step 2

From the graph decide whether the additive model or the multiplicative would be more appropriate. The additive is more appropriate when the trend is fairly stable (it looks 'flat' on the graph) whilst the multiplicative is more appropriate where the trend is rising or falling over time.

Step 3

Calculate a centred moving average trend (based on 12-period totals for monthly data and four-period totals for quarterly data).

Step 4

Calculate the deviations from the trend.

- For the additive model subtract the trend from the actual data in each period.
- For the multiplicative model divide the actual data in each period by the trend for that period.

Step 5

Calculate seasonal factors for each period.

- For each period (month/quarter) total the deviations and average.
- Total the average deviations across all the periods. For the additive model the deviations should total to zero. For the multiplicative model the deviations should sum to 4 for quarterly and 12 for monthly series.
- If necessary adjust the average deviations to give the seasonal variation.

Check that the seasonal variations total to zero for the additive model and to 4 or 12 for the multiplicative. It is easy to make an arithmetic mistake in the calculations and this is one way of checking that you have not.

Step 6

Examine the calculated trend and seasonal factors and compare these with your original graph to see that there are no obvious errors or miscalculations.

Step 7

If appropriate calculate the seasonally adjusted series.

- For the additive model subtract the seasonal factor for a given period from the actual value.
- For the multiplicative model divide the actual figure by the seasonal factor for that period.

FORECASTING A TIME SERIES

Management will be interested in the results of such analysis not only in terms of quantifying the trend and the seasonal variations but also in terms of forecasting future values of the variable under analysis. To forecast such a series requires two sets of forecasts:

Forecast of variable = Forecast of trend + Forecast of seasonal variation

That is, in order to forecast a future value for the variable we are analysing we need to forecast a future value for the trend and also a future value for the seasonal variation. For example, suppose we wanted to forecast sales of microcomputers for 1996 IV. We would need to forecast the trend value for this quarter and also forecast the seasonal variation in this quarter.

The forecast of the seasonal variation is quite straightforward. It is generally assumed that the seasonal variation already quantified will remain constant in the immediate future. That is, since we have measured the seasonal factor for quarter IV as +7.946 (using the additive model) then we assume this will also be the seasonal variation for the next fourth quarter (i.e. for 1996 IV). So, all we really have to try and forecast is the trend value for this quarter.

There are a number of sophisticated trend forecasting methods available but they tend to use some fairly complex mathematics. We shall look instead at a method which is fairly reliable as long as the trend is reasonably constant. The method we shall look at is forecasting the trend using regression.

Forecasting the trend using regression

If the trend, or part of it, is relatively linear then regression can be applied, using the technique from the previous chapter. The Y variable consists of the trend values calculated using moving averages (in Table 13.2). The X variable is chosen to represent time. That is, our regression equation will be:

$$Y = f(X)$$

where Y is the trend variable and X is a variable measuring time. If we assume a linear equation then we wish to estimate an equation:

$$Y = a + bX$$

To estimate this equation using regression we have to create a special variable to measure time (the X variable). We do this quite simply. If we set the first time period with a value of 1, the second time period as a value of 2 and so on we will then have a data set as shown below:

		Sales	Trend	Time
1992	I	86.7		
	II	94.9		
	III	94.2	98.0	1
	IV	106.5	101.3	2
1993	I	105.9	103.4	3
	II	102.4	105.6	4
	III	103.1	107.6	5
	IV	115.2	109.3	6
1994	I	113.7	111.3	7
	II	108.0	114.8	8
	III	113.5	118.6	9
	IV	132.9	121.6	10
1995	I	126.3	125.0	11
	II	119.4	128.1	12
	III	128.9	130.5	13
	IV	142.3	132.4	14
1996	I	136.4	132.9	15
	II	124.6		16
	III	127.9		17
	IV			18

Typically, X will take a simple series of values starting at 1, 2, 3, ..., up to t where t is the number of periods for which we have trend values. We see from the table above that X takes a value of 1 in 1992 III (which is the first period for which we have a trend, Y, value) and just increases by 1 each period. We have an X series up to $X = 18$ which is the X value in 1996 IV, the period we wish to forecast for. We can now calculate a regression equation using $X = 1,15$ and Y as the corresponding trend values. The resulting regression output is shown below:

$$Y = 94.96952 + 2.644642X$$

(and we note from the accompanying statistics that the r is 0.995 implying a very high fit of points on the estimated regression line). To forecast the trend in 1996 IV we substitute $X = 18$ into the regression equation:

$$Y = 94.96952 + 2.644642X$$
$$= 94.96952 + 2.644642(18)$$
$$= 142.573$$

That is, we estimate the trend for 1996 IV as 142.573. To forecast sales in this quarter we now take the forecasted trend and the corresponding seasonal factor:

$$\text{Sales forecast} = 142.573 + 7.946 = 150.5 \text{ (to 1 DP)}$$

So, we forecast actual sales in 1996 IV to be 150.5.

Note that we should not expect this forecast to be especially accurate. It assumes that:

- the trend will continue unchanged;
- the seasonal factor will continue unchanged;
- there will be no random or residual element in that quarter.

However, it is an estimate of the future that management can use to help in their decision-making.

Student activity

Suppose we decide instead to use the multiplicative model. What would the sales forecast for 1996 IV have been? What would the sales forecast for 1997 I be?

Using the multiplicative model we still use the same principles. For 1996 IV our trend forecast remains unchanged (since the trend is the same in both models). The seasonal factor for quarter IV is 1.067606 so our sales forecast would be:

Sales forecast = 142.573 × 1.067606 = 152.2 (to 1 DP)

Notice that the forecast from the multiplicative model is slightly different from that from the additive model because of the differing seasonal factors. We must be careful about using what we think is the most appropriate model for the data we are analysing.

Similarly our sales forecast for 1997 I would be:

Trend forecast:

$X = 19$
$Y = 94.96952 + 2.644642X = 145.218$
Sales forecast = 145.218 × 1.020001 = 148.1

SUMMARY

We have seen in this chapter how a time series will typically contain two major influences – a trend and a seasonal pattern. Because management typically wish to ascertain where a change in a variable has occurred it is necessary to be able to quantify both the trend and the seasonal effects. This is done through a process of time series decomposition, breaking the series into its component elements. This allows us to produce a seasonally adjusted set of data which has had the seasonal pattern removed. This allows us to see the underlying patterns in the variable.

Now that you have completed this chapter you will appreciate that:

- It is necessary to apply time series techniques to many business variables which are collected on a quarterly or monthly basis.

- The trend is the underlying long-term movement in the variable and can be estimated using a moving average calculation.
- The seasonal pattern represents the average change that will occur in the variable from one part of the year to another.
- The two common methods of decomposition are the additive and multiplicative models. The additive model is to be preferred where the trend is reasonably stable.
- Both models allow us to produce a seasonally adjusted series for a variable. This is the variable that management should examine to assess fundamental movements in the variable.

EXAMPLE

Finally, let us turn our attention to a real example and illustrate how such a technique might be used. From the *Monthly Digest of Statistics* published by the CSO we have obtained data on two variables:

- the number of passengers uplifted by UK airlines on scheduled domestic flights;
- the number of passengers uplifted by UK airlines on scheduled international flights.

The data covers the period 1987 to 1994 and is on a monthly basis. The data for each month relates to monthly averages and is shown in 000s. We will see the data in a table later but, for example, in January 1987 the figures show 574.2(000) for domestic services and 1,200.3(000) for international services. Effectively, the data shows the number of passengers carried by UK airlines each month on both domestic flights and international flights.

It is not difficult to see why the data might be of interest and why it might be useful to calculate both a trend and the seasonal factors. It is not only the airlines that would be interested in both long-term trends and also seasonal fluctuations but a number of other organizations also. The companies with franchises at the UK airports (duty free shops, food and drink shops, etc.) will have an interest as will the UK Customs and Immigration service!

So, we shall apply our time series technique to the two series. First of all, we shall graph the data to get an overall view of patterns. Figure 13.4 shows a time series graph of the two variables. We see that both series follow a similar, but not identical, pattern over this period, with domestic services below international. We see that domestic services appear to have a fairly 'flat' trend whilst international services appear to have a strong upward trend. We also note that for international services in particular a large drop in passengers uplifted occurred in February 1991.

Our first task is to calculate a suitable trend for both series. Without showing the full calculations Table 13.9 shows the two trends and Fig. 13.5 shows these trends and the actuals.

We see that the two trends are similar. Both show an increasing trend until the middle of 1990 followed by a decline in the trend until the middle of

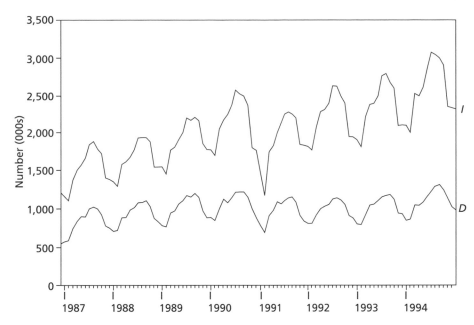

Fig. 13.4   Passengers uplifted: international (I) and domestic (D)

1991 since when the trends have steadily increased (note that we need to be a little careful about making direct comparison between domestic and international because of the different scales used in the diagram). If management are interested in comparing the two trends directly then one ready method is to show the two trends as an index series (as we discussed in Chapter 5).

If we set each trend to a value of 100 in month 7 of 1987 (the first month for which we have a trend value) and calculate an index for each subsequent month we obtain Fig. 13.6. We see that for the first two years the relative trends are quite similar. After 1989, however, although the trends follow a similar profile, in relation to each other they begin to diverge with international showing a much stronger upward growth from 1991 onwards than domestic.

We decide to use the multiplicative model for both sets of calculations and obtain the seasonal variations shown in Tables 13.10 and 13.11. (Notice that this time we are aggregating across the rows rather than down the columns to make it easier given the size of the table.) Both tables show the individual monthly deviations from their respective trends. These have then been averaged across the months, adjusted so that they total to 12 with the final seasonal factor for each month shown.

To facilitate comparison we can show both sets of seasonal factors on a graph, as in Fig. 13.7. We see that the two sets of seasonal factors are extremely similar with both showing seasonal factors above 1 during the summer months (May to October) and below 1 during the rest of the year.

We can also develop a forecast for both series, although we shall illustrate simply with reference to the international series. Referring back to Fig. 13.5, clearly the trend has not been stable over this entire period and it would not be appropriate to estimate a trend using regression for the entire period. However, on closer inspection the trend from January 1993 has remained

Table 13.9
Passengers uplifted and trends

		Domestic	Trend	International	Trend				Domestic	Trend	International	Trend
1987	1	574.2		1,200.3		1991	1		763.0	1,001.0	1,526.3	1,970.2
	2	591.1		1,110.7			2		688.6	993.1	1,164.2	1,946.9
	3	734.3		1,372.5			3		913.9	986.7	1,741.4	1,927.5
	4	830.1		1,503.3			4		969.6	980.6	1,822.1	1,911.2
	5	898.3		1,564.2			5		1,075.9	975.0	1,985.3	1,905.5
	6	900.8		1,664.5			6		1,067.1	971.4	2,095.8	1,909.5
	7	1,013.4	842.9	1,846.2	1,543.8		7		1,102.5	972.1	2,247.7	1,923.7
	8	1,022.5	853.9	1,889.5	1,557.9		8		1,136.4	978.4	2,266.0	1,960.2
	9	1,013.4	865.4	1,794.3	1,574.1		9		1,137.4	983.5	2,246.9	1,998.4
	10	931.9	873.8	1,723.0	1,587.0		10		1,063.1	984.9	2,193.7	2,030.4
	11	787.4	880.0	1,403.9	1,595.3		11		896.1	983.7	1,831.9	2,062.2
	12	751.3	888.6	1,375.2	1,604.0		12		831.0	980.7	1,824.0	2,088.4
1988	1	707.5	896.4	1,355.8	1,612.6	1992	1		803.1	980.5	1,803.6	2,116.9
	2	721.4	901.9	1,294.0	1,618.4		2		800.2	980.7	1,763.5	2,146.9
	3	879.6	908.1	1,578.0	1,626.0		3		925.9	978.5	2,059.6	2,170.3
	4	887.1	915.7	1,606.9	1,637.7		4		990.6	975.0	2,270.8	2,186.7
	5	989.3	923.2	1,661.5	1,650.0		5		1,026.5	973.0	2,300.9	2,198.8
	6	1,015.8	929.9	1,775.7	1,663.4		6		1,045.0	973.8	2,408.4	2,207.8
	7	1,085.7	936.1	1,939.6	1,678.9		7		1,119.4	973.7	2,618.5	2,216.3
	8	1,082.5	940.9	1,935.7	1,693.8		8		1,124.3	972.4	2,615.3	2,221.6
	9	1,102.0	945.5	1,931.2	1,708.3		9		1,097.2	973.6	2,459.3	2,228.9
	10	1,026.3	952.2	1,866.5	1,724.1		10		1,017.2	977.1	2,375.9	2,238.5
	11	871.2	959.2	1,554.7	1,742.5		11		895.9	979.8	1,939.8	2,245.4
	12	829.9	966.0	1,546.3	1,762.7		12		850.2	982.8	1,931.9	2,251.7
1989	1	778.0	973.2	1,557.0	1,782.8	1993	1		781.9	985.8	1,898.8	2,260.1
	2	764.4	979.8	1,451.7	1,802.8		2		788.5	988.1	1,796.5	2,271.8
	3	947.6	986.9	1,767.7	1,824.1		3		967.1	992.1	2,201.2	2,285.5
	4	980.2	995.5	1,797.4	1,848.1		4		1,033.5	997.1	2,361.1	2,300.9
	5	1,063.5	1,004.2	1,910.6	1,872.7		5		1,048.7	1,000.5	2,376.3	2,314.8
	6	1,105.2	1,009.8	2,011.4	1,894.6		6		1,093.8	1,004.2	2,483.9	2,327.2
	7	1,170.1	1,015.4	2,187.3	1,912.8		7		1,143.6	1,009.2	2,745.0	2,341.2
	8	1,156.9	1,023.0	2,168.5	1,932.2		8		1,154.6	1,013.8	2,768.4	2,356.0
	9	1,196.2	1,030.0	2,209.0	1,954.5		9		1,163.5	1,019.2	2,636.1	2,375.7
	10	1,138.5	1,038.6	2,163.6	1,981.8		10		1,070.5	1,022.0	2,568.4	2,392.9
	11	967.7	1,044.4	1,849.4	2,011.1		11		923.2	1,023.3	2,080.3	2,406.9
	12	867.8	1,046.9	1,776.0	2,039.3		12		913.6	1,028.1	2,089.3	2,430.9
1990	1	875.8	1,050.5	1,765.5	2,069.5	1994	1		837.1	1,036.2	2,076.7	2,458.5
	2	848.7	1,054.7	1,708.2	2,099.3		2		845.4	1,046.6	1,975.0	2,481.0
	3	1,030.3	1,057.8	2,045.9	2,124.4		3		1,039.5	1,056.9	2,494.5	2,503.4
	4	1,104.0	1,058.3	2,174.0	2,143.5		4		1,027.2	1,065.4	2,480.1	2,527.2
	5	1,080.1	1,057.8	2,237.0	2,149.7		5		1,086.6	1,073.7	2,595.0	2,548.4
	6	1,147.7	1,056.9	2,362.5	2,147.1		6		1,172.0		2,840.7	
	7	1,213.5	1,051.6	2,560.7	2,136.5		7		1,258.7		3,049.1	
	8	1,215.4	1,040.3	2,512.0	2,103.8		8		1,288.0		3,004.0	
	9	1,211.5	1,028.7	2,467.7	2,068.5		9		1,278.0		2,939.0	
	10	1,134.7	1,018.3	2,362.8	2,041.1		10		1,161.0		2,836.7	
	11	959.5	1,012.5	1,799.9	2,016.0		11		1,030.4		2,321.9	
	12	854.8	1,009.0	1,761.1	1,994.4		12		967.1		2,316.5	

Source: Monthly Digest of Statistics.

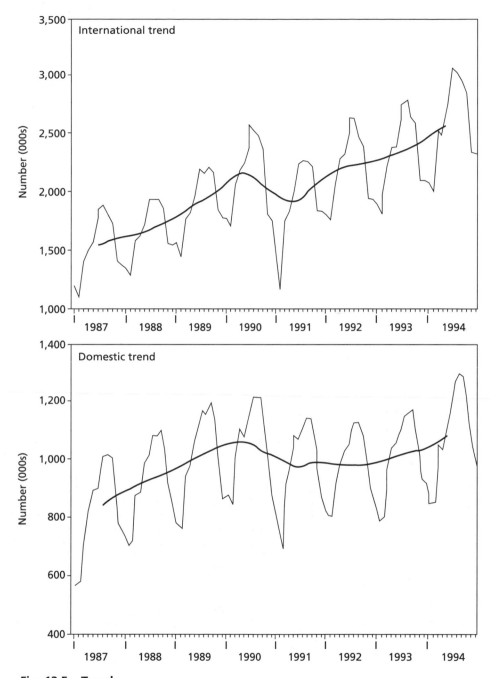

Fig. 13.5   Trends

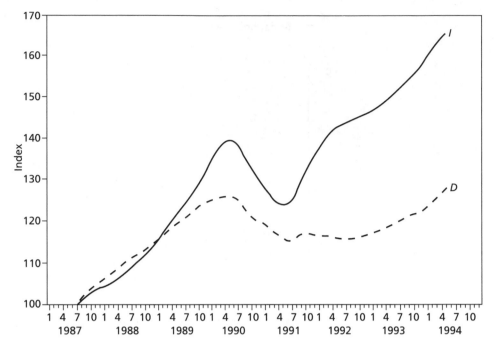

Fig. 13.6   Trend index

**Table 13.10
Seasonal factor calculations: domestic**

Month	Deviations							Average deviation	Adjust-ment	Seas-onal factor
1		0.7893	0.7994	0.8337	0.7622	0.8191	0.7931	0.8079	0.8007	0.9996	0.8004
2		0.7999	0.7801	0.8047	0.6934	0.8159	0.7980	0.8078	0.7857	0.9996	0.7854
3		0.9686	0.9602	0.9740	0.9262	0.9462	0.9748	0.9836	0.9619	0.9996	0.9616
4		0.9687	0.9847	1.0432	0.9887	1.0160	1.0365	0.9641	1.0003	0.9996	0.9999
5		1.0717	1.0591	1.0211	1.1035	1.0549	1.0482	1.0121	1.0529	0.9996	1.0525
6		1.0924	1.0945	1.0859	1.0985	1.0731	1.0892		1.0889	0.9996	1.0885
7	1.2022	1.1598	1.1523	1.1539	1.1342	1.1496	1.1332		1.1550	0.9996	1.1546
8	1.1974	1.1505	1.1309	1.1684	1.1615	1.1562	1.1388		1.1577	0.9996	1.1572
9	1.1710	1.1655	1.1614	1.1777	1.1565	1.1270	1.1415		1.1572	0.9996	1.1568
10	1.0664	1.0778	1.0962	1.1143	1.0794	1.0410	1.0475		1.0747	0.9996	1.0743
11	0.8948	0.9083	0.9265	0.9476	0.9109	0.9144	0.9022		0.9150	0.9996	0.9146
12	0.8455	0.8591	0.8289	0.8472	0.8473	0.8651	0.8886		0.8545	0.9996	0.8542

relatively stable and linear so this was used to produce the regression line for the trend equation:

$$Y = 2,224.957 + 18.02777X$$

with X as the time variable taking a value of 1 from January 1993. The equation has an r value of 0.992. If we wish to produce a forecast for January 1995 (given our data only goes to December 1994) we let $X = 25$ and

Table 13.11
Seasonal factor calculations: international

Month	Deviations							Average deviation	Adjust- ment	Seas- onal factor
1		0.8408	0.8733	0.8531	0.7747	0.8520	0.8401	0.8447	0.8398	1.0001	0.8399
2		0.7996	0.8052	0.8137	0.5980	0.8214	0.7908	0.7961	0.7750	1.0001	0.7750
3		0.9705	0.9691	0.9630	0.9035	0.9490	0.9631	0.9964	0.9592	1.0001	0.9593
4		0.9812	0.9726	1.0142	0.9534	1.0385	1.0262	0.9814	0.9953	1.0001	0.9954
5		1.0070	1.0202	1.0406	1.0419	1.0464	1.0266	1.0183	1.0287	1.0001	1.0288
6		1.0675	1.0617	1.1003	1.0976	1.0909	1.0673		1.0809	1.0001	1.0810
7	1.1959	1.1553	1.1435	1.1986	1.1684	1.1815	1.1725		1.1737	1.0001	1.1738
8	1.2129	1.1428	1.1223	1.1940	1.1560	1.1772	1.1750		1.1686	1.0001	1.1687
9	1.1399	1.1305	1.1302	1.1930	1.1243	1.1034	1.1096		1.1330	1.0001	1.1331
10	1.0857	1.0826	1.0918	1.1576	1.0804	1.0614	1.0734		1.0904	1.0001	1.0905
11	0.8800	0.8922	0.9196	0.8928	0.8883	0.8639	0.8643		0.8859	1.0001	0.8860
12	0.8573	0.8773	0.8709	0.8830	0.8734	0.8580	0.8595		0.8685	1.0001	0.8686

estimate the trend at 2,675.65. Applying the calculated seasonal factor for January of 0.8399 this produces a forecast of international passenger uplifts for January 1995 of 2,244.9. The actual value (from a later edition of *Monthly Digest of Statistics*) was 2,295.7 so we have a forecast error of only 2%, although as ever we should treat such a forecast as indicative on the assumption that trend and seasonal effects remain unchanged and there is no undue random effect in January.

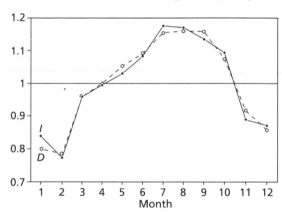

Fig. 13.7   Seasonal factors

SELF-REVIEW QUESTIONS

1 *Why is it necessary to undertake time series analysis?*

2 *What are the three main components of a time series?*

3 *How is the trend estimated?*

4 *Why is it necessary to 'centre' the moving averages?*

5 *How are the seasonal factors determined?*

6 *What is meant by the 'seasonally adjusted' series?*

STUDENT EXERCISES

1   For the example used at the end of this chapter find out what happened in 1991 that affected the number of passengers uplifted by so much.

For the remaining exercises in this chapter you are advised to use a spreadsheet to perform the calculations (the data files are available on the accompanying data disk). For each set of data you should:

- graph the data;
- decide on whether the additive or multiplicative model is preferred;
- calculate the trend;
- calculate the seasonal factors;
- comment on the trend and seasonal factors in the context of the problem;
- produce a forecast of the variable for a future time period then collect data on the variable from published sources to assess how accurate your forecast was (and what may have caused it to be different from the actual value that occurred).

All data has been taken from the *Monthly Digest of Statistics*.

2   The data below relates to the UK and shows the number of live births, marriages and registered deaths:

		Live births (000)	Marriages (000)	Deaths (000)
1989	1	189.4	54.7	169.9
1989	2	199.5	110.5	155.8
1989	3	198.6	155.9	143.1
1989	4	189.8	70.7	188.9
1990	1	191.3	52.9	177.8
1990	2	202.4	114.3	154.3
1990	3	207.5	138.7	143.5
1990	4	197.3	62.7	166.3
1991	1	194.5	45.6	179.5
1991	2	199.2	101.9	155.8
1991	3	205.9	146.2	143.6
1991	4	192.9	62.3	167.3
1992	1	195.8	41.7	176.8
1992	2	198.7	100.5	149.7
1992	3	201.5	138.5	142.8
1992	4	185.0	60.9	161.9
1993	1	184.4	41.7	172.8
1993	2	192.1	100.5	155.1
1993	3	198.7	138.5	145.7
1993	4	186.6	60.9	184.0
1994	1	188.0		
1994	2	190.0		
1994	3			
1994	4			

3 The data below relates to England and Wales and shows notifiable offences recorded by the police, as a total, those classed as burglary and those classed as theft and handling stolen goods.

		Total offences (000)	Burglary (000)	Theft (000)
1988	1	971.2	229.6	499.5
1988	2	925.7	198.0	484.6
1988	3	887.4	184.0	468.1
1988	4	931.6	206.1	479.1
1989	1	942.2	213.3	479.6
1989	2	947.8	192.7	499.1
1989	3	957.0	192.3	505.2
1989	4	1,023.8	227.7	528.8
1990	1	1,080.9	252.3	555.2
1990	2	1,111.3	231.6	586.3
1990	3	1,110.3	233.4	590.5
1990	4	1,241.0	289.5	642.4
1991	1	1,251.1	298.9	649.3
1991	2	1,326.2	292.0	701.1
1991	3	1,315.0	289.3	703.8
1991	4	1,383.8	339.2	706.9
1992	1	1,392.9	347.5	704.6
1992	2	1,376.7	313.9	716.5
1992	3	1,363.4	316.4	707.5
1992	4	1,458.8	377.5	723.1
1993	1	1,448.3	380.7	708.9
1993	2	1,406.4	336.5	714.2
1993	3	1,349.4	315.6	687.8
1993	4	1,322.1	336.8	641.0
1994	1	1,360.2	341.6	651.3
1994	2	1,333.9	310.6	652.8
1994	3	1,246.4	281.5	625.2
1994	4	1,310.8	324.3	629.7

How reliable do you think the trend for total offences will be in terms of representing the level of crime in England and Wales?

4 The data below shows sales by the gas and public electricity supply systems in the UK to industrial customers and to domestic customers.

		Gas		Electricity	
		Industrial	Domestic	Industrial	Domestic
		million therms	million therms	tera watt hours	tera watt hours
1988	1				
1988	2	1,256	1,810	23.10	19.69
1988	3	1,037	1,128	22.16	17.80
1988	4	1,411	3,221	24.21	26.28
1989	1	1,517	3,766	24.80	28.04
1989	2	1,356	1,881	24.08	20.19
1989	3	1,077	962	23.09	17.20
1989	4	1,568	3,305	24.29	26.84
1990	1	1,709	3,742	25.02	28.30
1990	2	1,260	1,827	24.32	20.21
1990	3	1,088	1,098	23.43	17.73
1990	4	1,621	3,584	25.40	27.56
1991	1	1,658	4,332	25.66	30.64
1991	2	1,244	2,253	23.51	21.76
1991	3	1,031	996	23.48	17.68
1991	4	1,514	3,814	24.21	28.02
1992	1	1,544	4,208	24.79	30.61
1992	2	1,175	1,867	23.54	20.56
1992	3	1,175	1,189	22.82	18.78
1992	4	1,861	3,999	23.09	29.35
1993	1	2,035	4,264	23.61	30.03
1993	2	1,833	1,852	22.85	21.55
1993	3	1,810	1,268	22.91	19.08
1993	4	2,512	4,222	24.39	29.74
1994	1	2,721	4,475	24.76	31.16
1994	2	2,262	2,147	23.78	20.92
1994	3	2,112	1,109	22.09	19.69
1994	4	2,668	3,513	23.82	28.30

5 The data below shows road casualties in Great Britain in terms of the total number, those killed and those involving pedal cyclists. How do you think the data might be used to assess the impact of a government campaign to improve road safety for pedal cyclists?

		Total	Killed	Pedal cyclists
1989	1			
1989	2	83,305	1,186	7,660
1989	3	87,747	1,422	8,800
1989	4	92,712	1,533	6,199
1990	1	81,015	1,278	5,609
1990	2	84,522	1,254	7,188
1990	3	87,051	1,267	7,804
1990	4	88,553	1,418	5,821
1991	1	70,217	969	4,643
1991	2	77,702	1,047	6,586
1991	3	81,667	1,203	8,304
1991	4	81,683	1,349	5,270
1992	1	71,756	971	4,738
1992	2	75,395	1,004	7,179
1992	3	80,185	1,078	7,299
1992	4	83,337	1,176	5,539
1993	1	67,179	850	4,657
1993	2	76,513	900	6,806
1993	3	79,566	947	7,345
1993	4	82,762	1,117	5,260
1994	1	73,496	878	4,788
1994	2	74,942	793	6,520
1994	3	79,313	930	7,719
1994	4	87,438	1,049	5,786

6 The data below shows the number of new registrations of vehicles for two types: private cars and goods vehicles.

		Private cars (000)	Goods vehicles (000)
1989	1	209.4	9.3
	2	192.3	8.8
	3	213.3	10.1
	4	186.2	10.1
	5	192.1	9.9
	6	167.8	8.6
	7	48.0	2.8
	8	491.7	8.2
	9	164.3	6.4
	10	147.7	4.8
	11	141.1	4.4
	12	87.4	2.8
1990	1	199.7	4.3
	2	161.6	4.1
	3	202.5	4.6
	4	155.8	4.4
	5	167.6	3.6
	6	136.8	3.7
	7	43.0	1.9
	8	421.5	5.4
	9	148.8	3.9
	10	125.8	3.0
	11	115.6	3.0
	12	63.6	2.1
1991	1	159.6	2.7
	2	119.0	2.3
	3	166.0	3.0
	4	116.0	2.3
	5	113.7	2.2
	6	94.0	2.3
	7	33.5	1.1
	8	358.3	3.5
	9	121.0	2.4
	10	99.0	2.7
	11	98.0	2.2
	12	59.3	1.9

		Private cars (000)	Goods vehicles (000)
1992	1	146.0	2.1
	2	105.0	2.1
	3	137.7	3.0
	4	129.5	2.2
	5	116.6	2.0
	6	97.6	2.4
	7	30.5	1.3
	8	363.8	3.8
	9	114.7	2.5
	10	105.3	2.8
	11	102.4	2.5
	12	78.9	2.0
1993	1	157.9	2.1
	2	120.9	2.3
	3	152.2	2.5
	4	127.3	2.4
	5	128.8	2.4
	6	105.6	2.6
	7	33.7	1.2
	8	424.4	4.6
	9	128.0	4.5
	10	121.5	2.6
	11	122.2	3.2
	12	72.1	2.1
1994	1	190.0	2.5
	2	137.0	2.7
	3	172.9	3.7
	4	134.0	2.9
	5	141.0	3.1
	6	124.2	3.2
	7	31.9	1.4
	8	434.1	5.9
	9	135.8	4.0
	10	116.4	4.2
	11	121.2	4.6
	12	70.4	3.0
1995	1	179.7	3.9
	2	144.5	3.9
	3	169.2	4.4
	4	126.5	4.4
	5	144.0	3.6

14 BUSINESS MATHEMATICS: FINANCIAL DECISIONS

INTRODUCTION

In this, the final, chapter we turn our attention to the use of mathematical techniques in the area of business finance and financial decision-making. It will not have escaped your attention that much of business decision-making is concerned with money. Organizations – and the people who manage them – are often concerned with finance in one form or another. Businesses generate profits and have to determine where that profit should be invested for maximum return. Finance needs to be arranged to support investment plans and alternative sources of finance must be compared and evaluated. Public sector organizations must strive to provide quality services at minimum cost. Much of the financial mathematics covered in this chapter is based on the idea of interest and it is with this that we begin. Later in the chapter we shall see how such interest calculations can be applied to projects and decisions. The purpose of this chapter is not to turn you into an accountant but rather to develop understanding of key concepts and techniques used in financial decision-making.

The use of logarithms and anti-logarithms is essential for a number of the calculations in this chapter. Go back and read the appropriate part of Chapter 2 if you're not sure about these.

> UP TO
> 8.8% P.A.
> TAX FREE
> INCOME

LEARNING OBJECTIVES

By the end of this chapter you should be able to:

- explain the terms investment, return and interest;
- calculate compound interest;
- calculate effective interest rates;
- explain the difference between nominal and effective interest rates;
- explain what is meant by discounting;
- calculate present values;
- apply discounting principles to calculate the net present value of an investment project.

INVESTMENTS, RETURN AND INTEREST

The basic principles of many financial decisions are based on some simple ideas with which you are probably already familiar. Some of the terms that are used, however, may not be familiar and it is important to understand the terminology that is used in financial decision-making as well as the principles involved in the relevant calculations.

We begin by introducing three key terms:

- investment;
- return;
- interest.

Corporate Bond PEP 8·5%

In very general terms an investment is an amount of money allocated to a particular purpose or to a particular project. As individuals, for example, we might invest some of our savings into a bank or building society. A business might invest some of its income into the construction of a new factory or the purchase of new equipment. A hospital might invest in a new X-ray machine. A college or school might invest in more PCs for students to use. Underpinning the idea of an investment, however, is the notion of a return on that investment – often (but not always) expressed in terms of a monetary return. That is, as individuals or as a business we might expect to have a sum of money returned to us at some time in the future that was larger than the sum of money we originally invested.

8% TREASURY STOCK

Student activity

For your birthday someone gives you a present of £500. You decide that you do not need the money at the moment so you go to your local building society and put the money into a savings account. Next year you decide that you would like to use the money to go on holiday. You go to the building society, ask for your money back and the building society gives you £550.

What was the size of the financial return? How much interest will your investment earn, both in £s and as a percentage?

The amount you originally put into the account would be the investment: £500. The amount of money the building society gives you – £550 – is the financial return on your investment. In this case the return is £50 greater than your original investment. What you have effectively done for the past year is to give the building society the use of your money: the £500. During this time the building society has been able to use the money for its own purposes – perhaps investing in the stock market, lending the money to another individual. By allowing the building society to use your money during this period you would probably expect some reward or incentive.

Typically this incentive is provided by the building society in the form of *interest*: a payment made in return for the loan of a sum of money, here £50 or 10% of the initial investment (of £500). The principle behind this reward is that you have 'sacrificed' your £500 for a year. After all you could have used it now to go on holiday rather than wait a year (with the associated concept that you have 'sacrificed' your holiday for a year). In giving the money to the building society you have made an investment. It is reasonable to expect a financial return on this investment given the implicit sacrifice you have made (otherwise why would you bother making the sacrifice in the first place?).

In the case of many investments this return is the interest paid on the investment. Let us suppose that the building society offers to pay you interest of 10% per year, usually written as *per annum* or 10% p.a. At the end of the first year you would expect an interest payment on your investment of £500 of 10%. That is:

10% of £500 = £50

This £50 would be the interest on your investment with the building society. Let us suppose that you decide to leave the original £500 *and* the interest of £50 in the building society account for a second year.

Student activity

How much interest would you expect at the end of the second year?

The answer to this is: it depends on what type of interest the building society is paying. We must distinguish between what is known as *compound interest* and *simple interest*.

SIMPLE AND COMPOUND INTEREST

In general there are two such types of interest payment:

- simple interest where interest is paid only on the original investment;
- compound interest where interest is paid both on the original investment and any interest from previous years added to the investment.

If it were simple interest you would get:

Investment: £500
Year 1 interest: £50
Year 2 interest: £50

and so on.

If it were compound interest you would get:

Investment: £500
Year 1 interest: £50
Year 2 interest: £55 , made up of £50 on the original investment and 10% interest on the Year 1 interest (i.e. 10% of £50).

Student activity

Construct a simple table with Years 1 to 5 as the rows. Show one column as the value of the investment each year assuming simple interest and the second column assuming compound interest.

The simple interest calculation is straightforward: interest is £50 per year. For compound interest it will be helpful to show the actual interest earned each year as well:

Year		Simple interest		Compound interest	
		Investment	*Interest*	*Investment*	*Interest*
1		500	50	500	50
2		550	50	550	55
3		600	50	605	60.50
4		650	50	665.50	66.55
5		700	50	732.10	73.21
End year	5	750		805.31	

For simple interest we have interest at £50 a year for five years giving a total return of £750 (£500 + £250 interest). For compound interest the total return is £805.31 (£500 + £305.31 interest), considerably higher. Notice also that the amount of investment + interest at the end of one year is the investment at the start of the following year.

Clearly, for more complex problems we do not want to have to resort to these step-by-step calculations for interest each year. We can, however, use the principles of compound interest to produce a number of useful formulae that provide shortcuts to many compound interest calculations that we might want to make. What we have in our example is:

Original investment: £500
Interest for Year 1:
    10% of £500 or 0.1(500)   with the rate of interest as a decimal

giving at the end of year 1:

$$£500 + 0.1(£500) = £550$$

We can rearrange this as: $£500(1 + 0.1)$ which is obviously equal to $£550$ but written in a different way. At the end of year 2 we would then have:

$$£550 + 0.1(£550) = £605$$

That is the amount we had invested at the end of year 1 ($£550$) and the interest earned during year 2 ($£55$). This can be rewritten as $£550(1 + 0.1)$. But $£550$ is exactly the same as $£500(1 + 0.1)$ that we wrote earlier so we can write:

$$£550(1 + 0.1)$$

as: $£500(1 + 0.1)(1 + 0.1)$

or: $£500(1 + 0.1)^2$

Student activity

Find an expression like the last one showing how we would calculate compound interest for the end of year 3.

At the start of year 3 (end of year 2) our investment was $£605$ so at the end of year 3 we would have:

$$£605(1 + 0.1)$$

or: $£500(1 + 0.1)^3$

A pattern to the calculations begins to emerge. We had:

Year 1 $£500(1 + 0.1)$
Year 2 $£500(1 + 0.1)^2$
Year 3 $£500(1 + 0.1)^3$

and it doesn't take a mathematical genius to figure out how we would calculate the total for year 4.

You will probably see that we could quite easily develop this formula for any year we wanted and it would give us the amount of our investment at the end of that year. If we use the following symbols:

P: the principal, or original investment
V: the future value of the investment
r: the rate of interest as a decimal
t: the number of years we invest

we can write a general formula:

$$V = P(1 + r)^t$$

for calculating the future value of any investment at any rate of interest for any number of years. Check this carefully for the specific formula we had for years 1, 2, 3 to convince yourself that it is the same.

Student activity

Resisting the temptation to spend the money you decide that you are going to leave your investment of £500 in the building society account for the next five years. What will the investment have increased to at the end of this time, assuming compound interest rates don't change?

Using the formula we have the following values:

$P = £500$
$r = 0.1$
$t = 5$

and then:

$$V = 500(1.1)^5$$

To work this out we must use logarithms. Using a calculator we take the logarithm of 1.1 (as 0.04139268515 on my calculator) and multiply this by 5 (to give 0.20696342579) and then take the anti-log of this number (often shown on a calculator as 10^x) to give 1.61051. This is the value of $(1.1)^5$. If we now multiply £500 by 1.61051 we get £805.26 which will be the return on your investment of £500 after five years at 10% p.a. compound interest.

The formula we have developed can easily be rearranged to allow us to perform related but different calculations. Suppose that we know that in five years' time we will need to spend £20,000 – perhaps to buy a new car, or to replace a machine in a factory. We have the opportunity of investing a sum of money now at 8% per annum interest. How much do we need to invest now so that our investment will be worth £20,000 in five years? The information we have is:

$r = 0.08$
$t = 5$
$V = £20,000$

and P is unknown.

So we know three of the four variables in the formula we have been using. If we rearrange the formula we can use it to calculate P. We have:

$$V = P(1 + r)^t$$

or rearranging by dividing through by $(1 + r)^t$ we get:

$$P = \frac{V}{(1 + r)^t}$$

This allows us to calculate P if we know the value of the other three variables (which we do). Here we have:

$$P = \frac{20,000}{(1 + 0.08)^5} = \frac{20,000}{1.4693281} = £13,611.66$$

That is if we invest £13,611.66 now at 8% per annum for five years the investment will have increased to £20,000 in five years' time. Clearly for a business which knows that it will need to replace equipment at some time in the future or that it will need to have access to a sum of money for repaying a loan the formula can be very helpful for indicating how much money needs to be invested now in order to generate a sufficient sum in the future to buy the replacement equipment.

We can also use our formula in a third way. Suppose you have £2,000 available now that you can afford to invest. However, you also know that in three years' time you want to go on a round-the-world trip which, you estimate, will cost you £3,000 in total. What return on your investment will you need to be able to afford the trip? This time we know:

$$P = 2,000$$
$$V = 3,000$$
$$t = 3$$

and it is now r which is unknown. We had:

$$V = P(1 + r)^t$$

If we divide through by P:

$$V/P = (1 + r)^t$$

If we take the t root of both sides:

$$\sqrt[t]{(V/P)} = (1 + r)$$

and subtracting 1 from each side gives:

$$\sqrt[t]{(V/P)} - 1 = r$$

Substituting the values we know (V, P, t) we then get:

$$\sqrt[3]{(3,000/2,000)} - 1 = r$$
$$\sqrt[3]{1.5} - 1 \qquad = r$$

We now take the log of 1.5 (0.17609125905), divide by 3 (0.05869708635) and take the anti-log to get 1.1447 as the value of $\sqrt[3]{1.5}$. From this we subtract 1 to get 0.1447 as the value of r as 14.47%. That is, you need an investment with a rate of interest of almost 15% if your £2,000 is to be worth £3,000 in three years' time.

With this sort of complex calculation it is worth checking your answer by reference to the original formula using $P = 2,000$, $r = 0.1447$ and $t = 3$ (you should of course get £3,000 as the answer).

In summary then we can find:

$$V = P(1 + r)^t$$

or: $$P = \frac{V}{(1 + r)^t}$$

or: $$r = \sqrt[t]{(V/P)} - 1$$

where:

P: the principal, or original investment;
V: the future value of the investment;
r: the rate of interest as a decimal;
t: the number of years we invest.

NOMINAL AND EFFECTIVE INTEREST

However, not all investments involve interest payments which are annual. Interest on an investment or on an amount borrowed may be calculated semi-annually, quarterly, monthly or even daily. Let us consider your investment of £500 that we started with at the beginning of the chapter. We saw that after five years at a rate of 10% it would have increased to £805.26 with the interest added at the end of each year. However, suppose the building society now added interest to your account not at the end of the year but at the end of each month. How would this affect the return on your investment at the end of five years?

The formula we derived for calculating future values can still be used but we need to alter the values we use for r and t to take into account we are now getting interest monthly rather than annually. r at 10% p.a. is the same as 1/12 of this each month or 0.00833% per month as a decimal. t refers to the number of periods interest is added. We have five years of 12 months so t will be 60. This then gives:

$$V = 500(1.00833)^{60} = £822.49$$

You can see that, because interest is now paid monthly, we use a monthly interest rate and there are now 60 months when interest is added to the account. The future value of the investment is now higher because the interest earned by the investment is being added every month rather than every year and this interest will in turn attract interest for the rest of the five-year period.

5.60%
5.7% APR
(variable)

In such a situation it can be helpful to distinguish between the *nominal* rate of interest and the *effective* rate of interest. The rate of 10% p.a. is known as the nominal rate. The rate actually earned over the year is known as the effective rate or as the annual percentage rate (APR). You may well see the APR figure quoted in advertisements exhorting people to borrow money or take out credit to finance their consumer purchases. The APR can be calculated using the formula:

$$APR = (1 + \underline{r})^t - 1$$
$$t$$

where r is the nominal rate;

t is the number of periods per year that interest is paid.

Student activity

Using the formula calculate the APR in the last example.

In this example we have:

$t = 12$ (the number of periods per year interest is paid)
$r = 0.10$ (10% as a decimal) the nominal rate

and we then calculate:

$$APR = (1 + \frac{0.10}{12})^{12} - 1$$

$$= (1 + .00833)^{12} - 1$$

$$= 1.1047 - 1$$

$$= 0.1047 \text{ or } 10.47\%$$

The effective or annual rate of interest earned on the account is, then, 10.47%.

It is important to understand properly what the APR figure shows. It indicates that an investment paying 10% p.a. interest on a monthly basis and an investment paying 10.47% p.a. on an annual basis are actually the same. It would not matter which investment we made. Both would produce the same future value at the end of the year.

A similar process applies to money borrowed. You may well see, for example, a bank advertising loans for 10% p.a. interest but with a different, and higher, APR quoted (say 12.3%). The reason for this is as follows. Suppose you borrow £1,200 for a year. You will be charged £120 interest so in total you will have to repay the bank £1,320 (£1,200 + £120). However, your repayments will almost certainly be spread through the year rather than be just one payment in 12 months' time. If we assume 12 equal repayments over the year this means that at the end of the first month you will repay the bank £100, at the end of the second month another £110 and so on. What this actually means is that, although you borrowed £1,200, you actually only had the use of this money for the first month. Since you had to pay some of it back at the end of the first month you have the use of less than £1,200 in month 2, less again in month 3 and so on. Effectively this means that you are paying more than 10% interest since, although the amount of interest is constant at £120, it represents more than 10% on the average amount of the loan you actually have over the whole year.

DISCOUNTING

Interest rate calculations are particularly important to financial decisions which relate to a project or an investment taking place over a period of time. The manager needs to be able to compare the financial consequences of one investment with those of another to decide which is preferable. The principle behind such decision-making is the concept of *present value* and we shall examine what present value means, how it is calculated and how it is used in decision-making.

TIME AND PREFERENCE

One important concept at the heart of present value is what is known as *time preference*: given a free choice and other things being equal we would normally prefer a sum of money now to the same amount of money at some stage in the future. Suppose a relative offers to give you £250 now or £250 in one year. Which would you choose and why?

You will almost certainly decide to take the £250 now. There will be a number of factors which will influence your decision:

- You may want the cash now because you have something specific you want to spend it on or because you need to pay some outstanding bills.
- You might think prices will rise over the next year making the £250 in a year's time worth less in terms of what it will buy.
- There may be uncertainty about the future. Can you be sure that you would get the £250 next year and that your relative wouldn't change their mind?

Unit trust savings schemes vs lump sum investment – value at September 1, 1995 of £1,000 after 3, 5 and 10 years

Unit trust sector	Investment route	3 years	5 years	10 years
UK general	Monthly savings*	1,137	1,298	1,671
	Lump sum	**1,595**	**1,710**	**3,274**
UK equity income	Monthly savings	1,141	1,305	1,686
	Lump sum	**1,655**	**1,687**	**3,541**
UK growth	Monthly savings	1,143	1,309	1,625
	Lump sum	**1,640**	**1,694**	**3,224**
UK smaller cos.	Monthly savings	1,197	1,401	1,633
	Lump sum	**1,784**	**1,776**	**3,281**
International growth	Monthly savings	1,114	1,319	1,639
	Lump sum	**1,716**	**1,770**	**3,069**
Japan	Monthly savings	1,001	1,125	1,284
	Lump sum	**1,640**	**1,257**	**3,176**
North America	Monthly savings	1,199	1,484	1,912
	Lump sum	**1,864**	**2,359**	**2,882**
Europe	Monthly savings	1,186	1,362	1,743
	Lump sum	**1,712**	**1,587**	**3,811**
Building society deposits	*Monthly savings*	*1,048*	*1,099*	*1,324*
	Lump sum	*1,099*	*1,264*	*1,843*

Footnotes: *Monthly savings = £50; investments are on an offer-to-bid basis, with net income reinvested
Sources: Autif, HSW, Micropal, Investment Intelligence

FT Source: *Financial Times*, 20 October 1995

However, the most important point influencing our decision is that of *time preference*: having the money *now* allows us to buy things with it that we can enjoy over the next 12 months. Alternatively we could take the £250 now and invest it so that it would be worth more than £250 in one year. In a case like this our decision as to what to do is a fairly easy one. In other cases it might be more difficult.

Student activity

Your relative now tempts you with either £250 now or £260 in one year. What would your decision be?

This time our decision is not quite as easy. If we had decided originally to wait a year before getting the money we would have received no 'reward' for sacrificing the use of the £250 in the intervening year. Now, however, we are getting such a reward – an extra £10 if we're willing to 'sacrifice' the £250 for a year. The difficulty we now have is to decide whether this sacrifice/reward is worthwhile.

Let us consider the alternatives. We could take the £250 now and invest it in a building society account. If we do this it would earn interest over the next 12 months. If we decide to take the £260 in one year we will have sacrificed the interest we could have earned on the original £250. This suggests that a comparison would help us choose between the two alternatives. Suppose the current interest rate offered by building societies is 5% p.a. If we took the £250 now and invested it then it would be worth £262.50 in one year (250 × 1.05). The alternative is to wait and get £260 in one year. Clearly we would decide to take money now since the 'reward' being offered of an extra £10 in one year's time is not enough (but of course we are ignoring all the other factors that we listed earlier which might influence the decision). We can use the rate of interest in this way to help us decide what to do in simple situations like this.

It may also have occurred to you that our decision will be affected by the rate of interest that we could earn.

Student activity

Assume the rate of interest were 4% (not 5%). Would this affect your decision to take the £250 now (forgetting all other possible factors). What about if the interest rate were 3%?

If we conveniently forget about all other factors except time preference then at a rate of interest of 4% the £250 now would have grown to £260 (250 × 1.04) in one year's time: exactly the same as we are being offered anyway. Purely on a time preference basis we would be indifferent as to whether we got £250 now or £260 in a year (although of course no one but an idiot would forget about all the other possible influences as to which choice to take). If the interest rate were 3% then £250 now would have increased to £257.50 in a year (250 × 1.03). In such a case – forgetting all other factors – then it would be better to take the £260 in a year's time rather than the £250 now.

PRESENT VALUE

To help us choose between financial alternatives we do not want to have to perform interest rate calculations like that in the last activity. For complex problems these can be quite awkward. What we can do instead is to calculate something known as the *present value* of a future sum of money. Consider the £260 in one year's time. We can ask the question: what is the value of this future sum of money now (i.e. in the present)? Or, put another way, what sum would we be prepared to accept now instead of £260 in a year's time?

We can use the principles of interest rate calculations to help us. We can approach the question by saying: let us calculate the sum of money we would have to invest now (at *present*) for this to be worth £260 in one year. Obviously in order to do this we need to know the interest rate. Let us suppose the interest rate is 5%. Then we can use the present value formula:

$$PV = \frac{V}{(1 + r)^t}$$

to work out the present value (PV). You will see that this is effectively the same as one of the formulae that we used in the previous section. V represents the sum of money in the future; r is the interest rate and t the number of years in the future we are calculating. Here we would have:

$$PV = \frac{V}{(1 + r)^t}$$
$$= \frac{260}{(1.05)^1} = £247.62$$

So the present value of £260 in one year's time is £247.62. This means that if we had £247.62 *now* it would be worth exactly the same to us as £260 in one year's time, with a current rate of interest of 5%.

You can probably see how we can use this PV. If we were offered £247.62 now or £260 in one year we would not be bothered which we chose since both are effectively worth the same. However, in our original problem we were offered not £247.62 now but £250. Since the sum we are offered now is worth more than the PV of the alternative (£260 in one year) it would be logical to choose the sum now: the £250. So, the calculation of the PV of a future sum can help us choose between alternatives.

459

This may seem a complex and laborious approach to what is quite a simple choice. However, we shall shortly be looking at more complex situations and it is important that you understand what the PV measures and how we use it to compare alternatives and make a choice between those alternatives.

Student activity

What is the present value of £270 in two years' time at a rate of interest of 5%?

The calculation uses the formula as before:

$$V = £270$$
$$r = 0.05$$
$$t = 2$$
$$PV = \frac{270}{(1.05)^2} = £244.90$$

That is, the present value of £270 in two years' time is £244.90. If we were now offered a choice simply between £260 in one year and £270 in two years' time then we would choose to have £260 in one year since its PV is higher than the alternative: 247.62 as against 244.90.

Discount factors

Another way of describing the calculation we have just performed is discounting: reducing the future sum of money back to the present using the current interest rate.

Sometimes the formula for PV is shown in a slightly different way:

$$PV = V \times \frac{1}{(1 + r)^t}$$

where the term:

$$\frac{1}{(1 + r)^t}$$

is known as the *discount factor*: the factor by which we multiply a future sum to obtain its present value.

Obviously the calculation would give the same answer as before as it is simply presented in another format. The discount factor for year 1 with r at 5% (0.05) would be:

$$\frac{1}{(1 + r)^t} = \frac{1}{(1.05)} = 0.95238$$

and for year 2 would be:

$$\frac{1}{(1 + r)^t} = \frac{1}{(1.05)^2} = 0.90703$$

We would then use these discount factors to calculate the present values:

PV of £260:
260 × 0.95238 = 247.62

PV of £270:
270 × 0.90703 = 244.90

Sometimes in exam questions the discount factors may be provided without you having to calculate them. This also explains why the calculation is often referred to as *discounting* a cash value – we are discounting a future sum back to the present.

INVESTMENT APPRAISAL

To help us see the importance of PV calculations we shall use the following example. A company is considering purchasing a new machine for use in the production of some product. It is estimated that the machine will have a useful life of five years and at the end of that time will have to be scrapped at a zero value. The machine is estimated to save £3,000 a year in staff costs. The firm also has the option of either buying the machine outright at a cost of £10,000 or of leasing the machine from the supplier. Leasing would cost the firm £1,000 now and then £2,000 a year for the next five years. The firm is trying to decide:

(a) whether acquiring the machine is worthwhile at all;
(b) if it is worthwhile, should it buy or should it lease?

Assume the current rate of interest is 6% p.a.

The way we can start to answer this is to consider the alternative use of the money that would be spent either buying or leasing the machine. After all the company could simply invest this money in a bank or building society and earn 6% interest for the next five years. The alternative use of the money is to buy the equipment and reduce staff costs. We can use the principles of present value to evaluate the investment opportunity.

Cash flows

The first thing we need to do is to show the financial consequences of the project in the form of what is known as a *cash flow* table. Such a table brings together and shows over the five-year period:

- the cash inflows – cash coming into the business, or savings in expenditure as a result of the investment;
- the cash outflows – cash being spent by the business or going out of the business as a result of the investment.

461

The difference between the two – cash inflows less cash outflows – is known as the *net cash flow*. We can then use this net cash flow information to try to reach a decision.

Let us illustrate just by looking at the option of buying the equipment. We can work out the appropriate flows for each year of the investment. At the beginning of the project – the present time – we have a cash outflow of £10,000 and no cash inflows since the firm will have to spend £10,000 *now* on buying the machine. Net cash flow will then be –£10,000. Conventionally we denote this period – the present – as Year 0. This would give:

Year	Cash inflow £	Cash outflow £	Net cash flow £
0	0	10,000	−10,000

For year 1, the next time period, the cash inflow will represent the labour cost savings. We are told that these are estimated at £3,000 over the next year. There are no cash outflows in year 1 so the net cash flow will be £3,000. The cash flow table then is:

Year	Cash inflow £	Cash outflow £	Net cash flow £
0		10,000	−10,000
1	3,000	0	3,000

You can see how we are building up the table year by year. The calculations for years 2–5 are the same and the completed table is then:

Year	Cash inflow £	Cash outflow £	Net cash flow £
0		10,000	−10,000
1	3,000	0	3,000
2	3,000	0	3,000
3	3,000	0	3,000
4	3,000	0	3,000
5	3,000	0	3,000
Total	15,000	10,000	5,000

We have assumed that the staff cost savings occur at the end of each year to make the calculation easier. In practice they would occur continuously. We see from the table that the project generates a net cash flow of £5,000 after five years, that is the total savings are £5,000 more than the cost.

Student activity

Construct a similar table for the leasing option.

For the leasing option the table would be as follows:

Year	Cash inflow £	Cash outflow £	Net cash flow £
0		1,000	−1,000
1	3,000	2,000	1,000
2	3,000	2,000	1,000
3	3,000	2,000	1,000
4	3,000	2,000	1,000
5	3,000	2,000	1,000
Total	15,000	11,000	4,000

The cash inflows stay the same since we make the same staff cost savings as with the buy option. The cash outflows are different, however. We must pay out £1,000 now (year 0) followed by five payments of £2,000 in the next five years. This option shows a net cash flow of £4,000. It is tempting to decide that the project should go ahead by buying the machine since this has the higher net cash flow: £5,000 as opposed to £4,000 for leasing. However, this simple view does not take into account the timings of these cash flows. Although the buy option shows a larger net cash flow it also has a large negative cash flow at the very start of the project (−£10,000) whilst the lease option has the negative cash flows spread out fairy evenly over the five years.

Based on our earlier discussion it is clear that to make a proper judgement we need to calculate the present value of this project: the value now of this stream of net cash flows. This is easily done using the PV principles.

Let us consider the PV of the buy option. What we need to do is work out the PV of the net cash flow in each year. If we then total these we will have the *net present value* for the project. The calculations are shown below:

Year	Net cash flow	Discount factor	PV
0	−10,000	1	−10,000
1	3,000	0.943396	2,830.19
2	3,000	0.889996	2,669.99
3	3,000	0.839619	2,518.86
4	3,000	0.792093	2,376.28
5	3,000	0.747258	2,241.77
	5,000		2,637.09

We have used the discount factor approach and for years 1–5 calculated the discount factor to be used at a rate of 6% p.a. (for year 5, for example, this is $1/1.06^5$). We then multiply the net cash flow in each year by the discount factor in that year to give the PV of that year's net cash flow. So, for example, £3,000 in year 5 has a PV of £2,241.77 (3,000 × 0.747258). If we sum these PVs across the life of the project we get £2,637.09 – the net present value (NPV) of the project.

The NPV allows us to determine – in present value terms – whether a project is worthwhile or not. First, we note that the NPV for the buy option is positive. A positive NPV implies that a project is worthwhile since it generates a positive net present value. A negative NPV would indicate a project that was not financially worthwhile: the PV of the cash outflows exceeds the PV of the cash inflows. Second, it follows from this that the higher the NPV the more worthwhile is the project. This implies that if we calculate the NPV of the lease option and compare it to that of the buy option we can see which of the two options is preferable, in NPV terms.

Student activity

Calculate the NPV for the lease option. Which of the alternatives – lease or buy – would you recommend and why?

The calculations for the lease options are:

Year	Net cash flow	Discount factor	PV
0	–1,000	1	–1,000
1	1,000	0.943396	943.40
2	1,000	0.889996	890.00
3	1,000	0.839619	839.62
4	1,000	0.792093	792.09
5	1,000	0.747258	747.26
Total	4,000		3,212.37

So, the NPV for the lease option is £3,212.37 – also positive and higher than for the buy option. This implies that, based on this information and ignoring any other factors, the lease option is to be preferred. It has a positive NPV implying that in PV terms the project is worthwhile and its NPV is greater than the alternative of buying the machine. The reason for this, of course, is to do with the timings of the net cash flows. Effectively the NPV calculations give more importance to earlier net cash flows than to later ones. Given that for the buy option the earliest net cash flow is a large negative value (–£10,000) then the lease option is to be preferred.

However, you will probably also realize that the NPV is determined in part by the interest rate (which is used to calculate the discount factors). A different interest rate will produce a different NPV and an organization will be well advised to undertake some sensitivity analysis of the calculations: seeing whether their decision might change if the interest rate changes. Although this takes us beyond our current analysis it is clear that such calculations are readily performed using a spreadsheet package. It is also clear that we could easily include in our analysis more realistic aspects of such a problem including tax, depreciation, loan repayments if money is borrowed, the effects of expected inflation and so on. The general principles, however, remain unchanged.

SUMMARY

In this chapter we have introduced the ideas of investment and financial return on investments. Financial returns are often based on the interest to be paid on a sum of money and we have seen how formulae can be developed to allow us to calculate such interest payments. We have also seen that we must distinguish between simple and compound interest and between nominal and effective interest rates. We also developed the concept of present value: the value now of a future sum of money at a given interest rate. We saw that present value allows us to compare sums of money received at different times and to indicate a preference as to which we would choose. The principles of present value are particularly useful in investment appraisal where we can calculate the net present value of a project at a given rate of interest to assess whether the project is financially viable.

Now that you have completed this chapter you will appreciate that:

- Interest payments are the financial return for the use of money over time.

- Simple interest is a constant payment on the original sum, the principal, invested.

- Compound interest is a payment on the principal plus any previous interest payments.

- The effective rate (or the annual percentage rate, APR) is the rate of interest actually earned or charged.

- The present value indicates what a future sum is worth now at a given rate of interest and present value calculations allow us to compare amounts of money at different times.

- The net present value (NPV) of a project is the discounted value of all cash flows (both inflows and outflows).

- A negative NPV implies that the PV of the outflows is greater than that of the inflows and so the investment is not worthwhile.

- A positive NPV implies that the PV of the inflows is greater than that of the outflows and so the investment is worthwhile.

EXAMPLE

A local printing firm is considering purchasing a new piece of equipment. The equipment would allow the firm to offer the latest service in multi-colour printing of publicity and advertising leaflets (the kind that get pushed through everyone's letterbox advertising local companies, restaurants, pubs, social events). At present the firm cannot offer this type of printing service to its customers and is losing this business to its competitors. The printing equipment will cost £600,000 to buy and will have a scrap value of £5,000 at the end of six years. Included in this price is a one-year service guarantee from the supplier of the equipment. Each additional year the equipment is in use the company intends to take out another service contract with the supplier at a fixed cost of £7,500, to be paid at the start of the year the service contract is to cover. Current rates of interest are 15% p.a. (although of course this rate might vary in the future). The firm has estimated that if it had the machine it could gain an extra £150,000 of business in the first year and the firm thinks that this part of the business would grow at about 3% p.a. The firm is trying to decide what to do.

Clearly we can develop a suitable cash flow table for the company and apply the principles of PV to the situation. Basically, we can ask the question: does this potential investment show a positive NPV after six years? If it does then the investment is potentially worthwhile (although of course there will be other factors for the company to take into account). If it does not then this effectively means that the company would be better off just sticking the £600,000 and the series of £7,500 payments into a bank account at 15% interest.

Let us first consider the cash flows arising from the additional business that the firm thinks would be generated if the new machine were purchased. We are told this is estimated at £150,000 in the first year and is expected to grow at 3% p.a. thereafter. Using compound interest principles we then have:

Year	Cash inflow	
0		
1	150,000	
2	154,500	$(150,000 \times 1.03)$
3	159,135	$(150,000 \times 1.03^2)$
4	163,909	$(150,000 \times 1.03^3)$
5	168,826	$(150,000 \times 1.03^4)$
6	173,891	$(150,000 \times 1.03^5)$

So, by year 6 – assuming the 3% growth rate materializes and stays constant – then annual income from this part of the business would have risen to £173,891. (Note that all figures have been rounded to the nearest £. Further accuracy really is not required for the project analysis.) However, we are also told that the machine will have a scrap value at the end of 6 years. This means that at the beginning of year 7 a further cash inflow of £5,000 will occur.

On the cash outflow side we know the firm will pay £600,000 for the machine at the start of the project (i.e. in year 0). However, there is also the matter of the annual service contract of £7,500. The first year's service contract is included in the machine cost. The service contract for the second year must be paid for at the start of year 2, that for year 3 at the start of year 3 and so on. This then gives a set of cash outflows:

Year	Cash outflow
0	600,000
1	
2	7,500
3	7,500
4	7,500
5	7,500
6	7,500

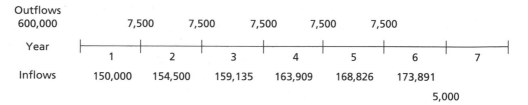

Fig. 14.1   Timing of cash flows

It can be very helpful with problems like this to use a simple time diagram to show all the relevant inflows and outflows, particularly when we need to be careful about exactly when some occur. The time diagram for this problem is shown as Fig. 14.1. This shows clearly when each cash flow occurs (for example, the scrap cash inflow at the beginning of year 7).

If we now use both the inflows and outflows we derive the net cash flow for the project.

Year	Cash inflow	Cash outflow	Net cash flow
0		600,000	−600,000
1	150,000		150,000
2	154,500	7,500	147,000
3	159,135	7,500	151,635
4	163,909	7,500	156,409
5	168,826	7,500	161,326
6	173,891	7,500	166,391
7	5,000		5,000
Total	975,261	637,500	337,761

We see that in simple cash flow terms the project generates a profit of about £338,000 since the total cash inflows are that much higher than the cash outflows. However, as we know, it is the timing of these cash flows that is critical to the viability of the project and not simply the total cash flow generated. We see that most of the cash outflow takes place at the start of the project whilst the higher cash inflows take place in the later years of the project. If we now obtain the discount factors at 15% and then the present values we have:

Year	Cash inflow	Cash outflow	Net cash flow	Discount factor	PV
0		600,000	−600,000	1	−600,000
1	150,000		150,000	0.869565	130,435
2	154,500	7,500	147,000	0.756143	111,153
3	159,135	7,500	151,635	0.657516	99,702
4	163,909	7,500	156,409	0.571753	89,427
5	168,826	7,500	161,326	0.497176	80,208
6	173,891	7,500	166,391	0.432327	71,935
7	5,000		5,000	0.375937	1,880
Total	975,261	637,500	337,761		−15,259

That is the NPV of the project is actually negative at −£15,000. This implies that once we have taken the timing of these cash flows into account the project is not viable (effectively the firm would be better off putting its £600,000 and payments of £7,500 into a bank and earning 15% interest for the next six years). This may seem somewhat surprising given the actual profit of the project of almost £380,000 but the reasoning again lies with the cash flow profile of the project.

Of course, from a management perspective the situation would not stop here. Simply because we have indicated that in NPV terms the project as specified is not worthwhile does not mean that we just abandon the idea. If the project is seen as strategically critical for the firm – perhaps in terms of its long-term viability or in terms of a planned expansion – then we need to look carefully at the project (and perhaps utilize other techniques we have looked at). Some of the ways we might do this would include the following:

- We could attach probabilities to the expected cash inflows arising from the additional business.

- We could use market research to quantify perhaps more precisely likely future growth in this part of the business. We have used a growth figure of 3% but detailed market research may provide a different, and possibly more accurate, estimate.

- If we have derived the 3% growth figure from market research we could use a confidence interval to provide a low and high estimate growth figure to assess the implications for the project viability.

- We might be able to use the forecasting techniques introduced in Chapters 12 and 13 to provide alternative forecasts of future growth.

- We might wish to approach the company selling the equipment to try to negotiate either a price reduction in the cost of the machine or perhaps some sort of staggered payment system where we pay part of the purchase cost each year (and of course using a spreadsheet we could easily quantify the impact this would have on our NPV calculations).

- We might also approach our friendly bank manager. At 15% the project is not viable but we know that the NPV will change if interest rates change. In fact using a spreadsheet we can readily calculate that at interest rates over 14.1% the project as it stands will have a negative NPV. At interest rates lower than 14.1% the project will have positive NPVs. We may be able to persuade the bank to lend us money at a rate of interest lower than 14.1% for this particular project.

In short, as with all the other techniques we have introduced in this text, the 'answer' that the technique provides is really just the start for management decision-making. Managers must not only be able to use and interpret such 'answers' but they must also be able to see how such 'answers' can be changed if we can alter parts of the problem/situation that we are analysing.

SELF-REVIEW QUESTIONS

1 *Why is interest paid on an investment?*

2 *What is the difference between simple and compound interest?*

3 *How would you calculate the rate of interest being earned in an account if you knew V, t and P?*

4 *What is meant by the APR?*

5 *What is meant by a present value?*

6 *What is meant by net present value?*

7 *Why is it necessary to use PV in project evaluations?*

STUDENT EXERCISES

1 A friend of yours wants to borrow some money from a bank. The bank advertisement says that the rate of interest charged on a loan is 15% p.a. But also shown are the words 'APR 17.3%'. Your friend has asked you to explain what this means.

2 You have some spare cash that you know you won't need for a while so you want to put it into a savings account. Wandering round the high street you see different banks offering differing savings schemes:

   Interest of 6.3% p.a. paid monthly
   Interest of 6.5% p.a. paid annually
   Interest of 6.2% p.a. paid daily
   Interest of 6.4% p.a. paid quarterly

   Which of the four accounts should you open and why?

3 A company knows that it will have to replace a piece of machinery in six years' time, at a cost of £35,000. If the current rate of interest is 12% what sum should be invested now to generate this sum in the future?

4 The same company has decided it can only afford to invest £10,000 now to finance the future replacement of the machine. What rate of return does it require on the investment?

5 For the example in the chapter concerning a buy/lease decision for equipment, calculate the NPV of the alternatives when the interest rate is 10% and again when the interest rate is 15%. Would you change your recommendation as to whether to lease or buy?

6   You have been left an investment in someone's will. The investment consists of £10,000 of government stock, paying 7% p.a. The stock is redeemable in eight years' time. What this means is that in eight years' time the government will repay the owner of the investment £10,000. Until then they will pay the owner of the investment £700 interest each year. The investment is transferable which means that if you want to you can sell it to someone else (but they will then get the interest payments and the final £10,000). Someone has expressed an interest in buying the security from you. How much would you sell it for? What assumptions have you made?

POSTSCRIPT

The first thing to say on reaching the end of the text is: congratulations!

The journey through the text – and the associated techniques and principles – has probably been a long and at times difficult one. We hope that you have found this material useful in your studies and in preparation for your exam and that you have been able to develop an understanding not just of the calculation methods but also of the potential for using such techniques and approaches in almost any organization. We hope that you have also understood that for any manager in any organization to be able to manage properly then appropriate quantitative skills are absolutely essential. Just as we would expect a manager to be able to read, to write, to use a computer, so most organizations today expect their managers to be numerate in a business sense. This does not mean that you need to be able to perform abstract mathematical calculations but rather that you have both an awareness of the techniques it is possible to apply in some situation and that you can evaluate the output from such techniques in a business and managerial context.

The bad news, though, is that the journey is not really over. Although we've introduced some of the more common techniques and approaches there are a lot more that you will find useful as a manager and we hope that this text has been sufficiently interesting and stimulating to encourage you to develop your skills and competence in the quantitative area more (when you have the time!).

You may find it useful to look at another text by the author* which develops some of the techniques introduced here but also provides reports and details of organizations actually applying these techniques in the real world.

Quantitative Methods for Decision Makers by Mik Wisniewski, Pitman Publishing, 1994, ISBN 0 273 03938 5.

APPENDIX 1

ANSWERS TO SELF-REVIEW QUESTIONS

Chapter 1

1 Primary data is generally data which has been collected directly for a particular statistical exercise or investigation. Secondary data relates to data originally collected for some other purpose than that to which it is now being used. An example might be the individual customer sales figures recorded by a supermarket's EPOS system. As primary data they may be used to provide information on total daily sales in a store. The data might then be used at a later date by head office, together with data on staffing levels in the store to assess productivity in the store. This would be classed as secondary data since the data was not originally collected for this purpose (and might then not satisfy exactly the primary needs).

2 A population refers to the entire set of data which potentially exists for some variable in which we are interested. A sample is a sub-set (or part of) this population. Again, with the supermarket example, the customer population would consist of all people who had ever used that supermarket. If we wished to assess the likely impact of some new product made available in the store we might seek the opinions of a sample of these customers. Naturally, we should wish to try to ensure that the sample selected was properly representative of the statistical population.

3 Following on from the example in **2**, it is frequently difficult, if not impossible, to collect and analyse data about an entire population. There might be too much data to collect, it might take too long or be too expensive, it might not be possible to actually identify or contact the entire population. For this reason we may have to resort to investigating only part of the population – a sample.

4 Descriptive statistics relate to the statistical analysis undertaken in order to provide a description of some set of data. Inferential statistics relates to the statistical analysis undertaken to try to reach conclusions about some statistical population based only on the descriptive statistical analysis of a sample of data.

5 Raw data is usually too much for a manager to usefully be able to assess in terms of any patterns or trends that may be emerging. Simply, a manager may suffer from 'information overload' with raw data. It is usually more appropriate to summarize or aggregate the data in some way so it makes it meaningful to a decision-maker.

6 If we wish to try to infer population characteristics from some sample set of data then we must be sure that the sample is properly representative of the population from which it was taken.

Chapter 3

1 The main stages in a data collection exercise can be summarized as:

(a) Determine the purpose of the exercise.

(b) Determine the information to be collected.

(c) Determine the method of data collection.

(d) Determine the sampling method to be used to select the sample.

(e) Carry out a pilot survey.

(f) Carry out the main survey.

(g) Validate the data and the collection methods.

(h) Analyse the data collected.

2 Bias is a term used to note that the sample drawn from a population may not be truly representative. If a sample is not fully representative it is said to be biased. For example, if we know the population contains 56% females but the sample contains 52% then the sample is biased towards males who are slightly over-represented in the sample.

3 Random sampling refers to those methods where each and every member of the population has an equal chance of being selected for the sample. Quasi-random methods refer to those methods which are not truly random. For example, we may choose the first item at random and then every nth item thereafter.

4 Systematic sampling and multi-stage sampling are the two major quasi-random sampling methods.

5 Non-random sampling methods may allow bias to be introduced into the sample selection.

6 Simple random sampling is where we choose items from the population to be included in the sample entirely at random, or by chance. Stratified sampling is random sampling but applied to specific strata or groups that make up the population: perhaps sex, age, ethnic origin.

7 We wish to ensure that the sample is properly representative of the population because our analysis will be on the sample. Any findings, conclusions and decisions that we come to about the characteristics of the population will be based on the sample data. If the sample is not properly representative then our findings and conclusions may not reflect the characteristics of the population.

Chapter 4

1 Percentages can be useful when we wish to see the component parts of some total amount or when the original numbers are changing through the table.

2 Tables should clearly indicate units of measurement used, the source of data used and the component parts of the table by the use of labels and should have a self-explanatory title.

3 Both types of table are similar. The percentage change table shows the percentage change in a variable between one time period and the next and it is possible to see the change in the variable only between each successive pair of time periods. An index table shows the variable as an index where in one time period the variable has been set to a value of 100. In every other period the actual value is then shown relative to the base period value. It is then possible to compare any two time periods in the table directly to assess the percentage change that has occurred.

4 A frequency table is a table showing a number of numerical intervals and the number – or frequency – of observations from a data set that fall into each interval.

5 A percentage change table can be useful when we are particularly interested in the change in some variable over a period of time and when the variable itself has changed considerably. Percentage change calculations then make it easier to see the relative change that has taken place between successive periods.

6 Ideally, a frequency table should have between five and 15 intervals. The purpose of a frequency table is to aggregate data so that we can distinguish its main features. Fewer than five intervals and we shall be aggregating the data too much and will lose much of the detail. More than 15 intervals and we shall not be aggregating the data sufficiently and will not be able to pick out the important characteristics.

Chapter 5

1 Sometimes the amount of data in a table may be too large to enable a manager to pick out the key patterns or trends in the variables shown in the table. By using appropriate diagrams we may be able to highlight key characteristics of the data in the table quickly and easily.

2 The disadvantages of a pie chart are that it is difficult to draw manually, it can only be applied to data which has a small number of groups or categories, it can be difficult to pick out details, and comparing one pie chart with another is difficult.

3 If the figures making up a component bar chart are changing rapidly over time it can be difficult to compare one component with another, or one component with itself. The use of percentages in such circumstances can help make such comparisons easier.

4 Tables and diagrams should clearly indicate units of measurement used, the source of data used and the component parts of the table or diagram by the use of labels and should have a self-explanatory title.

5 The size of each section of a pie chart is calculated by working out the percentage of the total represented by one component and then expressing this percentage as a proportion of 360°. This then represents the size of that 'slice' of the pie.

6 A scatter plot is drawn for two variables, denoted as X and Y. The Y variable is plotted on the vertical axis. Conventionally the Y variable is known as the dependent variable whilst the X variable is the independent or explanatory variable. We assume that the Y variable 'depends' on the X variable in some way.

Chapter 6

1 A frequency table should have between five and 15 intervals depending on the amount of data. The more data then in general the more intervals are appropriate.

2 The two main problems encountered when constructing a histogram are open-ended intervals in the frequency table and intervals of unequal widths.

3 An ogive is a graphical representation of the cumulative frequencies for a set of data. It might be shown in terms of actual numbers or as a percentage of the total.

4 Any one quartile divides the distribution into two parts. The three quartiles together divide the distribution into four equal parts.

5 A histogram shows the frequency of each interval as a bar. A frequency polygon shows the overall distribution of the data in the frequency table.

6 It may be better to show a histogram in percentage terms if we wish to compare the histogram for one set of data with that for a different set of data and the two data sets are of different sizes.

7 The frequency polygon uses the midpoints. An ogive uses the endpoints.

8 Unequal intervals are dealt with by choosing one interval width as the normal. The frequency for any interval with a different width is then adjusted accordingly.

Chapter 7

1 Statistics based on raw data tend to be more accurate because when calculating statistics for aggregated data it is often necessary to make assumptions about the data values.

2 Open-ended intervals occur at the beginning and end of frequency distributions. Typically the median value will occur within the distribution. When calculating the mean for aggregated data it is necessary to close such an interval by assuming a lower or upper limit to it. This assumption is not necessary for calculations involving the median.

3 The mean will tend to take a higher value than the median when there are a small number of high values in the data set. These will have the effect of pulling the mean away from the central part of the data.

4 The median is preferred to the mean when there are a small number of extreme values in the data set. These will have the effect of pulling the mean above or below the central part of the data.

5 If the median and mean for a data set were the same we would conclude that the distribution of the data was symmetrical.

6 The standard deviation measures dispersion around the mean. The quartile deviation measures variation around the median.

7 The statistic used to compare two or more standard deviations is the coefficient of variation.

8 A positive skew distribution leans to the left with a long tail to the right.

9 Any statistics based on aggregated or grouped data may be inaccurate because we have to make assumptions about the actual data values in order to perform the calculations. These assumptions may not be entirely accurate leading to inaccuracies in the statistics calculated.

Chapter 8

1 A probability can only take a numerical value between 0 and 1. A value greater than 1 cannot exist.

2 The general form of the addition rule is:

$$P(A \text{ or } B) = P(A) + P(B) - P(A \text{ and } B)$$

where A and B refer to two events.

3 The addition rule is used for events where we require the probability of either event occurring.

4 The general form of the multiplication rule is:

$$P(A \text{ and } B) = P(A) \times P(B|A)$$

where A and B refer to two events.

5 The multiplication rule is used where we require the probability of both events occurring.

6 Expected value is calculated by multiplying all outcomes by their respective probability and summing. It refers to the expected, or average, value in the long run.

7 $P(X) = 0.3$ indicates that event X has a probability of occurring of 0.3 or 30/100.

8 $P(X|Y)$ indicates the probability of X occurring given that Y has occurred.

9 A probability distribution is a distribution showing the probability of each and every outcome from some experiment.

10 A *Z* score is a means of standardizing a normally distributed variable. It expresses the difference between the mean of that distribution and any specific X value in terms of standard deviations.

11 The main features of the normal distribution are that it is symmetrical around the mean with all such distributions following the same general pattern, the only difference being the specific mean and standard deviation values.

12 Because every normal distribution is technically different, given the mean and standard deviation, we must standardize the particular normally distributed variable we are examining in order to be able to use pre-calculated tables of probabilities.

Chapter 9

1 The sampling distribution is a theoretical distribution. It shows the distribution of the means (or proportions) for all the different samples that could in principle be taken from some statistical population. The sampling distribution is normal.

2 The standard error is simply the standard deviation of the sampling distribution.

3 The Central Limit Theorem is important because it proves that the sampling distribution will be normal. This in turn allows us to use the probability principles of the normal distribution for statistical inference.

4 A 95% confidence interval takes its name from the fact that it represents a range of values within which, with a 95% probability, the sample mean/proportion and population mean/proportion will both occur.

5 A hypothesis test is a method of assessing whether a particular population value is likely given the sample information we have available.

6 H_0 is the null hypothesis in a test. It is the population characteristic/value that we cannot reject unless we bring sufficient statistical evidence to bear which indicates that the null hypothesis is unlikely to be correct at a given level of probability.

7 The critical statistic, Z_α, denotes the maximum difference, expressed in standard errors, that we can accept between the hypothesized population value and the observed sample value. If the calculated Z score exceeds Z_α we must reject H_0 and accept H_1 the alternative hypothesis.

Chapter 10

1 The independent variable, usually denoted as X, is the variable which is assumed to influence the dependent variable, usually denoted as Y.

2 For the slope of a linear function you would mark two points on the line of the function on the graph. For each point you would read the X and Y values. The slope would then be given as the ratio of the difference in Y to the difference in X.

3 A negative intercept means that the line crosses the Y axis where $Y < 0$.

4 A functional relationship means that there is some sort of dependency or relationship between the two variables.

5 The two parameters of a linear function are the intercept and the slope, denoted as a and b respectively.

6 We can normally find the solution to a set of linear equations either by using a graph or by applying the method of simultaneous equations.

7 The line with the positive slope will slope upwards from left to right whilst the other will slope downwards from left to right.

8 A line with a positive intercept will cross the Y axis where $Y > 0$ whilst one with a negative intercept will cross where $Y < 0$.

9 A linear function with a zero slope would be parallel to the X axis: Y would not change as X changed.

10 The advantage of using simultaneous equations is that such a method gives a precise solution to the problem. Using a graph it may be difficult to estimate precise values from the scales.

Chapter 11

1 In a quadratic equation of the form:

$$Y = a + bX + cX^2$$

it is the a term which indicates the intercept or constant value.

2 The c term in the quadratic can be used to tell us whether the quadratic takes the U-shape or the inverted U-shape. A negative c gives the inverted U and a positive c the U-shape.

3 The roots of a quadratic equation are the value for X which will give $Y = 0$. Graphically they show the points where the function intersects the X axis.

4 The turning point indicates where the slope of a function is zero and is literally where the slope is about to change direction. It can be found in different ways. We can find the turning point graphically. For a quadratic function we can apply a formula. For other functions we can apply the derivatives.

5 The derivative rule is a method for finding the derivative of any function. If we have a function of the form:

$$Y = kX^n$$

then its derivative is given by:

$$\frac{\mathrm{d}Y}{\mathrm{d}X} = nkX^{n-1}$$

6 The derivative is a function for the slope of the original function.

7 The derivative of a constant is zero since a constant has no slope.

8 By setting the derivative to zero and finding the corresponding value of X we find the turning point of the original function.

9 The second derivative is the derivative of the first derivative of the function.

10 The second derivative is calculated because it can be used to determine algebraically whether the turning point(s) found by using the first derivative are maximum or minimum.

Chapter 12

1 The line of best fit is the line of the regression equation. This is the line which, using the regression equations for estimating a and b, comes closest to the scatter of points from the data set. It is sometimes known as the least squares line, since regression is a technique which minimizes the squared deviations of the line from the data points.

2 A scatter diagram is essential because it provides a visual summary of the data we are trying to estimate a regression line for. A scatter diagram allows us to see whether there is any evident correlation between the two variables and whether this correlation appears linear. It also allows us to note any major deviation of data points from this pattern.

3 The Pearson correlation coefficient shows the strength of the linear relationship between two variables. It takes a value between −1 and +1. The closer to 1 then the stronger the linear correlation.

4 The correlation coefficient does not provide evidence of cause and effect since the correlation coefficient remains unchanged if we swap over the X and Y variables.

5 A correlation of 0 indicates that, literally, the two variables are totally uncorrelated: there is absolutely no connection between them in a numerical sense.

6 A forecast based on an interpolation uses an X value (to predict Y) which occurs within a numerical range we have already observed that X values take. An extrapolated forecast uses an X value which is outside this observed range. We are then in 'unknown' territory since we have no direct evidence of how Y relates to X once X takes a value outside the observed range.

7 The only difference lies in the direction of the relationship between X and Y. A positive correlation indicates that both variables change together in the same direction (as one increases the other increases). A negative coefficient indicates an inverse relationship: as one variable increases the other decreases.

Chapter 13

1 Time series analysis is needed so that we can quantify the different effects on some variable: the trend effect, the seasonal effect, the random effect. This will allow management to examine a time series and understand what is causing it to change at any given time and whether management action is needed as a result of this change.

2 The three main elements of a time series are the trend, the seasonal factor and the random/residual element.

3 The trend is estimated using the method of centred moving averages.

4 It is necessary to centre the moving averages because when we are dealing with an even number of time periods a simple average of these (to estimate the trend) will not line up with any specific time period. This means that we would then be unable to find the difference between the trend and a given actual figure.

5 The seasonal factors will be determined in slightly different ways depending on whether we use the additive or the multiplicative model. The additive model averages the trend deviations for each period in the year. These are then totalled and the averages adjusted until they total to 0 over the year. In the multiplicative model it is the trend ratios which are calculated. These are also averaged and again adjusted if they do not total to 4 over the year for a quarterly model or to 12 for a monthly model.

6 The seasonally adjusted series is the actual data with the seasonal factors removed. It shows the underlying trend in the variable together with any random/residual element.

Chapter 14

1 Interest is paid on an investment to persuade the investor to 'sacrifice' the sum of money involved for a given period of time.

2 Simple interest is calculated on the principal sum only. Compound interest is calculated on the principal plus any interest added to the principal from earlier periods.

3 We would use the formula:

$$i = \sqrt[t]{V/P - 1}$$

4 The nominal rate of interest is that quoted as being applied to an investment e.g. 10% p.a. The effective rate of interest, or annual percentage rate of interest (APR), is the rate that the investment actually earns over the year. There will be a difference between the two if interest is calculated on anything other than an annual basis.

5 A present value indicates the value now of a future sum of money.

6 Net present value is often applied to cash flows over some period of time. It is the present value of the difference between both cash inflows and cash outflows.

7 Because different projects will have different cash flows and different timings of cash flows we can compare them by converting such different cash flows to a common base: present value.

APPENDIX 2

BINOMIAL DISTRIBUTION

	$p =$	0.01	0.02	0.03	0.04	0.05	0.06	0.07	0.08	0.09
$n = 2$	$r \geq 0$	1.0000	1.0000	1.0000	1.0000	1.0000	1.0000	1.0000	1.0000	1.0000
	1	.0199	.0396	.0591	.0784	.0975	.1164	.1351	.1536	.1719
	2	.0001	.0004	.0009	.0016	.0025	.0036	.0049	.0064	.0081
$n = 5$	$r \geq 0$	1.0000	1.0000	1.0000	1.0000	1.0000	1.0000	1.0000	1.0000	1.0000
	1	.0490	.0961	.1413	.1846	.2262	.2261	.3043	.3409	.3760
	2	.0010	.0038	.0085	.0148	.0226	.0319	.0425	.0544	.0674
	3		.0001	.0003	.0006	.0012	.0020	.0031	.0045	.0063
	4						.0001	.0001	.0002	.0003
$n = 10$	$r \geq 0$	1.0000	1.0000	1.0000	1.0000	1.0000	1.0000	1.0000	1.0000	1.0000
	1	.0956	.1829	.2626	.3352	.4013	.4614	.5160	.5656	.6106
	2	.0043	.0162	.0345	.0582	.0861	.1176	.1517	.1879	.2254
	3	.0001	.0009	.0028	.0062	.0115	.0188	.0283	.0401	.0540
	4			.0001	.0004	.0010	.0020	.0036	.0058	.0088
	5					.0001	.0002	.0003	.0006	.0010
	6									.0001
$n = 20$	$r \geq 0$	1.0000	1.0000	1.0000	1.0000	1.0000	1.0000	1.0000	1.0000	1.0000
	1	.1821	.3324	.4562	.5580	.6415	.7099	.7658	.8113	.8484
	2	.0169	.0599	.1198	.1897	.2642	.3395	.4131	.4831	.5484
	3	.0010	.0071	.0210	.0439	.0755	.1150	.1610	.2121	.2666
	4		.0006	.0027	.0074	.0159	.0290	.0471	.0706	.0993
	5			.0003	.0010	.0026	.0056	.0107	.0183	.0290
	6				.0001	.0003	.0009	.0019	.0038	.0068
	7						.0001	.0003	.0006	.0013
	8								.0001	.0002
$n = 50$	$r \geq 0$	1.0000	1.0000	1.0000	1.0000	1.0000	1.0000	1.0000	1.0000	1.0000
	1	.3950	.6358	.7819	.8701	.9231	.9547	.9734	.9845	.9910
	2	.0894	.2642	.4447	.5995	.7206	.8100	.8735	.9173	.9468
	3	.0138	.0784	.1892	.3233	.4595	.5838	.6892	.7740	.8395
	4	.0016	.0178	.0628	.1391	.2396	.3527	.4673	.5747	.6697
	5	.0001	.0032	.0168	.0490	.1036	.1794	.2710	.3710	.4723
	6		.0005	.0037	.0144	.0378	.0776	.1350	.2081	.2928
	7		.0001	.0007	.0036	.0118	.0289	.0583	.1019	.1596
	8			.0001	.0008	.0032	.0094	.0220	.0438	.0768
	9				.0001	.0008	.0027	.0073	.0167	.0328
	10					.0002	.0007	.0022	.0056	.0125
	11						.0002	.0006	.0017	.0043
	12							.0001	.0005	.0013
	13								.0001	.0004
	14									.0001

	$p =$	0.01	0.02	0.03	0.04	0.05	0.06	0.07	0.08	0.09
$n = 100$	$r \geq 0$	1.0000	1.0000	1.0000	1.0000	1.0000	1.0000	1.0000	1.0000	1.0000
	1	.6340	.8674	.9524	.9831	.9941	.9979	.9993	.9998	.9999
	2	.2642	.5967	.8054	.9128	.9629	.9848	.9940	.9977	.9991
	3	.0794	.3233	.5802	.7679	.8817	.9434	.9742	.9887	.9952
	4	.0184	.1410	.3528	.5705	.7422	.8570	.9256	.9633	.9827
	5	.0034	.0508	.1821	.3711	.5640	.7232	.8368	.9097	.9526
	6	.0005	.0155	.0808	.2116	.3840	.5593	.7086	.8201	.8955
	7	.0001	.0041	.0312	.1064	.2340	.3936	.5557	.6968	.8060
	8		.0009	.0106	.0475	.1280	.2517	.4012	.5529	.6872
	9		.0002	.0032	.0190	.0631	.1463	.2660	.4074	.5506
	10			.0009	.0068	.0282	.0775	.1620	.2780	.4125
	11			.0002	.0022	.0115	.0376	.0908	.1757	.2882
	12				.0007	.0043	.0168	.0469	.1028	.1876
	13				.0002	.0015	.0069	.0224	.0559	.1138
	14					.0005	.0026	.0099	.0282	.0645
	15					.0001	.0009	.0041	.0133	.0341
	16						.0003	.0016	.0058	.0169
	17						.0001	.0006	.0024	.0078
	18							.0002	.0009	.0034
	19							.0001	.0003	.0014
	20								.0001	.0005
	21									.0002
	22									.0001

	$p =$	0.10	0.15	0.20	0.25	0.30	0.35	0.40	0.45	0.50
$n = 2$	$r \geq 0$	1.0000	1.0000	1.0000	1.0000	1.0000	1.0000	1.0000	1.0000	1.0000
	1	.1900	.2775	.3600	.4375	.5100	.5775	.6400	.6975	.7500
	2	.0100	.0225	.0400	.0625	.0900	.1225	.1600	.2025	.2500
$n = 5$	$r \geq 0$	1.0000	1.0000	1.0000	1.0000	1.0000	1.0000	1.0000	1.0000	1.0000
	1	.4095	.5563	.6723	.7627	.8319	.8840	.9222	.9497	.9688
	2	.0815	.1648	.2627	.3672	.4718	.5716	.6630	.7438	.8125
	3	.0086	.0266	.0579	.1035	.1631	.2352	.3174	.4069	.5000
	4	.0005	.0022	.0067	.0156	.0308	.0540	.0870	.1312	.1875
	5		.0001	.0003	.0010	.0024	.0053	.0102	.0185	.0313
$n = 10$	$r \geq 0$	1.0000	1.0000	1.0000	1.0000	1.0000	1.0000	1.0000	1.0000	1.0000
	1	.6513	.8031	.8926	.9437	.9718	.9865	.9940	.9975	.9990
	2	.2639	.4557	.6242	.7560	.8507	.9140	.9536	.9767	.9893
	3	.0702	.1798	.3222	.4744	.6172	.7384	.8327	.9004	.9453
	4	.0128	.0500	.1209	.2241	.3504	.4862	.6177	.7430	.8281
	5	.0016	.0099	.0328	.0781	.1503	.2485	.3669	.4956	.6230
	6	.0001	.0014	.0064	.0197	.0473	.0949	.1662	.2616	.3770
	7		.0001	.0009	.0035	.0106	.0260	.0548	.1020	.1719
	8			.0001	.0004	.0016	.0048	.0123	.0274	.0547
	9					.0001	.0005	.0017	.0045	.0107
	10							.0001	.0003	.0010
$n = 20$	$r \geq 0$	1.0000	1.0000	1.0000	1.0000	1.0000	1.0000	1.0000	1.0000	1.0000
	1	.8784	.9612	.9885	.9968	.9992	.9998	1.0000	1.0000	1.0000
	2	.6083	.8244	.9308	.9757	.9924	.9979	.9995	.9999	1.0000
	3	.3231	.5951	.7939	.9087	.9645	.9879	.9964	.9991	.9998
	4	.1330	.3523	.5886	.7748	.8929	.9556	.9840	.9951	.9987
	5	.0432	.1702	.3704	.5852	.7625	.8818	.9490	.9811	.9941

	$p =$	0.10	0.15	0.20	0.25	0.30	0.35	0.40	0.45	0.50
	6	.0113	.0673	.1958	.3828	.5836	.7546	.8744	.9447	.9793
	7	.0024	.0219	.0867	.2142	.3920	.5834	.7500	.8701	.9423
	8	.0004	.0059	.0321	.1018	.2277	.3990	.5841	.7480	.8684
	9	.0001	.0013	.0100	.0409	.1133	.2376	.4044	.5857	.7483
	10		.0002	.0026	.0139	.0480	.1218	.2447	.4086	.5881
	11			.0006	.0039	.0171	.0532	.1275	.2493	.4119
	12			.0001	.0009	.0051	.0196	.0565	.1308	.2517
	13				.0002	.0013	.0060	.0210	.0580	.1316
	14					.0003	.0015	.0065	.0214	.0577
	15						.0003	.0016	.0064	.0207
	16							.0003	.0015	.0059
	17								.0003	.0013
	18									.0002
$n = 50$	$r \geq 0$	1.0000	1.0000	1.0000	1.0000	1.0000	1.0000	1.0000	1.0000	1.0000
	1	.9948	.9997	1.0000	1.0000	1.0000	1.0000	1.0000	1.0000	1.0000
	2	.9662	.9971	.9998	1.0000	1.0000	1.0000	1.0000	1.0000	1.0000
	3	.8883	.9858	.9987	.9999	1.0000	1.0000	1.0000	1.0000	1.0000
	4	.7497	.9540	.9943	.9995	1.0000	1.0000	1.0000	1.0000	1.0000
	5	.5688	.8879	.9815	.9979	.9998	1.0000	1.0000	1.0000	1.0000
	6	.3839	.7806	.9520	.9930	.9993	.9999	1.0000	1.0000	1.0000
	7	.2298	.6387	.8966	.9806	.9975	.9998	1.0000	1.0000	1.0000
	8	.1221	.4812	.8096	.9547	.9927	.9992	.9999	1.0000	1.0000
	9	.0579	.3319	.6927	.9084	.9817	.9975	.9998	1.0000	1.0000
	10	.0245	.2089	.5563	.8363	.9598	.9933	.9992	.9999	1.0000
	11	.0094	.1199	.4164	.7378	.9211	.9840	.9978	.9998	1.0000
	12	.0032	.0628	.2893	.6184	.8610	.9658	.9943	.9994	1.0000
	13	.0010	.0301	.1861	.4890	.7771	.9339	.9867	.9982	.9998
	14	.0003	.0132	.1106	.3630	.6721	.8837	.9720	.9955	.9995
	15	.0001	.0053	.0607	.2519	.5532	.8122	.9460	.9896	.9987
	16		.0019	.0308	.1631	.4308	.7199	.9045	.9780	.9967
	17		.0007	.0144	.0983	.3161	.6111	.8439	.9573	.9923
	18		.0002	.0063	.0551	.2178	.4940	.7631	.9235	.9836
	19		.0001	.0025	.0287	.1406	.3784	.6644	.8727	.9675
	20			.0009	.0139	.0848	.2736	.5535	.8026	.9405
	21			.0003	.0063	.0478	.1861	.4390	.7138	.8987
	22			.0001	.0026	.0251	.1187	.3299	.6100	.8389
	23				.0010	.0123	.0710	.2340	.4981	.7601
	24				.0004	.0056	.0396	.1562	.3866	.6641
	25				.0001	.0024	.0207	.0978	.2840	.5561
	26					.0009	.0100	.0573	.1966	.4439
	27					.0003	.0045	.0314	.1279	.3359
	28					.0001	.0019	.0160	.0780	.2399
	29						.0007	.0076	.0444	.1611
	30						.0003	.0034	.0235	.1013
	31						.0001	.0014	.0116	.0595
	32							.0005	.0053	.0325
	33							.0002	.0022	.0164
	34							.0001	.0009	.0077
	35								.0003	.0033
	36								.0001	.0013
	37									.0005
	38									.0002

		$p =$ 0.10	0.15	0.20	0.25	0.30	0.35	0.40	0.45	0.50
$n = 100$	$r \geq 0$	1.0000	1.0000	1.0000	1.0000	1.0000	1.0000	1.0000	1.0000	1.0000
	1	1.0000	1.0000	1.0000	1.0000	1.0000	1.0000	1.0000	1.0000	1.0000
	2	.9997	1.0000	1.0000	1.0000	1.0000	1.0000	1.0000	1.0000	1.0000
	3	.9981	1.0000	1.0000	1.0000	1.0000	1.0000	1.0000	1.0000	1.0000
	4	.9992	.9999	1.0000	1.0000	1.0000	1.0000	1.0000	1.0000	1.0000
	5	.9763	.9996	1.0000	1.0000	1.0000	1.0000	1.0000	1.0000	1.0000
	6	.9424	.9984	1.0000	1.0000	1.0000	1.0000	1.0000	1.0000	1.0000
	7	.8828	.9953	.9999	1.0000	1.0000	1.0000	1.0000	1.0000	1.0000
	8	.7939	.9878	.9997	1.0000	1.0000	1.0000	1.0000	1.0000	1.0000
	9	.6791	.9725	.9991	1.0000	1.0000	1.0000	1.0000	1.0000	1.0000
	10	.5487	.9449	.9977	1.0000	1.0000	1.0000	1.0000	1.0000	1.0000
	11	.4168	.9006	.9943	.9999	1.0000	1.0000	1.0000	1.0000	1.0000
	12	.2970	.8365	.9874	.9996	1.0000	1.0000	1.0000	1.0000	1.0000
	13	.1982	.7527	.9747	.9990	1.0000	1.0000	1.0000	1.0000	1.0000
	14	.1239	.6526	.9531	.9975	.9999	1.0000	1.0000	1.0000	1.0000
	15	.0726	.5428	.9196	.9946	.9998	.10000	.10000	.10000	.10000
	16	.0399	.4317	.8715	.9889	.9996	.10000	.10000	.10000	.10000
	17	.0206	.3275	.8077	.9789	.9990	.10000	.10000	.10000	.10000
	18	.0100	.2367	.7288	.9624	.9978	.9999	.10000	.10000	.10000
	19	.0046	.1628	.6379	.9370	.9955	.9999	.10000	.10000	.10000
	20	.0020	.1065	.5398	.9005	.9911	.9997	.10000	.10000	.10000
	21	.0008	.0663	.4405	.8512	.9835	.9992	.10000	.10000	.10000
	22	.0003	.0393	.3460	.7886	.9712	.9983	.10000	.10000	.10000
	23	.0001	.0221	.2611	.7136	.9521	.9966	.9999	.10000	.10000
	24		.0119	.1891	.6289	.9245	.9934	.9997	.10000	.10000
	25		.0061	.1314	.5383	.8864	.9879	.9994	1.0000	1.0000
	26		.0030	.0875	.4465	.8369	.9789	.9988	1.0000	1.0000
	27		.0014	.0558	.3583	.7756	.9649	.9976	.9999	1.0000
	28		.0006	.0342	.2776	.7036	.9442	.9954	.9998	1.0000
	29		.0003	.0200	.2075	.6232	.9152	.9916	.9996	1.0000
	30		.0001	.0112	.1495	.5377	.8764	.9852	.9992	1.0000
	31			.0061	.1038	.4509	.8270	.9752	.9985	1.0000
	32			.0031	.0693	.3669	.7669	.9602	.9970	.9999
	33			.0016	.0446	.2893	.6971	.9385	.9945	.9998
	34			.0007	.0276	.2207	.6197	.9087	.9902	.9996
	35			.0003	.0164	.1629	.5376	.8697	.9834	.9991
	36			.0001	.0094	.1161	.4542	.8205	.9728	.9982
	37			.0001	.0052	.0799	.3731	.7614	.9571	.9967
	38				.0027	.0530	.2976	.6932	.9349	.9940
	39				.0014	.0340	.2301	.6178	.9049	.9895
	40				.0007	.0210	.1724	.5379	.8657	.9824
	41				.0003	.0125	.1250	.4567	.8169	.9716
	42				.0001	.0072	.0877	.3775	.7585	.9557
	43				.0001	.0040	.0594	.3033	.6913	.9334
	44					.0021	.0389	.2365	.6172	.9033
	45					.0011	.0246	.1789	.5387	.8644
	46					.0005	.0150	.1311	.4587	.8159
	47					.0003	.0088	.0930	.3804	.7579
	48					.0001	.0050	.0638	.3069	.6914
	49					.0001	.0027	.0423	.2404	.6178
	50						.0015	.0271	.1827	.5398

$p =$	0.10	0.15	0.20	0.25	0.30	0.35	0.40	0.45	0.50
51						.0007	.0168	.1346	.4602
52						.0004	.0100	.0960	.3822
53						.0002	.0058	.0662	.3086
54						.0001	.0032	.0441	.2421
55							.0017	.0284	.1841
56							.0009	.0176	.1356
57							.0004	.0106	.0967
58							.0002	.0061	.0666
59							.0001	.0034	.0443
60								.0018	.0284
61								.0009	.0176
62								.0005	.0105
63								.0002	.0060
64								.0001	.0033
65									.0018
66									.0009
67									.0004
68									.0002
69									.0001

APPENDIX 3
AREAS IN THE TAIL OF THE NORMAL DISTRIBUTION

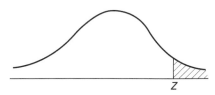

Z	.00	.01	.02	.03	.04	.05	.06	.07	.08	.09
0.0	.5000	.4960	.4920	.4880	.4840	.4801	.4761	.4721	.4681	.4641
0.1	.4602	.4562	.4522	.4483	.4443	.4404	.4364	.4325	.4286	.4247
0.2	.4207	.4168	.4129	.4090	.4052	.4013	.3974	.3936	.3897	.3859
0.3	.3821	.3783	.3745	.3707	.3669	.3632	.3594	.3557	.3520	.3483
0.4	.3446	.3409	.3372	.3336	.3300	.3264	.3228	.3192	.3156	.3121
0.5	.3085	.3050	.3015	.2981	.2946	.2912	.2877	.2843	.2810	.2776
0.6	.2743	.2709	.2676	.2643	.2611	.2578	.2546	.2514	.2483	.2451
0.7	.2420	.2389	.2358	.2327	.2296	.2266	.2236	.2206	.2177	.2148
0.8	.2119	.2090	.2061	.2033	.2005	.1977	.1949	.1922	.1894	.1867
0.9	.1841	.1814	.1788	.1762	.1736	.1711	.1685	.1660	.1635	.1611
1.0	.1587	.1562	.1539	.1515	.1492	.1469	.1446	.1423	.1401	.1379
1.1	.1357	.1335	.1314	.1292	.1271	.1251	.1230	.1210	.1190	.1170
1.2	.1151	.1131	.1112	.1093	.1075	.1056	.1038	.1020	.1003	.0985
1.3	.0968	.0951	.0934	.0918	.0901	.0885	.0869	.0853	.0838	.0823
1.4	.0808	.0793	.0778	.0764	.0749	.0735	.0721	.0708	.0694	.0681
1.5	.0668	.0655	.0643	.0630	.0618	.0606	.0594	.0582	.0571	.0559
1.6	.0548	.0537	.0526	.0516	.0505	.0495	.0485	.0475	.0465	.0455
1.7	.0446	.0436	.0427	.0418	.0409	.0401	.0392	.0384	.0375	.0367
1.8	.0359	.0351	.0344	.0336	.0329	.0322	.0314	.0307	.0301	.0294
1.9	.0287	.0281	.0274	.0268	.0262	.0256	.0250	.0244	.0239	.0233
2.0	.0228	.0222	.0217	.0212	.0207	.0202	.0197	.0192	.0188	.0183
2.1	.0179	.0174	.0170	.0166	.0162	.0158	.0154	.0150	.0146	.0143
2.2	.0139	.0136	.0132	.0129	.0125	.0122	.0119	.0116	.0133	.0110
2.3	.0107	.0104	.0102	.0099	.0096	.0094	.0091	.0089	.0087	.0084
2.4	.0082	.0080	.0078	.0075	.0073	.0071	.0069	.0068	.0066	.0064
2.5	.0062	.0060	.0059	.0057	.0055	.0054	.0052	.0051	.0049	.0048
2.6	.0047	.0045	.0044	.0043	.0041	.0040	.0039	.0038	.0037	.0036
2.7	.0035	.0034	.0033	.0032	.0031	.0030	.0029	.0028	.0027	.0026
2.8	.0026	.0025	.0024	.0023	.0023	.0022	.0021	.0021	.0020	.0019
2.9	.0019	.0018	.0018	.0017	.0016	.0016	.0015	.0015	.0014	.0014
3.0	.0014	.0013	.0013	.0012	.0012	.0011	.0011	.0011	.0010	.0010

INDEX